EMPOWERMENT
AND POVERTY REDUCTION

A Sourcebook

Contents

Foreword

This book is an outgrowth of *World Development Report 2000/2001: Attacking Poverty*, which identified opportunity, empowerment, and security as critical focus areas in the design and execution of poverty reduction strategies. The centrality of empowerment for development effectiveness has since been recognized in the World Bank's Strategic Framework, which identifies empowering poor people and investing in their assets as one of two priority areas for World Bank support to client countries. This book highlights the World Bank's current thinking on empowerment to improve development effectiveness.

Around the world 2.8 billion people, almost half the world's population, live on less than $2 a day. Unless we tap into the resources and capabilities of poor people themselves—expanding their freedom of choice and action and supporting their efforts to lift themselves out of poverty—the numbers of poor people around the world will only increase, and the impact of poverty on their lives will only worsen. The influence of poverty on poor people's lives is multidimensional, not simply through limited incomes and opportunities, but also through lack of education and health services, unsanitary living conditions, hunger, exhaustion, disease, insecurity, disregard, abuse, and a host of other issues.

Reducing poverty requires not only broad-based growth and improved governance at the national level, but also support to bottom-up approaches focusing on poor people and their roles and experiences in the development process. It requires increasing the resources dedicated to this goal, together with more responsible use of those resources. Further, it requires development approaches that are sustainable, so that programs and policies meant to improve people's lives today do not jeopardize their lives, or those of their children, tomorrow. In short, empowerment means changing not only what we do, but how we do it.

We hope this sourcebook will be useful in deepening both our understanding and our application of an empowering approach to poverty reduction. It marks the beginning of a collection of experiences that will evolve with our learning on the ground. We welcome your reactions and contributions to this ongoing work.

Gobind Nankani   Ian Johnson
Vice President   Vice President
Poverty Reduction   Environmentally and Socially
and Economic Management   Sustainable Development

Acknowledgments

This sourcebook was written by Deepa Narayan, Senior Adviser, Poverty Reduction and Economic Management (PREM), under the leadership of Nicholas Stern, Senior Vice President and Chief Economist, and Gobind Nankani, Vice President, PREM, with joint guidance from John Page, Director, Poverty Reduction Group, and Steen Jorgensen, Director, Social Development, all at the World Bank in Washington, D.C.

The book was prepared after extensive discussions, beginning in February 2001, on the empowerment framework and strategic actions that should be supported by the World Bank. The consultations involved over 1,000 people inside and outside the Bank. They included government officials, Bank staff, other donor representatives, and members of civil society in Indonesia, the Philippines, and Vietnam, as well as staff of the Asian Development Bank, the World Health Organization, the World Conservation Union, and the U.N. High Commission on Human Rights. The framework was further discussed within the Bank, as well as at a World Bank Institute–sponsored regional workshop on empowerment held in Hungary with participants from nine countries of Eastern Europe. A second regional workshop organized by the Latin America and Caribbean Region and held in Peru provided additional feedback. The framework was also discussed with external advisers on culture and empowerment and with the Social Development Board. Helpful feedback was also received from participants at two Bank-wide review meetings chaired by Nicholas Stern.

The book also benefited from discussions with Nisha Agrawal, Jehan Arulpragasam, Tamar Manuelyan Atinc, Kathy Bain, Lynn Bennett, Hans Binswanger, Anis Dani, Paula Donovan, David Ellerman, Norman Hicks,

Michael Klein, Alexandre Marc, Shaha Riza, Jean-Louis Sarbib, Sudhir Shetty, Veena Siddharth, Michael Walton, and Roberto Zagha.

Background research support was provided by Laura Bures, Simone Cecchini, Radha Seshagiri, and Talat Shah. Coordination support was provided by Bryan Kurey. The Tools and Practices were prepared by staff across the World Bank.

Acronyms and Abbreviations

ATM	Automated teller machine
BEEPS	Business Environment and Enterprise Performance Survey
CAS	Country Assistance Strategy
CDD	Community-driven development
CDI	Committee for Democracy in Information Technology (Brazil)
CGAP	Consultative Group to Assist the Poorest
CIDA	Canadian International Development Agency
CMU	Country Management Unit
CPPR	Country Portfolio Performance Review
CPRGS	Comprehensive Poverty Reduction and Growth Strategy (Vietnam)
DEC	Development Economics Vice Presidency (of the World Bank)
DFID	Department for International Development (U.K.)
ECA	Europe and Central Asia Region (of the World Bank)
ESW	Economic and sector work
FOIA	Freedom of Information Act
FSSAP	Female Secondary School Assistance Project (Bangladesh)
GDP	Gross domestic product
GUAPA	Guatemala Poverty Assessment
IBRD	International Bank for Reconstruction and Development (of the World Bank Group)

ICT	Information and communications technology
IDA	International Development Association (of the World Bank Group)
IDASA	Institute for Democracy in South Africa
IEC	Information, education, and communication
IFC	International Finance Corporation (of the World Bank Group)
IGR	Institutional and Governance Review
KDP	Kecamatan Development Project (Indonesia)
LAC	Latin America and the Caribbean Region (of the World Bank)
LLI	Local-level institutions
MASAF	Malawi Social Action Fund
MFI	Microfinance institution
MIGA	Multilateral Investment Guarantee Agency (of the World Bank Group)
NGO	Nongovernmental organization
OECD	Organisation for Economic Co-operation and Development
OED	Operations Evaluation Department (of the World Bank)
PAC	Public Affairs Centre (India)
PAD	Project Appraisal Document
PEAP	Poverty Eradication Action Plan (Uganda)
PER	Public Expenditure Review
PETS	Public Expenditure Tracking Survey
PPA	Participatory Poverty Assessment
PREM	Poverty Reduction and Economic Management Network (of the World Bank)
PRSC	Poverty Reduction Support Credit
PRSP	Poverty Reduction Strategy Paper
PSAL	Programmatic Structural Adjustment Loan
PSRL	Programmatic Social Reform Loan
RPO	Rural producers' organization
SEAF	Small Enterprise Assistance Funds
SECAL	Sector Adjustment Loan
SEWA	Self-Employed Women's Association (India)
SKS	Swayam Krishi Sangam (India)
SME	Small and medium enterprise
SPARC	Society for the Promotion of Area Resource Centers

UNDP	United Nations Development Programme
UNESCO	United Nations Educational, Scientific, and Cultural Organization
UNICEF	United Nations Children's Fund
UNIDO	United Nations Industrial Development Organization
USAID	U.S. Agency for International Development
WBES	World Business Environment Survey
WBI	World Bank Institute
WDR	*World Development Report*
ZAMSIF	Zambia Social Investment Fund
$	All dollar amounts used in this book are current U.S. dollars unless otherwise specified.

Summary

World Development Report 2000/2001: Attacking Poverty presents a multidimensional view of poverty. In particular, it underscores the importance of increasing poor people's access to opportunity, security, and empowerment for economic growth and poverty reduction. Building on *WDR 2000/2001*, the World Bank's Strategic Framework Paper identifies two priority areas for Bank support to client governments: (a) building the climate for investment, jobs, and growth, and (b) empowering poor people and investing in their assets. This book defines the World Bank's approach to empowerment for economic growth and poverty reduction. It is central to achieving the Millennium Development Goals.

A growing body of evidence points to the linkages between empowerment and development effectiveness both at the society-wide level and at the grassroots level. Empowerment approaches can strengthen good governance, which in turn enhances growth prospects. When citizens are engaged, exercise their voice, and demand accountability, government performance improves and corruption is harder to sustain. Citizen participation can also build consensus in support of difficult reforms needed to create a positive investment climate and induce growth. In addition, the empowerment agenda supports development effectiveness by promoting growth patterns that are pro-poor. This involves reducing inequalities by investing in poor people's capabilities through education and access to basic health care, as well as by increasing their access to land, financial capital, and markets.

Experience also demonstrates that empowerment can improve development effectiveness and pro-poor impact at the individual project level. Grassroots community involvement is a powerful tool for the production and maintenance of local public goods such as water supply, sanitation, schools, health, roads, and forest management, which in turn increase the development effectiveness of investments. Empowerment strategies at the project level are supported by civil liberties in society. Evidence shows that projects in countries with strong civil liberties—particularly citizen voice, participation, and accountability—significantly outperform projects in countries with weak civil liberties.

However, there remain many questions about what empowerment means, how it applies to the Bank's work, and what actions should be undertaken to move the empowerment agenda forward. This book addresses these three issues, taking into account the World Bank's mandate and comparative advantage in this field. The final section of the book documents tools and practices that can support the implementation of an empowering approach to poverty reduction.

The World Bank's comparative advantage in pursuing an empowerment agenda for poverty reduction lies in its relationship with governments around the world. The Bank is well placed to provide analysis, evaluation, advice, and financing on issues from governance to sector reform to economic growth. The Bank can convene stakeholders to stimulate debate, consensus, and coalition building for reform. It can support information disclosure, inclusion, and participation—particularly of poor people—and public accountability mechanisms in lending products and strategies. Finally, the Bank can support the strengthening of civil society and government institutions at the local and national levels.

The Meaning of Empowerment

Empowerment refers broadly to the expansion of freedom of choice and action to shape one's life. It implies control over resources and decisions. For poor people, that freedom is severely curtailed by their voicelessness and powerlessness in relation particularly to the state and markets. There are important gender inequalities, including within the household. Since powerlessness is embedded in a culture of unequal institutional relations, the book adopts an institutional definition of empowerment in the context of poverty reduction, which also helps draw out the relevance to the Bank's work:

> *Empowerment is the expansion of assets and capabilities of poor people to participate in, negotiate with, influence, control, and hold accountable institutions that affect their lives.*

Since poverty is multidimensional, poor people need a range of assets and capabilities at the individual level (such as health, education, and housing) and at the collective level (such as the ability to organize and mobilize to take collective action to solve their problems).

Empowering poor men and women requires the removal of formal and informal institutional barriers that prevent them from taking action to improve their wellbeing—individually or collectively—and limit their choices. The key formal institutions include the laws, rules, and regulations upheld by states, markets, civil society, and international agencies; informal institutions include norms of social solidarity, sharing, social exclusion, and corruption, among others.

Four Key Elements

Because state actions create the conditions in which poor people and other actors make decisions, the primary focus of this book is on state reform to improve provision of basic services, local and national governance, pro-poor market development, and access to justice. These reforms are premised on a mindset and values shaped by the view of poor people as partners and initiators of development rather than as problems. The book also highlights civil society roles to support pro-poor policies and actions at all levels.

Since social, cultural, political, and economic conditions vary and institutions are context-specific, reform strategies must vary as well. Although there is no single institutional model for empowerment, experience shows that certain elements are almost always present when empowerment efforts are successful. These elements act in synergy and strengthen the demand side of governance. The four key elements of empowerment that must underlie institutional reform are:

- *Access to information.* Information is power. Two-way information flows from government to citizens and from citizens to government are critical for responsible citizenship and responsive and accountable governance. Informed citizens are better equipped to take advantage of opportunity, access services, exercise their rights, and hold state and nonstate actors accountable. Critical areas where information is most important include state and private sector performance, financial services and markets, and rules and rights regarding basic services.

Information and communication technologies often play a pivotal role in broadening access to information.

- *Inclusion/participation.* An empowering approach to participation treats poor people as co-producers, with authority and control over decisions and resources devolved to the lowest appropriate level. Inclusion of poor people and other excluded groups in decisionmaking is critical to ensure that limited public resources build on local knowledge and priorities, and brings about commitment to change. However, in order to sustain inclusion and informed participation, it is usually necessary to change rules and processes to create space for people to debate issues, participate in local and national priority setting and budget formation, and access basic and financial services.

- *Accountability.* State officials, public employees, private providers, employers, and politicians must be held to account, making them answerable for their policies and actions that affect the wellbeing of citizens. There are three main types of accountability mechanism. Political accountability of political parties and representatives takes place increasingly through elections. Administrative accountability of government agencies is ensured through internal accountability mechanisms, both horizontal and vertical, within and between agencies. Social or public accountability mechanisms hold agencies accountable to citizens, and can reinforce both political and administrative accountability.

- *Local organizational capacity.* This refers to the ability of people to work together, organize themselves, and mobilize resources to solve problems of common interest. Organized groups and communities are more likely to have their voices heard and their demands met. When such membership-based groups federate at higher levels, they can gain voice and representation in policy dialogues and decisions that affect their wellbeing.

These four elements are already present in some of the Bank's ongoing work in projects, although investment in local organizational capacity is the least developed. They are much less present in policy loans and in analytical work. They also need to be reflected much more systematically in the Bank's Country Assistance Strategies, in its support for poverty reduction strategies, and in related mandates and analytical guidelines.

Application of Empowerment Approaches

Empowerment approaches can be applied across a broad range of the Bank's work. To provide some practical illustrations from Bank and non-Bank activities, this book focuses on application of the empowerment framework in five areas:

- Provision of basic services
- Improved local governance
- Improved national governance
- Pro-poor market development
- Access by poor people to justice.

In the past, strategies for improved governance and poverty reduction have focused on formal systems, with little connection to citizens and those working at the community level. An empowering approach to state reform can be viewed as strengthening the *demand side of governance* for greater public effectiveness. A demand-side approach focuses on creating laws, rules, and procedures that enable citizens and poor people's organizations to interact effectively with their governments. Such an approach invests in educating and informing citizens, in creating institutional mechanisms for their sustained inclusion and participation, and in enabling the emergence of strong poor people's organizations and citizens' groups.

Provision of Basic Services

This refers to improving poor people's access to and effective use of basic services including health care, education, water, and roads. The Bank supports government efforts to get resources down to the community level through a variety of institutional models: through private or public actors, through central agencies, sectoral agencies, or decentralized authorities of local government, through stand-alone sector projects or multisectoral community-driven development projects.

An empowering approach to provision of basic services focuses on a variety of co-production strategies. These include (a) putting information about government services and performance in the public domain; (b) designing mechanisms for inclusion and participation, including service delivery schemes that poor people can afford or demand-side financing strategies; and (c) promoting social accountability and local organizational capacity by giving community groups authority and control over key decisions and financial resources in community-driven development projects. These can be multisectoral, or they can be single-sector projects such as those in rural water supply and sanitation or education.

Improved Local Governance

Improved local governance is critical for better service delivery and greater responsiveness to poor people's priority problems. Decentralization and local government reform have so far focused primarily on the supply side of formal systems and not on strengthening the demand side through actions that enable citizens to effectively utilize the space created by new rules and regulations. Empowered local governments (with authority and resources) need to empower local communities through mechanisms that increase citizen access to information, enable inclusion and participation, increase accountability of governments to citizens, and invest in local organizational capacity. In general there has been insufficient attention to the relationship between citizens and local governments, and very few cases of investment in strengthening poor people's organizations or other local civil society intermediaries to enable them to play new roles effectively.

Improved National Governance

Macroeconomic policy choices are areas that are just beginning to open to societal engagement. Since national processes and policies determine poor people's access to resources and opportunities, it is critical that these processes incorporate the four empowerment elements. Actions include linking information from poor people to the process of national budget and policy formulation, as well as civil society involvement in expenditure tracking, or citizen feedback through social accountability mechanisms. This will require strengthening the capacity of poor people's organizations and other civil society groups to perform these new functions to keep national governments responsive and accountable.

Participatory processes are being incorporated in some policy-based lending, in programmatic loans, and in the formation of national poverty reduction strategies. Mechanisms are now needed to institutionalize participatory strategies and increase their effectiveness by incorporating the other three elements of the empowerment framework.

Pro-Poor Market Development

Poverty and vulnerability will not be reduced without broad-based growth fueled by private sector activity. However, economic growth cannot be sustained if poor people are excluded from optimal engagement in productive activities. While an overall investment climate that fosters entrepreneurship, job creation, competition, and security of property and benefit rights is crucial for poor people's involvement in market activities, it is not enough. Micro and small enterprises face constraints and exclusion that are not automatically corrected by improvements in the macro investment climate. Poor people are often excluded from equal access to economic opportunity because of regulations, discrimination, and lack of information, connections, skills, credit, and organization. Elements of empowering approaches can help to overcome many of these barriers that prevent poor people's entry into new markets. Changes in regulations can encourage private sector actors to innovate and develop new products that can potentially reach large numbers of poor people with financial and insurance products to manage vulnerability.

Access to Justice and Legal Aid

Rule of law and a functioning judicial system are important not only for the investment climate, but also for protecting poor people and their livelihoods. A new generation of judicial and legal reform projects is creating the legal environment for accountable governance and empowering poor people by increasing their access to justice through a mix of strategies. Currently, more than 400 Bank-financed projects have legal and judicial reform components. In addition, there are 30 freestanding projects in five regions. These projects focus on (a) improving administrative justice and making administrative decisions accountable and affordable to ordinary citizens; (b) promoting judicial independence and accountability; (c) improving legal education; (d) improving poor people's cultural, physical, and financial access to justice; and (e) public outreach and education.

Conclusion

Empowerment approaches focus on enhancing poor people's freedom of choice and action. Empowerment of poor people is an end in itself and is also critical for development effectiveness. It is not a stand-alone strategy but a way of doing development, grounded in the conviction that poor people themselves are the most invaluable partners in the task of poverty reduction. Empowerment approaches include behaviors that build people's self-confidence and their belief in themselves, and respect their dignity.

There are examples of this approach in ongoing work by the Bank and others, some of which are highlighted in this book. Systematic application of the four empowerment elements more broadly in the Bank's work will require leadership, contextualization, and capacity building, as well as incorporation of the elements in existing guidelines. Reliable data must be assembled to monitor empowerment processes and outcomes and to develop diagnostic tools to guide application across sectors. Nonetheless, there is certainly sufficient research and experience to move forward, learning through doing and through partnerships.

Chapter 1

Introduction

World Development Report 2000/2001: Attacking Poverty presents a multidimensional view of poverty. In particular, it underscores the importance of increasing poor people's access to opportunity, security, and empowerment for economic growth and poverty reduction. Building on *WDR 2000/2001*, the World Bank's Strategic Framework Paper identifies two priority areas for Bank support to client governments to increase development effectiveness: (a) building the climate for investment, jobs, and growth, and (b) empowering poor people and investing in their assets. This sourcebook defines the World Bank's approach to empowerment for economic growth and poverty reduction.[1]

There are many questions about what empowerment means, how it applies to the Bank's work, and what actions should be undertaken to move the empowerment agenda forward. This book addresses these three issues. To set the discussion in context, this introduction briefly summarizes the evidence linking empowerment to development effectiveness and then identifies the World Bank's comparative advantage in this field.

The book is organized in four chapters following the introduction. Chapter 2 defines empowerment from an institutional perspective and discusses the relationship between individual and collective assets and capabilities, particularly capability for collective action. There cannot be a single model for empowerment, given very different sociocultural, political, and institutional contexts; accordingly, the chapter describes four key elements of an empowering approach. It then goes on to identify some of the broad sets of conditions that help determine what kind of approach is feasible in different contexts.

Chapter 3 illustrates the application of an empowerment approach to five different areas of intervention by the Bank, and chapter 4 summarizes lessons learned to implement a systematic approach to empowerment. Chapter 5 consists of 20 "Tools and Practices" briefly describing relevant analytical tools and a selection of practices principally from the Bank's experience—ranging from the community to the country level—that support the empowerment of poor people.

Empowerment and Development Effectiveness

The need to deploy scarce development resources—whether in the form of finance or policy advice and technical assistance—as effectively as possible is a central development concern. This chapter very briefly explores three of the key channels through which empowerment enhances development effectiveness: through its impacts on good governance and growth, on helping growth to be pro-poor, and on the outcomes of development projects.[2] It is important to note that there is a synergistic relationship among these variables, and between key interventions to promote empowerment and effectiveness objectives. For example, support for broadening people's access to basic education and health care is central to the empowerment agenda; it is also critical for optimizing the long-run effectiveness of development strategies, including the creation of a dynamic investment climate. Finally, it should also be emphasized that empowerment, in the sense of enlarging people's choices and hence their freedom to take action to shape their lives, is much more than a means to other objectives; it is a good in itself, and a desirable goal of development.

Empowerment and Development Effectiveness: Good Governance and Growth

Good governance has increasingly been recognized as a crucial prerequisite for development effectiveness and the growth that it fosters. It is critical for ensuring a positive investment climate, and it has a two-way relationship with empowerment—that is, good governance promotes empowerment, and empowerment further enhances good governance. The components of good governance range very widely; some of its aspects and their relationship with empowerment and development effectiveness are briefly discussed below.

The rule of law is one of the foundations of good governance. According to Dollar and Kraay (2000), the availability (or absence) of impartial, dependable, and reasonably speedy judicial systems and associated enforcement mechanisms is important for the investment climate, and hence for countries' growth prospects. Kaufmann, Kraay, and Zoido-Lobatón (1999) found a large, significant, and causal relationship between the rule of law and the income of nations (and also between rule of law, higher literacy, and reduced infant mortality). In its equity (or inequity) aspects, the rule of law also affects empowerment: if poor people can obtain impartial justice, their freedom is enhanced. By the same token, empowerment can improve the quality of the judicial and enforcement system, especially by increasing the availability and dissemination of information about how the system works.

Corruption is both a symptom and a cause of poor governance. It undermines the investment climate and development effectiveness. It imposes heavy costs on poor people, who have fewer resources than the better-off to pay bribes. A study in Ecuador demonstrates that poor people and small firms pay more in bribes as a proportion of their income than the rich or large firms.[3] Empowering people through greater openness and participation can lead both to the availability of more information about the pervasiveness of corruption and to popular pressure to eliminate it—once again illustrating the two-way relationship between empowerment and good governance. One proxy for empowerment is the strength of civil liberties in society; Kaufmann (2000), using data from 150 countries, found that those with high levels of civil liberties had very low corruption, but that the level of corruption was four times higher in countries that were only partly free and 24 times higher in countries with no civil liberties.

One specific aspect of empowerment—enhanced women's rights and participation—deserves special mention in this context. Empowerment of women is associated with cleaner business and government, and better governance. Specifically, the greater their involvement in public life, the lower the level of corruption, even in countries with the same income, civil liberties, education, and legal institutions.[4] At the micro level, studies have shown that women in business are less likely than men to pay bribes to government officials, either because they have higher ethical standards or because they are more risk-averse. A study of 350 firms in Georgia found that firms managed by men are twice as likely to pay bribes as those managed by women. The difference drops but is still significant after controlling for firm size, sector, and education of owner or manager.[5]

Empowerment—through inclusion, voice, and accountability—can also promote social cohesion and trust, qualities that help reduce corruption, reinforce government and project performance, and provide a conducive environment for reform, with consequential benefits for development effectiveness and economic growth. Ritzen, Easterly, and Woolcock (2000) have demonstrated the importance of social cohesion and inclusiveness for generating the trust needed to implement reforms. Knack and Keefer (1997) have established the relationship between growth and measures of trust and civic cooperation. La Porta and others (1997) have demonstrated the positive relationships between trust and judicial efficiency, anti-corruption, bureaucratic quality, tax compliance, and civic participation. Rodrik (1999) has shown that countries with the steepest falls in growth after exogenous shocks after 1975 were those that were socially divided in terms of income inequality, ethnic and linguistic fragmentation or conflict, and social trust, and had weak institutions for managing conflict.

Extreme examples of the breakdown of social cohesion and trust are war and civil conflict. Their intuitively evident consequences have been confirmed by research. For example, Collier (2000) has shown that on average civil war reduces a country's per capita output by more than 2 percent a year compared to what it would otherwise have been.[6] A study of Indian states shows that civil strife leads to the worst investment climate and growth performance.[7]

An important aspect of poor governance, with adverse consequences for growth prospects, is the extent of "state capture" by large firms. Business Environment and Enterprise Performance Surveys carried out recently in 20 countries in Eastern Europe and Central Asia demonstrate the extent of this phenomenon and its effects in terms of firms' capacity to buy influence in parliamentary legislation, criminal and commercial courts, and decision making by central banks. The study shows that, between 1997 and 1999, "high capture" countries achieved only half the sales and investment of "low capture" countries. Again, however, the two-way relationship between empowerment and good governance comes into play. Good governance can promote empowerment by encouraging the growth of civil liberties—and countries with a high degree of empowerment in terms of civil liberties have low state capture.[8]

Finally, because development effectiveness and growth depend critically on public action, including well-designed and effectively deployed public spending on development priorities, sound public expenditure management is an essential aspect of good governance. Here again, aspects of empowerment, including provision of information to citizens and government commitment to transparency and accountability with respect to public spending, can play a critical role. When stakeholders, including civil society, the private sector, and intended beneficiaries (including poor people), can monitor public expenditure outcomes, performance can be enhanced. Public spending on education in Uganda provides a case in point. When Uganda instituted public monitoring of funds going to primary schools and school districts, the share of nonwage allocations actually reaching schools rose from 22 percent in 1995 to about 80 to 90 percent by 2000.[9] Here is an example of how key aspects of empowerment and government performance (and development effectiveness) go hand in hand: spending on improvements in education service delivery is critical for empowerment, while empowerment, in the form of citizen monitoring, is helping to ensure that public spending on education is actually reaching its intended beneficiaries—and thereby enhancing the effectiveness of public action and growth prospects.

Empowerment and Development Effectiveness: Making Growth Pro-Poor

There is a large cross-disciplinary literature and substantial development experience on the links between empowerment, growth, and poverty reduction (see especially Stern 2002; World Bank 2000c). Income poverty has fallen most rapidly in economies that have grown dynamically, and poverty has remained high or has increased in countries with poor growth records.

Experience also shows that growth alone is not enough to ensure substantial and sustainable poverty reduction. Country data indicate that similar growth rates can lead to very different poverty reduction outcomes.[10] For a given rate of growth, poverty will fall faster in countries where the distribution of income becomes more equal, as in Uganda, than in countries where it becomes less equal, as in Bangladesh.[11] And even where income distribution does not become more unequal with growth, country differences in initial inequality produce different poverty reduction outcomes for a given rate of growth. Hence, if poverty reduction is taken as a measure of development effectiveness, then the development effectiveness of growth efforts varies with levels of inequality.

A critical aspect of an empowering approach is to reduce inequality by broadening human capabilities (through, for example, universal basic education and health care, together with adequate arrangements for social protection)[12] and improving the distribution of tangible assets (such as land or access to capital). Such an approach can enhance the poverty-reducing impact of growth-inducing policies and investments by enabling poor people to more effectively participate in markets. The converse also applies. When inequality is high, poor people lack capabilities and assets (ranging from literacy to collateral for credit) and thus have difficulty taking advantage of economic opportunity. This limits a society's potential for growth in general and pro-poor growth in particular, and consequently the effectiveness of development efforts.[13]

Gender discrimination, whether legal or customary, is a particularly important aspect of inequality. By curtailing the economic contribution of half the population, overall prospects for growth and higher living standards are limited—a situation perpetuated into future generations by inadequate investment in female education.[14]

Empowerment also implies more participatory, bottom-up approaches to development objectives. There is now substantial agreement that approaches giving poor people more freedom to make economic decisions enhance development effectiveness at the local level in terms of design, implementation, and outcomes. A particularly striking example of the positive consequences of empowering people in these ways comes from China. Two major Chinese reforms, the Household Responsibility System and the Township and Village Enterprise movement, promoted poor people's participation and freedom to make economic choices in rural areas, releasing the entrepreneurial energies of the Chinese people and thereby helping China to achieve rapid pro-poor growth. The number of poor people in rural China fell from 250 million in 1979, the first year of reform, to 34 million in 1990, with about half of the decline occurring between 1978 and 1985.[15]

Finally, empowerment can have sociopolitical benefits for a country's poverty reduction efforts. As noted in the previous section, societies that take steps toward wider social inclusion, broader voice, and enhanced accountability of governments can better achieve the social consensus and capacity for collective action needed to carry through sometimes difficult reforms effectively. They are also more likely to have a greater degree of policy and political stability, both of which help to promote sustainable and equitable pro-poor development, broadly defined.

Empowerment and Development Effectiveness: Project-Level Evidence

The above discussion has concentrated mainly on economy-wide relationships between empowerment and development effectiveness. This section draws on evidence at the project level that confirms the critical role of empowerment in terms of development outcomes.

Analyses of both large sets of projects and individual operations confirm the relationship between empowerment—in terms of variables such as voice, participation, and civil liberties—and development effectiveness in terms of outcomes. Isham, Kaufmann, and Pritchett (1997) found a strong empirical link between civil liberties and the performance of 1,500 government projects in 56 countries. Countries with the strongest civil liberties had project rates of return that were 8 to 22 percent higher than those without, and the relationship held even when controlling for the level of democracy. Thus civil liberties, especially in the form of citizen voice based on information, participation, and public accountability, can enhance the effectiveness of government action.

Empowerment in terms of citizen inclusion and participation at the local level can help ensure that basic services reach poor people, and can lower operation and maintenance costs by comparison with centrally managed activities. A study by the Bank's Operations Evaluation Department (OED) found that Bank-financed projects managed by local communities were slightly more successful than those managed by other entities.[16] Empowerment through community involvement is particularly effective in the management of local public goods such as water supply, sanitation, forests, roads, schools, and health clinics.[17] The poverty targeting of village-level food-for-education programs is improved by community involvement.[18] More specifically, within the range of variables associated with empowerment, a detailed analysis of village water and sanitation committees in two Indian states found that water system effectiveness, operation, and maintenance were most strongly linked to transparency of information, followed by ownership, participation, and inclusion.[19]

Devolving authority and decisions to the local level is not necessarily a panacea. Improvements in outcomes depend critically on local conditions and on tailoring institutional design to meet them. For example, a study of the Aga Khan Rural Support Program in Pakistan found that community-specific factors such as social heterogeneity, communal inequality, and leadership (or lack of it) accounted for half of the variation in collective performance on local infrastructure maintenance, but that project design features could compensate for adverse community-specific factors.[20] Institutional mechanisms for ensuring effectiveness, and for preventing capture by local elites, varied from case to case and drew on understanding of local power structures and investment in local capacity.

Finally, project-level effectiveness can be enhanced by an aspect of empowerment referred to earlier: greater gender equality. Farm-level studies of households in Burkina Faso, Cameroon, and Kenya show that more equal control of inputs and farm income by women and men could raise farm yields by as much as a fifth of current output.[21]

Conclusion

This section has summarized some of the linkages between empowerment and development effectiveness in terms of good governance, pro-poor growth, and project-level outcomes. But it must be emphasized that empowerment—especially empowerment of poor people—remains an ideal rather than a reality in most developing societies. The Voices of the Poor study, conducted in 60 countries, has shown that, despite very different social, economic, and political contexts, poor people's experiences are pervaded by a common sense of powerlessness and voicelessness.[22] Working to enhance empowerment is thus a huge challenge for developing countries and their external partners. It is both a moral challenge and an intensely practical one. Reducing the human degradation of powerlessness and releasing the energies of people to contribute to their societies through empowerment are two sides of the same coin, and represent not only key inputs to development effectiveness but also criteria by which the development effort of the twenty-first century will be judged (box 1-1).

Box 1-1 Why Is Empowerment Important?

Empowerment is key for:

- Quality of life and human dignity
- Good governance
- Pro-poor growth
- Project effectiveness and improved service delivery

The World Bank's Role

The World Bank's comparative advantage in pursuing an empowerment agenda as an integral aspect of poverty reduction lies in its relationship with more than 100 governments around the world. The Bank's comparative advantage is, obviously, not to work at the community level but to advise governments based on analytical and evaluative work, to facilitate links to financial investment, and to enable others directly or indirectly to work on the empowerment agenda. The Bank is uniquely placed to provide support in four areas: (a) analysis, evaluation, and advice; (b) convening; (c) enabling; and (d) capacity building.

Analysis, Evaluation, and Advice

The Bank advises governments on a wide range of issues, from governance to sector reform to economic growth strategies, basing its advice on sound analysis and research and learning from investment projects that it co-finances with governments. Indeed, the Bank provides more advice on systemic changes than any other organization. The Bank is uniquely placed to conduct rigorous analyses on empowerment issues and their linkages to growth and poverty reduction. It is also uniquely placed to ensure that macro, micro, and institutional reforms are reciprocally reinforcing, and that they empower poor people by increasing their assets, capabilities, and access to services while improving economic efficiency. This is important for strategies that affect poor people as consumers (food, electricity, water, transport); as producers (farmers, entrepreneurs, employees); and as citizens (access to justice, education, health, protection from crime and warfare).

Convening

Empowering poor people requires new relations and partnerships based on respect and tolerance among government, the legislature, civil society, poor peoples' organizations, research institutes, the private sector, and donors. The Bank can play a very useful convening role in bringing the different stakeholders together to stimulate debate, consensus, and coalition building for reform.

Enabling

The Bank's focus on the four key elements of empowerment can create the space for other actors, both local and international, to support empowerment approaches that are not within the Bank's comparative advantage. The Bank can play a crucial role in supporting information disclosure and public accountability mechanisms to monitor economy-wide reform, public expenditures, and sector reform, all the way down to investments made in particular communities. Fostering a climate of transparency and public access to information can enable civil society and others to play important roles in creating accountable governments. It will create a demand for strong local capacity for research, analysis, monitoring, and evaluation of social and economic outcomes. Similarly, emphasizing the need for local organizational capacity will create space for local actors to work at the grassroots level. The Bank's comparative advantage is primarily in working with governments to change rules, regulations, and investment strategies to make possible the emergence of strong local organizations that can work as effective partners with their governments.

Capacity Building

Strong civil society and government institutions—at both the local and national levels—that learn consciously from their experience are essential for sustained poverty reduction. Bank-financed projects and programs that require local organizational capacity must also invest resources in building such capacity. In addition, the Bank has an important role to play in enabling long-term support to local institutions. In collaboration with other donors and the private sector, the Bank can support the capacity of in-country intermediary organizations, research institutes, and nongovernmental organizations (NGOs) that conduct poverty, institutional, social, and governance assessments. Local capacity to monitor, evaluate, and communicate information back to citizens, including poor people, is critical for improving the outcomes of government programs. The Bank can also facilitate a global network of learning from poor people's organizations and civil society intermediaries about the empowerment of poor people.

Notes

1. The empowerment framework will also feed into the World Bank's Social Development Strategy currently being developed (see World Bank 2002b).

2. A paper prepared for the April 2002 meeting of the World Bank–IMF Development Committee highlighted empowerment of poor people as a critical component of development effectiveness (Development Committee 2002).

3. Hellman and others 2000.

4. World Bank 2001c.

5. World Bank 2001c.

6. Collier also establishes the links between poverty, civil conflict, and economic dependence on the export of a single primary commodity (such as diamonds).

7. Dollar 2000.

8. Hellman and others (2000) note that action to reduce state capture can include encouraging societal voice, transparency in reform, political accountability, and increased economic competition.

9. Reinikka 2001; Reinikka and Svensson 2002.

10. Ravallion 2001.

11. Appleton and others 1999; Wodon 1997, 1999, 2000; World Bank 2000c.

12. Stern 2002.

13. A recent study of 15 Indian states shows that rural nonfarm output growth was more pro-poor in states that initially had higher literacy, farm productivity, and rural living standards relative to urban areas, and lower landlessness and infant mortality (Ravallion and Datt forthcoming). Another recent study comparing inequality in Brazil, Mexico, and the United States concludes that Brazil's high income inequality results from high inequality in access to education and claims on assets and transfers that generate nonlabor income (Bourguignon, Ferreira, and Leite forthcoming).

14. One study estimates that if the countries of South Asia, Sub-Saharan Africa, and the Middle East and North Africa had started with East Asia's 1960 gender gap in average years of education and had closed the gap at the rate achieved by East Asia between 1960 and 1992, their per capita income could have grown by 0.5–0.9 percentage points faster per year—a substantial increase over the rates actually achieved (World Bank 2001c).

15. Stern 2002.

16. OED 2000.

17. Baume, Juarez, and Standing 2001; Hoddinot and others 2000; Jimenez and Sawada 1998; Katz and Sara 1997; Narayan 1995; Venkataraman and Falconer 1998.

18. Galasso and Ravallion 2000. This study also found that targeting was worse in villages that were isolated or had higher land inequality.

19. Abhyankar and Iyer 2001; World Bank 2001h.

20. Khwaja 2000.

21. Dollar and Gatti 1999; Klasen 1999; World Bank 2001c.

22. Voices of the Poor is a multicountry research initiative undertaken to understand poverty from the perspectives of poor people. The findings were published in three volumes. *Can Anyone Hear Us?* (Narayan with others 2000) gathers the voices of over 40,000 poor women and men in 50 countries from the World Bank's participatory poverty assessments. *Crying Out for Change* (Narayan and others 2000) pulls together new fieldwork involving 20,000 poor men and women in 23 countries in 1999. *From Many Lands* (Narayan and Petesch 2002) offers regional patterns and country case studies.

Chapter 2

What Is Empowerment?

WDR 2000/2001 and the *Voices of the Poor* study establish that across very different social, cultural, economic, and political contexts the common elements that underlie poor people's exclusion are voicelessness and powerlessness. Confronted with unequal power relations, poor people are unable to influence or negotiate better terms for themselves with traders, financiers, governments, and civil society. This severely constrains their capability to accumulate assets and rise out of poverty. Dependent on others for their survival, poor women and men also frequently find it impossible to prevent violations of dignity, respect, and cultural identity.

This chapter first sets forth a definition of empowerment and then identifies four elements that appear—singly or in combination—in most successful attempts to empower poor people. Drawing on these elements, it then diagrams a conceptual framework that focuses on institutional reform to invest in poor people's assets and capabilities, leading to improved development outcomes. Finally, the chapter discusses how empowerment approaches vary by context.

Defining Empowerment

The term empowerment has different meanings in different sociocultural and political contexts, and does not translate easily into all languages. An exploration of local terms associated with empowerment around the world always leads to lively discussion. These terms include self-strength, control, self-power, self-reliance, own choice, life of dignity in accordance with one's values, capacity to fight for one's rights, independence, own decision making, being free, awakening, and capability—to mention only a few. These definitions are embedded in local value and belief systems.

Empowerment is of intrinsic value; it also has instrumental value. Empowerment is relevant at the individual and collective level, and can be economic, social, or political. The term can be used to characterize relations within households or between poor people and other actors at the global level. There are important gender differences in the causes, forms, and consequences of empowerment or disempowerment. Hence, there are obviously many possible definitions of empowerment, including rights-based definitions.[1]

In its broadest sense, empowerment is the expansion of freedom of choice and action.[2] It means increasing one's authority and control over the resources and decisions that affect one's life. As people exercise real choice, they gain increased control over their lives. Poor people's choices are extremely limited, both by their lack of assets and by their power-lessness to negotiate better terms for themselves with a range of institutions, both formal and informal. Since powerlessness is embedded in the nature of institutional relations, in the context of poverty reduction an institutional definition of empowerment is appropriate. This also helps draw out the relevance to Bank operations.

> *Empowerment is the expansion of assets and capabilities of poor people to participate in, negotiate with, influence, control, and hold accountable institutions that affect their lives.*

Poor People's Assets and Capabilities

Poor women and men need a range of assets and capabilities to increase their wellbeing and security, as well as their self-confidence, so they can negotiate with those more powerful. Because poverty is multidimensional, so are these assets and capabilities.

"Assets" refers to material assets, both physical and financial. Such assets—including land, housing, livestock, savings, and jewelry—enable people to withstand shocks and expand their horizon of choices. The extreme limitation of poor people's physical and financial assets severely constrains their capacity to negotiate fair deals for themselves and increases their vulnerability.

Capabilities, on the other hand, are inherent in people and enable them to use their assets in different ways to increase their wellbeing. Human capabilities include good health, education, and production or other life-enhancing skills. Social capabilities include social belonging, leadership, relations of trust, a sense of identity, values that give meaning to life, and the capacity to organize. Political capability includes the capacity to represent oneself or others, access information, form associations, and participate in the political life of a community or country.

Assets and capabilities can be *individual* or *collective*. Given lack of voice and power and deeply entrenched social barriers, even in many formal democracies, poor people are often unable to take advantage of opportunities to invest in their assets or exercise their individual rights.

For poor people, the capacity to organize and mobilize to solve problems is a critical *collective* capability that helps them overcome problems of limited resources and marginalization in society. Social capital, the norms and networks that enable collective action, allows poor people to increase their access to resources and economic opportunities, obtain basic services, and participate in local governance. There are important gender differences in social capital that need to be addressed.[3] Poor people are often high in "bonding" social capital—close ties and high levels of trust with others like themselves. These close ties help them cope with their poverty. Sometimes poor people's groups establish ties with other groups unlike themselves, creating "bridge" relations to new resources managed by other groups. Traditionally these ties have been unequal, as in patron-client relations. When poor people's organizations link up or bridge with organizations of the state, civil society, or the private sector, they are able to access additional resources and participate more fully in society.

Relationship between Individual and Collective Assets and Capabilities

There is a reciprocal relationship between individual assets and capabilities and the capability to act collectively. This two-way relationship holds true for all groups in society, although the focus here is on poor people. Poor people who are healthy, educated, and secure can contribute more effectively to collective action; at the same time, collective action can improve poor people's access to quality schools or health clinics. Poor people's freedom of choice and action can thus be expanded in various ways. Investments in health, education, and life skills are of intrinsic value and can also increase economic returns to the individual. Access to wage employment can increase security. This is not automatic, however, given the social, power, and communication barriers faced by poor people.

Poor people's organizations, groups, and networks, working with others, can mobilize resources to improve individual health, education, and security of assets. Working through representative community-based organizations, poor people can express their preferences, exercise voice, and hold governments and state service providers accountable for providing quality services in education, health, water, sanitation, agriculture, or other areas. Collective action through poor people's membership-based organizations can also improve access to business development and financial services, and to new markets where people can buy needed items and sell their produce.

These collective capabilities that allow poor people to mobilize and organize to solve problems have not yet been systematically included in strategies to reduce poverty.

Institutional Reform and Empowerment

In an institutional context, empowerment is about changing unequal institutional relationships. Institutions are rules, norms, and patterned behavior that may or may not take organizational form. The institutions that affect poor people's lives are formal and informal. Formal institutions include the laws and rules embedded in state, private sector, and civil society organizations at the local, national, and global levels, as well as international organizations. Informal institutions include, for example, norms of inferior or superior status, expectations of bribes, networks of kin, friends, and neighbors, informal restrictions placed on women inheriting property, or the cluster of practices surrounding treatment of widows.

State policies and the culture of state institutions shape the actions of all other actors: poor men and women, other excluded groups, the private sector, civil society including unions and faith-based organizations, and international agencies. When states are captured by the wealthy and powerful and become mired in a culture of corruption, clientism, exclusion, and discrimination, even well-meaning policies and programs fail to promote investment or reduce poverty. Hence it is important to address the culture, values, and ethics of institutions, since these can defeat formal rules. Findings from Voices of the Poor also establish that poor people long for institutions that listen and treat them with respect and dignity, even when these institutions cannot solve any problems.

Poor people are generally excluded from participation in state institutions that make the decisions and administer the resources that affect their lives. This is what leads poor people to conclude, "Nobody hears the poor. It is the rich who are being heard" or "When the rich and poor compete for services, the rich will always get priority."[4] To bring about systemic reform will require changing these unequal institutional relations that reflect a culture of inequality. Changing unequal institutional relations depends in part on top-down measures to improve governance—changes in the laws, procedures, regulations, values, ethics, and incentives that guide the behavior of public officials and the private sector. It also depends crucially on the presence of well-informed and well-organized citizens and poor people. This requires rules and laws and investment of public and private resources to *strengthen the demand side of governance*. These changes can create the conditions that enable poor women and men to exercise their agency.

Intermediate civil society groups have critical roles to play in supporting poor people's capabilities, translating and interpreting information to them, and helping link them to the state and the private sector. However, such groups have to stay vigilant to ensure that they really do represent poor people's interests and are accountable to them.

The social and cultural context is particularly important for empowerment approaches. Therefore both state reform and efforts to build poor people's assets and organizational capability must take forms that reflect local norms, values, and behaviors. Empowerment approaches will sometimes be controversial; for instance, local women's demands for autonomy and equal access to resources may run up against cultural norms of female exclusion. Reform processes must always try to build on cultural strengths to overcome exclusionary barriers and bring about pro-poor change.

No Single Model for Empowerment

An empowering approach to development puts poor people at the center of development and views them as the most important resource rather than as the problem. It recognizes and values their identity. This implies changes in the beliefs, mindsets, and behavior that outsiders bring to poverty reduction. An empowering approach thus builds on poor people's strengths: their knowledge, skills, values, initiative, and motivation to solve problems, manage resources, and rise out of poverty. It treats poor people as worthy of honor, respect, and dignity.

Since most societies are not socially homogenous but are marked by class, ethnicity, caste, religion, and gender differences, institutional strategies to empower poor people will necessarily vary. Strategies to enable poor women to inherit property will differ from strategies to make local schools accountable to parents or to have ethnic minority concerns reflected in national budgets. Each of these in turn will vary depending on the political, institutional, cultural, and social context.

Strategies also evolve and change over time in any given context. With time, there is generally a movement away from reliance on informal mechanisms toward formal mechanisms, and from direct and more time-intensive forms of participation toward indirect forms of participation. The latter include market mechanisms and paying fees for services rather than co-management.

The challenge, then, is to identify *key elements of empowerment* that recur consistently across social, institutional, and political contexts. Institutional design must then focus on incorporating these elements or principles of empowerment.

Four Elements of Empowerment

There are thousands of examples of empowering approaches that have been initiated by poor people themselves and by governments, civil society, and the private sector. Successful efforts to empower poor people, increasing their freedom of choice and action in different contexts, often share four elements:

- Access to information
- Inclusion and participation
- Accountability
- Local organizational capacity.

While these four elements are discussed separately below, they are closely intertwined and act in synergy.[5] Thus although access to timely information about programs, or about government performance or corruption, is a necessary precondition for action, poor people or citizens more broadly may not take action because there are no institutional mechanisms that demand accountable performance or because the costs of individual action may be too high. Similarly, experience shows that poor people do not participate in activities when they know their participation will make no difference to products being offered or decisions made because there are no mechanisms for holding providers accountable. Even where there are strong local organizations, they may still be disconnected from local governments and the private sector and lack access to information.

Access to Information

Two-way information flows from governments to citizens and from citizens to governments are critical for responsible citizenship and responsive and accountable governments. Informed citizens are better equipped to take advantage of opportunities, access services, exercise their rights, negotiate effectively, and hold state and nonstate actors accountable. Without information that is relevant, timely, and presented in forms that can be understood, it is impossible for poor people to take effective action. Information dissemination does not stop with the written word, but also includes group discussions, poetry, storytelling, debates, street theater, and soap operas—among other culturally appropriate forms—and uses a variety of media including radio, television, and the Internet. Laws about rights to information and freedom of the press, particularly local press in local languages, provide the enabling environment for the emergence of informed citizen action. Timely access to information in local languages from independent sources at the local level is particularly important, as more and more countries devolve authority to local government.[6]

Most investment projects and institutional reform projects, whether at the community level or at the national or global level, underestimate the need for information and underinvest in information disclosure and dissemination.[7] Critical areas include information about rules and rights to basic government services, about state and private sector performance, and about financial services, markets, and prices. Information and communications technologies (ICT) can play important roles in connecting poor people to these kinds of information, as well as to each other and to the larger society. Tools and Practices 1 provides some examples of this. Tools and Practices 7 provides detailed examples of information disclosure strategies used in different contexts.

To ensure responsiveness to poor people, governments also need to institute ways of collecting information about poor people's priorities and preferences. Mechanisms for systematic feedback from them must be institutionalized.

Inclusion and Participation

Inclusion focuses on the *who* question: Who is included? Participation addresses the question of *how* they are included and the role they play once included. An empowering approach to participation views poor people as co-producers with authority and control over decisions and resources—particularly financial resources—devolved to the lowest appropriate level.

Sustaining poor people's participation in societies with deeply entrenched norms of exclusion or in multiethnic societies with a history of conflict is a complex process that requires new institutional mechanisms, resources, facilitation, sustained vigilance, and experimentation. The tendency among most government agencies is to revert to centralized decision making and to hold endless public meetings without any impact on policy or resource decisions. "Participation" then becomes yet another cost imposed on poor people without any returns.

Inclusion of poor people and other traditionally excluded groups is also critical in priority setting and budget formation at the local and national level to ensure that limited public resources build on local knowledge and priorities, and build commitment to change. Participatory decision making is not always harmonious and priorities may be contested, so conflict resolution mechanisms need to be in place to manage disagreements.

Participation can take different forms. At the local level, depending on the issue, participation may be:

- direct
- representational, by selecting representatives from membership-based groups and associations
- political, through elected representatives
- information-based, with data aggregated and reported directly or through intermediaries to local and national decision makers
- based on competitive market mechanisms, for example, by removing restrictions and other barriers, increasing choice about what people can grow or to whom they can sell, or by payment for services selected and received.

Among the four elements of empowerment, participation of poor people in planning is the most developed in Bank projects and increasingly also in preparation of Bank Country Assistance Strategies (CASs).[8] In low-income countries, the process of preparing Poverty Reduction Strategy Papers (PRSPs) has opened new opportunities to institutionalize broad-based participation by poor people, citizens' groups, and private sector groups in national priority setting and policymaking.

Accountability

Accountability refers to the ability to call public officials, private employers, or service providers to account, requiring that they be answerable for their policies, actions, and use of funds. Widespread corruption, defined as the abuse of public office for private gain, hurts poor people the most because they are the least likely to have direct access to officials and the least able to use connections to get services; they also have the fewest options to use private services as an alternative.[9]

There are three main types of accountability mechanisms: political, administrative, and public. Political accountability of political parties and representatives is increasingly through elections.[10] Administrative accountability of government agencies is through internal accountability mechanisms, both horizontal and vertical within and between agencies. Public or social accountability mechanisms hold government agencies accountable to citizens. Social accountability can reinforce political and administrative accountability mechanisms.

A range of tools exists to ensure greater accounting to citizens for public actions and outcomes. Access to information by citizens builds pressure for improved governance and accountability, whether in setting priorities for national expenditure, providing access to quality schools, ensuring that roads once financed actually get built, or seeing to it that medicines are actually delivered and available in clinics. Access to laws and impartial justice is also critical to protect the rights of poor people and pro-poor coalitions and to enable them to demand accountability, whether from their governments or from private sector institutions.

Accountability for public resources at all levels can also be ensured through transparent fiscal management and by offering users a choice in services. At the community level, for example, this includes giving poor groups choice and the funds to purchase technical assistance from any provider rather than requiring them to accept technical assistance provided by government. Fiscal discipline can be imposed by setting limits and reducing subsidies over time. Contractor accountability is ensured when poor people decide whether the service was delivered as contracted and whether the contractor should be paid. When poor people can hold providers accountable, control and power shifts to them.[11]

Local Organizational Capacity

Since time immemorial, groups and communities have organized to take care of themselves. Local organizational capacity refers to the ability of people to work together, organize themselves, and mobilize resources to solve problems of common interest. Often outside the reach of formal systems, poor people turn to each other for support and strength to solve their everyday problems. Poor people's organizations are often informal, as in the case of a group of women who lend each other money or rice. They may also be formal, with or without legal registration, as in the case of farmers' groups or neighborhood clubs. Around the world, including in war-torn societies, the capacity of communities to make rational decisions, manage funds, and solve problems is greater than generally assumed.[12]

Organized communities are more likely to have their voices heard and their demands met than communities with little organization. Poor people's membership-based organizations may be highly effective in meeting survival needs, but they are constrained by limited resources and technical knowledge. In addition, they often lack bridging and linking social capital, that is, they may not be connected to other groups unlike themselves or to the resources of civil society or the state. It is only when groups connect with each other across communities and form networks or associations—eventually becoming large federations with a regional or national presence—that they begin to influence government decision making and gain collective bargaining power with suppliers of raw materials, buyers, employers, and financiers.[13]

Local organizational capacity is key for development effectiveness.[14] Poor people's organizations, associations, federations, networks, and social movements are key players in the institutional landscape. But they are not yet a systematic part of the Bank's analytical or operational work in the public or the private sector or in most sectoral strategies.[15] Tools and Practices 9 provides examples of investing in local organizational capacity in community-driven projects. Tools and Practices 13 provides examples of the roles played by poor people's organizations, such as farmers' organizations in rural areas and slum dwellers' associations in urban areas.

The Empowerment Framework

Figure 2-1 summarizes the empowerment framework outlined above, describing the relationship between institutions, empowerment, and improved development outcomes, particularly for poor people. State reform that supports investments in poor people and their organizations leads to improved development outcomes, including improved governance, better-functioning and more inclusive services, more equitable access to markets, strengthened civil society and poor people's organizations, and increased assets and freedom of choice.

Institutional reform to support empowerment of poor people means changing the relationship between the state and poor people and their organizations. It focuses on investing in poor people's assets and capabilities, both individual capabilities and the collective capacity to

FIGURE 2-1 Empowerment Framework

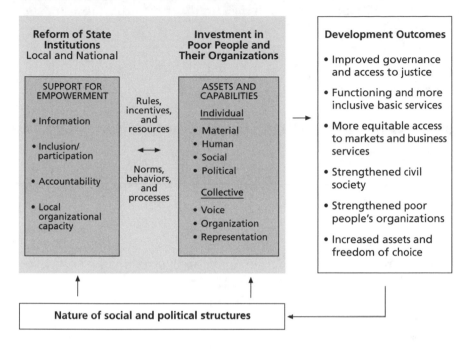

organize, to enable them to participate effectively in society and to interact with their governments, so as to strengthen the demand side of governance. State reform, whether at the national, state, or local government level, must focus on laws, rules, institutional mechanisms, values, and behavior that support the four elements of empowerment. Changes in formal rules and regulations must be connected to efforts to enable poor people and other citizens to interact effectively with their governments and to monitor governance.

The focus of reform is thus on: (a) designing mechanisms to support poor people's access to information; (b) supporting mechanisms for inclusion and participation; (c) creating social accountability mechanisms; and (d) investing in poor people's organizational capacity to solve problems. Direct participation of poor people and their representatives is not feasible or realistic in every context. Civil society intermediaries such as research institutes, NGOs, and faith-based organizations have important roles to play in carrying poor people's voices to local and national decision makers.

The kind of state reform that is feasible and relevant is conditioned by the country's social and political structures at a particular point in time. Over time, there are feedback loops that affect social and political structures, which then leads to changes in the state mechanisms for supporting empowerment. For example, as the importance of access to information becomes apparent, countries may execute new freedom of information acts and invest in information technology to ease public access to information.

Empowerment in Context: Conditions Vary

There is no single model for empowerment and no blueprint for the reforms required. What is possible and appropriate will vary by context. Nevertheless, it is possible to identify major influencing conditions:

- The nature of public action
- Patterns of social exclusion and conflict
- The extent of decentralization
- The strength of local-level institutions and civil society
- The extent of political freedom.

Nature of Public Action

Public action can vary from intervention at the local level to broad economy-wide changes. Depending on the nature of the "good" being provided at the local level, either some or all four features of empowerment will be important. If the provision of a public service or action at the local level is based on co-management with local communities, for example, in rural water supply or elementary education, all four principles including local organizational capacity become important. If, on the other hand, the service is government-managed and either requires few ongoing management inputs or is based on a fee for service, then institutional mechanisms to disseminate information to enable inclusion and downward accountability mechanisms may be sufficient.

If the public action is sector-wide or economy-wide, the most useful strategy is a process of consultation and debate to inform decision making, followed by information dissemination about the decision and institutionalized mechanisms for feedback from poor people and other citizens on the impact of policies. Ongoing and continuous participation may be inappropriate in most such cases.

Patterns of Social Exclusion and Conflict

All societies are stratified to a greater or lesser extent. When social cleavages are deep and systemic, access to services and opportunities is determined not by individual characteristics but by social structures and a culture of inequality that discriminate against or exclude entire social groups. The more powerful social groups control the entry and exit options of those excluded from full participation in social, economic, and political life at the community and national levels. In Latin America, for example, many people of indigenous or African descent continue to be excluded and discriminated against by the dominant culture, and they remain poor. In other places exclusion is based on caste, race, religion, or ethnicity, or on educational or economic distinctions. Gender is often a basis of exclusion.

Understanding patterns of social exclusion and the culture supporting exclusion is critical in making informed policy choices, as well as in designing interventions. The first step is making exclusion visible by gathering poverty statistics disaggregated by social group. Efforts to address exclusion may require changes in laws, rules, and regulations to remove discriminatory barriers. Additionally, to enable previously excluded groups to take advantage of new opportunities to participate, it may be necessary to invest in the capabilities of these groups in ways that they value.

When societies are affected by conflict, the history of that conflict will condition the nature of intervention. Of the 47 countries included in the Heavily Indebted Poor Countries debt initiative, 20 (43 percent) are conflict-affected. In the last decade alone, 90 new conflicts, largely intrastate in nature, have erupted worldwide.[16] If a conflict is based on social exclusion, then reconciliation, peace, and nation building must include actions to develop "bridging" social capital that increases interaction over time between previously warring social groups.

Extent of Decentralization

The idea behind decentralization is that moving decision making closer to people will lead to better public decisions that reflect local priorities. It is possible for community members to participate in local governance in countries that have devolved authority, resources, and decision making to lower levels of government and political bodies.

However, decentralization is unlikely to lead to improved governance and greater equity if it does not reach down into communities, enable informed input into public decisions, and provide incentives to local governments to empower local communities and be accountable to their input.

In highly centralized countries, community-driven demonstration projects can help establish the credibility of local groups to manage resources and develop their communities. However, these experiences should be closely monitored, and results should be evaluated and disseminated to inform national policies aimed at creating decentralized governance structures appropriate to that country.

Strength of Local-Level Institutions and Civil Society

Interventions at the local level require groups that include or represent poor people's interests. This in turn requires understanding local-level institutions, their leadership patterns, their activities, and their outreach. Such institutions tend not to be registered or to have formal status. When history, politics, war, migration, or policies have eroded local-level institutions and poor people's organizations, strategies that presume strong local organizations will not work without investment in these organizations over a period of time. Emergence of invisible and dormant local-level institutions can be encouraged by changes in legislative and administrative rules and regulations that allow these groups to access resources, including information.

Civil society institutions, from research institutes to parliaments to labor unions, are important intermediaries and actors in the domain of public action. Rules and regulations may limit their activities, their access to financing, their ability to associate, their access to information, and their independence. In certain contexts, changing the overall rules and regulations that influence the strength of civil society may be more productive than other interventions.

Extent of Political Freedom

It is important to understand the political context in order to develop strategies that work. Political freedoms—particularly freedom of information, a free press, freedom of speech and public debate, freedom to form associations and unions, and equal access to justice—condition the institutional reform that is feasible. In an environment where these freedoms are limited, three strategies are possible. The first is to establish pilot projects as special enclaves in which to test out what works; however, scaling up is only feasible when the enabling environment changes. The second is to establish transparency and free flow of information to the public and downward accountability mechanisms, at least in Bank-financed projects, to ensure effective use of funds. The third, which may be the most appropriate entry point, is to enlarge freedom in economic decisions and activities of producers, buyers, and sellers.

Notes

1. A review of definitions of empowerment reveals both diversity and commonality. Most definitions focus on issues of gaining power and control over decisions and resources that determine the quality of one's life. Most also take into account structural inequalities that affect entire social groups rather than focusing only on individual characteristics. The UNICEF Women's Equality and Empowerment Framework emphasizes women's access, awareness of causes of inequality, capacity to direct one's own interests, and taking control and action to overcome obstacles to reducing structural inequality (UNICEF 2001). The United Nations Development Programme's Gender Empowerment Measure focuses on inequalities in economic and political participation and decision-making power and power over economic resources (UNDP 1995). Other writers explore empowerment at different levels: personal, involving a sense of self-confidence and capacity; relational, implying ability to negotiate and influence relationships and decisions; and collective (Rowlands 1997). The definition used by the International Fund for Agricultural Development includes both access to productive resources and the capacity to participate in decisions that affect the least privileged (Popular Coalition to Eradicate Hunger and Poverty 1995). In an extensive exploration of the term empowerment, Kabeer (1999, 2001) focuses on three dimensions that define the capacity to exercise strategic life choices: access to resources, agency, and outcomes.

2. Amartya Sen (1985, 1999) has written extensively on the importance of substantive freedoms and the individual freedom to choose and achieve different outcomes.

3. Narayan and Shah 2000b.

4. Narayah and others 2000.

5. A recent survey of public officials in Bolivia shows that municipalities with greater transparency and citizen involvement have greater poverty reduction, and less bribery and job purchase (World Bank 2001g). A detailed analysis of village water and sanitation committees in 45 randomly selected villages in two states in India with Bank-financed water supply and sanitation projects found water system effectiveness to be

most strongly linked to transparency of information, followed by ownership, participation, and inclusion (Abhyankar and Iyer 2001; World Bank 2001h).

6.   A study of decentralized governance in the Philippines and Uganda found that the absence of local media and press coverage of local government activities left citizens dependent on local leaders and officials for information. People had more independent information from the media about national government policies and activities than about their local governments. Uninformed people cannot hold governments accountable (Azfar, Kähkönen, and Meagher 2001; World Bank 2001a).

7.   A key strategy that has emerged for effective management of local public goods is the creation of user groups. However, a recent survey of 2,400 user group members in three Bank-financed natural resource projects in three states in India revealed that approximately two-thirds of members did not attend user group meetings because "information about meetings is not available to group members." Most members did not know the rules about group finances or how funds were managed or spent (Alsop and others 2001).

8.   Studies by the Bank's Operations Evaluation Department establish that participation of poor people in projects increased from 40 percent in 1994 to 70 percent in 1998. In Country Assistance Strategies it increased from 24 percent in 1995 to 73 percent in 2000. However, only 12 percent of projects were participatory during implementation and only 9 percent included participatory monitoring and evaluation, a key mechanism to foster accountability to community groups. The most frequently cited internal constraint on higher levels of participation was lack of financial resources (World Bank 2000b).

9.   Corruption is a regressive tax on the poor. A study in Ecuador found that as a proportion of their revenue, micro businesses paid four times as much in bribes as did large firms. The bribe cost to poor households was triple the cost to high-income households (Kaufmann, Zoido-Lobatón, and Lee 2000).

10.   As part of the PRSP process, parliamentarians in several countries have asked for support in capacity building to better discharge their legislative and oversight roles.

11.   An incentive analysis of strategies to combat corruption at the local level in the Kecamatan Development Project (KDP) in Indonesia concludes that effective incentives to curb corruption include easy public access to information, particularly financial information, use of local social norms and social institutions to stigmatize misuse and resolve conflicts, and socialization of communities and facilitators to understand their rights and become vigilant agents of anti-corruption. The KDP funds pass through fewer intermediaries with less red tape than elsewhere, and authority and control over resources is given to local communities rather than directly to contractors. On average sub-projects cost 20–30 percent less than other projects (Woodhouse 2002).

12.   An in-depth study of 48 villages across Indonesia found that 38 percent of all community development activities had been initiated by communities themselves without any government involvement. These outperformed government-initiated activities on every outcome measure: extent to which they reached beneficiaries, use of facilities,

maintenance, and women's participation. Despite this, there was no linkage between this community capacity and government-initiated community development activities (Chandrakirana 1999; Narayan with others 2000).

13. As part of the PRSP process, labor unions are increasingly being involved; in West Africa this includes farmers' associations.

14. An analysis of 18 case studies of the best-known large-scale rural development programs across Asia, Africa, and Latin America concludes that a "critical success factor is creating organizational capabilities at local levels that can mobilize and manage resources effectively for the benefit of the many rather than just the few" (Krishna, Uphoff, and Esman 1997, p. 2). An econometric analysis of 121 rural water supply projects found local organizational capacity to be key in sustainable functioning of water systems (Narayan 1995; Isham, Narayan, and Pritchett 1995). A study in Tanzania found that higher village-level social capital measured by membership in groups of particular characteristics generated higher household incomes (Narayan and Pritchett 1997). In Côte d'Ivoire, when responsibility was shifted from central governments to water user groups, breakdown rates were reduced from 50 to 11 percent and costs fell nearly 70 percent. However, these results were sustained only where well-functioning community organizations existed (Hino 1993).

15. While the language of user groups, self-help groups, and community groups has been incorporated in many Bank-financed projects, the emphasis has been narrowly instrumental, focusing on participation in particular management tasks, which does not necessarily build local organizational capacity. A recent large-scale study on user groups in India, where over 40 percent of Bank-financed investment projects depend upon local organizations such as user groups, is instructive. The authors conclude that although user groups work well in the delivery of project benefits, current strategies do not foster sustainable participation of excluded groups or local ownership. The groups are unlikely to serve as the basis for longer-term local organizations (Alsop and others 2001). The cohort of Bank-financed community-driven projects that gives community groups authority and control over resources is more likely to build long-term local organizational capacity. However, evaluations of this capacity are still in the early stages.

16. For more information and a useful typology of conflict and phases of conflict, see von Meijenfeldt 2001.

Chapter 3

Applying Empowerment Principles

The four elements of empowerment—information, inclusion/participation, accountability, and local organizational capacity—can be combined to create more effective, responsive, inclusive, and accountable institutions. Such institutions enable poor people to develop their own capabilities, increase their assets, and move out of poverty.

The state has a central role to play in providing the right incentives to improve the performance of public and private providers. The state can change rules and the culture of exclusion and inequality, remove constraints, encourage choice, and enforce accountability, while ensuring access by the poor. This can only be achieved within an overall policy environment that focuses on improving governance and encourages innovation and experimentation by public and private actors to develop institutional mechanisms that reach the poor.

This chapter draws on the World Bank's operational experience, while also including some non-Bank experiences, to illustrate actions that the Bank can support directly or enable others to undertake. It applies the empowerment framework to five important areas for poverty reduction:

- Provision of basic services
- Improved local governance
- Improved national governance
- Pro-poor market development
- Access to justice and legal aid.

The experiences are organized by the extent to which they depend primarily on one or another element of empowerment, although to some extent the elements are interdependent. Thus accountability is never possible without access to information. Strengthening local organizational capacity requires access to information, participation, and accountability of service providers to poor people.

Institutional demands are the simplest for access to information and the most complex for investing in local organizational capacity. The larger the number of empowerment elements needed to achieve desired outcomes, the higher the institutional demands. Hence, if effectiveness of a public action can be improved by focusing on increasing access to information or by instituting mechanisms for accountability to citizens, or by designing new products that will enable the inclusion of poor people, then this should be given preference, rather than focusing on participatory processes and co-management strategies that require strong capacity on the part of poor people's organizations and provider agencies.

Because the empowerment elements are so closely intertwined, most of the policies and projects described in the following sections incorporate more than one of the elements. Each project has been placed in a matrix according to the element it most clearly exemplifies, but this should be seen as a helpful lens for understanding the importance of the empowerment principles, not as a hard-and-fast classification of the projects. Many of the projects are described in more detail in the Tools and Practices in chapter 5.

Provision of Basic Services

Recognizing the urgency of delivering sustainable basic services including health care, education, water, roads, and basic infrastructure to the majority of poor people, the World Bank's Strategic Framework Paper endorses the Millennium Development Goals as a frame of reference.[1] The Bank supports government efforts to get resources down to the community level through a variety of institutional models. Implementation can be carried out by private or public actors, by central agencies, sectoral agencies, or decentralized authorities of local government, through stand-alone sector projects, or through multisectoral community-driven development projects. A new emphasis on performance is changing mindsets, shifting the indicators of project success from inputs to outcomes on the ground.

Sector policies and projects necessarily vary in the extent to which they adopt all four elements of empowerment. Although it is difficult to completely disentangle the four empowerment elements, this section highlights three different strategies for providing effective services to poor people, based on the nature of the good or service to be provided and the institutional strategies possible in particular contexts. The first focuses on improving access to information, primarily by putting information about government performance in the public domain. The second makes use mainly of mechanisms for inclusion and participation. It includes private sector strategies that depend on designing access to basic services that poor people can afford, as well as demand-side financing strategies, particularly in education and health. The third focuses on local organizational capacity and includes all four elements of empowerment acting in synergy. Examples include a variety of multisectoral community-driven development projects, as well as single-sector projects such as those in rural water supply and sanitation (table 3-1).

Access to Information

Relevant information enables people to access public or private services. With information about service schedules, for example, people can rely on buses for travel or time their visits to health clinics during the hours they are open. Information and communications technology can play a pivotal role. The placement of computer kiosks in public spaces in rural areas allows villagers to access their land records, such as through the

Table 3-1 Provision of Basic Services, Examples Classified by Major Empowerment Element

Information	Inclusion/participation	Local organizational capacity
Gyandoot information technology project, Madhya Pradesh, India	Female Secondary School Assistance Project, Bangladesh	Kecamatan Development Program, Indonesia
Cellular telephones, India and Bangladesh	Education voucher program, Colombia	Social Development Fund, Romania
Program for Pollution Control, Evaluation, and Rating (PROPER), Indonesia	Privatization of utilities, Bolivia	Irrigation Rehabilitation Project, Albania
Water Districts Development Project, Manila, the Philippines	Identification cards for women, Egypt	
Public Expenditure Tracking Survey, Uganda		

Gyandoot program in Madhya Pradesh, India. This is not only convenient, but also cuts down on corruption and increases poor people's security over their land. In Bangladesh, poor landless women who are members of Grameen Bank take loans to buy cellular phones, which they then make available to other villagers for a fee. Analysis of use patterns there as well as among members of the Self-Employed Women's Association (SEWA) in India shows that women use telephones to access information about basic services, such as hours of clinics, opening of markets, and availability of drugs and doctors.[2] (See also Tools and Practices 1 on ICT.)

Analysis of Public Expenditure Tracking Surveys (PETS) in Uganda, Tanzania, Ghana, and Honduras found that asymmetric information had negative effects on the flow of funds to the local level and on service delivery.[3] When local officials or citizens do not know their monthly entitlement, it is impossible for them to demand accountability.[4]

Putting information in the public domain to inform people about private sector or public sector performance is the first step in building pressure for change. The private sector is often easier to influence through release of such information because of risks to reputation and the impact on the "bottom line." In the case of a Nike subcontractor in Vietnam that remained immune even to pressure from government officials, an international information campaign became instrumental in improving local labor and environmental practices.

Indonesia's PROPER program, which rated the pollution performance of factories and ensured the strategic dissemination of pollution ratings through the media, is a good example of the use of information to improve private sector performance. Each factory was assigned a color rating of gold, green, blue, red, or black, with gold meaning world-class performance on environmental standards while black indicated factories causing serious environmental damage. Under threat of public disclosure, a number of factories improved their performance. Many others changed their practices once their color ratings, names, locations, managers, and parent companies were released to the media and public. Altogether, the proportion of plants not in compliance with environmental regulations fell from 65 percent when PROPER began in June 1995 to 47 percent by September 1996. The number of firms in compliance increased by 50 percent over this period. Information also empowered local communities to negotiate better environmental arrangements with factories.

A public performance audit of the privatized Metro Manila Waterworks and Sewerage System provides citizens and service providers with easy-to-understand information on service quality, reliability, and satisfaction. Performance is measured using a system of established benchmarks, putting pressure on concessionaires to improve their performance. Conversely, audits of public performance with no links to accountability mechanisms create only weak incentives to change.

Experimentation with using the power of information in the public domain to improve state performance in provision of basic services is just beginning. Some of these experiences are discussed in the sections on improving local and national governance.

Inclusion and Participation

State policies and programs can be effective by focusing on information dissemination to help poor people make informed choices while at the same time designing institutional mechanisms and products that enable poor people to opt in. This is facilitated by changes in the policy and regulatory framework. Institutional design, product development, and needed policy changes can be informed by public consultations, as well as by a range of studies including institutional analysis, poverty and social analysis, beneficiary assessments, economic analysis, and willingness-to-pay studies. In all these cases community groups do not play management roles. Rather, the emphasis is on collecting information about beneficiaries in their broader cultural and institutional context to design institutional mechanisms for their inclusion.

In Egypt, issuing of identification cards and birth certificates to poor women enabled them to access services and resources from which they had been previously excluded. Within one year, 20 poverty-focused NGOs that had been trained in the procedures for obtaining identification cards and birth certificates helped to empower more than 80,000 poor women to draw pensions, claim inheritances, obtain passports, access microcredit, register for literacy classes, and find employment in the formal sector. A mass media campaign has resulted in publicity in the national media, and dialogue with government authorities has started to simplify the civil registration process. More than 200 NGOs are now working on this issue.[5]

In Bangladesh, where enrollment of girls in secondary education is extremely limited, creatively designed scholarships appropriate to the local social, cultural, and economic context have tipped the cost-benefit calculations of parents in favor of the decision to send girls to secondary schools. Parent-teacher associations or other community-level organizations do not play a management role. Rather, there is heavy investment in disseminating information about the scholarships and motivating parents to send their girls to school through television commercials, radio spots, and discussions with opinion leaders, including religious leaders.

Scholarships are given directly to girls through passbook accounts. This process greatly increases the social status of young girls, who then directly pay other costs to the schools (see Tools and Practices 10, on empowerment in education, for more information).

In Colombia, a carefully designed voucher program to increase poor children's choice in and access to secondary education is based on understanding poor people's aspirations as well as the broader institutional context of both public and private secondary schools. It invests in information dissemination to parents and students, but again, parent-teacher associations do not play a key management role.[6]

The question of how privatized public utilities can achieve efficiency with equity is just beginning to be addressed. The strategies will vary for provision of water, sanitation, electricity, telephones, or transport. Provision of water supply and sewerage to low-income households can be made affordable through use of lower-cost technologies, options in levels of service desired, contribution of labor by households, and payment in installments. These changes in design and policies, combined with dissemination of information about the new rules, can enable poor households to be included.[7] However, the processes of managing equitable pricing and sustainable systems of private delivery of public services are proving to be difficult.

Local Organizational Capacity

All four elements of empowerment become important and local organizational capacity becomes critical when community groups are expected to take on long-term management roles to initiate, implement, operate, and maintain basic services in collaboration with state officials. To ensure that communities are willing to take on increasingly demanding roles, and to improve access and the functioning of services, an increasing number of sector agencies are handing over control and authority over investment resources and decisions to community groups. In many community-driven development (CDD) projects, innovation is initiated from within government ministries, championed by a small group that builds strategic alliances across different levels of government and with outsiders. The approach is based on learning by doing, including learning from communities (box 3-1).[8]

The results are impressive, particularly in management of natural resources, provision of local infrastructure, and primary education. In the Andhra Pradesh Joint Forest Management Program in India, more

> ### Box 3-1 An Empowerment Approach to CDD Projects
>
> - Understand local social structures and institutions
> - Identify clear rules and mechanisms for community control and authority
> - Invest in information, downward accountability, and local organizational capacity so poor people can make effective use of new opportunities
> - Empower local agency staff to support poor people and their organizations
> - Assess progress and track outcomes, including changes in social relations and community organizations

than 5,000 village protection committees involving a million village women and men have rejuvenated 1.2 million hectares of degraded forests. In El Mezqital, Guatemala, a dormant municipal development project was redesigned to establish cooperatives to manage housing loans and community services in a squatter community. Housing loan repayments cost no more than households earlier spent on buying water from vendors.[9] In Albania, 408 water users' associations have grouped into 21 federations covering 200,000 families, or one-third of the entire population. The associations are self-financing and manage entire irrigation schemes; they have improved delivery of water to those at the end of irrigation schemes and increased cost recovery from zero dollars in 1994 to $700,000 in 2000.[10] Educational outcomes such as enrollment rates have increased dramatically through reform based on management partnerships with parents, community groups, and village education committees in contexts as diverse as El Salvador, Madagascar, and Uttar Pradesh in India (see Tools and Practices 10).

Multisectoral CDD projects are extremely important in getting resources to the grassroots, particularly in contexts of geographic isolation, weak governance, high corruption, and post-conflict recovery. Over time, strong links need to be made with local government structures. The Kecamatan Development Project in Indonesia, despite a financial and political crisis and a highly centralized government structure, was able to reach 10 million people in 12,000 villages with subprojects. Evaluations establish that 60 percent of the people reached are among the poorer groups and 40 percent are women. In the Romania Social

Development Fund, the participatory process includes training and investing in local organizational capacity and tracking changes over time. A social capital survey recorded higher levels of trust among people in villages participating in the project than among those in villages without projects. In northeast Brazil, a gradual shift since 1985 from large integrated rural development projects to community-driven approaches has resulted in 93 percent of resources now reaching communities, compared to 20 percent earlier.[11]

Many of the newer CDD projects invest more in information dissemination, accountability, and local capacity building; the latter is achieved through the assistance of trained facilitators, through learning by doing, and by giving community groups direct access to funds and the authority to hire and fire workers and contractors. Information disclosure strategies include putting information about local budgets on public blackboards or walls as well as funding journalists, NGOs, and other third-party actors to monitor and publicize projects. (See Tools and Practices 9 for case studies of CDD projects.)

There is also reason for caution. CDD projects, like all projects, are subject to capture by elites. Success varies with the social, economic, and political features in each community. Many CDD projects still do not systematically invest in the capacity of local organizations, and many lack clear indicators to track empowerment, as this has not been a clearly identified objective of projects. A recent OED evaluation of social funds concludes that while social funds are highly effective in delivering small-scale infrastructure, they do not expand community capacity or social capital.[12] Most projects have not led to the development of permanent and autonomous community organizations that can build networks across communities and eventually a regional or national presence. There are some exceptions. In Africa a few capacity-building projects support the evolution of national and regional farmers' associations as well as pastoralist networks. (See Tools and Practices 13 on poor people's organizations for an example from Burkina Faso.)

Improved Local Governance

Improved local governance is critical to better service provision and greater responsiveness to poor people's priority problems. To improve local governance, local governments with authority and resources need to empower local communities through mechanisms that increase citizen access to information, enable inclusion and participation, increase accountability of governments to citizens, and invest in local organizational capacity. Decentralization and local government reform have so far focused primarily on the supply side of formal systems and not on strengthening the demand side through actions that enable citizens to effectively utilize the space created by new rules and regulations. Experiences in Bolivia, India, the Philippines, and Uganda demonstrate that when space is created by new rules but there is a lack of investment in information dissemination and local organizational capacity of civil society and poor people's organizations, poor people cannot participate effectively in local governance.[13] There has been insufficient attention to the relationship between citizens and local governments.

Focus on the demand side of improved local governance is just beginning. Although still few, there are some important examples of efforts to increase access to information, design mechanisms for inclusion and participation, and build in mechanisms of accountability to citizens. On the other hand, in the context of local government reform, there do not appear to be any strong cases of investment in strengthening poor people's organizations or other local civil society intermediaries so they can effectively play the new roles assigned to them (table 3-2).[14]

Access to Information

The right to information through independent sources is fundamental to improving local governance. When citizens cannot find out what local governments are doing and how they spend their funds, governments have little incentive to improve performance, monitor their own performance, or publish the results. It is important that the right to

Table 3-2 Improving the Demand Side of Local Governance, Examples Classified by Major Empowerment Element

Information	Inclusion/participation	Accountability
Right to information laws, India	Women's inclusion in Panchayat Raj institutions, India	People's Voice Program, Ukraine
Citizen report cards in Bangalore, India	Participatory planning and budgeting, Porto Alegre, Brazil	Law on popular participation and decentralization, Bolivia
Municipal websites with performance information, Argentina	Citizen involvement in municipal tax decisions and rule making, Argentina and Venezuela	Citizen referendum to recall elected mayors, Madhya Pradesh, India

information be guaranteed by law. In Rajasthan, India, the struggles of Mazdoor Kisan Shakti Sangathan to gain copies of bills, vouchers, and employment rolls of government development projects not only exposed local corruption and led to corrective action in some cases, but also prompted consideration of a national right to information law.

Municipal governments are beginning to create websites that enable citizens to interact with government, access certificates, register property, and give governments feedback on their performance. In Latin America, the World Bank is interconnecting the municipal websites of 10 capital cities to encourage exchange of experiences as well as public engagement. In Argentina, the Cristal project uses the Internet to disseminate in an easily understood format all information concerning the use of public funds in different programs.[15] The site is audited externally by Foro Transparencia, a group of 15 nongovernmental organizations concerned with government transparency.

Citizen feedback on government performance can be a useful tool for improving local governance. Fed up with unresponsive, poorly performing, and corrupt government agencies, citizens' groups in Bangalore, India, conducted surveys of government performance and made the information available to the public and the press to create pressure for reform. In 1993 the Public Affairs Centre in Bangalore initiated citywide citizen "report cards" for public services. Citizens were asked to rate the quality, adequacy, and efficiency of services such as water, transport, electricity, the municipal office, and police, and the findings were publicized in the media. This led to discussions with heads of agencies about needed reform, and in some cases services improved. The methodology has spread to other states and was recently administered countrywide in India (see Tools and Practices 16).[16]

Bangalore is also becoming known for its Swabhimana initiative, in which volunteer engineers and architects, tired of shoddy public construction, monitor the city's public works directly at the site, providing public information on all aspects of the contract—thus increasing contractors' accountability.[17]

Inclusion and Participation: Planning, Budgeting, Rule Making, and Management

Citizen participation in planning, budget allocation, and rule making initiated by mayors can improve governance and the delivery of services, and can also help mayors get re-elected. To be meaningful this must be in the context of hard budget constraints to avoid generation of "wish lists." Citywide strategies for poverty reduction can help bring different stakeholders together across sectors for more effective poverty reduction.[18] In Colombia, municipalities are using "co-participation" with local communities as the means to respond to community priority needs in construction and maintenance of public works. Opinion surveys show improved sectoral allocation as well as greater citizen trust of local officials. Similar findings are emerging from Bulgaria, Croatia, Romania, Serbia, and Ukraine .

Participatory planning and budgeting involves citizens through group meetings. Information collected is aggregated into neighborhood priorities for government budgetary allocations. The approach was pioneered by the city of Porto Alegre, Brazil, in 1988, and has been institutionalized there through the support of successive mayors. In a typical year only 200 of the 1,500 requests for public projects received can be financed. Between 1996 and 1998 more than $260 million was spent on projects selected by participants, the vast majority of them carried out in underserviced and poorer districts. As of June 2000, it was estimated that nearly 100 municipalities and five states in Brazil were implementing some aspects of citizen engagement in budgetary allocations.[19] (See Tools and Practices 6 for more information on participatory budgeting.)

In order to improve city governance, curtail corruption, and build social consensus around unpopular decisions such as raising taxes, some cities are institutionalizing citizen referendums. In the city of Mar del Plata, Argentina, a newly elected mayor called for a referendum on 26 public works to be constructed during his term. The plan was to improve infrastructure to attract tourists, with the costs to be covered by a tax to be paid over four years. The vote was positive, the work was completed on schedule, and the mayor was reelected.[20] In Campos Elias, Venezuela, municipal performance on public access to information, productivity, cost effectiveness, and corruption improved by more than 50 percent in one year. The results were attributed to participatory budgeting, public and computerized tracking of information on municipal performance, setting up of a Tripartite Auditing Commission that included citizens, and creation of a functioning Office for Development and Citizen Participation.[21]

Citizen involvement in setting new rules can break deeply entrenched practices of state capture. In the municipality of Moron in the province of Buenos Aires, Argentina, the government together with the city council called for public hearings to design criteria for the award of the city government's largest tender, for waste collection. The public hearings led to changes in tender specifications that allowed new companies to bid, kept on workers already under contract, and were based on outputs rather than inputs. As a result, the contract cost decreased by 30 percent.[22]

In the presence of deep social inequities, it is difficult to initiate change without rules and laws that require inclusion and participation of excluded or marginalized groups in local governance. In India's cultural context, it took a constitutional amendment—requiring that one-third of the councilors in *panchayats* (village-level councils) be women—to create opportunities for women's voices, priorities, and leadership in local governance. While in many *panchayats* women have emerged as effective leaders, in others cultural norms and lack of a support system and training still limit women's roles.[23]

Accountability

Access to information is a prerequisite for accountability. As noted above, citizen monitoring of government performance through citizen "report cards" or "scorecards," followed by workshops in which citizens discuss findings with government officials, attended by wide media coverage, is an effective tool to build citizen demand for better local government performance. And when governments put in place social accountability mechanisms, the impact of information can be even more powerful.

In Ternopil and Ivano-Frankivsk, Ukraine, the People's Voice Program created citizen scorecards on public services after getting the two mayors involved as champions of the process.[24] The surveys revealed widespread dissatisfaction with service quality, and widespread bribe-taking was reported. Fifty percent of respondents claimed that government services were not provided according to rules and regulations. In Ternopil, the municipality responded by opening one-stop service centers where people can pay for all municipal services. In Ivano-Frankivsk, education reform is encouraging greater citizen involvement through newly created education advisory groups and parent councils, and citizens' groups and the municipality are working together to address other identified problems.[25] In summer 2001, the scorecard method was expanded to two other municipalities in Ukraine. Similar work has been undertaken in Bulgaria, Croatia, and Serbia, creating new partnerships of trust between citizens and city governments.

Bolivia's Law on Popular Participation, adopted in 1994, incorporates indigenous people's organizations into municipal decision making, and empowers "community vigilance committees" to investigate municipal decisions and activities and stop central government transfers to local government if the annual plan does not respond to community demands. Without institutional mechanisms it is difficult to sustain citizen engagement to improve local governance for poverty reduction. While citizen engagement laws create the possibility of changes in both Bolivia and in India, results have been uneven, reflecting uneven local capacity to access information, mobilize, organize, assert leadership, and demand accountability.[26]

In India, the Madhya Pradesh state assembly passed a law in 1999 empowering dissatisfied citizens to recall an elected mayor mid-term through a citizen referendum—the first law of its kind in India. The new law, inspired by similar referendum laws in Switzerland, states that if three-quarters of local legislators pass a resolution against a directly elected mayor who has completed two years in office, a referendum will be held to decide the mayor's fate. In the coal mining town of Anooppur, 5,519 of the 8,799 eligible voters voted to oust the corrupt mayor in April 2001.[27] It should be noted, however, that without strong citizens' groups and poor people's organizations, such laws can become political tools, leading to changes in mayors almost every year as happened in some municipalities in Bolivia.[28]

Improved National Governance

Macroeconomic policy and choices are areas that are just beginning to open to societal engagement. While the ultimate decisions, like all development decisions, involve technical expertise, discussion with those who are affected offers multiple advantages. It helps clarify the causal links and assumptions underlying policy tradeoffs and choices; it leads to discussions about the institutional capacity needed to implement reforms and alliances that will have to be built with different parts of society; it builds social consensus on the importance of the reform; it gives the reformers room to maneuver against narrower political interests; it educates all involved in the process; and it helps identify and develop needed compensatory mechanisms for the poorest and most adversely affected citizens.

Some progress has been made in demonstrating the value of information tools in the public domain as well as consultative processes. Progress on linking information collected to mechanisms of accountability to poor people and citizens' groups is just beginning. Sector reform loans and credits, as well as budget support loans and credits, *assume* that local capacity exists at all levels of civil society to collect and analyze information and engage effectively with governments to keep them accountable. None of the budget support loans/credits are directly supported by capacity-building operations (table 3-3). Except in Uganda, the capacity to conduct participatory poverty diagnostics so far has not been institutionalized at the national level, either in government or in local universities or other civil society organizations. Local and national capacity of civil society organizations to participate effectively in these new roles deserves urgent attention.

Public sector reform processes that focus on rationalizing and tracking public expenditures as well as modernizing financial management systems are critical first steps toward internal and public accountability. Public participation and public access to key information in forms that can be understood can further increase government accountability for improved performance.

Participatory processes in the development of national poverty reduction strategies, particularly in connection with the preparation of PRSPs in low-income countries, have become a central part of efforts to reach societal consensus on priorities for government expenditure as well as for policy reform. These processes can lay the foundation for public accountability to citizens. Since national processes and policies determine poor people's access to resources and opportunities, it is critical that these processes incorporate the four empowerment elements.[29]

Table 3-3 Improving National Governance, Examples Classified by Major Empowerment Element

Information	Inclusion/participation	Accountability
National government websites, Argentina	Poverty Reduction Strategy Paper processes in several countries	Poverty Reduction Support Credit, Uganda
Freedom of Information Act, Romania	Participatory Poverty Assessments, Uganda and Vietnam	Citizen report card on pro-poor services, the Philippines
Programmatic Structural Adjustment Loan, Latvia	Social Partnership Agreement, Ireland	Programmatic Social Reform Loan, Peru
	Coal Sector Adjustment Loan, Russia	

Access to Information

New levels of transparency and accountability are made possible by the use of information and communications technology in what is becoming known as e-governance. As mentioned earlier, in Argentina, for example, the national government is putting on the Internet in easy-to-understand formats all information regarding use of public funds, not only the amount devoted to different programs but also how these funds are administered.[30] The goal is to inform citizens so that they can exercise more effective control over their elected representatives and government officials (see also Tools and Practices 1).

An increasing number of countries are also enacting new laws to support free access to information about government performance in an effort to curb corruption and increase responsiveness and efficiency. In Romania, for example, a public opinion survey revealed high levels of corruption, but neither the media nor citizens had any access to information. In response, the Romanian Academic Society built a domestic coalition of Romanian NGOs, media, and political organizations that put forward a Freedom of Information Act, which became law in October 2001.

The Latvia Programmatic Structural Adjustment Loan I (PSAL I) includes some measures to ensure public access to information, including information about anti-corruption efforts and about court decisions and rulings (see Tools and Practices 5).

Inclusion and Participation

Inclusion of poor people in national processes can be indirect, through gathering information about what poor people want and about their priorities and experiences in gaining access to resources and public services. When decision-making processes are opened up, even indirectly, to a range of new stakeholders who have different perspectives, there is potential for conflict. Management of participatory processes for complex reform, for national budgeting, or even just for information gathering—as through Participatory Poverty Assessments—*requires significant investment in trust and relationship building* (box 3-2). This has both cost and time implications. Whether in Bolivia, Bulgaria, Guinea, the Philippines, Uganda, Ukraine, or Vietnam, new relations and functioning pro-poor partnerships would not have emerged without the time and finances to allow the

> ### Box 3-2 Improving Governance
>
> - Invest in convening poor people, other citizens, private sector interests, and other stakeholders with governments
> - Invest in building new alliances, trust, and common interests among stakeholders
> - Expect ups and downs; invest time, patience, and goodwill
> - Support a culture of debate, dialogue, and action, with public monitoring of government performance
> - Invest in citizen report cards on government expenditures, follow-the-money surveys, and measurement of service delivery outcomes

parties to meet, get to know each other, change processes, and eventually work together as partners.

The more complex and controversial the reform process, the more critical the investment in consultative processes, consensus building, and setting up of joint steering committees that include civil society and the private sector. These conclusions are confirmed by the PRSP experiences, for example in Bolivia, Kenya, and Uganda. The consultative process used to develop the Morocco Gender Action Plan, which has been controversial in the country, has also had to deal with conflicting perspectives and tensions.[31]

In South Africa, a recent study concludes that the lack of alliances between the government and labor unions undermined implementation of needed macroeconomic reform.[32] In Latin America, heads of state from Bolivia, Colombia, Ecuador, Honduras, Nicaragua, and Paraguay have requested help in managing multi-stakeholder involvement in the design and implementation of anti-corruption strategies. Without this kind of investment, reforms flounder, as is evident in the recent cancellation of the $300 million second tranche of the Safety Net Sectoral Adjustment Loan in Indonesia—an outcome that reflected both the breakdown of trust between citizens' groups and the government and the lack of progress in public accountability mechanisms.

Participatory Poverty Assessments (PPAs) as well as nationwide surveys are important tools to inform national policies and budgetary allocations. In both Uganda and Vietnam, PPAs provided critical new insights missed by survey data. Government ownership of the PPA process ensured that findings were used. In Uganda, the government substantially increased its investments in water supply and increased the flexibility of use of district budgetary allocations to enable districts to respond to local needs. In Vietnam, the PPA findings have led to projects targeting urban poverty as well as issues of ethnicity and gender. In one province, revenue raising at the commune level was found too burdensome, regressive, nontransparent, and poorly accounted for. This issue is being investigated in a national public expenditure review. The study also found poor implementation of the Grassroots Democracy Decree. As a result, mechanisms are being considered to stimulate two-way flows of information, including piloting by the government of a citizen report card on delivery of basic services. (See Tools and Practices 3 on empowerment in the Vietnam country program, and Tools and Practices 20 on participatory poverty diagnostics.)

The process of "social partnership agreements" in Ireland is a good example of the high payoffs in economic and social stability that can be achieved through broad stakeholder involvement in macroeconomic decision making. The Irish discussions are based on government economic forecasts. Over the last ten years, an institutional framework has emerged in which the government, the private sector, and civil society representatives including labor unions come together to participate in major socioeconomic decisions. Popular support for reform is one of the factors credited with restoring competitiveness, maintaining industrial peace, and providing an environment for investment and growth, making Ireland a "Celtic Tiger."[33] (See also Tools and Practices 6 on participatory budgeting.)

The Russia Coal Sector Adjustment Loan provides a different kind of example. The reform was undertaken to address an array of problems: declining productivity despite $2.7 billion in subsidies, wages not paid on time, mine closures, and increasing militancy among miners. The backdrop was one of instability, with five changes in prime minister and four different leaders of the coal agency between 1996 and 2000. Institutional redesign was based on consultations with those affected, mapping the blockages in flows of policies, information, and funds, and adopting measures to overcome these identified blockages. While problems remain, subsidies to the industry decreased in 2000 to $0.28 billion, one-third of which was reoriented to social protection and community development. The productivity of mines improved by 77 percent, and 98 percent of laid-off and disabled workers received their benefits directly and on time. (See Tools and Practices 5 for a more detailed discussion of the Russian coal sector reforms.)

Accountability: Citizen Monitoring

For citizen feedback to affect decision making, information has to be in the public domain; it has to be collected quickly on a key set of core performance indicators, using quantitative, qualitative, and/or participatory methods; and it has to be available to decision makers who have to be held accountable to respond to feedback. This is particularly relevant in the context of budget support loans with yearly decision points for release of the next year's tranche.

Three kinds of monitoring activities are particularly important: public expenditure tracking or follow-the-money studies; monitoring the delivery of basic services to the poor; and citizen surveillance to track the impact of macroeconomic adjustment policies. There is growing experience in these areas through the use of a variety of data gathering techniques. These include national citizen scorecards and household surveys on key basic services, "social weather surveys," beneficiary assessment surveys, Core Welfare Indicators Questionnaire surveys, budget tracking surveys, PPAs, and participatory monitoring and evaluation.[34]

Social accountability procedures that provide civil society and local communities with access to information they need to effectively monitor government performance are beginning to be a feature of some recent budget support loans.

The Uganda Poverty Reduction Support Credit (PRSC) includes independent and multi-stakeholder monitoring of government performance, including tracking flow of funds, corruption, and service delivery. It is expected that results of civil society monitoring will eventually be incorporated as part of decision triggers. The monitoring approach builds on the success of the Uganda Public Expenditure Tracking Survey, essentially a follow-the-money survey (see also Tools and Practices 5).[35]

The citizen report card methodology has recently been applied at the national level in the Philippines as a follow-up to the poverty assessment. The survey was undertaken by the World Bank in collaboration with an independent and credible local survey research organization, Social Weather Stations. The questionnaire focused on awareness, access, use, and satisfaction related to pro-poor public services in five areas: health care, primary education, housing, water, and subsidized rice distribution. The National Department of Budget and Management has agreed to institutionalize the report card on services. A government oversight agency will conduct studies and results will inform national budgeting processes.

Over the long term governments can only be responsive to citizen priorities if there are institutional mechanisms for citizen engagement and feedback from the community, district, and state levels to the national level. These mechanisms need to support poor people's and citizens' access to information, foster inclusion and participation, ensure accountability, and invest in local organizational capacity.

The Peru Programmatic Social Reform Loan (PSRL), designed to support the government's medium-term social reform program, includes many features to enable poor people and other citizens to hold governments accountable for their performance. These elements include public access to information, institutional mechanisms for public debate and monitoring, widely known performance benchmarks, and a well-publicized national ombudsman's office to establish a complaint redress mechanism. Citizen involvement mechanisms build on the follow-up to the 1997 poverty assessment, when the government of Peru created *mesas de concertación*, inclusive forums for deliberately plural public debate and action. These roundtables were created at all levels of society from the community to the district level to inform national decision making. Participants include local communities, civil society, local and national government, as well as the donor community. They have recently been institutionalized through a presidential decree and are now responsible for monitoring all public expenditures as well. The PSRL will be monitored by more than 100 of these multi-stakeholder *mesas*. However, funds for these major capacity-building efforts are raised through a variety of ad hoc grant mechanisms (see Tools and Practices 5).

Local Organizational Capacity

As yet there are no systematic efforts to invest in capacity building of research institutes and citizens' groups to monitor government performance. On the other hand, where such capacity already exists, it has been used. Examples include Social Weather Stations in the Philippines, the Open Society Institute in Hungary, the Institute of Public Finance in Croatia, the Institute for Democracy in South Africa (IDASA), and the Public Affairs Centre in India. Long-term investments are needed in such institutes and in field-based NGOs and poor people's organizations to empower citizens to engage meaningfully with their governments and be sources of independent monitoring information. The value of such efforts can be seen from the role played by SMERU (Social Monitoring and Early Response Unit) in Indonesia, which was created at the height of the financial crisis. The institute now functions as an independent public policy monitoring agency whose data are trusted and used by national policymakers.

Pro-Poor Market Development

E conomic empowerment is critical for poor people's wellbeing. Freedom from hunger, adequate income, and security of material assets are central issues in poor people's lives. Even in natural disasters such as floods and earthquakes, poor people often refuse at peril of their lives to leave their meager assets, knowing that lost assets mean a slow but just as certain death. In Gujarat, India, work by the Self-Employed Women's Association is demonstrating that post-earthquake rehabilitation efforts that focus on physical reconstruction without simultaneously focusing on livelihoods do not address poor people's central concerns, and result in long-term destitution.

Poverty and vulnerability will not be reduced without broad-based growth fueled by private sector activity. Economic growth cannot be sustained if poor women and men, who may be 50 percent or more of a country's population, are excluded from optimal engagement in productive activities. Involvement of such large numbers of poor people in more productive livelihoods can only happen when a country's overall domestic investment climate fosters entrepreneurship, job creation, competition, and security of property or benefit rights. This is not enough, however. While the overall business climate for investment is important, micro and small enterprises face constraints and exclusion that are not automatically corrected by improvements in the macro investment climate. Hence the need for "liberalization from below." Poor people are often excluded from equal access to economic opportunity because of regulations, because they lack information, connections, skills, credit, and organization, and because of discrimination. Elements of empowering approaches can help overcome many of these barriers that prevent poor people's entry into new markets and limit their productivity despite their unremitting hard labor.

Understanding the business investment climate for farmers, microentrepreneurs, and small and medium businesses—as well as for large firms—is critical to inform policy change that supports economic development and increases productivity, security, and empowerment. Governments can accelerate the development of markets for financial and nonfinancial services appropriate for poor women and men by promoting innovation in products and delivery mechanisms, and by building institutional capacity. A *market-oriented approach* to these services is critical to avoid unsustainable and ineffective public programs. A key component is carefully structured and time-bound subsidies within an overall approach incorporating market features, product innovation, and wide dissemination of institutional innovations.

This section highlights the application of the four empowerment elements to support poor women's and men's entrepreneurship through: (a) business development services for micro, small, and medium enterprises; (b) financial services; and (c) microinsurance and housing loans. The use of different empowerment elements across these three activities is highlighted in table 3-4. Tools and Practices 11 highlights innovations that support micro, small, and medium enterprises, while Tools and Practices 12 highlights innovations in provision of financial services to the poor. Local and international NGOs and international agencies have played important roles in supporting innovations by

Table 3-4 Pro-Poor Market Development, Examples Classified by Major Empowerment Element

Information	Inclusion/participation	Local organizational capacity
GrameenPhone, Bangladesh	One-stop shops, Bali, Indonesia	Metalworkers' and hammock makers' networks, Honduras and Nicaragua
E-commerce: Novica.com, PeopLink.org	Urban Property Rights Project, Peru	Rice millers' association, Cambodia
Self-help groups, credit ratings, Andhra Pradesh, India	Banefe, Chile	SEWA microinsurance, India
Smart cards, India and Swaziland	New MFIs, Bolivia and Kosovo	SPARC guarantee loan, India
ATM banking, South Africa		

subsidizing research and development, experimentation, and investment in organizational development. However, in almost all cases, achieving financial viability was central in the experimentation.

Business Development Support Services for Micro/SMEs

In many developing countries, poor people work primarily in the informal sector, surviving through a patchwork of economic activities or employed by small and medium enterprises (SMEs). The informal sector is responsible for 83 percent of new jobs in Latin America and the Caribbean and 93 percent of new jobs in Africa.[36]

Large numbers of poor people, particularly poor women, make a living through informal activities, although not everyone in the informal sector is poor. In India 90 percent of the nonagricultural workforce is in the informal sector with little access to financial services or social protection. In Peru, micro and small enterprises account for 95 percent of all firms in the country and provide 50 percent of national employment and 60 percent of employment in urban areas.[37] In Bangladesh, microenterprises account for 90 percent of all firms in the manufacturing sector, and 40 percent of total employment.[38] In Macedonia, small enterprises of less than 20 employees account for 39 percent of the gross domestic product (GDP) and 25 percent of employment.[39] Despite these statistics, development of micro, small, and medium enterprises does not feature prominently in development plans of most developing countries.

The World Bank Group already makes substantial investments in microenterprises and SMEs, 7 percent of overall lending in 2001.[40] As yet, however, there is virtually no economic and sector work on the investment climate, constraints, and innovations needed specifically to support the microentrepreneurial activity of poor people and SMEs.[41] However, the recently issued private sector development strategy provides the basis for sector-specific strategies and further analytical work through firm surveys that include microenterprises.[42]

Access to information and information technology

Micro, small, and medium enterprises face information asymmetries in two ways: in their own access to market- and business-related information, and as providers of services to poor people. Informational costs of isolation and low volume can be reduced through formation of groups, associations, business clusters, and franchising, discussed later in the context of investing in local organizational capacity. Innovative use of information technology and telecenters can cut down transaction costs, and enable microentrepreneurs and SMEs to connect to information about markets more effectively.

The experience of the "telephone ladies" of Grameen Bank demonstrates that it is possible to increase economic returns to poor people by changing nothing more than their access to information about market prices. Grameen Telecom (financed in part by the International Finance Corporation [IFC]) provides commercial phone service in rural areas of Bangladesh through local entrepreneurs. Grameen members, mostly women, many of them illiterate, take loans to buy and operate cellular telephones, charging villagers by the minute for calls. Studies show that 50 percent of the calls are made by poor people, mainly for economic reasons; these include checking out the current price of goods before a meeting with a purchaser, finding prices in various markets before deciding where to go to sell goods, and consulting with doctors and medicine providers. It is estimated that the phones generate real savings of between $2.70 and $10.00 for calls that substitute for travel between villages and Dhaka, the capital.[43] The telephone women are able to repay their loans in a year, and they call the telephones a more reliable investment than cows. As of March 2002, about 10,000 village phones were in operation. However, the model has worked in part because it is based on an already established revenue collection system through the networks of existing groups managed by Grameen Bank.[44]

Poor people's associations and networks in many parts of the world are wiring up to connect to each other and to markets. In Mexico, the Information Network for Indigenous Organizations includes 19 organizations that use the Internet to exchange information, access market and technological information, and market products.[45] In Guatemala, a MicroNet project that scaled up from an InfoDev project will establish 10 MicroNet centers that are technology-based, integrated information business development centers by 2004. The centers will assist 25,000 micro businesses run primarily by indigenous Mayan women and those associated with more formal organizations.[46]

Micro producers and intermediaries have also turned to e-commerce, both retail and business-to-business, to improve sales and profits. In Kenya, the Naushad Trading Company, which sells local wood carvings, pottery, and baskets, went online two years ago and has seen its annual revenues grow from $10,000 to over $2 million. African Crafts Online receives between 5,000 and 25,000 hits per month. Novica, which has been rated by Media Metrix as one of 500 most visited sites in the world, charges no listing fees for artisans and experienced a fivefold increase in sales in 2000. It offers more than 8,500 craft items from 13 countries. Other innovations include Viatru and PeopLink.[47]

SMEs can also benefit from information and communications technology applications. In the Philippines 99 percent of firms are microenterprises and SMEs, employing 55 percent of the country's labor force. An IFC equity investment in E-Planters aims to create a joint venture company to offer web-hosting services for SMEs to grow their businesses via the Internet at an affordable cost. The company is being formed through a partnership of Planters Development Bank, the largest SME bank in the Philippines, with the Asian Institute of Management, the chamber of commerce, and VICOR, a California-based technology company.[48]

Finally, governments are simplifying registration procedures through use of information technology in many countries. In Andhra Pradesh, India, land registration offices throughout the state now help citizens register land within one hour; it used to take days, accompanied by bribes. Within six months of the change, 80 percent of all land transactions were being electronically processed. This has increased government revenue, decreased corruption and uncertainty, and increased public demand for similar improvement in other government services.[49]

Changing regulation for inclusion and participation

Regulations, corruption, and complicated business licensing and property registration procedures limit and add costs to poor people's entrepreneurial activity. Poor women and men with limited information, contacts, and cash are the least able to pursue property or business registration, or buy protection (box 3-3). They therefore remain excluded or vulnerable to high levels of exploitation and harassment. Stories about how many steps it takes to register property or obtain a license, and about locked up "dead capital," have been made legendary by Peruvian economist Hernando de Soto's work. In Peru, 70 percent of urban properties are unregistered, with 14 different agencies involved in conferring each title. In Lima, it takes six hours a day for 289 days to register a small garment workshop operated by one worker; the cost is $1,231, or 31 times the monthly minimum wage. In Egypt a person who wants to register a lot on state-owned desert land must complete 77 bureaucratic procedures at 31 public and private agencies, a process that takes between 5 and 14 years.[50]

> ### Box 3-3 Improving Market Access of the Poor
>
> - Diagnose and discuss overall domestic investment climate through firm surveys, which include poor people's microentrepreneurial activities
> - Understand the constraints felt by poor entrepreneurs and their associations and networks
> - Understand the constraints felt by private providers in targeting the poor
> - Identify strategies for overcoming disadvantages of small size and distance from formal institutions
> - Promote dialogue between poor people's organizations, government officials and policymakers, and the private sector to initiate pro-poor regulatory change and encourage innovation in the private sector
> - Provide graduated subsidies to broker new linkages between poor people and their organizations, on the one hand, and markets and formal financial systems, on the other hand, with provision primarily by private sector actors
> - Consider ways of increasing poor people's access to information technology

In Indonesia, red tape is a particular deterrent to small businesses, which are subject to innumerable inspections, levies, and high licensing fees. While official license fees are approximately $400—very high for a small entrepreneur faced with other start-up costs—the actual costs are often three times as much, as papers are pushed from one office to another. In Zimbabwe, registration of companies takes over a year; the average official cost of registering a tourist company after obtaining various certificates and paying various guarantees is $14,000, which makes it difficult for community groups to initiate community-based cultural and wildlife tourism.[51]

Urban vendors probably face more restrictive municipal laws and police harassment than any other entrepreneurs. In Durban, South Africa, 60 percent of the estimated 20,000 street vendors are women. There are an estimated 200,000 street vendors in Mumbai, India.[52] Street vendors' associations have successfully worked with municipal officials to create marketplaces, lower license fees, and set expectations of new behavior from policemen.[53]

"One-stop shops" for business licenses and permits introduced by the regent of Gianyar in Bali, Indonesia, show how more efficient licensing procedures not only support small entrepreneurs but can also increase tax revenues—by 75 percent in this case.[54] In Durban, South Africa, citywide development planning strategies have included consultations with street vendors' associations and programs of support to address their needs. In India, the government of Gujarat has removed regulations that required gum collectors, almost all of them poor women, to sell at low prices only to a handful of government-licensed gum buyers.

The Peru Urban Property Rights Project, based on thorough research conducted by a Peruvian research institute, supported regulatory reform and procedural streamlining that helped almost 7 million Peruvians secure land titles collectively worth more than $4 billion by August 2000.[55] The technical and institutional procedures are based on learning from pilots and detailed diagnostic studies that illuminated how processes work in reality. Pilot projects established that the value of 300,000 new titles doubled within four years and led to the emergence of private mortgage and consumer credit markets.

Accountability

Simple and transparent business and licensing procedures increase the accountability of service providers. Use of information technology rather than judgments made by officials or buyers increases transparency of information and hence accountability to users. The National Dairy Development Cooperative in India collects milk daily from 75,000 villages through 60,000 milk collection societies involving 10 million members. Dairy farmers deliver their milk to the cooperative's collection centers every morning and evening. Building on the existing organization, the Indian Institute of Management introduced a computerized system with integrated electronic weights, electronic fat-testing machines, and plastic readers at 3,000 collection centers. This has led to greater transparency, faster processing, shorter queues, and immediate payment to farmers. A dairy information portal is currently being piloted in two cooperative villages in the Kheda District of Gujarat, enabling farmers to access business-related information.[56]

Market-based approaches instill accountability by imposing market discipline and hard budget constraints. All business enterprise development should comply with national environmental and labor standards. Deregulation and privatization of utilities, water, electricity, and telecommunications raise important policy issues about achieving efficiency with equity. This work is just beginning. Innovative solutions are being sought through analyses and stakeholder discussions that involve providers, regulators, and users, particularly trade associations and poor people.[57]

Finally, enforcement depends on the extent to which a country's judicial and court system functions effectively. What is important for poor people is access to legal aid and conflict resolution mechanisms that are within their reach.

Local organizational capacity

The key challenge in providing market-oriented business support services to micro and small entrepreneurs is helping them to overcome the disadvantages of being small, scattered, and unorganized (box 3-4). Various linking strategies have emerged to provide services to support microenterprises and SMEs, including formation of networks and associations; business clusters; franchising, leasing, and subcontracting; and business incubators. For illustrative purposes two of these strategies are discussed here: formation of networks/associations and business clusters. Both demonstrate how carefully structured public subsidies can overcome market failures in collective action to benefit the poor.

Formation of networks and associations. Just as community facilitators bolster local organizational capacity for management of local public services, formation of networks and producers' associations is a key

---

Box 3-4 Key Steps to Overcome Barriers of Small Size and Isolation of Micro Producers

- Clarify property rights
- Strengthen membership-based groups, organizations, and networks of poor people
- Educate and link groups with formal financial systems and service providers
- Support the creation of business clusters
- Use information technology to connect people to each other and to markets
- Support changes in regulatory framework to encourage the private sector to provide services to the poor
- Create incentives for the private sector to develop new products and organizations to "downscale" services; upgrade semiformal institutions and create new microfinance institutions; and franchise services and innovate to reach large producer organizations

strategy to overcome the drawbacks of being small and powerless in the enterprise world. Networks are groups of firms that cooperate on joint development projects to solve common problems. In Honduras, the United Nations Industrial Development Organization (UNIDO) piloted the idea of "network brokers" to work with small businesses that have similar characteristics and growth constraints by bringing them together. Network brokers provide some analysis of common problems and encourage members to take collective action to solve their problems. This could mean, for example, pooling their resources to purchase raw materials in bulk, applying for a loan together, sharing equipment, and eventually diversifying production and seeking new markets. The only subsidy to the network is the services of the network broker; these are initially free and over a period of time move to fee for service.

A metalworkers' network in Tegucigalpa, Honduras started with 11 enterprises of four workers each. Within five years, the network had purchased large equipment and established a separate independent enterprise to manage the new equipment and provide services to network members. Sales have increased by 200 percent, employment by 15 percent, and fixed assets by 98 percent. An independent training foundation of network brokers financed by public and private sources has emerged to support the development of new networks.[58]

Similarly, in Nicaragua, 11 hammock producers who compete in the local market have formed a horizontal network and collectively broken into the export market in Europe. Pooling their resources, they have been able to incorporate environmentally friendly features and improve the quality and standardization of their hammocks. As a result, by 1999 they were exporting 3,000 hammocks per month. As a consequence of the involvement of Nicaraguan government officials in this UNIDO-financed project, networking promotion has become a keystone of the government's policy in private sector development.[59]

In Cambodia, a capacity-building grant from the IFC-managed Mekong Project Development Facility is helping to revive one of the country's key industries, rice production, by supporting the emergence of rice millers' associations in eight provinces. Three-quarters of Cambodia's population work in agriculture, with the majority producing rice. Rice millers' associations include hundreds of small producers and a couple of large firms. The initial task was to overcome lack of information, communication, and technology, and a history of social distrust. The eight networks, which have been successful in improving productivity and access to markets, have now created a national Federation of Rice Millers

Associations so as to negotiate better prices for their members, handle higher-volume orders, dialogue with government, and learn about global markets. The group is currently piloting an Internet-based RICENET, managed by a student-run firm, to connect all members to each other and to regional and global suppliers and buyers.[60]

Formation of business clusters. When a large concentration of small businesses all compete with each other, unable to break into new markets or improve product design, competition drives down prices and can lead to self-exploitation strategies. In this environment, a cluster approach to development of business services can be a viable option to achieve collective efficiency.

In Jaipur, India, famous for its ethnic hand-block print fabric, a UNIDO-supported intervention helped 500 small firms employing 10,000 workers to increase their profitability, improve their product quality, and access new export markets by pursuing a cluster strategy. The first steps were to increase communication, build trust, analyze problems, and develop a common vision of problems and needed collective action. Over time, this led to revitalization of a dormant artisans' association, the Calico Printers Co-operative Society; this in turn led to the creation of a common showroom and an independent Consortium of Textile Exporters. Private service providers such as the National Institute of Fashion Technology have stepped in to provide fashion design advice, a credit scheme has been extended through the Small Industries Development Bank of India, and a market is gradually developing for consulting on export strategies, Internet technology, bulk purchasing, and product marketing for small enterprises.[61]

Other successful examples of small business clusters penetrating national and global markets include shoe exporters in Brazil's Sinos Valley and stainless steel surgical instrument manufacturers in Sialkot, Pakistan.

Access to Financial Services

It is estimated that more than 500 million poor people worldwide operate profitable micro and small enterprises, yet less than 4 percent receive financial services from sources other than moneylenders or friends and family.[62] In order to expand outreach and serve the large majority of microentrepreneurs in poor households and those managing small and medium enterprises, the lessons learned through a quarter-century of NGO intermediation have been applied to attract private sector involvement in provision of financial services to the poor. The institutional models vary, building upon existing strengths and innovative use of technology, and adapting outreach strategies and products to meet the demands of poor rural and urban clients.[63]

The recent entry of the private sector is reflected in statistics. By 1995, in a survey of 200 microfinance institutions, NGOs made up more than half the sample but accounted for only 9 percent of total outstanding loans and 4 percent of outstanding loan balances. This is in part because of the growth of commercial and savings banks and credit unions. These figures also reflect the fact that NGOs offer the smallest loans and work with the poorest borrowers. NGOs generally offer more social services than banks, invest much more in the capability of poor people, educate poor people about financial systems, and prepare them for participation in formal financial institutions.[64]

Technological innovations to reduce information and transaction costs

Two types of technological innovation are improving information access and reducing transaction costs in connecting poor people to financial markets. The first is credit scoring. While it is a standard statistical method used to calculate the risk of lending based on a customer's profile, credit history, and other relevant factors, credit scoring is only now being applied in developing countries to connect micro producers to formal financial systems. Microfinance institutions trying out this system include FUNDES in Panama, Financiera Familiar in Paraguay, and Orion in Peru.[65]

In India, a performance scoring system to enable poor people's self-help groups to access formal financial systems is being piloted in a World Bank-financed district poverty project in the state of Andhra Pradesh. There are over 30,000 poor women's self-help groups with different credit histories, savings, and skills in self-management. The project is piloting a performance rating system that classifies these groups into three categories corresponding to indigenous equivalents of AAA, AA, or A credit risk ratings. The rating system has been developed in collaboration with financial institutions, the self-help groups, and the National Bank for Agriculture and Rural Development.

Increased competition and computer technologies are stimulating commercial banks to move their services down-market and NGOs to move up-market to retain their competitive edge and market share. Computerization, automated teller machines (ATMs), and smart cards are all tools whose potential is now being explored to reduce costs, establish reliable credit histories, and reach poorer clients more efficiently. These examples do not require local organizational capacity but represent innovations in new products that fit poor people's profiles and contribute to their asset accumulation.

Financial institutions in India and Swaziland are using a smart card with an embedded microchip containing information on a client's credit history to reduce transaction costs and establish credit history. In Swaziland, the Growth Trust Corporation, a business affiliate of Swazi Business Growth Trust (SBGT), issues a smart card to its small business clients. Clients use the cards to access funds and make payments at participating commercial banks around the country. The system enables SBGT to become a virtual bank running the country's largest banking network for low-income clients.[66] In a poor, arid district of Andhra Pradesh, India, where many villagers are in permanent debt to moneylenders, Swayam Krishi Sangam (SKS) provides general, seasonal, emergency, and consumption loans at different rates to the poorest women. SKS combines group solidarity with issuing smart cards to members and handheld computers to workers to reduce the transaction costs of financial information recording. The organization plans to add a read-only computer in villages so that villagers can more regularly check their accounts.[67]

In South Africa, First National Bank and ABSA, a large banking group, have rapidly increased the number of ATMs in black townships and rural areas. ATMs are used to deliver pension checks to villages too small to be serviced by bank branches. ATMs have reduced theft of checks and fraudulent claims by 15 to 20 percent.[68]

Standard Bank of South Africa has developed "E Plan" to reach small depositors while keeping costs low. E Plan outlets are colorful nontraditional kiosks, conveniently located and open to sidewalks, with video displays for entertainment and information. ATM screens are graphics-driven because of high levels of illiteracy. Customers are helped by three or four friendly assistants who speak several local languages. E Plan offers a single savings account for deposits and cash withdrawals, and all money in accounts with more than $56 earns interest. The accounts have proven to be very popular in part because poor clients who live in high-crime areas can protect their money from being stolen right out of their hands.[69]

In 1997 Standard Bank converted close to half a million low-balance customers to E Plan and attracted 600,000 new customers within a period of 10 months. By 1998 there were approximately 1.4 million

E Plan account holders. Forecasts for 2002 were for 50 million E Plan transactions—42.5 percent of all Standard Bank of South Africa transactions (for more information, see Tools and Practices 1).[70]

Inclusion and participation

The search for new markets by the private sector, combined with regulatory change and the desire for poverty reduction, is bringing about changes in the way financial services are provided to poor people. Institutional innovations to promote poor people's use of formal financial services include "downscaling" of products offered by commercial banks; "upgrading" of existing semiformal financial institutions or creation of new microfinance institutions; and regulatory change.

Downscaling. This refers to provision of financial services to poorer clients than an institution has previously served, and can be undertaken by state-owned commercial and development banks, private microfinance institutions (MFIs), or consumer credit companies. The Bank Rakyat Indonesia is a good example of downscaling, reaching poorer clients through its autonomous Unit Desas.[71]

In Chile, where financial liberalization is fairly advanced, commercial banks have moved into the microfinance sector in a big way, outperforming NGOs in their outreach and cost of delivery within five years of market entry. The entry of commercial banks was facilitated by time-bound government subsidies. Banefe, a commercial bank with 22,000 clients, Bandesarrollo, a socially conscious private bank with 16,600 clients, and Banco del Estado, a state-owned bank with 8,290 clients, have all gained additional clients and offered a wider range of products, while the market share of NGOs has rapidly declined.[72]

Upgrading and new MFIs. BancoSol in Bolivia grew directly out of the success of an NGO, PRODEM, that could not mobilize savings because of legal restrictions. By 1991 PRODEM had provided $27.6 million in loans with an average loan size of $273. To overcome the restrictions on savings mobilization, BancoSol was created in 1992, the first private commercial bank to cater specifically to microenterprises. By 1999 BancoSol had a loan portfolio of $63.8 million with 76,200 clients primarily in the informal sector, an average loan size of $828, and a 30 percent return on equity. Increased competition has forced BancoSol to diversify and simplify its products, including granting individual loans to better-off and repeat clients who dislike the solidarity group requirements.[73]

IFC and other agencies are providing equity capital and capacity-building grants to enable large, credible microfinance NGOs to spin off new financially profitable MFIs. Between 1991 and 2001, ACCION International's network of MFIs in Latin America and the Caribbean disbursed over $3 billion in loans averaging $600 to more than 2 million microentrepreneurs, with 98 percent loan repayment rates. The network serves home-based workers as well as street vendors, carpenters, and other self-employed micro producers, many of them women. In Mexico, ACCION International recently provided technical assistance and direct investment to enable affiliate Compartamos to spin off its microfinance activities into a separate for-profit entity, Financiera Compartamos SA, that is expected to help Compartamos triple its number of borrowers in the coming years. In 2001, with support from the World Bank's SME Capacity Building Facility, ACCION began expansion of its model to Africa.[74]

New microenterprise banks are proving to be commercially viable even under very difficult conflict circumstances, as in Kosovo. IFC formed a successful partnership with a German firm, Internationale Projekt Consult GmbH, to start Micro Enterprise Bank of Kosovo. The bank turned a profit in its first six months, and the partnership has now been extended through an $85 million package of grants and equity investment to start up commercially viable microcredit banks in several other countries, including Bulgaria, Georgia, Ghana, Kazakhstan, Macedonia, Moldova, the Philippines, and Romania. Start-up costs include training, fundraising, and management support services.[75]

Regulatory change. Financial market liberalization will not automatically result in the emergence of microcredit institutions unless regulations that prevent their entry into financial markets change. These include tax laws and the civil code as well as banking laws. For example, regulations about large capital requirements can discourage the establishment of microfinance banks. In the Philippines, new banking regulations permit the establishment of more microfinance banks. They have exempted MFIs from requiring applicants to provide the usual amount of collateral, income and expenditure statements, and tax forms. The new regulations also set much lower capital requirements—$100,000 as opposed to a minimum of $50 million for commercial banks.[76]

In Bolivia and Peru, new regulations have allowed the creation of specialized nonbank financial intermediaries for micro and small businesses: Private Financial Funds (PFFs) and Caja de Los Andes in Bolivia, and Small and Microenterprise Development Entities (EDPYME) in Peru. These are regulated financial intermediaries that have advantages over commercial banks in terms of lower capital, reserve, and provision requirements, leaner cost structures, and greater flexibility and responsiveness. Many commercially oriented NGOs and new commercial companies in Bolivia are becoming PFFs. As a result, outreach has increased dramatically, although some of these funds are experiencing serious repayment problems. Increased competition is bringing about further changes in the MFIs. It is now estimated that one-third of Bolivia's 600,000 microenterprises are reached by one of the MFIs.[77]

Local organizational capacity

Building local organizational capacity through poor people's groups and federations is a fundamental part of the microfinance revolution on which other elements depend. The two principles that have been established in the last few decades of microfinance lending are that poor people can borrow and repay on commercial terms and that poor people have high demand for convenient savings instruments. Many of the institutional innovations depend on the capability of poor people, particularly the poorest, to form groups. Group-based methodologies that allow the poor to use their social capital as a collateralizable asset reduce both risks and transaction costs to the microfinance institution and enable poor people to overcome their lack of material collateral and engage in shared learning.

Many of the other innovations that lead to financial viability take advantage of this group presence. These include frequent repayment in small amounts; incentive-based innovations to overcome information asymmetries that include starting with small, short-term loans and building up the size over time for those with a good track record of repayment; and requiring a certain amount of up-front savings to establish the client's commitment and ability to service a loan. Finally, insistence on high discipline in repayment has meant a shift from treating poor people as beneficiaries to treating them as clients and customers capable of managing their own business affairs.

Groups are such an important part of reaching poor people, and particularly the poorest, that they form the base on which other institutional mechanisms mentioned earlier rely. These include using information technology to track credit history, or to educate and raise awareness on other social issues.

Group-based lending, however, is not always appropriate. Individual lending is more appropriate and less cumbersome to individuals with a credit history, greater education and skills, higher income, and need for larger loans. It is also appropriate where conflict or deep social divisions exist, and in certain urban contexts.

Managing Vulnerability: Insurance and Housing

Poor people need access to finance not only for direct income generation but also to overcome shocks and to safeguard personal and household wellbeing. Ownership of homes with secure tenure and some sort of insurance against shocks, including health shocks, are important in reducing poor people's vulnerability. However, high start-up capitalization requirements regulating insurance companies currently prevent the entry of smaller companies that cater to a poorer segment of the population. Two areas of innovation are microinsurance and housing loans. Microinsurance schemes provide poor people with some protection against costs associated with illness, death, theft, or damage to property. Housing loans provide much-needed asset security and support poor people's home-based income-generation activities.

All promising examples are based on poor people's groups or their capacity to organize. The Self-Employed Women's Association (SEWA) in India provides an integrated social security scheme to its members, who are primarily poor women in the informal sector, especially home-based workers and street vendors. The scheme involves subsidies from the Life Insurance Corporation of India and the United India Insurance Company and covers all basic lifetime risks: death, widowhood, personal accident, sickness, maternity, and loss of assets, working equipment, and housing. Insurance can be purchased either by paying a yearly premium or by making a one-time fixed deposit into SEWA's bank, with interest on the deposit used to pay the annual premium. As of December 2000, the scheme covered almost 30,000 members.[78] In 2002, SEWA is exploring ways to strengthen the financial base of the social security scheme and to achieve long-term financial and administrative sustainability at levels of premiums that its members can support. Ultimately, SEWA hopes to expand coverage to all members and their families.

Other efforts to provide insurance to poor women and men include Delta Life Insurance Company Ltd in Bangladesh, which provides microinsurance through Grameen Bima and Gono Bima.[79] In Cambodia, the Research and Technology Exchange Group (GRET), a French NGO, is running an experimental program to provide health insurance and access to primary health care facilities to poor families in two communes close to Phnom Penh.[80]

In several countries, poor people's associations and cooperatives are working with local authorities and banks to address their need for secure tenure and housing, particularly in urban slum areas. In Mumbai, India, Mahila Milan, a member of the National Slumdwellers Federation, has been able to acquire land, housing, and basic infrastructure services for its members. It first mobilized members' own savings, then negotiated land with local authorities and accessed additional finance through the Housing and Finance Development Corporation of India.

Large poor people's organizations also need access to larger bridge or guarantee loans to help them expand outreach. It has been difficult even for large poor people's organizations engaged in productive activities to obtain loans from commercial banks. Recently, however, the Society for the Promotion of Area Resource Centers (SPARC), an Indian NGO with an equity of $530 and thus no balance sheet or collateral, received a $9.5 million guarantee loan from a private commercial bank based on its track record of community service. This enabled SPARC to win a construction contract for 320 community toilets in Mumbai to expand services to the poor through the Slumdwellers Federation.[81]

In Quezon City, the Philippines, the legally registered Payatas Scavengers Association addresses the needs of 300,000 scavengers living on a 15-hectare municipal dumping ground. Formation of the group has led to savings mobilization and legal land acquisition for its members, aided by loans for housing repairs and land purchase. By mid-1999, the association's members had saved $283,000 and were negotiating with the government for provision of basic services and pro-poor regulatory changes.[82] In Guatemala, 50,000 squatters have formed cooperatives and acquired land through legal means and are repaying 15-year loans without default.[83] In Peru, MiBanco, a microfinance institution with over 70,000 microenterprise borrowers, has developed a successful program of housing loans that resemble microfinance loans more than mortgages, to help poor people upgrade and rehabilitate their homes in progressive stages. The system relies on both well-trained loan officers and good management information systems to track loans and repayment histories.[84]

Access to Justice and Legal Aid

A new generation of judicial and legal reform projects is creating the legal environment for accountable governance and empowering poor people by increasing their access to justice through a mix of strategies (table 3-5). How these projects incorporate empowerment elements is described in detail in Tools and Practices 14.

Table 3-5   Increasing Poor People's Access to Justice, Examples Classified by Major Empowerment Element

Information	Inclusion/ participation	Accountability	Local organizational capacity
All four projects include mechanisms to ensure public access to information	Judicial Reform Project, Guatemala Judicial Reform Project, Ecuador	Supreme Court modernization, Venezuela	Urban Property Rights Project, Peru

The goal of legal and judicial reform is to build legal systems based on the rule of law, with laws that are publicly known and are enforced in a predictable way and through transparent mechanisms. The rules must apply equally to all citizens, and the state must also be subject to the rules. The quality of legal norms in a society and the manner in which they are administered have direct impacts on the extent to which citizens have a voice in the decision-making process. How state institutions comply with the law greatly affects the daily lives of citizens, particularly poor people who are least able to protect themselves from abuse of their rights. The extent to which a society is law-bound affects its national income as well as its levels of literacy and infant mortality.[85]

Clearly defined property and benefit rights, and confidence that these rights can be fairly and efficiently defended against encroachment if necessary, are critical to inducing hundreds of thousands of individuals and groups to make investment decisions that contribute to economic growth and poverty reduction.

The World Bank's approach to and support for legal reform have evolved from an initial narrow focus on commercial law and matters most closely related to economic development and foreign investment to a much broader understanding of legal reform from the perspective of all stakeholders, particularly the poor. From this perspective, reform is not just a technical challenge of building courts, increasing the number of judges, and providing computers, but entails more fundamental changes in governance and social norms, aimed at ensuring justice for all. It is also recognized that laws without foundation in social values and the cultural context will remain void of meaning and hence will not be implemented. This has led to two important changes.

First is the use of participatory processes and consultation to create ownership of needed change and to ensure that new laws are informed by those most affected.[86] Second is recognition of the importance of understanding customary laws and traditional conflict resolution institutions, and supporting these as appropriate. Customary laws can be discriminatory of women and other excluded groups.

Currently, more than 480 Bank-financed projects have legal and judicial reform components. In addition, there are 35 freestanding projects in four regions that undertake such reform through knowledge dissemination, capacity building, and reform of laws. Judicial and legal reform projects focus on: (a) improving administrative justice, and making administrative decisions accountable and affordable to ordinary citizens; (b) promoting judicial independence and accountability; (c) improving legal education; (d) improving poor people's cultural, physical, and financial access to justice; and (e) public outreach and education.

To ensure that legal reform processes incorporate the perspectives of all those affected, most projects start with broad stakeholder participation involving those within the legal system such as judges and public administration officials, as well as businesses, NGOs, and citizens. Judicial sector assessments are becoming standard practice to guide the reform process.

Recent projects have established creative long-term relationships with civil society groups. Their roles extend from working in partnership with judges to ensure accountability and transparency, as in Venezuela; to social communication, outreach, and citizen education, as in Ecuador; to institutional assessment, monitoring, and evaluation, as in the Peru Urban Property Rights project.

Inclusion and participation of poor people is ensured through a range of mechanisms. The Guatemala Judicial Reform project is training judges and other court personnel in local languages and cultures. Projects in Colombia, Guatemala, and Peru are experimenting with decentralized court services as well as services offered by traveling judges and public defenders. NGOs are providing low-cost legal services in Ecuador even though costs of transportation may still be too high for poor people in remote areas. To reduce costs as well as provide speedy hearings, some countries including El Salvador use alternative dispute resolution mechanisms. In El Salvador, the Procuraduría General offers counseling, mediation, and other services to women with family problems that can often be resolved without resorting to courts.

Rules and laws are reflections of culture and society. Gender-based discrimination is embedded in the laws of many countries. A World Bank-sponsored review of laws in Nepal identified 54 laws that discriminate against women. These include laws that prohibit transfer of the mother's citizenship to children, that make married daughters ineligible to inherit property, and that require a husband's consent for women's admission to certain educational institutions.[87]

Notes

1. World Bank 2001f.

2. Narayan and Shah 2000a.

3. The Uganda PETS is described in more detail in the section of this chapter on improving national governance, and all four PETS are described in Tools and Practices 18.

4. Reinikka and Svensson 2002.

5. Internal memo prepared by Carmen Niethammer, 2001. See also http://www.developmentmarketplace.org/

6. Angrist and others 2001; King, Orazem, and Wohlgemuth 1998; King and others 1997; Patrinos and Ariasingam 1997.

7. Estache, Foster, and Wodon 2001; Ryan and Sara n.d.

8. The Bank approved $1.4 billion in CDD projects and components in fiscal 2001, and this was expected to increase to $2 billion in fiscal 2002. Projects channel funds either directly to local communities, or through local government, NGOs, and private firms, or directly through central government, or they give community groups authority over investment decisions. All institutional models try to develop the optimal synergy between community groups and other actors.

9. Kessides 1997; Venkataraman and Falconer 1998.

10. See Tools and Practices 13 on poor people's organizations. For more information on the Albania Irrigation Rehabilitation Project, see the website of the International Network on Participatory Irrigation Management at http://www.inpim.org/Countries/Albania/albania.html

11. World Bank 2001b.

12. As of May 2001, the Bank operated 98 social fund projects in 58 countries with a total investment of $3.5 billion. Of closed projects, 96 percent were rated satisfactory—well above the Bank average. Thirty-two percent of social funds include community capacity building among their objectives; community empowerment was mentioned in 18 percent of projects, and social capital in 5 percent. The report concludes that since each community processes just one subproject, overall, social funds have operated as users rather than producers of social capital (Rawlings, Sherburne-Benz, and VanDomelen 2001; World Bank 2001e).

13. A large study of decentralized governance institutions of the Panchayat Raj based on over 2,000 interviews in 53 villages in Rajasthan and Madhya Pradesh, India, establishes that the majority of villagers (65 percent) did not attend a single *gram sabha* (village council) meeting in the previous year and that barely 7 percent attended meetings regularly. Further analysis revealed that the *gram panchayat*'s development initiatives were the least valued of all development activities since villagers felt that they had no influence, and there was a lack of transparency and high levels of corruption. Using econometric analysis, the study concludes that the addition of one more source of information to a person's repertoire increases participation by more than five percentage points (Alsop, Krishna, and Sjoblom 2001). For information on experiences with decentralization in Bolivia, the Philippines, and Uganda, see Azfar, Kähkönen, and Meagher 2001; Faguet 2000; World Bank 2000a.

14. An analysis of 38 municipalities across Bolivia revealed that the Law of Popular Participation has had little impact where political parties, as opposed to local organizations and rural unions, have a strong presence. Where local organizational life is weak, narrow interests take precedence over the wider interests of the municipality and the community as a whole (Faguet 2000).

15. See http://www.ayudaurbana.com and http://www.cristal.gov.ar

16. Paul 2002; Paul and Sekhar 2000.

17. For additional information about Swabhimana, see http://www.savebangalore.org/ and http://www.pacindia.org/

18. Citywide strategies for poverty reduction are being undertaken in approximately 80 cities around the world, including Cali, Colombia; Kampala, Uganda; Haiphong, Vietnam; and Johannesburg, South Africa.

19. World Bank 2001d.

20. Ocampo 2001.

21. de Asis 2000.

22. Ocampo 2001.

23. Chattopadhyay and Duflo 2001; Jain 1996; Vyasulu and Vyasulu 1999.

24. Ternopil Urban Development Agency 2000.

25. ICPS 1999.

26. For evidence from Bolivia see Faguet 2000; Grootaert and Narayan 2001; for evidence from India see Alsop, Krishna, and Sjoblom 2001; Jain 1996; Vyasulu and Vyasulu 1999.

27. Abdi 2001; *the Hindu* 2001.

28. The 38 municipalities included in a survey in Bolivia had an extraordinary total of 92 mayors in the first 3.5 years of the 1996–2000 term. More than a quarter of these municipalities had a new mayor every year of the four-year term (Faguet 2000).

29. Several reviews of participatory processes highlight both the weaknesses and strengths of experiences to date. All agree that the PRSP has opened up new opportunities for

citizen engagement in identifying priorities and influencing poverty strategies. Most reviews also highlight the need to deepen, broaden, and institutionalize the participatory processes. See http://www.worldbank.org/poverty/strategies/review/index.htm

30. See http://www.cristal.gov.ar

31. See http://www.femmesdumaroc.ma/plan.asp

32. de Silva 2001.

33. Achievements include a budget surplus in 1999 of more than 1.1 billion Irish pounds compared to a deficit of 1.4 billion pounds in 1986. This has allowed the government to increase expenditures on health by 150 percent, on education by 84 percent, and on welfare by 70 percent since 1987, while unemployment has been reduced from 17.5 percent to under 5 percent. Society-wide policy and wage agreements have helped maintain social stability.

34. In India, the Millennial Public Service Survey, which applied the citizen scorecard methodology to a sample of over 36,000 households across 24 Indian states, has just been released and widely discussed in the media. The survey provides citizen ratings on the performance of five basic public services of special concern to poor people: drinking water, health and sanitation, education and child care, the public distribution system, and road transport (Paul 2002). In Guyana, the World Bank is supporting efforts by the government to strengthen monitoring and evaluation capacities in the key line agencies with those responsibilities, and to pilot a community-based participatory monitoring and evaluation system designed to engage poor communities directly in PRSP monitoring.

35. Reinikka 2001.

36. WIEGO 2000a,b.

37. Cisneros 1997.

38. Hallberg 1999.

39. IFC 2001b. IFC data are from 1998.

40. The World Bank Group's investment in SMEs between 1997 and 2001 reached $8.31 billion (World Bank 70 percent, IFC 25 percent, and Multilateral Investment Guarantee Agency [MIGA] 5 percent). Fifty percent of this support goes to small enterprises, 31 percent to medium-size enterprises, and 19 percent to microenterprises. No IFC investments are targeted to microenterprises. Most of the support is direct firm-level assistance, through financial markets in general and assistance with regulations and policies. In fiscal 2001, 7 percent of the World Bank Group's overall investment was in SMEs. Fourteen percent or $1.82 billion of IFC's current portfolio is invested in SMEs either directly or through financial markets, primarily in Europe and Central Asia Region (ECA), Latin America, and Africa. The World Bank's current SME portfolio of $5.96 billion is predominantly in the Latin America and the Caribbean Region (LAC), followed by Africa and East Asia. Investments are spread across sectors, with the largest shares in agriculture (41 percent), finance (15 percent), and social protection (11 percent), and smaller percentages in

environment, education, power, transport, and urban development (Webster, Kochar, and Raissian 2001).

41. Some country studies, such as the one by Kapoor, Mugwara, and Chidavaenzi (1997) on Zimbabwe and the IFC's work on country mapping (2000b), touch on the issue of assessing investment climate and constraints of SMEs.

42. World Bank 2002c.

43. Richardson, Ramirez, and Haq 2000.

44. Bayes, von Braun, and Akhter 1999; Narayan and Shah 2000a. Also see the Grameen Phone website at http://www.grameenphone.com/village.htm

45. See the Information Network for Indigenous Organizations website at http://www.laneta.apc.org/rci/

46. See the Guatemala MicroNet Project website at http://www.worldbank.org/pics/pid/gt55084.txt

47. See the following websites: Naushad Trading Company (http://www.ntclimited.com/); African Crafts (http://www.africancrafts.com/); Novica (http://www.novica.com/); Eziba (http://www.eziba.com/); PeopLink (http://www.PeopLink.org/).

48. World Bank 2002a.

49. Bhatnagar 2000b.

50. de Soto 2000, 2001.

51. Bell, Peters, and Ndiweni 1995; Carlton and Hancock 2000; Kapoor, Mugwara, and Chidavaenzi 1997.

52. WIEGO 2000a,b.

53. WIEGO 2000a,b.

54. Tesoro 2000.

55. Panaritis 2001; World Bank 1998.

56. Bhatnager 2000a.

57. See Estache, Foster, and Wodon 2001. Also see the World Bank's Smart Business Smart Development website at http://www.worldbank.org/business

58. Ceglie and Dini 1999.

59. Ceglie and Dini 1999.

60. IFC 2000a. See also http://www.mpdf.org

61. Clara, Russo, and Gulati 2000.

62. Microcredit Summit 2000; Women's World Banking 1995. The Microcredit Summit brings together practitioners, advocates, educational institutions, donors, international financial institutions, and NGOs with the goal of reaching 100 million of the world's poorest families with credit by the year 2005.

63. Recent analyses of successful microfinance institutions emphasize three elements of support by international agencies: capacity building of MFIs; steps to foster formal market linkages; and promotion of policy reform. Two additional factors are focus on

financial viability and innovation based on the needs of poor customers (Ledgerwood 1999; Rhyne 2001).

64. Ledgerwood 1999.

65. IDB 1998; Schreiner 2000. Good financial management systems are a prerequisite for credit scoring systems and other such innovations.

66. Nelson 1999.

67. Microfinance Gateway 1999.

68. Nelson 1999.

69. Paulson and McAndrews 1998.

70. Paulson and McAndrews 1998.

71. Mukherjee 1997; Patten, Rosengard, and Johnson 2001.

72. Baydas, Graham, and Valenzuela 1997; Christen 2000.

73. Glosser 1994; Otero and Rhyne 1994.

74. IFC 2001a.

75. IFC 2000c.

76. Lucas 2001; Vogel, Gomez, and Fitzgerald 1999.

77. IDB 1998.

78. McCord, Isern, and Hashemi 2001.

79. Ahmed 2001.

80. CGAP 2001.

81. Balaram 2001a,b.

82. Microenterprise Best Practices 2000.

83. Kessides 1997.

84. Malhotra, Brown, and García forthcoming.

85. Dollar 2000; Hellman and others 2000; Kaufmann, Kraay, and Zoido-Lobatón 1999.

86. The Guatemala Judicial Reform project involved stakeholder consultations with over 1,000 individuals and organizations, including judges, law schools, private sector interests, and civil society groups. Similarly, a recently completed study that gathers the voices of 200 judges, lawyers, legislators, business people, journalists, academics, and development assistance officials from five countries in Eastern Europe and Central Asia forms the basis of dialogue for reform and raises awareness of the potential for reform in that region (Dietrich 2000).

87. Ofosu-Amaah 2001.

Chapter 4

Lessons Learned

A society's formal and informal institutions are a reflection of its history, culture, politics and geography. Approaches to empowering poor people to participate in governance and market activity and invest in their own assets are necessarily context-specific. There is much to be learned from the innovations featured in projects and policies, and these lessons need to be more systematically incorporated into poverty reduction strategies.

When poverty reduction is viewed through an empowerment lens, it becomes clear that, in addition to specific policies and institutional mechanisms, the *how* of development or process issues are of great importance. Box 4-1 highlights ten broad lessons, including process lessons, that have been learned across very different contexts. These should be kept in mind when considering an empowering approach to development in any context.

Overall, what emerges from analyses of projects and analytical work is the progress made in establishing partnerships with poor people in the co-production of local public goods, particularly basic education, and in management of natural resources. However, many projects of these types, both single-sector and multisector, need to invest more systematically in information disclosure, social accountability, and local organizational capacity. This is essential in helping to overcome the risk of capture by local elites and in achieving long-term sustainability. Few projects as yet systematically track changes in levels of empowerment and local organizational capacity.

Much more attention needs to be paid to strengthening the demand side of governance in projects and policies related to improving local and

Box 4-1 Lessons Learned

Respect, trust, and social relations matter. Development policy is not an exact science. The best technical ideas have to be communicated, owned, and defended within a given country. It takes time, skills, resources, and patience to build consensus and trust. Without this investment in participatory processes, agreements remain fragile as key actors who have opposed each other in the past have little opportunity to build trust or confidence in each other. Breakdown of agreements interferes with reform processes and feeds narrow political opportunism.

Participatory processes and conflict management go together. Participatory processes that bring different stakeholder groups together to make decisions about setting priorities, changing rules, and allocating resources are by definition potentially conflictual. Therefore, participatory processes should have clearly defined rules of engagement as well as rules and mechanisms for resolving conflict and disagreements that are known and agreed to by all.

Change is brought about by champions and alliances in country. Almost every case of large-scale change involves strong innovators in country, both within and outside government. Innovations and support for policy reform spread when alliances are built across classes and sectors. Innovations also get internalized best through peer learning and horizontal exchanges, such as between ministers, mayors, or communities. Outsiders have important roles to play in supporting this process and disseminating information across boundaries.

Bringing key actors together is vital. Large-scale change for effective poverty reduction happens when changes occur in the relations between the four key actors: the state, the private sector, civil society, and poor people. Policy and institutional design forums that bring them together to listen to each other and work together are key. Each actor has strengths that can complement the strengths of others.

Four empowerment elements act in synergy. Access to timely and understandable information, inclusion and participation, accountability, and investment in local organizational capacity all reinforce each other to deliver better poverty reduction outcomes. While much progress has been made on participation, the other three principles—investment in access to information, downward accountability mechanisms, and local organizational capacity—may be even more important. Work in these areas will need to be refined over time through action learning.

Direct, intensive forms of participation are not always appropriate. It is important to be clear on the purpose and value added of participatory

(box continues on following page)

Box 4-1 (continued)

processes that involve poor people, since participation costs to them can be high. Sometimes all that is needed is information from poor people about their priorities and resources and the constraints that guide their decisions, whether these are about which water sources to use or whether to send a child to school. This information can then be used to design policies and programs that best fit the needs of poor women and men in a particular context.

Poor people's realities are the starting point. A mindset driven by looking at the world through the eyes of poor women and men and then searching for the best-fit policies for that political, economic, social, and institutional context will prevent many mistakes. This must be complemented by an attitude of learning by doing.

Local capacity is systematically underestimated. Local capacity, particularly poor people's capacity to make rational decisions and effectively manage development resources, is usually underestimated. Given the opportunity, poor people often manage resources more efficiently than other agencies, although they may need resources to hire technical expertise in some areas. Also frequently underestimated are local research institutes and local government staff. The problem is often lack of incentives or active disincentives, or lack of funds to take initiative, rather than lack of basic competence.

Poor people's membership-based organizations are overlooked. In many parts of the world poor women and men have organized beyond communities into federated networks with representation at the national level. Such networks include producers' associations, farmers' associations, slum dwellers' networks, and trade unions. These organizations, as well as other civil society organizations such as business management institutes and chambers of commerce, are important actors that need to be part of policy dialogue and project implementation where appropriate.

Changes in rules and institutional processes enable large-scale change. The poverty reduction challenge is to bring about change on a large scale. This implies replicating successful experiences. This in turn requires changes in the enabling policy and regulatory regimes that are informed by successes, failures, poor people's experiences, and institutional realities. Changing rules is not enough. Implementing new rules requires educating stakeholders at all levels, including government officials, about the new rules, and getting buy-in; acknowledging the need for changes in values and behaviors; supporting institutional capacity to implement and manage change processes; ensuring public accountability; and monitoring, evaluating, and refining the rules based on experience.

national governance. Even where formal rules have changed to enable poor people and other citizens to participate in decisions about local resource allocation, lack of information and weak organizations of poor people and civil society prevent effective use of the new rules and regulations and accountability mechanisms. Strategies for improved governance and poverty reduction have focused on formal systems, with little connection to those working at the community level. The challenge is to connect changes in rules and regulations with efforts to strengthen the capacities of citizens, especially poor people, to monitor governance and hold governments accountable.

Budget support loans can combine access to information with accountability to citizens to improve pro-poor actions by governments. This shift is in the very early stages, and therefore this role for civil society organizations is new in most contexts. To be effective, citizen feedback must be linked to resource allocation or redesign decisions. There is thus a need to invest in the capacity of a wide range of civil society organizations including research institutes, NGOs with links to poor people, and poor people's organizations, to enable them to fulfill these new roles effectively.

The focus on outcome indicators and performance monitoring to improve development effectiveness provides important opportunities for citizen engagement. This requires a shift from participation in events to institutional mechanisms that engage poor people and other citizens in policymaking, expenditure tracking, and monitoring of basic service delivery in both PRSP and middle-income countries.

Especially where poverty is widespread, economic growth will be fueled by the productive efforts of millions of poor people who labor primarily in agriculture and in the informal sector. Actions to empower poor people economically include connecting them to information about markets, reducing transaction costs to service providers through use of information technology, simplifying registration and licensing procedures, and investing in poor people's business organizations, networks, and clusters. Understanding the investment climate for micro, small, and medium enterprises is therefore a central part of poverty reduction strategies. Poor people's access to economic opportunity can be enhanced by removing policy, social, informational, and infrastructure barriers that limit their access to markets. Firm surveys that include microenterprises can provide valuable information on the constraints faced by such entrepreneurs.

Rule of law, access to justice, and confidence in impartial justice are critical for economic growth and to protect basic rights and assets of citizens, and particularly poor people. Recent Bank-financed projects seek to increase poor people's access to justice by understanding and addressing constraints in a broader social and cultural context. Secure tenure rights and ownership of assets decrease poor people's vulnerability.

Conclusion

Drawing from WDR 2000/2001, Voices of the Poor, ongoing experience, and analytical work, this sourcebook lays out an approach to empowerment designed to help the World Bank increase development effectiveness and move toward the ultimate goal of poverty reduction and inclusive development.

Empowerment of poor people is an end in itself and is also critical for development effectiveness. An empowering approach is not a stand-alone strategy but a way of doing business for successful scaling-up. It is grounded in the conviction that poor people themselves are the most invaluable partners in the task of poverty reduction. In projects, policy-based lending and analytical work such as public expenditure tracking, the connection to citizens needs to be strengthened through focus on the four empowerment elements: access to information, inclusion/participation, accountability, and local organizational capacity. While these four elements are common to successful efforts, the processes must be context-specific.

Building on experience, these empowering approaches need to be deepened and reflected in the Bank's work across countries, networks, and sectors, and incorporated in analytical work and lending instruments. Leadership will be needed across the Bank's regions and networks with systematic efforts to support locally owned development and to continue to learn from experience. While much is known about empowerment, much remains to be learned. There is a vast monitoring and research agenda that needs to inform project design and implementation as well as policy reforms.

Organizations that adopt empowerment as a key goal must also adopt empowering processes and behaviors internally. Poor people express the desire to be treated with respect, honesty, care, and dignity in their encounters with institutions. Empowerment approaches by definition include behaviors that build people's self-confidence and their belief in themselves. Discussions about informal norms and behavior that support ownership, dignity, and respect need to be part of the dialogue of institutional reform in countries, in support organizations, and within the World Bank.

References and Background Papers

Abdi, S. N. M. 2001. "India: New Law Empowers Citizens to Sack Corrupt Mayor." *South China Morning Post* (Hong Kong), April 13.

Abhyankar, Sham, and Parameswaran Iyer. 2001. "Why Some Village Water and Sanitation Committees Are Better than Others." Internal presentation, March 27. World Bank, South Asia Region, Water and Sanitation Program, Washington, D.C.

Ahmed, Mosleh Uddin. 2001. "Delta Life Insurance Company Bangladesh." Presentation at Workshop on Innovations in Microfinance, World Bank Institute, Washington, D.C., March 20. Available: http://www.worldbank.org/wbi/banking/microfinance2001/presentations/uddinahmed.ppt

Alsop, Ruth, Anirudh Krishna, and Disa Sjoblom. 2001. "Inclusion and Local Elected Governments: The Panchayat Raj System in India." Social Development Paper 37. World Bank, South Asia Region, Social Development Unit, Washington, D.C.

Alsop, Ruth, Disa Sjoblom, Ceema Namazie, and Pawan Patil. 2001. "Community Level User Groups in Three World Bank Aided Projects: Do They Perform as Expected?" World Bank, India Country Management Unit and the Poverty Reduction and Economic Management Unit in South Asia, Washington, D.C.

Angrist, Joshua, Eric Bettinger, Erik Bloom, Elizabeth King, and Michael Kremer. 2001. "Vouchers for Private Schooling in Colombia:

Evidence from a Randomized Natural Experiment." NBER Working Paper W8343. National Bureau of Economic Research, Cambridge, Mass. Available: http://papers.nber.org/papers/W8343.pdf

Appleton, Simon, Tom Emwanu, Johnson Kagugube, and James Muwonge. 1999. "Changes in Poverty in Uganda, 1992–1997." Centre for the Study of African Economies, Oxford, U.K. Available: http://www.economics.ox.ac.uk/CSAEadmin/workingpapers/pdfs/9922text.pdf

Azfar, Omar, Satu Kähkönen, and Patrick Meagher. 2001. "Conditions for Effective Decentralized Governance: A Synthesis of Research Findings." University of Maryland, Center for Institutional Reform and the Informal Sector, College Park, Md. Available: http://www1.worldbank.org/publicsector/decentralization/synthesispaper.pdf

Balaram, Gunvanthi. 2001a. "Community Service Gives Credibility." *Times of India* (Bombay), August 17.

_____. 2001b. "NGO Cashes in on Track Record, SPARC History." *Times of India* (Bombay), August 17.

Baume, Elaine, Mercedes Juarez, and Hilary Standing. 2001. "Gender and Health Equity Resource Guide." University of Sussex, Institute of Development Studies, Brighton, U.K. Available: http://www.ids.ac.uk/bridge/Reports/Geneq.pdf

Baydas, Mayada, Douglas Graham, and Liza Valenzuela. 1997. "Commercial Banks in Microfinance: New Actors in the Microfinance World." Microenterprise Best Practices. Development Alternatives, Inc., Bethesda, Md. Available: http://www.mip.org/pdfs/mbp/commer.pdf

Bayes, Abdul, Joachim von Braun, and Rasheeda Akhter. 1999. "Village Pay Phones and Poverty Reduction: Insights from a Grameen Bank Initiative in Bangladesh." ZEF, Bonn. Available: http://www.zef.de/download/zef_dp/zef_dp8-99.pdf

Bell, Robin, Geoffrey Peters, and Mehlo Ndiweni. 1995. "Zimbabwe: Financial Sector Assessment." GEMINI Technical Report 5. United States Agency for International Development, Bethesda, Md.

Bhatnagar, Subhash. 2000a. "Empowering Dairy Farmers through a Dairy Information & Services Kiosk." E-Government Case Study. World Bank, Public Sector Group, Washington, D.C. Available: http://www1.worldbank.org/publicsector/egov/diskcs.htm

_____. 2000b. "Land/Property Registration in Andhra Pradesh." E-Government Case Study. World Bank, Public Sector Group, Washington, D.C. Available: http://www1.worldbank.org/publicsector/egov/cardcs.htm

Bourguignon, François, Francisco H.G. Ferreira, and Phillippe G. Leite. Forthcoming. "Beyond Oaxaca-Blinder: Accounting for Differences in Household Income Distributions." Draft. World Bank, Washington, D.C.

Carlton, Andy, and David Hancock. 2000. "ISTARN: An Experimental Approach to Informal Sector Business Support in Zimbabwe." International Labour Organization, Geneva. Available: http://www.ilo.org/public/english/employment/ent/papers/istgtz.htm

Ceglie, Giovanna, and Marco Dini. 1999. "SME Cluster and Network Development in Developing Countries: The Experience of UNIDO." Paper presented at the international conference on Building a Modern and Effective Development Service Industry for Small Enterprises, Rio de Janeiro, March 2–5. Available: http://www.ilo.org/public/english/employment/ent/papers/cluster.htm

CGAP (Consultative Group to Assist the Poorest). 2001. "GRET (Cambodia): Extending Health Insurance to Reduce Vulnerability." Pro-Poor Innovation Challenge Round 3. Washington, D.C. Available: http://www.cgap.org/html/mfis_funding_ppic.html

Chandrakirana, Kamala. 1999. "Local Capacity and Its Implications for Development: The Case of Indonesia. A Preliminary Report: Local Level Institutions Study." World Bank, Jakarta.

Chattopadhyay, Raghabendra, and Esther Duflo. 2001. "Women's Leadership and Policy Decisions: Evidence from a Nationwide Randomized Experiment in India." IED Discussion Paper 114. Boston University, Institute for Economic Development.

Christen, Robert Peck. 2000. "Commercialization and Mission Drift: The Transformation of Microfinance in Latin America." Consultative Group to Assist the Poorest, Washington, D.C. Available: http://www.cgap.org/assets/images/LAC_Commercializationfinal.pdf

Cisneros, Susana Pinilla. 1997. "Banking on the Poor: Peru's Small and Micro Enterprise Sector." Development in Practice 7 (2): 130–39.

Clara, Michele, Fabio Russo, and Mukesh Gulati. 2000. "Cluster Development and BDS Promotion: UNIDO's Experience in India." Paper presented at the international conference on Business Services for Small Enterprises in Asia: Developing Markets and Measuring Performance, Hanoi, April 3–6. Available: http://www.ilo.org/public/english/employment/ent/papers/unido.htm

Collier, Paul. 2000. "Economic Causes of Civil Conflict and Their Implications for Policy." World Bank, Washington, D.C. Available: http://www.worldbank.org/research/conflict/papers/civilconflict.pdf

de Asis, Maria Gonzalez. 2000. "Reducing Corruption: Lessons from Venezuela." *PREM Notes* 39 (May). World Bank, Development Economics Vice Presidency and Poverty Reduction and Economic Management Network, Washington, D.C. Available: http://www1.worldbank.org/publicsector/decentralization/PREMnote39.pdf

de Silva, Luiz Pereira. 2001. "Pro Poor Growth in South Africa." Internal presentation, April 17. World Bank, Poverty Reduction and Economic Management Network, Poverty Reduction Group, Washington, D.C.

de Soto, Hernando. 2000. *The Mystery of Capital: Why Capitalism Triumphs in the West and Fails Everywhere Else.* New York: Basic Books.

_____. 2001. "Why Capitalism Works in the West but Not Elsewhere." *International Herald Tribune,* January 5. Available: http://www.iht.com/articles/6349.html

Development Committee (Joint Ministerial Committee of the Boards of Governors of the Bank and the Fund on the Transfer of Real Resources to Developing Countries). 2002. "Development Effectiveness, Partnership, and Challenges for the Future." DC-2002-0006. Prepared by World Bank staff for the April 21, 2002 Development Committee meeting. World Bank and International Monetary Fund, Washington, D.C.

Dietrich, Mark K. 2000. *Legal and Judicial Reform in Central Europe and the Former Soviet Union: Voices from Five Countries.* Washington, D.C.: World Bank. Available: http://www4.worldbank.org/legal/publications/ljr_eca.pdf

Dollar, David. 2000. "Confederation of Indian Industries and World Bank Firm Analysis and Competitiveness Survey." Internal presentation, November. World Bank, Development Economics Research Group, Washington, D.C.

Dollar, David, and Roberta Gatti. 1999. "Gender Inequality, Income, and Growth: Are Good Times Good for Women?" World Bank, Development Research Group, Poverty Reduction and Economic Management Network, Washington, D.C. Available: http://www.worldbank.org/gender/prr/wp1.pdf

Dollar, David, and Aart Kraay. 2000. "Property Rights, Political Rights, and the Development of Poor Countries in the Post-Colonial Period." Draft. World Bank, Development Economics Research Group, Washington, D.C. Available: http://www.worldbank.org/research/growth

Estache, Antonio, Vivien Foster, and Quentin Wodon. 2001. "Infrastructure Reform and the Poor: Learning from Latin America's Experience." World Bank, LAC Regional Studies Program, WBI Studies in Development, Finance, Private Sector and Infrastructure Development, Washington, D.C.

Faguet, Jean-Paul. 2000. "Does Decentralization Increase Responsiveness to Local Needs? Evidence from Bolivia." Policy Research Working Paper 2516. World Bank, Development Research Group, Public Economics, Washington, D.C. Available: http://econ.worldbank.org/files/1332_wps2516.pdf

Galasso, Emanuela, and Martin Ravallion. 2000. "Local Knowledge vs. Local Accountability? Decentralized Targeting of an Anti-Poverty Program." World Bank, Development Research Group, Washington, D.C.

Glosser, Amy J. 1994. "The Creation of BancoSol in Bolivia." In Maria Otero and Elisabeth Rhyne, eds., *The New World of Microenterprise Finance: Building Healthy Financial Institutions for the Poor*. West Hartford, Conn.: Kumarian Press.

Grootaert, Christiaan, and Deepa Narayan. 2001. "Local Institutions, Poverty, and Household Welfare in Bolivia." Policy Research Working Paper 2644. World Bank, Social Development Department and Poverty Reduction and Economic Management Network, Washington, D.C.

Hallberg, Kristin. 1999. "Small and Medium Scale Enterprises: A Framework for Intervention." World Bank, Small Enterprise Unit, Private Sector Development Department, Washington, D.C.

Hellman, Joel S., Geraint Jones, Daniel Kaufmann, and Mark Schankerman. 2000. "Measuring Governance, Corruption, and State Capture: How Firms and Bureaucrats Shape the Business Environment in Transition Countries." Policy Research Working Paper 2312.

World Bank Institute and European Bank for Reconstruction and Development, Washington, D.C.

The Hindu. 2001. "Voters Exercise Rights to Recall." Online Edition, April 12, 2001. Available: http://www.hindu.com/2001/04/12/stories/14122123.htm

Hino, Toshiko. 1993. "Community Participation in 'Programme de restructuration de l'hydraulique villageoise' in Côte d'Ivoire." World Bank, Washington, D.C.

Hoddinott, John, Michelle Adato, Tim Besley, and Lawrence Haddad. 2000. "Participation and Poverty Reduction: Issues, Theory, and New Evidence from South Africa." IFPRI, Washington, D.C. Available: http://www.worldbank.org/poverty/wdrpoverty/background/adatoetal.pdf

ICPS (International Centre for Policy Studies). 1999. "People's Voice Project Survey in Ternopil: Report, July 30, 1999." UFE Foundation, World Bank Institute, International Centre for Policy Studies, and Canadian International Development Agency, Kiev, Ukraine. Available: http://www.icps.kiev.ua/docs/other/survey_ternopil_eng.pdf

IDB (Inter-American Development Bank). 1998. "Microfinance Meets the Private Sector." *Microenterprise Development Review* 1 (May). Available: http://www.iadb.org/sds/doc/1274eng.pdf

IFC (International Finance Corporation). 2000a. "A Rice Industry Revives: The Millers' Tale." *SME Facts* 1 (9). World Bank Group, Small and Medium Enterprise Department, Washington, D.C.

_____. 2000b. "Country Mapping." *SME Facts* 1 (7). World Bank Group, Small and Medium Enterprise Department, Washington, D.C.

_____. 2000c. "IFC and 'Internationale Projekt Consult Finance': Microcredit Start-ups in Developing Countries." Press Release 00/115. World Bank Group, Small and Medium Enterprise Department, Washington, D.C.

_____. 2001a. "ACCION International." *SME Facts* 2 (3). World Bank Group, Small and Medium Enterprise Department, Washington, D.C.

_____. 2001b. "FYR Macedonia Review." SME Country Mapping. World Bank Group, Small and Medium Enterprise Department, Washington, D.C. Available: http://ifcnet.ifc.org/sme/cm/html/macedonia_overview.html

Isham, Jonathan, Daniel Kaufmann, and Lant Pritchett. 1997. "Civil Liberties, Democracy, and the Performance of Government Projects." *World Bank Economic Review* 11 (2): 219–42.

Isham, Jonathan, Deepa Narayan, and Lant Pritchett. 1995. "Does Participation Improve Performance? Enabling Causality with Subjective Data." *World Bank Economic Review* 9 (2): 175–200.

Jain, Devaki. 1996. "Panchayat Raj: Women Changing Governance." United Nations Development Programme, New York. Available: http://www.undp.org/gender/resources/mono5.html

Jimenez, Emmanuel, and Yasuyuki Sawada. 1998. "Do Community-Managed Schools Work? An Evaluation of El Salvador's EDUCO Program." World Bank, Development Research Group, Washington, D.C. Available: http://www.worldbank.org/education/economicsed/finance/demand/related/latin/educo.doc

Kabeer, Naila. 1999. "The Conditions and Consequences of Choice: Reflections on the Measurement of Women's Empowerment." UNRISD Discussion Paper 108. United Nations Research Institute for Social Development, Geneva.

_____. 2001. "Resources, Agency, Achievements: Reflections on the Measurement of Women's Empowerment." In *Discussing Women's Empowerment—Theories and Practice*. SIDA Studies No. 3. Swedish International Development Cooperation Agency, Stockholm.

Kapoor, K., D. Mugwara, and I. Chidavaenzi. 1997. "Empowering Small Enterprises in Zimbabwe." Discussion Paper 379. World Bank, Washington, D.C.

Katz, Travis, and Jennifer Sara. 1997. "Making Rural Water Supply Sustainable: Recommendations from a Global Study." United Nations Development Programme and World Bank, Water and Sanitation Program, Washington, D.C. Available: http://www.wsp.org/pdfs/global_ruralstudy.pdf

Kaufmann, Daniel. 2000. "'Unbundling' Governance and Corruption: Some New Empirical Findings and Collective Action Approaches." Presentation given at Anti-Corruption Summit, World Bank Institute, Washington, D.C., September. Available: http://www.worldbank.org/wbi/governance

Kaufmann, Daniel, Aart Kraay, and Pablo Zoido-Lobatón. 1999. "Governance Matters." Policy Research Working Paper 2196. World

Bank, Development Research Group, Washington, D.C. Available: http://www.worldbank.org/wbi/governance/pdf/govmatrs.pdf

Kaufmann, Daniel, Pablo Zoido-Lobatón, and Young Lee. 2000. "Governance and Anticorruption: Empirical Diagnostic Study for Ecuador." Processed. World Bank, Washington, D.C.

Kessides, Christine. 1997. "World Bank Experience with the Provision of Infrastructure Services for the Urban Poor: Preliminary Identification and Review of Best Practices." World Bank, Environmentally Sustainable Development, Transportation, Water, and Urban Development Department, Washington, D.C. Available: http://www.worldbank.org/html/fpd/urban/publicat/service_provision.pdf

Khwaja, Asim Ijaz. 2000. "Can Good Projects Succeed in Bad Communities? Collective Action in the Himalayas." Harvard University, Cambridge, Mass.

King, Elizabeth, Peter F. Orazem, and Darin Wohlgemuth. 1998. "Central Mandates and Local Incentives: The Colombia Education Voucher Program." Working Paper Series on Impact Evaluation of Education Reforms, Paper No. 6. World Bank, Development Economics Research Group, Washington, D.C.

King, Elizabeth, Laura Rawlings, Marybell Gutierrez, Carlos Pardo, and Carlos Torres. 1997. "Colombia's Targeted Education Voucher Program: Features, Coverage, and Participation." Working Paper Series on Impact Evaluation of Education Reforms, Paper No. 3. World Bank, Development Economics Research Group, Washington, D.C.

Klasen, Stephan. 1999. "Does Gender Inequality Reduce Growth and Development? Evidence from Cross-Country Regressions." World Bank, Development Research Group, Poverty Reduction and Economic Management Network, Washington, D.C. Available: http://www.worldbank.org/gender/prr/wp7.pdf

Knack, Stephen, and Philip Keefer. 1997. "Does Social Capital Have an Economic Payoff? A Cross-Country Investigation." *Quarterly Journal of Economics* (November): 1251–88.

Krishna, Anirudh, Norman Uphoff, and Milton Esman, eds. 1997. *Reasons for Hope: Instructive Experiences in Rural Development.* West Hartford, Conn.: Kumarian Press.

La Porta, R., Florencio Lopez de Silanes, Andrei Shleifer, and Robert Vishny. 1997. "Trust in Large Organizations." *American Economic Review* 87 (2): 333–38.

Ledgerwood, Joanna. 1999. *The Microfinance Handbook*. Washington, D.C.: World Bank.

Lucas, Daxim L. 2001. "Microfinance Firms Exempted from Collateral Requirements." *Business World* (Philippines), February 8.

Malhotra, M., W. Brown, and A. García. Forthcoming. "Micasa: Financing the Progressive Construction of Low-Income Families' Homes at Mibanco." Draft. Case study prepared for the Cities Alliance Shelter for the Poor Series, Cities Alliance, Washington, D.C.

McCord, Michael J., Jennifer Isern, and Syed Hashemi. 2001. "Microinsurance: A Case Study of An Example of the Full Service Model of Microinsurance Provision." MicroInsurance Centre Case Studies, Nairobi, Kenya. Available: http://www.microinsurancecentre.org

Microcredit Summit. 2000. "Empowering Women with Microcredit: 2000 Microcredit Summit Campaign Report." Washington, D.C. Available: http://www.microcreditsummit.org/campaigns/report00.html

Microenterprise Best Practices. 2000. "Housing Microfinance Initiatives: Synthesis and Regional Summary: Asia, Latin America, and Sub-Saharan Africa with Selected Case Studies." Microenterprise Best Practices Project, Development Alternatives/USAID, Bethesda, Md. Available: http://www.mip.org/pubs/mbp/housingmicrofinanceinitiatives.htm

Microfinance Gateway. 1999. "Swayam Krishi Sangam (SKS): Smart Cards to Sustainably Serve the Poorest." Consultative Group to Assist the Poorest, Washington, D.C. Available: http://www.cgap.org/assets/images/SKS.pdf

Mukherjee, Joyita. 1997. "State-Owned Development Banks in Microfinance." CGAP Focus Note 10. Consultative Group to Assist the Poorest, Washington, D.C. Available: http://www.cgap.org/html/p_focus_notes10.html

Narayan, Deepa. 1995. "The Contribution of People's Participation: Evidence from 121 Rural Water Supply Projects." Environmentally Sustainable Development Occasional Paper Series 1. World Bank, Washington, D.C.

Narayan, Deepa, and Lant Pritchett. 1997. "Cents and Sociability: Household Income and Social Capital in Rural Tanzania." Policy Research Working Paper 1796. World Bank, Social Development Department and Development Research Group, Washington, D.C.

Narayan, Deepa, and Talat Shah. 2000a. "Connecting the Local to the Global: Voices of the Poor." World Bank, Washington, D.C. Available: http://www.worldbank.org/poverty/voices/globcoal/dec00/narsha.pdf

_____. 2000b. "Gender Inequity, Poverty & Social Capital." Draft. World Bank, Poverty Reduction and Economic Management, Washington, D.C.

Narayan, Deepa, with Raj Patel, Kai Schafft, Anne Rademach, and Sarah Koch-Schulte. 2000. *Voices of the Poor: Can Anyone Hear Us?* New York: Oxford University Press for The World Bank. Available: http://www.worldbank.org/poverty/voices/reports.htm#cananyone

Narayan, Deepa, Robert Chambers, Meera Shah, and Patti Petesch. 2000. *Voices of the Poor: Crying Out for Change.* New York: Oxford University Press for The World Bank.

Narayan, Deepa, and Patti Petesch, eds. 2002. *Voices of the Poor: From Many Lands.* New York: Oxford University Press for The World Bank.

Nelson, Eric. 1999. "Financial Intermediation for the Poor: Survey of the State of the Art." African Economic Policy Discussion Paper 10. Development Alternatives, Inc., Bethesda, Md.

Ocampo, Luis Moreno. 2001. "State Capture: Who Represents the Poor?" *Development Outreach* (winter). World Bank Institute, Washington, D.C. Available: http://www1.worldbank.org/devoutreach/winter01/article.asp?id=100

OED (Operations Evaluation Department). 2000. "Lessons on Community-Driven Development." *Lessons and Practices* 12. World Bank, Washington, D.C.

Ofosu-Amaah, A. Waafas. 2001. "Gender and Access to Justice." Internal memorandum, December 27. World Bank, Poverty Reduction and Economic Management, Gender Division, Washington, D.C.

Otero, Maria, and Elisabeth Rhyne, eds. 1994. *The New World of Microenterprise Finance: Building Healthy Financial Institutions for the Poor.* West Hartford, Conn.: Kumarian Press.

Panaritis, Elena. 2001. "Do Property Rights Matter? An Urban Case Study from Peru." Global Outlook: International Urban Research Monitor 1 (April): 20–22. Woodrow Wilson International Center for Scholars and U.S. Department of Housing and Urban Development, Washington, D.C.

Patrinos, Harry Anthony, and David Lakshmanan Ariasingam. 1997. Decentralization of Education: Demand-Side Financing. Washington, D.C.: The World Bank. Available: http://www.worldbank.org/education/economicsed/finance/demand/demfin/dsf_index.htm

Patten, Richard H., Jay K. Rosengard, and Don E. Johnson Jr. 2001. "Microfinance Success Amidst Macroeconomic Failure: The Experience of Bank Rakyat Indonesia During the East Asian Crisis." World Development 29 (6): 1057–69.

Paul, Samuel. 2002. Holding the State to Account: Citizen Monitoring in Action. Bangalore, India: ActionAid Karnataka Projects–Books for Change.

Paul, Samuel, and Sita Sekhar. 2000. "Benchmarking Urban Services: The Second Report Card on Bangalore." Public Affairs Centre, Bangalore, India.

Paulson, Jo Ann, and James McAndrews. 1998. "Financial Services for the Urban Poor: South Africa's E Plan." Policy Research Working Paper 2016. World Bank, Washington, D.C.

Popular Coalition to Eradicate Hunger and Poverty. 1995. "Empowerment of the Poor." Discussion Paper 1. Conference on Hunger and Poverty, Brussels, November 20–21.

Ravallion, Martin. 2001. "Growth, Inequality and Poverty: Looking Beyond Averages." World Bank, Development Research Group, Washington, D.C.

Ravallion, Martin, and Gaurav Datt. Forthcoming. "Why Has Economic Growth Been More Pro-Poor in Some States of India than Others." Journal of Development Economics.

Rawlings, Laura, Lynne Sherburne-Benz, and Julie VanDomelen. 2001. "Letting Communities Take the Lead: A Cross-Country Evaluation of Social Fund Performance." Draft. World Bank, Human Development Network, Social Protection Unit and Poverty Reduction and Economic Development Network, Poverty Analysis Unit, Washington, D.C.

Reinikka, Ritva S. 2001. "Public Expenditure Tracking Surveys." World Bank, Development Economics Research Group, Washington, D.C. Available: http://www1.worldbank.org/publicsector/pe/trackingsurveys.htm

Reinikka, Ritva, and Jakob Svensson. 2002. "Assessing Frontline Service Delivery." World Bank, Development Research Group, Public Services, Washington, D.C.

Rhyne, E. 2001. *Mainstreaming Microfinance: How Lending to the Poor Began, Grew, and Came of Age in Bolivia.* West Hartford, Conn.: Kumarian Press.

Richardson, Don, Ricardo Ramirez, and Moinul Haq. 2000. "Grameen Telecom's Village Phone Programme: A Multi-Media Case Study." Canadian International Development Agency, Guelph, Ontario. Available: http://www.telecommons.com/villagephone/index.html

Ritzen, Jo, William Easterly, and Michael Woolcock. 2000. "On 'Good' Politicians and 'Bad' Policies: Social Cohesion, Institutions and Growth." World Bank, Development Research Group, Washington, D.C.

Rodrik, Dani. 1999. "Where Did All the Growth Go? External Shocks, Social Conflict, and Growth Collapses." *Journal of Economic Growth* 4 (4): 385–412.

Rowlands, Jo. 1997. *Questioning Empowerment: Working with Women in Honduras.* Oxford, U.K.: Oxfam Publishing.

Ryan, Andrea, and Jennifer Sara. n.d. "Ghana Community Water Supply and Sanitation Project." Community Driven Development Case Study. World Bank, Environmentally and Socially Sustainable Development Network, CDD Secretariat, Washington, D.C.

Schreiner, Mark. 2000. "Credit Scoring for Microfinance: Can It Work?" Paper presented at the III Foro Interamericana de la Microempresa, Barcelona, August 23. Available: http://www.iadb.org/sds/doc/micmschreinere.pdf

Sen, Amartya. 1985. "Well-being, Agency and Freedom. The Dewey Lectures 1984." *The Journal of Philosophy* 82 (4): 169-221.

_____. 1999. *Development as Freedom.* New York: Knopf.

Stern, Nicholas. 2002. *A Strategy for Development*. Washington, D.C.: World Bank.

Ternopil Urban Development Agency. 2000. "Reforming of Education Policy in the City of Ternopil." People's Voice Project, International Center for Policy Studies, Ternopil, Ukraine. Available: http://www.icps.kiev.ua/docs/other/ternopil_education_eng.pdf

Tesoro, José Manuel. 2000. "Big Little Problems: Small Businesses Want Jakarta Off Their Backs." *Asiaweek* 26 (37), September 22. Available: http://www.asiaweek.com/asiaweek/magazine/2000/0922/biz.enterprises.html

Tikare, Seema, Deborah Youssef, Rita Hilton, Paula Donnelly-Roark, and Parmesh Shah. 2001. "Organizing Participatory Processes in the PRSP." In World Bank, *Poverty Reduction Strategy Sourcebook*. Washington, D.C.: World Bank. Available: http://www.worldbank.org/poverty/strategies/chapters/particip/orgpart.htm

UNDP (United Nations Development Programme). 1995. *Human Development Report 1995: Gender and Human Development*. Oxford, U.K.: Oxford University Press.

UNICEF (United Nations Children's Fund). 2001. "The Women's Equality and Empowerment Framework." New York. Available: http://www.unicef.org/programme/gpp/policy/empower.html

Venkataraman, Arjunamurthy, and Julia Falconer. 1998. "Rejuvenating India's Decimated Forests through Joint Action: Lessons from Andhra Pradesh." Rural Development Project Brief. World Bank, Washington, D.C.

Vogel, R., A. A. Gomez, and T. M. Fitzgerald. 1999. "Regulation and Supervision of Microfinance: A Conceptual Framework." Draft. Microenterprise Best Practices Project, Development Alternatives/USAID, Bethesda, Md. Available: http://www.mip.org/pdfs/mbp/regulation_and_supervision.pdf

von Meijenfeldt, Roel. 2001."Comprehensive Development Framework and Conflict-Affected Countries: Issues Paper." Processed. World Bank, CDF Secretariat, Washington, D.C.

Vyasulu, Poornima, and Vinod Vyasulu. 1999. "Women in Panchayati Raj: Grassroots Democracy in India (Malgudi Experience)." Paper presented at the UNDP Meeting on Women and Political Participation: 21st Century Challenges, New Delhi, March 24–26.Available: http://magnet.undp.org/events/gender/india/VYASULU3.htm

Webster, Leila, R. Kochar, and Feresteh Raissian. 2001. "World Bank Group Support for SMEs." Presentation at the World Bank, Washington, D.C., April 4.

WIEGO (Women in Informal Employment Globalizing and Organizing). 2000a. "Annual Report 2000." Cambridge, Mass. Available: http://www.wiego.org/papers/2000report.pdf

_____. 2000b. "Women in the Informal Economy." Brochure. Cambridge, Mass. Available: http://www.wiego.org/papers/brochure.pdf

Wodon, Quentin. 1997. "Food Energy Intake and Cost of Basic Needs: Measuring Poverty in Bangladesh." *Journal of Development Studies* 34: 66–101.

_____. 1999. "Growth, Inequality, and Poverty: A Regional Panel for Bangladesh." Policy Research Working Paper 2072. World Bank, Washington, D.C.

_____. 2000. "Public Works Employment and Workfare Programs: Optimizing the Timing of Benefits for Poverty Reduction." World Bank, Poverty Reduction and Economic Management Network, Washington, D.C.

Women's World Banking. 1995. "The Missing Links: Financial Systems That Work for the Majority." New York. Available: http://www.womensworldbanking.org/english/2000/2700.htm

Woodhouse, Andrea. 2002. "The Dynamics of Rural Power in Indonesia." World Bank, East Asia and Pacific Social Development Group, Washington, D.C.

World Bank. 1998. "Urban Property Rights Project, Peru (P039086)." Project Appraisal Document. Latin America and Caribbean and Public Sector Management, Washington, D.C.

_____. 2000a. "Bolivia: From Patronage to a Professional State." Bolivia Institutional and Governance Review, Volume I: Main Report, No. 20115-BO. Poverty Reduction and Economic Management Network, Latin America and Caribbean Region, Washington, D.C.

_____. 2000b. "Participation Process Review." Draft, October 27. Operations Evaluation Department, Washington, D.C.

_____. 2000c. *World Development Report 2000/2001: Attacking Poverty.* New York: Oxford University Press. Available: http://www.worldbank.org/poverty/wdrpoverty/report/index.htm

_____. 2001a. "Decentralization and Governance: Does Decentralization Improve Public Service Delivery?" *PREM Notes* 55 (June). Development Economics Vice Presidency and Poverty Reduction and Economic Management Network, Washington, D.C.

_____. 2001b. "Empowering the Poor through Decentralization: Brazil Rural Poverty Alleviation Program." *Social Development Notes* 51. Environmentally and Socially Sustainable Development Network, Washington, D.C.

_____. 2001c. "Engendering Development: Through Gender Equality in Rights, Resources, and Voice." New York: Oxford University Press.

_____. 2001d. "Porto Alegre: Brazil Participatory Approaches in Budgeting and Public Expenditure Management." Civic Engagement in Public Expenditure Management Case Study. Social Development Department, Participation Thematic Group, Washington, D.C. Available: http://www.worldbank.org/participation/web/webfiles/cepemcase1.htm

_____. 2001e. "Social Funds: A Review of World Bank Experience." Operations Evaluation Department, Washington, D.C.

_____. 2001f. "Strategic Directions for FY02–FY04: Implementing the World Bank's Strategic Framework." Washington, D.C. Available: http://www.worldbank.org/html/extdr/strategypapers/directions.pdf

_____. 2001g. "Voice of the Poor and Taming of the Shrew: Evidence from the Bolivia Public Officials' Survey." Draft, February 15.

_____. 2001h. "Why Some Village Water and Sanitation Committees Are Better than Others: A Study of Karnataka and Uttar Pradesh (India)." Field note. South Asia Region, Water and Sanitation Program, New Delhi. Available: http://www.wsp.org/pdfs/sa_ybetter.pdf

_____. 2002a. "Information and Communication Technologies: A World Bank Group Strategy." Global Information and Communication

Technologies Department, Washington, D.C. Available: http://info.worldbank.org/ict/ICT_ssp.html

_____. 2002b. "Issues Paper for a World Bank Social Development Strategy." Draft. Social Development Department, Washington, D.C.

_____. 2002c. "Private Sector Development Strategy: Directions for the World Bank." Private Sector Development Department, Washington, D.C. Available: http://www.worldbank.org/strategy/index.asp

Chapter 5

Tools and Practices

Tools and Practices 1

Information and Communications Technology as a Tool for Empowerment

Information and communications technology (ICT) is creating economic, social, and political empowerment opportunities for poor people in the developing world.[1] Although most poor people remain isolated from the new information revolution, cellular phones, telecenters,[2] and other innovative solutions are in fact beginning to provide low-cost ways for poor people to access ICT (box 5-1). As these technologies open communication and spread information, ICT is helping poor people overcome powerlessness and voicelessness even while structural inequities exist in the distribution of traditional assets such as education, land, and finance.[3]

Exploiting the potential of ICT to improve the lives of poor people, however, is not automatic and requires supportive policies and strategic project design. The primary factor for reaching poor people is low-cost access to information infrastructure. Inadequate or absent connectivity and unstable power supply limits usage and jeopardizes the economic viability of most ICT projects. Rigorous and regular monitoring, evaluation and beneficiary impact assessment are necessary for determining whether benefits of using ICT outweigh costs, as well as ensuring sustainability.[4]

This note was prepared by Simone Cecchini and Talat Shah, under the overall guidance of Deepa Narayan (PREMPR).

Box 5-1 Innovative and Creative Solutions to Bring ICT to Poor People

The **Simputer** (Simple, Inexpensive, Multilingual Computer), developed by scientists at the Indian Institute of Science and a software company in Bangalore, is a user-friendly and inexpensive handheld computing device, particularly suitable for illiterate people. The device features locally relevant icons, touch-sensitive screens, and text-to-speech functions in different Indian languages. The Simputer can be adapted to meet a range of functions, including micro-banking, data collection, Internet access, and agricultural information. At a price tag of about $250 each, Simputers are designed to be shared by a local community of users, for example, a village *panchayat* or school. A shopkeeper can even purchase a Simputer, renting it out to individuals for a user fee. "Smart card" technology personalizes the device by storing individual user profiles that are updated when inserted into the Smart card interface.*

In Kothmale, Sri Lanka, a joint project between the United Nations Educational, Scientific, and Cultural Organization (UNESCO), the Ministry of Posts, Telecommunications, and the Media, the Sri Lanka Broadcasting Corporation, and the Telecommunications Regulatory Commission of Sri Lanka uses the **radio** as an interface between rural people and the Internet. A daily one-hour live radio program is broadcast during which an announcer and a panel of resource persons browse the Internet, responding to listener requests in real time. This process enables the project to overcome linguistic barriers to Internet use by non-English-speakers. In addition to the live program, the Kothmale community radio station maintains a public rural database, primarily by packaging public domain information often requested by listeners for off-line use. The radio station also functions as a mini-Internet service provider by offering Internet access points at two public libraries located within the radio's target area and running an Internet café at the radio station (Grace and others 2001).

In Uganda, a **CD-ROM** produced by the International Women's Tribune Center in partnership with International Development Research Center's Nairobi Office, is providing business training and best-practice information to women microentrepreneurs. "Rural Women in Africa: Ideas for Earning Money," developed both in English and in local languages, is available for use at rural telecenters, which enables the process of peer learning among groups of women entrepreneurs. By using sound and visuals, the CD-ROM content is accessible to women with low levels of education. In addition to providing useful information, the new tool was designed to give first-time computer users a positive experience, which has encouraged them to continue to use computers as well as other new technologies.**

---

*   Mathew 2001 and Reuters 2002. A smart card looks like a plastic credit card and has a microprocessor or memory chip embedded in it. The chip stores electronic data and programs that are protected by security measures enabling controlled access by appropriate users. Smart cards provide data portability, security, convenience, and transparency of financial records and transactions.

**   Available at the International Women's Tribune Center website at http://www.iwtc.org/!start.html

Appropriate content, effective intermediaries, and local ownership are additional key considerations for realizing the empowerment potential of ICT. To become truly relevant for poor people, ICT applications must make content available in local languages and, to the greatest extent possible, convey concepts with visuals and graphics. Before launching an ICT project, the information needs of a community should be thoroughly assessed in a participatory process that includes the active involvement of the target community. Further, ICT projects are more likely to reduce poverty when they are carried out by organizations and grassroots intermediaries that have appropriate incentives and a proven track record in working with poor people.

This note highlights how ICT can empower poor women and men in four broad areas: provision of basic services; improved local and national governance; support for entrepreneurship; and, access to financial services.

Provision of Basic Services

ICT is being used in the provision of basic services such as education and health care, particularly among the rural poor and urban slum dwellers. Relatively low cost and widespread use make radio and television effective tools for delivering education to isolated rural areas. Telecenters use these traditional technologies as well as computers to conduct distance learning and virtual education. In addition to traditional curricula, telecenters can provide customized training in ICT for marginalized groups with low levels of education. These activities are creating new opportunities in the job market.[5]

In health care, telemedicine helps the poor by alleviating the cost and hardship of long-distance travel for medical attention and diagnosis. E-mail and medical list-serves deliver recent medical findings at minimal cost to health workers who lack research and technological facilities.[6] ICT is creating efficiencies by simplifying medical data collection, record management, and paper filing processes. Worldwide experience in applying ICT to delivery of basic services indicates that even illiterate adults and children quickly learn to use icon-based applications.

Education

In Brazil, the **Committee for Democracy in Information Technology** (CDI) provides computer and civics training to young people living in urban slums, or *favelas*. Founded by former teacher Rodrigo Baggio,

CDI emerged from the belief that computer literacy can maximize employment opportunities and promote democracy and social equity. Along with training in word processing, database management, accounting programs, and web design, CDI teaches civic participation, nonviolence, human rights, environmental awareness, health, and literacy. After a three- or four-month course, graduates typically find well-paid jobs, start microbusinesses, or become certified teachers within the organization. Some graduates decide to go back to traditional school and complete their formal education. Many others put their computer skills to work in various community activities, including health education and AIDS awareness campaigns. In addition to serving the urban poor, CDI has extended its model to indigenous communities, the blind, prisoners, and the mentally ill.

The first Information Technology and Citizenship School opened in Rio de Janeiro's Santa Maria *favela* in 1995. CDI has since established some 350 schools in 19 states in Brazil, training more than 166,000 children and youth. Although some schools, supported by foundations, offer free computer training, most maintain a symbolic fee of $4 per student to cover administrative costs and pay instructors.[7] Students who cannot afford to pay have the option to volunteer in exchange for classes.

CDI schools are created through partnerships with community organizations, NGOs, and religious groups. Communities have complete ownership of the schools, including their physical space, and are responsible for staffing, management, and maintenance. To develop a CDI partner school, a community sets up a coordinating committee to assess local demand, identify potential instructors and a suitable location, and establish security measures for the computers. Over the course of three to six months, CDI trains the instructors, works with the school to obtain a hardware donation from sponsors, and helps the school install the computers. After a school has been established, CDI serves as a partner and consultant but does not manage the school's day-to-day activities.

CDI is funded through partnerships with the government, the private sector, foundations, and international organizations, as well as individuals and local businesses that donate computer hardware and software. In 2001, Microsoft donated $5 million in software, the Gates Foundation granted $400,000, infoDev granted $150,000, and the IDB committed $250,000 to help CDI expand in Brazil and other Latin American countries. Other partners include Dell, Exxon, McKinsey, SSI

Server, the Starmedia Foundation, Xerox, and UNESCO. The CDI model has been exported to Chile, Colombia, Japan, Mexico, and Uruguay, countries where there is now a CDI international office, and will soon reach Angola, Guatemala, and South Africa.[8]

The World Bank Institute's **World Links for Development (WorLD)** program provides training in the use of technology in education for teachers, teacher trainers, and students in developing countries, and connects them via the Internet to counterparts in developed countries for collaborative learning. The program also offers telecommunications policy advice for education sector professionals in developing countries, as well as monitoring and evaluation support. Begun in 1997, the WorLD program is currently active in more than 20 countries in Asia, Africa, Latin America, and the Middle East, reaching nearly 160,000 students and teachers. The program supports the establishment of a network cluster, consisting of a resource center and five satellite schools, in each location in a participating country. Each resource center will have 10 to 15 networked computers and a central server with an Internet connection. Satellite schools each have one computer and a monitor to organize access for teachers and students.

An independent review of the program in 1999–2000 found that, while the provision of computer hardware and software was significant, the program's most important contribution was the provision of professional development to enhance teachers' technological and pedagogical skills. Teachers reported that the program had the greatest impact on their capacity to design and prepare projects for students, learn more about their subject matter, and have students work in groups. Seventy-eight percent of WorLD teachers indicated that student knowledge about the use of computers had increased a great deal as a result of working with them. The WorLD program has helped to cultivate pockets of innovation in schools using ICT to improve education and communication. Sixty-three percent of WorLD teachers reported that their students use computers to interact with students and teachers in other countries, compared with 9 percent of non-WorLD teachers.[9]

Health

In India, infoDev and CMC Ltd. are working together to optimize scarce health care resources in the southern state of Andhra Pradesh using handheld computing technology. The **Information-Based Health Care**

Delivery project seeks to reduce paperwork, improve data accuracy, and empower village health care workers to provide timely care and information. The impetus for the project came from the Indian government's interest in improving the effectiveness of preventive health programs in that state and alleviating the heavy burden of data collection and paperwork on health care workers.

The project, which began in 1994 and has been piloted in two sites in the Nalgonda district of Andhra Pradesh since June 2001, aims at increasing the efficiency of auxiliary nurse midwives (ANMs).[10] ANMs are a small group of women who shoulder most of the responsibility for health care delivery in the vast and densely populated rural areas of that state. Each one serves 5,000 people, typically residing in different villages and hamlets, often located several miles apart. ANMs administer immunizations, advise on family welfare, and educate people about mother-child health programs. Along with health care delivery, ANMs are also responsible for data collection and record keeping on the rural population's growth, birth rate, and immunization rate.

Handheld computers, or personal digital assistants (PDAs), are expected to facilitate data acquisition and transmission to the primary health centers, saving up to 60 percent of the ANMs' work time. Redundant entry of data prevalent in paper registers will be eliminated, and ANMs' monthly reports will be generated automatically, making data electronically available for further analysis and compilation at higher levels of the health care system.

The PDAs, whose navigation is based on icons representing villages, households, and individuals, are designed to cater to the literacy levels of the health workers. Each icon, when tapped with the PDA's pen, leads to a more specific record with information on immunization status, diseases, and other conditions. Health workers are extensively trained in the use of the pocket computers, which can have screens translated into the local Telugu language.

Challenges to the project included delays caused by technical problems and by frequent changes in end-user requirements. For instance, the households list on the PDAs was initially presented in the order the ANMs typically visit their villages—house by house—but there were cases in which the ANMs administered health services by assembling all villagers in one place. This entailed searching for individuals rather than for households on the PDAs, and required substantive changes to search features.[11]

ICT As a Tool to Improve Governance

E-government refers to the use of ICT by government agencies to transform relations with citizens and businesses. ICT can serve a variety of different ends for improving governance: from better delivery of government services to citizens to improved interactions with business and industry, from citizen empowerment through access to information to more efficient government management. The resulting benefits include less corruption and increased transparency. Information disclosure and the possibility of interacting with public officials can build pressure for improved government accountability at both the local and national levels (box 5-2).[12]

Box 5-2 Enabling More Effective Participation at the Local, National, and Global Levels

In Mexico City, the NGO **Women to Women** used e-mail connections with women's groups in California to obtain information on the business practices, profit structures, and ownership of a textile company that had announced plans to build a plant in their community. As a result, they were better prepared for negotiations with plant officials and management as well as with local government.

In India, the women's rights NGO **Sakshi** faced difficulties in lobbying for sexual harassment legislation. With help from international women's networks through the Internet, Sakshi was able to receive advice and technical assistance on legal issues surrounding sexual harassment. As a result of these online discussions, the group was successful in convincing the Indian Supreme Court to establish sexual harassment guidelines in workplaces and brought the issue within the purview of human rights violations (World Bank 2002c).

Women have used the Internet for organizing and lobbying at the regional and international levels for many years, beginning most notably in 1995 with the U.N. World Conference on Women in Beijing. In 1999, to prepare for Beijing+5—the fifth anniversary of the Beijing Conference—more than 40 women's media networks formed **WomenAction.** WomenAction has developed global and regional websites on women's issues and has also initiated workshops to train women from all regions in the construction of websites, facilitated regional and national dialogues, and repackaged information downloaded from the Internet for its constituents (Carr and Huyer 2001).

E-government can be implemented in different stages. Initially, departments and agencies use the Web to post information about themselves for the benefit of citizens and business partners. At a second stage, these sites become tools for two-way communication, allowing citizens to request feedback on a particular issue. At a third stage, websites facilitate a formal, quantifiable exchange, such as renewing a license, paying a fine, or enrolling in an education course.[13] At a final stage, a portal integrates the complete range of government services and provides a path to them that is based on need and function, not on department or agency.[14]

Improving Local Governance

ICT can play an important role in improving local governance, connecting poor people to local leaders, reducing transaction costs, and better connecting the poor to services.

In Madhya Pradesh, India, **Gyandoot**, a government-owned computer network, is making government easily accessible to villagers, reducing the time and money they spend trying to get to and through public officials, and giving them immediate and transparent access to local government data and documentation.

Gyandoot started in January 2000 in Dhar, a district where 60 percent of the 1.7 million inhabitants live below the poverty line. The program was launched with the installation of a low-cost rural Intranet kiosk that initially connected 20 villages and was later expanded to another 11. The entire district was wired for Rs. 2.5 million (about $55,000) in less than a year. The average cost incurred by the village committee (*panchayat*) in establishing a single kiosk was Rs. 75,000 (about $1,650). Information kiosks (*soochanalayas*), generally located in *panchayat* buildings, have been placed in villages that have block headquarters, hold weekly markets, or are located on major roads, so that each kiosk can cater to about 25 to 30 villages. The entire network of 40 kiosks thus covers more than 600 villages and reaches half a million people.

Kiosks are run by local operators along commercial lines. The operators pay an annual license fee of Rs. 5,000 to the district council (*zila panchayat*) and earn a monthly gross income between Rs. 1,000 and Rs. 5,000 from user fees. Because most villagers are barely literate and electronic financial transactions in India are not yet legal, an operator to assist users and a physical office for making payments are needed. After two years, only a few kiosks have proven to be commercially viable.

Villagers now use Gyandoot to keep track of the cost of fruits and vegetables in the region's wholesale market. Gyandoot provides the prevailing rates for prominent crops at auction centers for a charge of Rs. 5. It also furnishes information on previous rates and on the volume of incoming agricultural produce. They pool their resources and catch a bus to the place offering the best deals, cutting out the middlemen traders. Sometimes this means trucking their produce 400 miles to Mumbai to earn 40 percent more than they would at home. Other times villagers decide to hold on to their produce until prices are higher in local markets.

Gyandoot also provides documents on land records for a charge of Rs. 15, thus helping the poor fight fraudulent land claims. In the words of a villager: "The farmers need these land records every season to get crop loans, and the *patwari* [keeper of land records] extracts a heavy price every season. Bribe him and he will redraw your map at your neighbor's expense. Ask him for old records and he will tell you that they are lost, burnt, or damaged for good. In the digital database we can retrieve land records for Rs. 15 instead of the minimum bribe of Rs. 200 plus transport costs." As a consequence, some local politicians and the lower-level bureaucracy, perceiving a loss of power, have attempted to sink the program.

Other services offered include an online registration of applications for caste, income, and domicile certificates, a public complaint line for reporting broken pumps, unfair prices, absentee teachers, and other problems, as well as an auction facility to trade land, agricultural machinery, equipment, and other commodities. Applications for drivers' licenses and school examination results are among the most accessed services. Gyandoot also offers e-mail services in Hindi connecting village-level institutions with block and district offices.

Challenges encountered in the implementation of the project include problems with the power supply and with the dial-up connection—as most of the local rural telephone exchanges do not operate with optical fiber cable. Poor or intermittent connectivity can reduce the economic viability of the kiosk and decrease the motivation level of the kiosk operator to be a partner in the project.

Around 40,000 people have used Gyandoot's services since the project's inception. Following the success of the initiative, the government of Madhya Pradesh has issued a tender to set up similar information kiosks across the state. Drishtee.com, an Indian software company, intends to replicate the Gyandoot model nationwide and has already expanded the project in northern India, reaching Sirsa in Haryana,

Shahdol and Seoni in Madhya Pradesh, and Jallandhar in Punjab. Additional pilot projects are to be launched soon in Gujarat and Maharashtra.[15]

Improving National Governance

ICT has the potential to improve national governance by increasing transparency and accountability; allowing greater access to information about representatives, institutions, decisions, laws, and regulations affecting poor people's lives; and providing mechanisms for contacts between poor people and leaders and decision-making bodies at the national level.

In Argentina, the government's **Cristal** website provides information to citizens so that they can exercise more effective control over their political representatives.[16] The Cristal website was launched in early 2000 to fulfill the mandate of Argentina's September 1999 Fiscal Responsibility Law, which required the state to publish information related to the administration of public funds. The website includes information on the execution of budgets to the lowest level of disaggregation; purchase orders and public contracts; payment orders submitted to the National Treasury; financial and employment data on permanent and contracted staff and those working for projects financed by multilateral organizations; an account of the public debt; inventory of plant and equipment and financial investments; outstanding tax and customs obligations of Argentine companies and individuals; and regulations governing the provision of public services.

After initial problems—stemming from lack of content on many pages of the website—a new version of Cristal was launched in August 2000. Between the launch and March 2001, visits to the website increased by about 200 percent. The website is currently organized into three thematic areas: "The State Within Reach of All," which explains how public monies are redistributed between the national government and provinces; "Goals and Results," which gathers information on all national policies to evaluate their management and the manner in which public funds are allocated; and "Accountability and Representatives," which presents information related to the fight against corruption, both in government and in the nongovernmental sector. Tutorials explain each of the themes in a clear and easy-to-grasp fashion. Users can also interact with website staff, with responses given within 24 hours.

This initiative is proving significant not only because it seeks to improve governmental transparency, but also because many agencies have started to improve their data gathering practices in response to Cristal's requests. Cristal is audited externally by Foro Transparencia, a coalition made up of 15 nongovernmental organizations concerned with government transparency.[17]

ICT as a Tool to Support Poor People's Entrepreneurship

By connecting people to markets, ICT can stimulate poor people's entrepreneurship and the development of businesses in underdeveloped areas. ICT allows poor people to access important market and business-related information in a more timely and efficient manner. For example, isolated farmers can use ICT to access essential agricultural information such as data on crops, input prices, weather conditions, and credit facilities. Further, electronic bulletin boards and databases can help farmers to share innovations and technical information.[18]

Commercial possibilities for micro producers in developing countries have been multiplied by the Internet, with its capacity to connect producers directly to buyers. By cutting out layers of middlemen, e-commerce has the potential to increase the income of poor producers by giving them a greater share of the final sale price, sometimes 10 times what they would get in traditional trade. Through online sales, artisans can assess which products sell better and tailor production accordingly.[19] E-commerce in developing countries, however, is still in its infancy. Despite increasing volumes, net profits are generally low because a large portion of the sales price goes to high delivery and payment charges.[20]

Access to Markets and Business-Related Information

In Bangladesh, **Grameen Phone** provides commercial phone service in rural areas through local entrepreneurs, usually poor women, who own and operate cellular phones that typically serve an entire village.[21] Women entrepreneurs borrow about $350 at 22 percent interest from the Grameen Bank to purchase a handset. They then sell telephone services to other villagers, making a living and paying off their loan, usually within a year. This creates a self-employment opportunity for a woman in each village and provides all villagers with access to telephones.

Grameen Phone started its operations in Dhaka in 1997 and later expanded to rural areas. By March 2002, about 10,000 village phones were in operation, catering to an estimated 15 million people. Rural telephones are very profitable, bringing in revenues per phone of $93 a month, twice as much as Grameen Phone's urban mobile phones. However, rural phones represent less than 2 percent of the phones used on Grameen Phone's network and therefore bring in only 8 percent of the company's total revenue. The company's profitability thus still depends on its urban business.

Village phones, on average, serve 70 customers a month. The average income of the "phone ladies" is estimated at more than $700 a year after covering all costs, more than twice the country's annual per capita income. In larger villages, individual phone revenues can be more than $12,000 per year, although revenues are falling in areas with multiple telephones. High and, so far, secure returns have led many women to regard these telephones as their "modern cows."

Estimates show that village phones generate savings (or revenues) of between $2.70 and $10.00 per call. This is not only because phone calls would otherwise be extremely expensive, but also because very important information is exchanged. About 50 percent of the calls are made for economic reasons, mainly by poor people. Users (40 percent of them women) call relatives and friends, often overseas, to request remittances or medical help; farmers and traders call city markets to find out the prices of agricultural produce. In villages with phones, eggs and poultry sell for higher prices, the cost of information is much lower (25 percent of prior costs, which included a trip to town), the cost of feed is lower, and diesel prices are more stable. Prices paid by traders for raw materials and crafted goods have risen, because sellers have more pricing information. Exchange rates for currency from expatriates have improved. Furthermore, the phones offer the villagers additional benefits such as improved law enforcement, faster and more effective communications during disasters, and stronger kinship bonding.

The Grameen Phone experience has shattered many myths about the capabilities of poor rural women. Even illiterate women who have never seen a telephone have mastered the skills quickly, gained confidence, and earned new status and respect in their communities as owners of a powerful and desirable asset. Telephone owners have greater freedom than before to move about the villages as they deliver messages or take the phones to users, charging a higher fee for the service. Women learn about medical information and the status of markets in Dhaka by overhearing conversations. Some have developed a sophisticated functional knowledge of international currency markets. "She used to cook for the elites," said the neighbor of one of these phone ladies. "Now she is invited by them."

Looking to the future, Grameen Telecom plans to set up cyber kiosks in rural villages. "The cell phone will be followed by the Internet, faxing, and worldwide networking," says Grameen Bank's Mohammed Yunus, who hopes that telecommunications will revolutionize the cognitive world of the villagers. In 1999, the International Finance Corporation signed an agreement to lend $16.7 million and invest $1.6 million in equity toward expanding Grameen Telecom, now the largest cellular phone operator in Bangladesh. The Asian Development ment Bank and the Commonwealth Corporation are providing parallel financing in the form of loan and equity investments.[22]

E-Commerce: Connecting Small Artisans to Markets

PEOPLink is a nonprofit corporation formed in 1995 to build a global network of trading partners that can provide services to community-based artisan producer groups. PEOPLink currently works with more than 100 trading partners—local NGOs with relationships to grassroots groups such as craft cooperatives and peasant leagues—in Africa, Asia, and Latin America. PEOPLink functions both as a business-to-consumer (B2C) business, connecting poor producers to customers through the Internet, and as a business-to-business (B2B) broker and escrow agent for wholesale opportunities, connecting producers with firms in industrial countries.

Artisans represented by the local NGO trading partners, the majority of them women, are organized into community-based producer groups. They are talented artisans who have developed their skills over generations but who have not had the resources to connect directly to the global marketplace. Traditionally, they have sold their goods through a long, complicated chain of middlemen who pay them low prices and then mark up the items many times on the way to the final consumer.

Through e-commerce, PEOPLink helps artisans improve their terms of trade. It has placed great emphasis on training and developing a set of equipment, software, and procedures that enables trading partners to work with electronic communications for improved product design and sales. Trading partners are equipped with digital cameras and trained to photograph artisan products and load the photos onto the PEOPLink e-commerce website. They also receive online training and product development support to build their own websites and online catalogues. PEOPLink staff usually travel to the country where the trading partner is located and do a series of demonstrations to demystify the technology for clients with limited exposure to Internet applications. Additional technical support is provided in specific areas such as product design, quality control, packing, shipping, and creation of a coordinated global distribution and payment system.

Daily sales for each artisan range between $50 and $500, with up to 90 percent of the sales price going to artisans. Examples of PEOPLink's wide range of trading partners include the Kuna Mola Cooperative, Tiendas Camari, and the Community Crafts Association of the Philippines. Kuna Mola is a cooperative of 1,200 indigenous Kuna women living on the San Blas Islands off the Caribbean coast of Panama, who produce intricate reverse appliqués based on their traditional dress. Tiendas Camari serves 98 community producer groups representing more than 8,000 artisans in the highlands of Ecuador producing both handicrafts and foodstuffs. The Community Crafts Association of the Philippines (CCAP) serves 21 producer associations and 30 family-based groups with more than 2,000 artisans, 90 percent of whom are women. CCAP is a well-established institution with more than $700,000 in annual exports.[23]

Support to Innovators

In India, the **Honey Bee Network** is making poor people's innovations and traditional knowledge visible through a multimedia and multi-language database of solutions to local development problems. The database contains more than 10,000 innovations in text form collected from 4,000 villages and presented in seven languages, as well as over 100 innovations in multimedia format. The information is disseminated both through the Honey Bee newsletter and through stalls at religious fairs, which receive more than 400 visitors per day. Linkages between farmers, rural extension workers, and researchers in agricultural institutions will be strengthened by the creation of a knowledge network supported by an infoDev grant in 2000. This network will allow extension workers and researchers to transmit information by sound or picture files to facilitate communication with farmers who are illiterate.

The Honey Bee Network is a concrete example of the democratization of knowledge through horizontal networking. Local communities and individual innovators, even those who are illiterate, can use the network to learn from each other across large geographic distances and across cultures. Many of the innovations are extremely simple but can significantly improve the efficiency of farm workers, small farmers, and artisans. Innovative solutions have included a tilting bullock cart, a simple device to fill nursery bags, an improved pulley for drawing water, and a gum scrapper used by women to collect gum from thorny bushes or trees. The database also features a large number of small machineries, herbal pesticides, veterinary medicines, new plant varieties, and agronomic practices developed by small farmers.

Scouting and documenting innovations, however, is not enough. Some of the innovators actually experienced increased frustration after being featured in the database. They know that despite doing good work, they remain poor. There is therefore a need to commercialize these innovations, which in turn requires an incubator fund, a microventure capital fund, and the protection of intellectual property rights.

In 1993 Honey Bee was strengthened by the formation of the Society for Research and Initiatives for Sustainable Technologies and Institutions (SRISTI). Since then, Honey Bee has scaled up significantly, with the creation of a regional microventure promotion fund, the Gujarat Grassroots Innovation Augmentation Network (GIAN), and a national register for innovations, the National Innovation Foundation (NIF).

GIAN was created in 1997 in collaboration with the Gujarat state government, which as of June 2001 contributed $300,000 to convert innovations from the Honey Bee database into viable enterprises. Innovators are given access to risk capital and to technical know-how to turn their innovations into a product that can be commercialized. As of June 2001, GIAN incubated several innovations into products, filed nine patents on behalf of grassroots innovators, and licensed some of the innovations to entrepreneurs on a district-wide basis with the license fee going to innovators. Honey Bee intends to set up similar venture promotion funds in other states in India.

The National Innovation Foundation was set up in March 2000 to replicate the Honey Bee model all over the country, with $5 million from the Indian Department of Science and Technology at Ahmedabad. The NIF will develop a national register of inventions and innovations, link innovations, investments and enterprises, connect excellence in formal and informal sciences, set up incubators, and help in changing society's mindset to ensure respect, recognition, and reward for grassroots innovators who often face indifference or contempt. In 2001, NIF organized a national contest for scouting innovations, and more than 1,800 proposals were received from all over India.[24]

Support to Small Farmers

The milk cooperative movement initiated by India's National Dairy Development Board serves 600,000 households daily, making it one of the largest cooperatives in the world. Dairy products are marketed in 500 towns and milk is collected through 96,000 village milk collection societies in 285 districts, involving 10 million farm families. Approximately 16.5 million liters of milk are procured daily with an annual value of Rs. 780 billion (about $16 billion).[25]

About 2,500 collection centers in Gujarat have introduced a computerized system with integrated electronic weights, electronic fat-testing machines, and plastic readers. This has increased transparency and led to faster processing, shorter queues, and immediate payment to farmers. Formerly, the fat content in milk was calculated through a cumbersome measurement process hours after the milk was received. Even if they delivered milk daily, farmers were paid only every 10 days and had to trust the cooperative society staff's manual calculations of the quality and quantity of milk. Malfeasance and underpayment to farmers, although difficult to substantiate, were commonly alleged.

With the computerized system, dairy farmers now receive immediate payment and save considerable time with shorter queues at milk collection centers. Farmers delivering milk to the cooperative collection centers are given a plastic card as a form of identification. The card is dropped into an electronic reading machine that transmits the identification number to a personal computer. The milk is then emptied into a steel trough and the weight is instantly displayed to the farmer and communicated to a computer. A sample is also fed into a machine that determines its fat content in seconds, displaying it to the farmer and transmitting it to the computer. The computer calculates the amount due to the farmer on the basis of the milk's fat content. The total value of the milk is then printed on a payment slip and given to the farmer, who collects the payment at an adjoining window. In many centers the entire transaction takes no more than 30 seconds. The more than 50,000 dairy farmers who use the computerized system benefit from a more transparent, efficient, and effective cooperative delivery system.

The Centre for Electronic Governance at the Indian Institute of Management, Ahmedabad has developed a Dairy Information System Kiosk (DISK) software package, which is being pilot tested in two cooperative villages in the Kheda District, Gujarat. DISK has two main components: an application with enhanced database and reporting that includes a complete history of all milch cattle owned by the farmers, and a dairy portal connected to the Internet through which producers can make business transactions, order supplies, access information and government documents, and exchange information with each other. Farmers will also be able to learn about dairy innovations through a multimedia database, the Honey Bee Network (see above).[26]

Access to Financial Services

Computerization, smart cards, and automated teller machines (ATMs) reduce costs for financial institutions, enabling them to reach clients more efficiently. Poor people and microbusinesses, therefore, can gain broader access to financial services.

Even the most efficient MFIs are in fact spending between 35 percent and 51 percent of their average loan outstanding on operating costs. Smart cards with an embedded microchip containing information on the clients' credit history, along with software systems that provide loan tracking, financial projections, and branch management information, help microfinance institutions (MFIs) reduce transactions costs. By lowering costs, smart cards and software systems can make MFIs financially sustainable more quickly and in a position to reach a large number of poor people.[27] In addition to smart cards, ATMs, allowing cost-effective deposits and withdrawals, can make it possible for commercial banks to extend services to poorer townships and slums.[28]

Smart Cards for Microfinance

An Indian MFI, **Swayam Krishi Sangam** (SKS), introduced smart cards in August 2000 to reduce time spent by loan officers on copiously recording financial transactions at group meetings. SKS was set up in 1998 by Vikram Akula, a son of Indian immigrants to the United States, who was inspired by a visit to Muhammad Yunus and the Grameen Bank. SKS targets the poorest 20 percent of the population by focusing on the poorest regions and selecting individuals through key informant interviews and village surveys. As a result, SKS clients are considerably poorer than most MFI clients.

SKS currently operates four branches in Medak District, Andhra Pradesh, and serves about 2,200 female customers. SKS provides savings and loan products designed through participatory processes and disbursed through village collectives called *sangams*. As of June 2001, total disbursement was $165,000 with a repayment rate of 100 percent on income-generating loans (20 percent interest rate), seasonal loans, and emergency loans (0 percent interest rates). Most members take $50 general loans their first year and $100 their second, and use these funds for land and livestock-related enterprises.

At one of the four SKS branches, loan officers are piloting the smart card technology. At the branch office they download borrower information from a main computer terminal into a handheld computer before a group meeting. At the meeting, borrowers insert their smart cards into a reader in the handheld computer to review their accounts and record new transactions. Upon returning to their offices, loan officers upload information back into the main computer. A read-only handheld computer is left in the village for customers to check their balances on a regular basis. SKS plans to expand the use of the technology to all four branches.

Smart cards offer three important advantages for SKS. First, they lower the high cost of delivering financial services to the poor by reducing the time of weekly village meetings by as much as 50 percent, enabling field staff to conduct three or four village meetings per day instead of the typical two per day. Second, smart cards help SKS maintain sound financial standards and controls to prevent error and fraud. This is particularly important because microfinance involves a large number of transactions, thus leaving ample scope for error and fraud. Smart cards solve this problem by having a single data entry point on an "electronic passbook" that seamlessly links information from the village to the branch, up to the head office and even to donor and lending agencies. In addition, the smart card system enhances the ability of management to monitor operations and respond quickly to problems. Finally, smart cards promote SKS sustainability and enable the MFI to offer a wide range of flexible financial services to better meet the financial needs of the poor.[29]

Smart Cards for Small Businesses

In Swaziland, the Growth Trust Corporation, a business affiliate of **Swazi Business Growth Trust** (SBGT), with assistance from the U.S. Agency for International Development (USAID) and Development Alternatives, Inc., is issuing smart cards to its small business clients to allow them to get funds and make repayments at participating commercial bank branches around the country.

SBGT, acting as a "virtual bank," has provided Swaziland's four major banks and their branches in the country's two largest cities with battery-powered smart card reading terminals. SBGT maintains a line of credit with the commercial banks offering the service free of charge to its low-income clients. Transaction information, complete with cash flow analysis, is downloaded daily, enabling SBGT to accurately and easily monitor disbursements and repayments.

SBGT invested approximately $100,000 to develop its smart card technology and banking software. Smart card reading terminals cost $1,000 per unit; smart cards cost about $8 each, and can be reprogrammed after being returned by graduated borrowers. The system is becoming less expensive, as the cost of smart cards is falling rapidly and a less expensive ($500) reading terminal is being developed. In the future, SBGT plans to make transactions, including savings services, available to its customers by telephone and online.

ATMs to Bring Commercial Banking to the Poor

In 1993, the **Standard Bank of South Africa** created an affiliate, E Bank, to deliver basic banking services to the urban poor through ATMs conveniently located in townships. Historically, poor South Africans have opened direct deposit accounts with the banking system in order to avoid theft. Most wage laborers have passbook savings accounts that have high transaction costs because of high transaction fees and teller time. Long payday lines of one to two hours at banking halls are expected. Due to high levels of illiteracy, banks were unable to move these low-balance high-volume accounts to card-based accounts accessible through regular ATM machines.

E Bank combines innovative technology of modified ATM services with staff trained to help clients with basic electronic banking. E Bank outlets are situated in nontraditional kiosks open to the sidewalk, conveniently located in townships, with videos for entertainment or instruction, and are decorated with vibrant colors. In addition to text, the ATMs have a simplified screen that uses graphics to illustrate usage for illiterate customers. Each kiosk is staffed by three or four assistants who speak several local languages.

E Bank offers a single savings account (no checking, no passbook), and all accounts with more than R 250 ($56) earn interest. Clients can obtain cash, deposit savings, and transfer money to relatives and others in the system around the country. Depositors with regular minimum balances become eligible for drawings and prizes and even automatically receive a modest amount (R 1,500, or $333) of life insurance coverage.

More than 150,000 customers created E Bank accounts within its first year of operation. However, running E Bank as a stand-alone entity was not profitable as the number of transactions per machine was below the break-even point. In 1996 E Bank was folded back into Standard Bank and E Bank clients were transferred to a new E Plan; facilities were renamed Auto Bank E outlets. By 1998 there were approximately 1.4 million E Plan account holders using 70 Auto Bank E outlets. This amounted to more than 18 million Auto Bank E transactions, which make up 24.6 percent of all Standard Bank transactions. Forecasts for 2002 were for 50 million Auto Bank E transactions—42.5 percent of all Standard Bank of South Africa transactions.[30]

Notes

1.   ICT consists of hardware, software, networks, and media for collection, storage, processing, transmission, and presentation of information that can be in the form of voice, data, text, or images (World Bank 2002c).

2.   Telecenters are shared locations that provide access to ICT for educational, personal, social, and economic development (Reilly and Gómez 2001).

3.   Narayan and Shah 2000. The World Bank has hosted three international workshops on Global Coalitions for Voices of the Poor, involving many of the organizations and examples highlighted in this note. For more information, see http://www.worldbank.org/poverty/voices/globcoal/index.htm

4.   See Cecchini forthcoming; Narayan and Shah 2000.

5.   Examples include the infoDev-sponsored Project SITA (Study of Information Technology Applications) in India, Women's Net in South Africa, and the Street Children Telecenter project in Colombia and Ecuador.

6.   HealthNet, for instance, is using a diverse array of ICT technologies (including radio and telephone-based computer networks and low-earth-orbit satellites) to allow health care workers in 30 developing countries to access medical research, exchange data on emerging epidemics, and obtain information on the use of drugs and treatments.

7.   Even with such low fees, instructors teaching just eight classes per week receive almost twice Brazil's official minimum wage.

8.   For more information see the CDI website at http://www.cdi.org.br/. Also see Narayan and Shah 2000.

9.   Bloome 2000; de Alcántara 2001; SRI International 1999; SRI International 2000. Also see the WorLD program website at http://www.worldbank.org/worldlinks/

10.   The project began as a collaborative effort between the Indian government and Apple Computers. The first pilot project was conducted in the state of Rajasthan, near the city of Ajmer, between 1994 and 1995.

11.   infoDev 2001; Bhatnagar and Schware 2000; CMC Ltd. 2001.

12.   See the World Bank's e-government website at http://www1.worldbank.org/publicsector/egov/

13. In Brazil, for example, Serviço de Atendimento ao Cidadão (SAC) is a system of public service assistance created by the state government of Bahia. Mobile SAC units visit remote areas and allow geographically isolated populations access to some essential services, such as the issuing of birth certificates, identification cards, and labor identification cards (World Bank 2002c).

14. Symonds 2000. One example of such a portal is Singapore's eCitizen Centre at http://www.gov.sg/

15. Gyandoot 2001; Narayan and Shah 2000; Rajora 2002; World Bank 2002c.

16. See the Cristal website at http://www.cristal.gov.ar.

17. Radics 2001; World Bank 2002a.

18. Examples include Chile's rural information service for farmers' groups, as well as Agropol and Agrositio in Argentina.

19. E-commerce websites selling handicrafts made by small artisans from developing countries include Novica.com, OneNest.com, ElSouk, African Crafts Online, and many others. See Narayan and Shah 2000.

20. The United Nations Conference on Trade and Development (UNCTAD) has estimated the average annual turnover of e-commerce enterprises based in developing countries as between $2,000 and $30,000 a year. See UNCTAD 2001, p.192.

21. Grameen Phone was founded in 1996, when the Bangladeshi government was preparing to auction off private cell phone licenses to four companies. Fifty-one percent of Grameen Phone is owned by Telenor, a Norwegian company, and 35 percent by the Grameen Bank through its Grameen Telecom arm. The rest of the shares are owned by a Japanese trading house, Marubenu, and a group of Bangladeshi expatriates in the United States.

22. Burr 2000; Digital Opportunity Initiative 2001; Grameen Phone 2001 and 2002; Narayan and Shah 2000.

23. See the PEOPLink website at http://www.peoplink.org. Also see Digital Opportunity Initiative 2001; Narayan and Shah 2000.

24. Baramati Initiatives 2001; Bhatnagar and Schware 2000; Cecchini forthcoming; Gupta 2001.

25. NDDB 2001.

26. World Bank 2002b; Bhatnagar and Schware 2000. See also India's National Dairy Development Board website at http://www.nddb.org

27. In Africa, the financial and information service network provided by Pride Africa offers microfinance to a client base of 100,000 in five countries. The average loan size is $125 (Digital Opportunity Initiative 2001).

28. Akula 2000; Digital Opportunity Initiative 2001.

29. Akula 2000.

30. Paulson and McAndrews 1998.

Resources

Akula, Vikram Byanna. 2000. "Putting Technology to Work for Poverty Alleviation: A Draft Proposal for $151,030 to Develop Smart Cards for Microfinance." Swayam Krishi Sangam, Hyderabad, Andhra Pradesh, India.

Baramati Initiatives. 2001. "Honeybee Network Case Study." Prepared for the workshop on Achieving Connectivity for the Rural Poor in India, Baramat, Maharashtra, India, May 31–June 2. Available: http://www.baramatiinitiatives.com/cases/case4.htm

Bhatnagar, Subhash, and Robert Schware, eds. 2000. *Information and Communication Technology in Rural Development: Case Studies from India.* New Delhi: Sage Publications India. Available: http://www.worldbank.org/wbi/pubs_case37160.html

Bloome, Anthony. 2000. "The Bindura–World Links for Development Telecentre: Modest in Size, but Mighty in Impact." *TechKnowLogia* 2 (November/December).

Burr, Chandler. 2000. "Grameen Village Phone: Its Current Status and Future Prospects." Paper presented at international conference on Business Services for Small Enterprises in Asia: Developing Markets and Measuring Performance, Hanoi, Vietnam, April 3–6. Available: http://www.ilo.org/public/english/employment/ent/papers/grameen.htm

Carr, Marilyn, and Sophia Huyer. 2001. "Information and Communications Technologies: A Priority for Women in Developing Countries." Paper prepared for Once and Future Network Meeting on Gender and ITs in a Global Economy, Harvard University, May 1.

Cecchini, Simone. Forthcoming. "Can Information and Communications Technology Applications Contribute to Poverty Reduction? Lessons from Rural India." World Bank, Poverty Reduction and Economic Management Network, Washington, D.C.

CMC Ltd. 2001. "India Health Care Project. 4th Quarterly Report." Submitted to infoDev. Hyderabad, India.

de Alcántara, Cynthia Hewitt. 2001. "The Development Divide in a Digital Age. An Issues Paper." Programme Paper 4. United Nations

Research Institute for Social Development, Technology, Business and Society Program Area, Geneva. Available: ftp://ftp.unicc.org/unrisd/outgoing/pp/tbs/hewitt.pdf

Digital Opportunity Initiative. 2001. "Creating a Development Dynamic: Final Report of the Digital Opportunity Initiative." New York. Available: http://www.opt-init.org/framework.html

Grace, Jeremy, Charles Kenny, and Christine Qiang, with Jiu Liuard Taylor Reynolds. 2001. "Information and Communication Technologies and Broad-Based Development: A Partial Review of the Evidence." World Bank, DECRA Research Project, Washington, D.C.

Grameen Phone. 2001. "Village Phones." Available: http://www.grameenphone.com/village.htm

_____. 2002. Grameen Phone Newsletter, March 2002. Available: http://www.grameenphone.com/news/new.htm

Gupta, Anil K. 2001. "Building Upon Grassroots Innovations: Articulating Social and Ethical Capital." SRISTRI, Ahmedabad, India. Available: http://209.249.15.51/users/know-net/papers/A34.htm

Gyandoot. 2001. "A Community-Owned, Self Sustainable and Low Cost Rural Intranet Project." Available: http://www.gyandoot.nic.in/gyandoot/intranet.html

Heeks, Richard. 1999. "The Tyranny of Participation in Information Systems: Learning from Development Projects." Development Informatics Working Paper 4. Institute for Development Policy and Management, University of Manchester, U.K. Available: http://idpm.man.ac.uk/idpm/di_wp4.htm

infoDev. 2001. "infoDev Quarterly Report: Second Quarter 2001." The World Bank: Washington, D.C. Available: http://www.infodev.org/library/qr201.pdf

Mathew, Ciny. 2001. "Simputer: Netdevice for DCs." *Information Technology in Developing Countries* (10) 3. Available: http://www.iimahd.ernet.in/egov/ifip/dec2000.htm

Michiels, Isabel, and L. Van Crowder. 2001. "Discovering the Magic Box: Local Appropriation of Information and Communication Technologies." *SD Dimensions* (June). Food and Agriculture Organization of the United Nations, Sustainable Development Department, Communications for Development Group. Available: http://www.fao.org/sd/2001/KN0602a_en.htm

Narayan, Deepa, and Talat Shah. 2000. "Connecting the Local to the Global: Voices of the Poor." Framework paper prepared for workshop on Local to Global Connectivity for Voices of the Poor, December 11–13. World Bank, Poverty Reduction and Economic Management Network, Poverty Reduction Group, Washington, D.C. Available: http://www.worldbank.org/poverty/voices/globcoal/dec00/narsha.pdf

National Dairy Development Board (NDDB), India. 2001. *Annual Report for the Year 2000–2001*. Gujarat, India. Available: http://www.nddb.org/annualreport.html

Paulson, Jo Ann, and James McAndrews. 1998. "Financial Services for the Urban Poor: South Africa's E Plan." Policy Research Working Paper 2016. World Bank, Development Research Group, Washington, D.C.

Radics, Axel. 2001. "Cristal: Transparencia en la Gestión Pública." *Revista Probidad* 14 (May–June). Special edition on corruption in Argentina. Buenos Aires, Argentina. Available: http://www.probidad.org/revista/014/art14.html

Rajora, Rajesh. 2002. *Bridging the Digital Divide: Gyandoot—The Model for Community Networks*. Tata McGraw-Hill, New Delhi.

Reilly, Katherine, and Ricardo Gómez. 2001. "Comparing Approaches: Telecentre Evaluation Experiences in Asia and Latin America." *Electronic Journal on Information Systems in Developing Countries* 4 (3):1–17. Available: http://www.is.cityu.edu.hk/ejisdc/vol4/v4r3.pdf

Reuters. 2002. "Simputer for the masses set for takeoff." March 6, 2002. Available: http://zdnet.com.com/2100-1103-852805.html

SRI International. 1999. "World Links for Development: Accomplishments and Challenges. Monitoring and Evaluation Annual Report 1998–1999." SRI Project P03617. SRI International, Center for Technology in Learning, Menlo Park, Calif. Available: http://www.worldbank.org/worldlinks/english/assets/SRI_WorLD_report-view.pdf

_____. 2000. "World Links for Development: Accomplishments and Challenges. Monitoring and Evaluation Annual Report 1999–2000." SRI Project P10533. SRI International, Center for Technology in Learning, Menlo Park, Calif. Available: http://www.worldbank.org/worldlinks/english/assets/SRI_M-E_Annual_Report_1999-2000.pdf

Symonds, Matthew. 2000. "The Next Revolution: After E-Commerce, Get Ready for E-Government." *The Economist,* 24(June): 53–59. Available: http://www.economist.com/surveys/showsurvey.cfm?issue=20000624

UNCTAD. 2001. *E-Commerce and Development Report.* United Nations: New York and Geneva. Available: http://www.unctad.org/en/pub/ps1ecdr01.en.htm

World Bank. 2002a. "Cristal: A Tool for Transparent Government in Argentina." E*Government Website, Argentina Case Studies. Poverty Reduction and Economic Management, Public Sector Group, Washington, D.C. Available: http://www1.worldbank.org/publicsector/egov/cristal_cs.htm

_____. 2002b. "Empowering Dairy Farmers through a Dairy Information & Services Kiosk." E*Government Website, India Case Studies. Poverty Reduction and Economic Management, Public Sector Group, Washington, D.C. Available: http://www1.worldbank.org/publicsector/egov/diskcs.htm

_____. 2002c. "Information and Communication Technologies: A World Bank Group Strategy." Global Information and Communication Technologies Department, Washington, D.C. Available: http://info.worldbank.org/ict/ICT_ssp.html

Tools and Practices 2

Empowerment and the World Bank's Country Assistance Strategy for Indonesia

Drawing from the most recent poverty report on Indonesia prepared by the World Bank, the Bank's *Indonesia Country Assistance Strategy Fiscal Year 2001–2003* emphasizes policies and programs designed to help empower Indonesia's poor and vulnerable. This note outlines the poverty report's treatment of empowerment issues and then describes how they are taken up in the CAS, including specific lending and nonlending activities. It concludes with a review of the Bank's support for community-driven development programs.

The Poverty Report

Poverty Reduction in Indonesia: Constructing a New Strategy (October 2000) discusses up front the close link between poverty and governance issues. The report notes that it is pointless to discuss recommendations for actions the government can take to reduce poverty "without first considering the government's *capability, accountability,* and *incentive* to embark upon an ambitious poverty reduction program."[1] The report points out that democratization and decentralization are changing the fundamental design of governance in Indonesia,

This note was prepared by Jessica Poppele.

and that the *nature* of these changes in governance will matter for the poor, suggesting three basic elements for emphasis:

- *Information*. Poverty reduction programs should break the "monopoly on information" held by previous administrations. Wide publicity through multiple channels about the content of programs before and during program implementation should be given high priority and budget. A criterion for program success should be the extent of awareness created among primary target groups (such as the poor, and the most disadvantaged among the poor).

- *Voice*. The voices of poor people should be included in public expenditure allocation, in program design, and in public sector implementation. Programs to reach the poor should strive to give them at least as much choice as the non-poor, rather than limiting the poor to government suppliers only. But choice is not possible in all situations, and in many cases "public goods"— such as roads and police services—are necessarily used by all citizens in the community. In these cases, citizen voices, especially those of poor people and women, must be sought directly in making decisions and in monitoring services.

- *Accountability*. Decision makers at all levels should be accountable to the people for each stage of planning, budgeting, implementing, and monitoring public programs and projects. In particular, officials should be accountable for outcomes: Do people find the public services useful to them, in line with what they need, and are they kept up over time? This will mean creating a new ethic of public service, reorienting civil service incentives, and gradually increasing the rule of law and transparent law enforcement.

After making this fundamental link between governance and poverty, the report discusses specific policies and programs in two broad areas of action: a *policy environment* conducive to raising the incomes of the poor, and *effective public services* that reach the poor in the core areas of government responsibility.

Policy Environment

The first area of action assumes that, for the most part, families and individuals will escape poverty and reduce their vulnerability through their own efforts. The economic policies pursued by government can either stymie or assist these individual efforts. A policy framework to create an environment in which individuals can make progress contains three elements that raise empowerment issues:

- *Resumption of rapid sustainable growth.* Policies that lead to a growing economy with rising real wages, expanding employment, and limited inflation will create an environment for poverty reduction. But for the poor to benefit fully from growth, the government must take steps to eliminate corruption; maintain open internal trade (which benefits poor farmers); enable small and medium enterprises to thrive; and raise rural incomes (through productivity improvements).

- *Economic empowerment of the poor.* For growth to be an effective route to poverty reduction, the poor must have equitable access to assets and fair returns for their products. Policies affecting the markets for labor, capital (finance, savings), land, and natural resources will be key determinants.

- *Poverty-focused public expenditures.* Allocations of public expenditures that maintain fiscal balance and enable decentralization while benefiting the poor are a third key element of economic policy. Three actions are essential: looking at what subsidies can be eliminated (as most benefits go to the rich and there are more direct ways of helping the poor); examining the pattern of spending across and within sectors to see who benefits; and supporting a regional transfer system that reduces inequality.

Effective Public Service Delivery

The second area of action concerns issues of effective public service delivery, starting with local governance and including basic health and education, basic infrastructure, mobility and access, and safety nets. In each of these areas, the report focuses on factors that affect *how well* these services are provided and how responsive they are to the needs of citizens.

- *Local governance that puts people first.* Decentralization will hand over public service delivery and development responsibilities to subnational governments. The report looks at the areas and ways in which the basic ingredients of good governance should be considered in local elections, civil service structures, budget processes, and program design, and in responsible spending of public monies, so that decentralization can actually improve public service delivery.

- *Basic health, education, and infrastructure that meet the needs of the poor.* The report discusses various ways to reorient service delivery to be more responsive to local needs, especially those of the poor. These include better incentives for civil servants, "demand side" measures to give providers feedback and provide accountability for adequate services for the poor, and creating a "broker" or "facilitator" function that helps the poor make their voices heard.

- *Safety nets for the poorest and measures to help vulnerable groups cope with shocks.* The report notes two groups who need special attention. One is a small number of chronically poor people, primarily those who lack earning power (widows, orphans, the socially excluded, the physically disabled) and thus require some basic income assistance. The other, larger group consists of people who need a temporary hand after losing a job or falling ill: not a safety net, but a temporary safety trampoline or cushion to prevent a drop into chronic poverty and propel them back into productive activity.

The Country Assistance Strategy for Indonesia

The same ideas that shape the poverty report form the core of the Country Assistance Strategy. The CAS states:

The overarching goal of the Bank Group's CAS will be to reduce poverty and vulnerability in a more open and decentralized environment. This will require attention to government policies that promote broad-based economic growth as a key requirement for poverty reduction. At the same time, the quality of growth matters to make it sustainable and genuinely pro-poor. But it is not just what government does, not just how much the government spends, but how well its services are provided. Strong improvements in governance will be critical to winning back confidence from private investors and giving voice to the poor. With the far reaching decentralization of government functions just around the corner, actions will be required to build strong governance both at the national and local levels to ensure effective public service delivery to the poor.[2]

The CAS then elaborates three broad priority areas, each of which gives special attention to empowerment and governance issues.

Sustaining Economic Recovery and Promoting Broad-Based Growth

This first CAS area explains how the Bank will promote pro-poor policies and public expenditures in the context of other actions to support economic recovery and growth.

- *Keeping rice prices affordable and internal trade open, and supporting rural development through provision of basic infrastructure, credit, research, and extension services.* The Bank will continue to provide policy advice in these critical areas and will use investment programs that emphasize empowerment in rural development.
- *Helping to empower the poor through access to secure possession of land and natural resources and increasing the availability of financial services to them.* The Bank is working to encourage stakeholder dialogue on forestry and land policy. It is also undertaking analytical work and supporting preparation of a Land Management Policy Development Program to help reverse past practices of land allocation and distribution that disadvantaged the poor. The Bank's support for microfinance will focus on increasing access by the poor and strengthening institutions, rather than on credit subsidies. A rural finance project is foreseen for fiscal 2003.
- *Helping to keep a poverty focus in public expenditures, including looking hard at which subsidies can be eliminated and supporting poverty reduction by local governments.* The Bank will continue to support the government's policy of reducing fuel subsidies and redirecting funds to pro-poor programs. To help encourage poverty agendas at the local level, through budget transfer, the Bank will focus on the fiscal transfer framework, as well as on the minimum standards of service delivery. These will be addressed through policy advice and technical assistance, and

in the context of proposed projects in health, education, and basic infrastructure.

Building National Institutions for Accountable Government

This CAS area notes that "strong improvements in governance" will be critical to giving voice to the poor. Actions in this area rely heavily on analytical and advisory activities addressing, at the national level, legal and judicial reforms, civil service reforms, decentralization, and the government's fiduciary controls.

Delivering Better Public Services to the Poor

The national-level governance agenda is complemented by and overlaps with this third CAS area. Here the Bank's strategy looks at Indonesia's decentralization and democratization reforms as an opportunity to support empowerment on three fronts: supporting improvements for more accountable and transparent public sector management at the local level; building community participation features, where appropriate, into sectoral projects (for example, empowering water users' associations); and expanding projects that work through communities linking up to local government from below.

During the CAS period, Indonesia's "big bang" decentralization offers the biggest hope for—and significant risks to—public service delivery. Decentralization makes possible more accountable and transparent government by bringing government closer to the people. However, in light of international experience, it is clear that decentralization will not lead automatically to these empowerment outcomes. To encourage such reforms, the Bank strategy proposes that donor support be directed toward subnational governments that have put pro-poor reforms into practice, that is, those who have taken steps toward more transparent, accountable, and demand-responsive public service delivery. To begin to get to know local governments and identify reformers, the country strategy includes a process for deeper engagement with local governments and civil society organizations in three provinces and 10 cities through consultations and public expenditure reviews. This activity is expected to begin supporting efforts by the selected local governments to become more transparent and accountable to citizens, to learn from local stakeholders ways to address key development challenges in the regions, and to build an analytical foundation for the selection of regions in which the Bank could operate.

Concurrent with the Bank's engagement with local governments on public sector management reforms, sectoral studies and projects are investigating and pushing ahead with empowerment reforms. Water sector management provides a good example. Under an umbrella of broad institutional and regulatory reforms, supported by the Bank's Water Sector Adjustment Loan, national, provincial, and river basin-level authorities are being set up with membership from civil society and other stakeholders to improve accountability. The reforms also require local governments to apply demand-driven and participatory approaches for planning, building, and maintaining rural water infrastructure.

To help put these reforms into practice, the Java Irrigation Improvement and Water Management Project has been establishing self-governing water users' associations across Java since 1997. By 2001 more than 360 of these were operational, with membership from over half a million rural households. These associations (whose members are the users of irrigation services) elect their leaders, collect irrigation fees, take the lead in operation and maintenance of the infrastructure, and allocate water. In some districts (*kabupatens*), part of the irrigation budget is being transferred to these water users' associations for the operation and maintenance on a matching basis. Preliminary evidence suggests that productivity and rural income have improved, and water and finance are being used more efficiently. A grant from the Netherlands will allow this approach to be piloted off Java. A new investment loan, Water Resource Management Program (FY03), will help take improved governance, accountability, and water user empowerment objectives to the next stage.

The World Bank's Role in Community-Driven Development in Indonesia

Bank-funded community empowerment projects have been built upon an Indonesian tradition of (troubled) "bottom-up" planning. Indonesia has for some time made the provision of basic infrastructure for villages—addressing problems of access to education, health, and safe water—a development priority. Studies all pointed to the lower costs, higher quality, and greater ownership that comes from community participation. However, in all cases, the top-down government budget transfer system was clumsy and slow to respond to the so-called bottom-up planning that was in place. Furthermore, reviews of community programs on the ground showed recurrent problems of elite capture and political manipulation. Simply building infrastructure was not enough without a more conducive environment for planning and managing it.

Large-scale Bank and government sector work and operational replies to the systemic problems of bottom-up planning started in the mid-1990s, with the Local-Level Institutions study (LLI, FY98) on the one side, and the Water Supply and Sanitation for Low-Income Communities project (WSSLIC, FY92 Board) and the Village Infrastructure Project (VIP, FY95 Board) on the other. WWSLIC was the first project sponsored by the government of Indonesia to bring communities into project decision making by requiring them to contribute both in cash and in kind. The project combined community participation in water supply and sanitation planning with integrated hygiene and sanitation education in order to improve villagers' health; another project benefit was to free up time spent carrying water for other productive activities. Other early projects, such as the National Watershed Management and Conservation Project (NWMCP, FY93 Board), had piloted the direct transfer of funds to community groups. But it was the VIP that pioneered direct resource transfers on a large scale to villages across Java. Funds were used by villagers to build rural infrastructure despite initial skepticism that the system (and villagers) could respond effectively.

The LLI study documented the systemic mismatches between community priorities and development investment decisions, and regional agricultural area development projects were restructured in light of these lessons. The LLI study identified the growing gap between government agencies and community organizations and pointed to the social processes that were creating these gaps. The key finding from that study was the potentially positive role that community institutions could play in local development despite the many ways in which they were being undermined by the "New Order" approach of the government, which sought to limit the involvement of civil society. The Bank's Poverty Assessment (FY01) also stressed the close linkages between local governance reform, demand-responsive public services, and a revived strategy for poverty reduction. These findings harmonized well with academic work on social capital, and with work being done in other countries on community-driven development.

The Bank's strategy for community development has evolved along with the government's own changing perspective on decentralization and local reform. However, the heart of this strategy has been the use of projects to create "facts on the ground" that show that properly designed community empowerment programs lead to higher returns, greater benefits for the poor (including better accountability for and more transparent use of funds), and more sustainable outcomes. World Bank contributions to these types of programs have concentrated less on detailed sector work per se than on setting the operational precedents for pushing to the next level. Thus, the first Village Infrastructure Project provided the design machinery for communities, on a large scale, to receive funds directly and manage them in accountable ways. Lessons from WSSLIC and the NWMCP pilot also lent support to rooting rural infrastructure in community empowerment. The NWMCP Implementation Completion Report of 2000 affirmed: "Direct involvement of primary stakeholders in planning, implementation, and management of key activities, for example, conservation and village infrastructure works, is important for realizing sustainable project development." Once there was a system in place for transferring and managing money and projects at the village and community levels, other projects began to make use of this mechanism for various approaches to development assistance.

Beginning in the mid-1990s, new project approvals shifted steadily away from big-contract, large-scale infrastructure toward putting more funds directly under community control. In the mid-1990s less than 10 percent of new Bank approvals were directed to communities, but by the latter part of the decade this had risen to one-third; and from fiscal 1999 to 2001 more than 50 percent of approvals—with as much as 75 percent in one year—were for community empowerment. For example, the Decentralized Agriculture and Forestry Extension Project (FY00 Board) is piloting ways to help extension workers better respond to farmers' needs by giving communities more control over project funds. The Second Water Supply and Sanitation for Low Income Communities Project (FY00 Board) adopted the Village Infrastructure Project fund-channeling mechanism to take community participation to the next stage in the health sector. The value of community empowerment approaches is not limited to rural areas. The Urban Poverty Project (FY99 Board) has shown that the incomes of poor city-dwellers can also be raised through community-driven approaches. Older projects were also restructured based on community-driven success. After languishing in problem status for more than two years, two regional area development projects (Nusa Tenggara and Sulawesi) were restructured in the late 1990s to put control in the hands of villagers. These projects are now back on track for successful outcomes.

The Kecamatan Development Project (KDP) broke new ground with its ambitious coverage and open menu. The first KDP began in 1998 and will have disbursed $273 million (IBRD and IDA funds) by early 2002. Of the 67,500 villages in Indonesia, more than 12,000 of the poorest villages have participated in KDP so far, with a total beneficiary population of almost 10 million people. Building from VIP, the first kecamatan (subdistrict) project focused on broadening the range of stakeholders involved in decision making, including a renewed regulatory and advisory role for the decentralized district governments and, for the first time, an institutionalized role for civil society monitors. KDP also opened up project menus so that for the first time villagers were engaged in fully participatory and transparent budgeting. By the second year the project was disbursing $100 million. Seventy-five percent of the village grants were used to build economic infrastructure including roads (62 percent of all economic infrastructure projects), bridges (10 percent), irrigation (8 percent), and clean water (7 percent). Economic infrastructure built through KDP methods costs as much as 30 percent less than that built using traditional approaches in the same places. The remaining 25 percent of KDP village grants was used for economic activities.

Poverty benefits from the village investments have been large. Seventy-seven percent of KDP's loan beneficiaries are believed to be among the poorer members of their communities, and 38 percent have been women. Nearly 5 million people received wages for their labor on project works in KDP's first year, and because the project sets wages below the local agricultural minimum, nearly all of the wage amount is paid to the poor and vulnerable. Ex-post reviews show average rates of return of 30 to 40 percent to rural infrastructure built through KDP, virtually all of which is captured by villagers. A sample of the subdistricts that were included in the first year of the project found that 60 percent of the participants in project meetings were poor, and 40 percent were women.

The second KDP (FY01 Board) continues this program, with an increasingly explicit governance-poverty linkage. At $325 million, the project accounts for 75 percent of the Bank's FY01 lending program to

Indonesia. The heart of the project is the activities that increase communities' abilities to assess their development needs and involve local governments and other stakeholders in solving them. However, while the program presumes that representative institutions are fundamental for successful service delivery to the poor, a responsive technical support structure is still needed to ensure the quality of whatever it is that communities build with their resources. As a result, the new project places greater emphasis on developing local technical capacities for design, management, and maintenance.

Note

1. World Bank 2001b, p. vii.
2. World Bank 2001a, p.19.

Resources

World Bank. 2001a. "Country Assistance Strategy of the World Bank Group in Indonesia." Report No. 21580-IND. Indonesia Country Management Unit, East Asia and Pacific Region and the International Finance Corporation, East Asia and Pacific Department, Washington, D.C.

World Bank. 2001b. *Poverty Reduction in Indonesia: Constructing a New Strategy.* Environment and Social Development Sector Unit, East Asia and the Pacific Region, Washington, D.C.

Tools and Practices 3

Empowerment in the Vietnam Country Program

Following adoption of the *doi moi* ("renovation") strategy in 1986 and the introduction of a series of economic reforms, Vietnam experienced GDP growth rates averaging 8 percent per year between 1990 and 1997. Absolute poverty declined from 58 percent in 1993 to around 37 percent in 1998, while the number of people below the "food poverty line" dropped from 25 percent to 15 percent. Trends in nonmonetary indicators of welfare confirmed that living standards were improving. Access to health, education, and infrastructure services expanded for the bulk of the population.

The shift toward a market-oriented economy also brought some changes in the political structures of the country. According to the new constitution adopted in 1992, the Communist Party remains the leading organ of the state, but is bound to operate within the framework of the law and the constitution. The constitutional and legislative powers of the National Assembly, whose members are elected through universal suffrage and secret ballot, were also expanded.

In recent years, the government has taken significant steps to improve communication and to encourage a two-way flow of information and views. In 1998 a Grassroots Democracy Decree was passed, which established the legal framework for the participation of citizens in local decision-making processes at the commune level and their right to "monitor" local government expenditures. Although the capacity of citizens

This note was prepared by Carrie Turk.

to participate actively remains constrained, especially by their lack of awareness of their rights and entitlements, the decree is viewed as a step toward enhancing the transparency and accountability of local government officials.

Building Blocks for a Strengthened Empowerment Agenda

The 1998 Country Assistance Strategy

The World Bank's early assistance to Vietnam focused on rehabilitation of infrastructure that had been devastated during the consecutive wars, and on restoration of the basic health and education systems. The program was designed to gain high rates of return from these investments and made an impact on poverty by easing constraints to broad-based growth. The most recent Country Assistance Strategy, in 1998, was designed to support government efforts to restore growth momentum, which had faltered in the late 1990s as a result of the regional economic crisis. This CAS emphasizes the need to concentrate on the quality of growth, with a more explicit focus on poverty, social issues, and rural development. The CAS also emphasizes the need to develop clearer links between individual projects and policy dialogue and to give greater attention to improving the efficiency of public administration—particularly the accountability of the public sector.

The 1998 CAS included a number of elements that were intended to give poor people a stronger voice in project planning and in the broader processes of government planning and budgeting. These included:

- Introduction of two community-driven development projects in some of the poorest parts of the country (the Community Based Rural Infrastructure Project and the Northern Mountains Poverty Reduction Project), which delegate both planning and resource management responsibilities to the commune level;
- Plans for implementing Participatory Poverty Assessments in poor regions to form an integral part of a collaborative poverty assessment;
- Initiatives to enhance transparency and accountability in the use of public funds through increased decentralization and participation. These include a Public Expenditure Review; a Participatory Provincial Partnership with the United Nations Development Programme (UNDP) and Oxfam GB to strengthen

participatory planning in Tra Vinh Province; and work to strengthen local civil society.

With the exception of planned support for strengthening local civil society (which, ultimately, the government decided not to take advantage of), these initiatives have provided a firm basis for future efforts to forge a stronger link between poor households and decision-making processes. The Community Based Rural Infrastructure Project was approved by the Board in June 2001 ($102.78 million), and the Northern Mountains Poverty Reduction Project was approved in October 2001 ($110 million). The PPAs have had widespread impact, and the Public Expenditure Review led to a comprehensive program of follow-up activities, several of which are related to improved financial accountability of local authorities to poor communities.

The PPAs and "Vietnam: Attacking Poverty"

Despite the important achievements of the 1990s in reducing poverty and raising living standards for nearly all groups in Vietnam, the PPAs highlighted the extent to which poorer households felt alienated from decision-making and policymaking processes.[1] These studies emphasized the constraints that poor people face in accessing basic information on matters of importance to their lives. Findings suggested that some groups had less voice than others: women, ethnic minorities, and unregistered migrants were particularly unlikely to participate in decision-making processes. Drawing on these findings, the poverty assessment "Vietnam: Attacking Poverty" placed issues of local governance and grassroots democracy at the heart of the discussion on social equity. A number of new initiatives are now planned to respond to the issues raised, as described below.

The process of implementing the PPAs and integrating the findings fully into the poverty assessment sought to involve government policymakers, at both the central and local levels, as much as possible. The establishment of a governance structure made up of many stakeholders—the Poverty Working Group—was key to generating buy-in and consensus on the findings.[2] As a result, issues that were sensitive and rarely discussed in public policy debate, such as findings on voicelessness and powerlessness, were brought to the fore with the agreement of government counterparts. It was felt that the way in which the PPAs had been implemented, as much as the information they generated, was important in raising the profile of some of these empowerment issues. The government used the PPAs as background information in the preparation of the interim PRSP and several of the areas flagged as strategically important are derived from the PPAs. These include improving the dissemination of information on legal rights to poor households; strengthening a two-way dialogue between local authorities and poor households; creating an enabling environment for poor households to take part in local economic development plans; and creating a legal framework to enable communities to maintain and manage resources provided through development projects.[3]

A Future Empowerment Agenda

Initiatives Underway

Experience in implementing the 1998 CAS and the findings of the PPAs led directly to several initiatives. First, the findings of the Ha Tinh PPA—that the methods of raising revenue at the commune level were burdensome, regressive, nontransparent, and poorly accounted for in some parts of the country—led to the inclusion of further work in the Public Expenditure Review. Conducted with the Ministry of Finance, this study concluded that households were subject to a complex range of fees and contributions that were confusing to households and commune officials alike. This in turn limited the potential for poor households to question the legitimacy or calculation of charges. In addition, the finding that few, if any, communes in the study area were making any serious attempts to implement the Grassroots Democracy Decree (which requires commune authorities to publish and publicly discuss commune plans, budgets, and expenditures) compounded the impression that ordinary citizens are remote from local financial decision making. The Ministry of Finance responded to this by drawing up new regulations governing revenue collection at this level.

Second, in response to findings in the PPAs that there were pockets of very severe poverty in urban areas, a decision was made to refocus the urban component of the assistance strategy to develop a stronger emphasis on community-identified needs and poverty reduction objectives. This led to the preparation of a community-based urban upgrading program, beginning with participatory surveys of how poor and vulnerable groups prioritize solutions to problems regarding access to housing and infrastructure.

Third, plans have been established to assist the government in gathering feedback from households on their views about the quality, efficiency, and usefulness of public service delivery. In the longer term it is hoped that this feedback can be incorporated into household survey work to yield a more accurate national picture of access to and quality of public services, broken down by socioeconomic group. It is hoped that ultimately a link could be made between client assessments of public services and resource allocation.

Fourth, the Ministry of Finance would like to address some of the transparency and accountability issues at the commune level as part of their follow-up to the Public Expenditure Review. They have requested assistance in investigating ways in which budget and expenditure information could be made more readily accessible and comprehensible to poor households. At the time of writing, this was being pursued in collaboration with a local NGO, which specializes in disseminating information on legal rights.

Future Work

Production of the next CAS has been delayed slightly to allow the government of Vietnam to complete its PRSP, which it calls the Comprehensive Poverty Reduction and Growth Strategy (CPRGS). Future assistance strategies, on the part of the World Bank and some other donors, will be closely aligned to the CPRGS. It follows that the future agenda of empowerment work depends to a large extent on the strategic direction set out by the government in its CPRGS. This highlights the need to develop stronger mechanisms for meaningful consultations with poor households and vulnerable individuals during preparation of the CPRGS. The absence of a vibrant local civil society that includes poor peoples' organizations is a gap in this respect, and the development of robust processes for participation by poor households in the preparation of the CPRGS is a priority area of concern for the World Bank and many other donors.

The government of Vietnam, in cooperation with the World Bank, has adopted several strategies for approaching this, and for developing mechanisms for stakeholders to monitor progress against strategic targets. The World Bank has coordinated village-level consultations on the CPRGS to discuss whether villagers' diagnosis of poverty is adequately addressed by the proposed strategies. The Poverty Task Force (formerly the Poverty Working Group) is assisting the government in developing a monitoring framework for the CPRGS by preparing a series of eight papers on core development goals and outcome targets. At the time of writing, discussions had already involved more than 100 policymakers and practitioners who have agreed on the importance of including goals to make government more transparent, accountable, predictable, and participatory.[4]

Notes

1.   Poverty Working Group 1999.
2.   Turk 2001.
3.   Government of the Socialist Republic of Vietnam 2001.
4.   Government of Vietnam-Donor-NGO Poverty Task Force 2001.

Resources

Government of the Socialist Republic of Vietnam. 2001. "Interim Poverty Reduction Strategy." Hanoi. Available: http://www.worldbank.org/poverty/strategies/index.htm

Government of Vietnam-Donor-NGO Poverty Task Force. 2001. "Report of the Haiphong Workshop. Localizing the International Development Goals: The Vietnam Development Targets." Hanoi.

Poverty Working Group. 1999. "Vietnam: Attacking Poverty." Vietnam Development Report 2000. Joint Report of the Government of Vietnam-Donor-NGO Poverty Working Group. World Bank, Washington, D.C.

Turk, Carrie. 2001. "Linking Participatory Poverty Assessments to Policy and Policymaking: Experience from Vietnam." Policy Research Working Paper 2526. World Bank, Development Research Group, Washington, D.C.

Tools and Practices 4

Peru Portfolio Review through an Empowerment Lens

After the publication of *Voices of the Poor* and *World Development Report 2000/2001: Attacking Poverty,* it became clear to the Country Management Unit (CMU) for Peru that empowerment is central to economic growth and poverty reduction strategies. The question that followed was how and with what results the Bank was incorporating empowerment in its assistance strategy and ongoing operations in Peru, and how that could be improved.

A Glance at the Peru Portfolio

Given that the country team was winding up implementation of the 1997 CAS, a first step was to look into the country portfolio. As part of the annual Country Portfolio Performance Review (CPPR), the CMU assessed how the eight Bank-financed projects underway in Peru were contributing to empowerment of the project beneficiaries. The specific objectives of the exercise were to:

- Analyze and identify to what extent empowerment was included within the project design and project activities, and with what mechanisms; and
- Identify ways to improve empowerment in the projects.

This note was prepared by Keta Ruiz.

143

Two consultants were engaged, under the oversight of the Country Officer and guidance of other Bank staff,[1] to undertake the following activities: (a) an overall desk review of project-related Bank documents; (b) preparation of an interview guide; (c) interviews of government project directors, project staff, and Bank task managers; (d) presentation and discussion, during the CPPR, of the findings of the desk review and interviews; and (e) preparation of a report summarizing the main findings of the exercise.[2]

Principal findings of the exercise were as follows:

- Although the term "empowerment" has only recently come into wider use, the Bank has been striving for the last few years to include in its projects in Peru some elements of empowerment through the concepts of participation, equity, transparency, and sustainability. These elements were included in most project designs and formed part of the ongoing supervision and evaluation of the projects.

- Although these elements have been included in projects to varying degrees, the empowerment objective, understood as the creation of capabilities and sharing of power with project beneficiaries, was not included in all logical frameworks. Input, output, and outcome indicators to measure empowerment were also missing.

- Empowerment is relevant to, and could be applied differently in, each of the Bank-financed projects in Peru. There are a few projects (education, health, rural development, and indigenous peoples) where empowerment has been a central element of design and implementation. In other cases (urban water rehabilitation and infrastructure, urban property rights) empowerment has been achieved indirectly through the project. For example, by earning property rights through the Urban Property Rights Project, poor Peruvians have gained access to an economic asset that allows them to enter the formal economy and creates new opportunities.[3]

- There was the risk of "Babelization" of the concept of empowerment, given the novelty, complexity, and ambiguity of the term, the heterogeneity of the projects, and the professional diversity of project directors and staff.

- There was also the risk that the objective of the exercise would be trivialized if project directors, staff, and Bank teams adopted it simply because it is an institutional requirement and not because they are convinced of its importance or relevance.

Building a Common Understanding

Given the risks outlined above, it was decided that the next step after the CPPR exercise should be to build a better understanding of empowerment and its operationalization in project work. For this purpose, two workshops, each addressing four of the eight projects, were organized with the participation of Bank staff and government project directors. The specific objectives of the workshops were to:

- Provide an opportunity for analyzing empowerment and reaching a better common understanding of the concept within the project teams;
- Define mechanisms for the monitoring and evaluation of empowerment in the projects; and
- Provide an opportunity for the project teams to exchange experiences of the way empowerment was included in their projects.

During the workshops, project teams briefly explained their project objectives, how they understood empowerment, and how empowerment of beneficiaries was being achieved through their projects. They also discussed the key elements of empowerment and some intended and unintended effects of its operationalization, and applied the concept through working teams that reviewed project activities and monitored indicators related to empowerment.

The discussions yielded several common understandings about what empowerment entails in the context of Peru's project work; these can also be applied more broadly in operational work. First, empowerment is a process that responds to endogenous and exogenous factors. It therefore cannot have a set target, but rather is a matter of level or degree. Second, empowerment implies a change in the power relationship among project directors, operational project staff (intermediary clients), and beneficiaries. Third, capacity building and a clear understanding of empowerment at the level of both project directors and intermediary clients, but especially of the beneficiaries, is indispensable for the effectiveness and sustainability of this change in power relationships.

Other key questions discussed during the workshops included:

- Who to empower? Although the ultimate target is project beneficiaries, it became clear that it is also important to empower intermediary clients, because it would be difficult for them to promote empowerment of project beneficiaries if they are not empowered themselves.

- How to carry out the process? A main element is to ensure consultation with and participation of the beneficiaries throughout the project cycle.
- Why empower? In addition to the understanding that empowerment of poor people is central to economic growth and poverty reduction, it is also important to consider that it is key to project sustainability.

Working with the Project Teams and Beneficiaries: The Peru Irrigation Rehabilitation Project

As the workshops drew to a close, participants emphasized the need to carry out similar exercises with intermediary clients and also to observe in the field how "empowered" project beneficiaries may have actually become. It also was apparent that more detailed work was necessary to clarify the logical framework and indicators to be used in operationalizing empowerment. Work on this is being piloted in the Peru Irrigation Rehabilitation Project, an $85 million project approved by the Board in 1996 to increase the productivity of more than 50,000 families cultivating approximately 65 percent of the existing irrigation schemes (200,000 hectares) on the coast of Peru.

The project has achieved only some of its original objectives because of slow implementation caused by initial delays, restructuring due to changes in priorities as a result of El Niño, and lack of counterpart funds. The establishment of decentralized decision making by associations of water users, however, is one of the specific objectives on which significant progress has been made. Of the 64 water users' associations, 52 now have technical managers and 60 have followed awareness courses; in addition, the water law has been changed to make water users less dependent on the Ministry of Agriculture. The project is also reducing the role of the state in the irrigation sector. Elections of representatives of water users' associations have been held for all irrigation schemes, in hopes that this will enable the associations to be run more efficiently and less under the direct control of the Ministry of Agriculture. Cost recovery of investment, operation, and maintenance in irrigation systems is slow, but there has been progress. As of 2001, 20 water users' associations (30 percent of the total number) had recovered 75 percent of water charges (compared to 5 percent two years before), and only 25 associations were recovering less than 50 percent of the water charges.

Through interviews and workshops with intermediary clients of the project, along with field visits to assess how "empowered" the project beneficiaries had become, a number of additional steps were identified for increasing the effectiveness and sustainability of the project. These include:

- Reassigning budget items to activities that strengthen empowerment of the water users' associations and water committees, especially capacity building, technical assistance, and required equipment;
- Strengthening the project board by including not only irrigation experts, Ministry of Agriculture authorities, and representatives of the private sector, but representatives of the water users' associations as well;
- Promoting experience-sharing among project beneficiaries by setting up a technical exchange system; and
- Linking project beneficiaries to technical assistance and hydraulic engineering services providers (universities, consulting firms) so that beneficiaries can hire them directly for the rehabilitation and maintenance of their irrigation infrastructure.

Finally, it is essential to take steps to simplify, unify, and select indicators in the project logical framework in order to measure progress achieved in the empowerment process. These should include indicators that will: (a) measure the management capacity of the water users' associations, such as increase in revenues, percentage allocated to operations and maintenance, and percentage of beneficiaries who are satisfied with the management of the association; and (b) measure the organization and technical management of the farmers, such as percentage of farmers who participate in the decisions of the water users' associations and percentage of farmers who are satisfied with the quality of the technical assistance they receive from the associations.

Notes

1.   The Regional Adviser for Poverty Reduction, the Regional Civil Society Coordinator, and the Civil Society Specialist for Peru contributed to the preparation of the terms of reference for the consultants and also contributed as advisers to the process.

2.   This note draws heavily from the consultants' report.

3.   See Tools and Practices 14 for more information on this project.

Tools and Practices 5

Social Accountability Mechanisms in Programmatic and Structural Adjustment Loans

There are three main types of accountability mechanisms that assist in making governments answerable for their decisions, policies, and use of resources:

- *Political accountability* mechanisms ensure that political parties and representatives are responsive to the needs of their constituents. This is carried out increasingly through elections.
- *Internal accountability* mechanisms focus on improving the administrative performance of government agencies, both horizontal and vertical, within and between agencies.[1]
- *Public or social accountability* mechanisms include a range of tools that promote greater accounting by government citizens. Social accountability can reinforce political and administrative accountability mechanisms.

Social accountability mechanisms have become a feature of recent budget support, adjustment, and public and sectoral reform loans. Recent examples of loans with provisions for social accountability

This note was prepared by Laura Bureš, with input from Magui Moreno Torres, under the overall guidance of Deepa Narayan.

include the Guinea Decentralization Project, the Tanzania Public Sector Reform Project, the Guatemala Financial Management and Judicial Reform projects, the PSRLs to Thailand and Peru, the PRSC approved for Uganda, the Sector Adjustment Loans (SECALs) to the Russian coal sector, and the PSALs to Latvia. Examples from Uganda, Russia, Latvia, and Peru follow.

Uganda Poverty Reduction Support Credit

The first Poverty Reduction Support Credit of $150 million was approved in 2001 for Uganda. The PRSC is planned as a series of annual programmatic structural adjustment credits with clear performance benchmarks, outcome indicators, and policy measures. The reform program supported by the first PRSC aims to: (a) improve public service delivery through efficient and equitable use of public resources; (b) improve governance by increasing transparency and participation, fighting corruption, and reforming public services, procurement, financial and human resource management, and monitoring and evaluation; and (c) increase access to and quality of basic services, including education, health care, water, and sanitation.[2]

What Problems Will the PRSC Address?

In Uganda, public service delivery currently focuses on inputs and implementation processes rather than on the end results of policies and programs. Major problems include insufficient clarity and consistency of sector outcome/output indicators, targets, and service standards, and lack of systematic feedback from public service users. Monitoring and evaluation activities and reporting requirements are uncoordinated and often place a considerable burden on weak local governments. Accounting for public expenditure is lax because of disregard for timely and regular recording of transactions, sidestepping of controls, and lack of financial discipline.

In addition, transparency and accountability in both government and NGO service delivery are also weak, community participation and the use of participatory approaches and methods remain mostly ad hoc, and corruption is widespread, especially in the judiciary, the police, and the health services. Access to information about public sector performance and practices is limited. In this area, Uganda has had success in recent years with using information to improve government accountability and performance, most notably in the case of the Public Expenditure Tracking Surveys in the education and health sectors.[3] The PRSC will build on Uganda's success with these surveys and information disclosure to improve accountability.

What Accountability Mechanisms Does the PRSC Introduce?

Social accountability

To improve social accountability, the PRSC will support Uganda in efforts to monitor public service delivery and expenditures and increase citizens' access to information about their government. Over the three-year period, the government of Uganda and/or civil society and other stakeholders will:

- Monitor public service delivery and corruption on a regular basis through surveys;
- Implement regular expenditure tracking surveys in basic services;
- Establish a common monitoring and evaluation system linked to performance in basic service sectors;
- Improve citizens' access to public information, including tabling an Access to Government Information bill in Parliament;
- Post public notices of conditional and other grants at service delivery points;
- Publish budget performance reports;
- Prepare and implement a communication strategy for the budget process and fiscal policy;
- Increase availability of public information on fiscal transfers at local levels;
- Streamline reporting requirements for local governments;
- Develop, publish, and implement government pay and procurement reform strategies;
- Harmonize NGO policy and a code of conduct for using participatory approaches.

Surveys and monitoring. The country will institutionalize surveys similar to the Public Expenditure Tracking Surveys in other sectors and will streamline the numerous ongoing monitoring and evaluation activities.

Key monitoring mechanisms for poverty and sector-level outcomes include three independent annual surveys (household, service delivery, and integrity surveys). Periodic Participatory Poverty Assessments, enterprise surveys, and annual expenditure tracking surveys in basic service sectors will be carried out. A poverty monitoring and evaluation strategy has been prepared as well.

Monitoring is increasingly a joint effort between the Ugandan government, IDA, and other donors for the Poverty Eradication Action Plan (PEAP)/PRSP. Monitoring the progress in reform program implementation and its impact will follow the PRSP review mechanism, taking into account information collected in citizen and civil society monitoring activities. The Ugandan government will make quarterly reports on progress in each program area. The reform program sets clear quantitative and qualitative benchmarks for three years, and the government and IDA will agree on PRSC II and PRSC III on an annual basis.

Access to information. In March 2001, the Ministry of Information, in collaboration with the Ministry of Ethics and Integrity, reviewed the Official Secrets Act in light of best practices regarding access to government information. The cabinet is working to approve principles of access to government information, and it is hoped that the Ministry of Information will table an Access to Government Information bill in Parliament by April 2004.

Also in March 2001, the Ministry of Finance, Planning, and Economic Development produced a citizens' guide to the budget process.

Internal accountability

To improve internal accountability, the PRSC will support efforts to:

- Improve accounting and auditing systems at the central and district levels of government;
- Improve the flow of funds to frontline service delivery;
- Coordinate financial management reform and update the legal-institutional framework;
- Increase collaboration among judicial and law enforcement agencies.

These efforts are expected to improve the financial management, accounting, and auditing processes and improve coordination and accountability between government agencies and institutions.

Russia Coal Sector Adjustment Loans

The World Bank has supported Russia's coal sector restructuring program through two Coal Sector Adjustment Loans (Coal SECAL I, $500 million; and II, $800 million) between 1996 and 2000.[4]

What Problems Did the Coal SECALs Address?

Transition from the Soviet period

Years of poor management of the coal sector during the Soviet period, combined with a drop in demand in the early 1990s, significantly damaged the sector's economic viability. The coal sector was second only to agriculture in the magnitude of the government subsidies it received. By 1993, subsidies had reached unsustainable levels, exceeding 1 percent of Russia's GDP. There was little relationship between the amount of subsidy and the output of the mines. In addition, the coal sector was suffering from enormous inefficiencies and ever-worsening safety conditions, while the system of wage payments had collapsed. Wages went unpaid for an average of 8 to 16 months, and when workers were paid, they were often paid in kind—in shoes, glass, or sugar. The capacity of municipal governments was very limited, and systems for resource transfers related to the coal sector were not in place.

Government instability, secrecy, and loss of public trust

There was a high level of instability as a result of turnover in top government positions, which hindered reforms. Between 1996 and 2000, Russia had five prime ministers, seven deputy prime ministers who were also the formal conveners of the Inter-Agency Coal Commission, six ministers of energy, and four leaders of the coal agency. In addition, there were major constraints on information flows within government. Top officials had very little access to information, which tended to be hoarded by lower-ranking officials who had a stake in the status quo. Trust in government generally and in the coal sector particularly was extremely low. According to a survey of mining households in 1995, one-fifth of the households did not trust any organization to distribute money or assistance. Only 5 percent trusted RosUgol, less than 3 percent trusted regional coal companies, 3 percent trusted the regional government, and 8 percent trusted trade unions.

What Were the Outcomes of the Coal Sector Reforms?

Outcomes on the ground

- *Subsidies to the coal sector decreased* from $2.76 billion in 1994 to $0.28 billion in 2000. These subsidies have been reoriented from soft budget support of an unproductive sector to the delivery of social protection and community development. (Of the coal subsidy for the year 2000, 31 percent was directed to social protection.)

- Over the same six-year period, *productivity of mines increased* from 764 tons per worker per year to 1,355 tons per worker per year—a 77 percent improvement in productivity. The imposition of hard budget constraints in the coal sector created incentives for managers to focus on productivity.

- *Delivery of social protection improved.* All workers laid off from closed or continuing mines have received their benefits directly, in full, and on time, as verified through multiple sources in government and through social impact monitoring. All disabled workers from closed mines have received their benefits in full and on time. The delivery of benefits has allowed citizens to participate in economic activity to a greater extent.

- *Coal worker salaries and conditions improved.* In Siberia, salaries are now paid 100 percent in cash and reach 30,000 rubles per month.

Organizational outcomes

- *New roles for existing organizations.* The Treasury's role was expanded to make it the central agency in the new system for accountability, delivery of benefits, and management of subsidies. For the delivery of benefits to disabled miners, the Social Insurance Fund (SIF) agreed to deliver benefits initially out of funds from the Ministry of Energy and, in the longer term, from fees collected from the coal mines. In the SIF, a culture of delivery and a pattern of predictability were established, as benefits were delivered in full and on time.

- *Mechanisms established for intra-governmental participation.* The Inter-Agency Coal Commission provides a forum for discussion and resolution of issues by bringing all government stakeholders together. An interministerial group for tranche releases ensures that the necessary actions have been taken by different stakeholders in order to produce outcomes in a timely manner.

Institutional outcomes

- Across government agencies, rules were created establishing *clear links between allocations and outcomes*. Budgets now clearly state the categories of subsidy, the recipients of subsidies, and the mechanisms of delivery and accountability.
- *Checks and balances between government ministries* are now in place for enforcement of rules. Mechanisms are also in place to secure the participation of government agencies in reform and decision-making processes.
- Because new government rules and resolutions have been translated into corresponding action, and because they have been geared toward long-term solutions for the coal sector, they may have long-term positive effects on the *credibility of the state* by satisfying citizens' expectations.
- The new accountability mechanisms introduced in government for coal sector reform have also set *precedents for reform in other sectors* of the Russian economy.
- *Local municipalities*, which had initially opposed accountability mechanisms pertaining to local development funds, found the new accountability mechanisms helpful because they protected local officials from intense pressure from other stakeholders.

What Accountability Mechanisms Did the Coal SECALs Introduce?

Reform of the coal sector included several important accountability mechanisms such as process mapping and stakeholder mapping, greater information sharing and transparency, mechanisms providing for consultation with and participation of stakeholders, checks and balances between ministries for budget allocation and enforcement of rules, and financial auditing and accountability processes.

Process mapping was used to build accountability for outcomes by tracing flows in three key areas:

- Flows of money relating to the delivery of social protection;

- Flows of policies and decision making relating to the closure of mines;
- Flows of information among government ministries and officials, and to the public.

Mapping the flows of money allocated for social protection from the very top all the way to intended recipients showed that one flow passed through the federal, regional, and local governments to communities, while another flow went from the federal government to the national coal company to regional coal companies, then to the mines, and finally to miners. At each point in the flow, correspondence between the formal rules and actual practices was checked, and major breakdowns were revealed. Coal companies and mine managers had enormous discretion and soft budgets with scant accountability to recipients for delivery of funds. There was little predictability in flows of money for social protection.

Mapping the flows of policies revealed the gaps between policy intention and reality. For example, though policy dictated that 300 billion rubles were to be spent on social protection in 1996, less than 35 percent of miners received their funds; though only eight mines were to close, 60 mines closed without legal due process. The mapping between stated policy and actual outcomes also showed uncertainty among miners about when mines would close and what their entitlements were, and there were no procedures in place to inform miners of their rights.

Mapping the flows of information showed that low-level government officials often kept information from high-ranking officials, and ministries typically failed to share information with each other. For example, the Ministry of Finance classified most information as "national secrets." In response, the Bank established neutral mechanisms for gathering and analyzing information from multiple sources, cross-tabulated the information to find areas of agreement and disagreement, and ensured timely delivery of information at monthly and quarterly intervals.

Stakeholder mapping was also important because stakeholders provided critical information on processes and were able to recommend catalytic mechanisms for institutional interventions.[5] Stakeholder mapping at the local level showed that accountability and transparency were problematic given the absence of budgeting and accounting procedures. In response, mechanisms were established to ensure that all payments were directed through the Treasury to constrain the discretion of local governments. The reform included provisions for government to provide miners, their families, and their communities with adequate and timely information about the reform program, its implementation, their entitlements, and mechanisms for legal recourse during restructuring.

Internal accountability was strengthened as budget allocations were checked by several ministries as well as the Bank, and rules for internal processes, oversight mechanisms, and financial auditing were put in place. Floating loan tranches provided flexibility to reassess and respond to unanticipated issues and focused the attention of key government officials on the coal sector several times a year.

Participatory processes were created to improve accountability at the regional, local, and community levels:

- Social partnership mechanisms that included various groups of residents in coal regions were developed by strengthening the regional Inter-Agency Coal Commissions set up in 1994–95 and establishing commissions in coal regions that did not yet have them.
- At the local level, an association of mayors of mining cities was created and funded to bring mayors together to discuss impacts of reform and ways of enhancing local capacity.
- Oversight committees, including the local heads of administrations and representatives of various affected groups, were formed to plan, coordinate, and implement a local strategy for development, determine social protection for laid-off workers and residents of mining communities, and create guidelines for disbursement of funds for local programs.
- Workers, communities, and unions were also brought into the process as stakeholders. Two labor unions were awarded contracts of $400,000 each to promote workers' awareness of their rights and to engage in monitoring programs.
- Social impact monitoring was also conducted at the local level to monitor and assess the delivery of benefits and the impact of coal sector reforms on miners, their families, and mining communities. Federal government and Bank officials traveled to the field repeatedly to meet directly with workers.

Latvia Programmatic Structural Adjustment Loans

In the late 1990s, Latvia faced the difficult last stages of transition in which the lack of efficiency and effectiveness in government were the main impediments to achieving a full-fledged market economy and sustained economic growth. Latvia continued to have difficulty in privatizing the remaining large state enterprises, and the country's system of public administration continued to permit widespread corruption. The World Bank provided a Programmatic Structural Adjustment Loan (PSAL I, $40.41 million) to Latvia in 2000 to support the country's ongoing reform process.[6] PSAL I was intended to assist in the country's efforts to improve the credibility, efficiency, and effectiveness of the public sector in public service delivery; to support private-sector-led growth; to fortify the economy against external shocks; and to prepare Latvia for European Union (EU) accession by improving public sector management and reducing corruption. Over the three-year period, three programmatic structural adjustment loans were planned to support these reforms.

What Problems Did PSAL I Address?

Corruption
Recent Bank research has classified Latvia as a country with medium levels of administrative corruption and high levels of state capture. Inefficiency and corruption in the delivery of public services have undermined public welfare and disproportionately hurt the country's most vulnerable people, who cannot afford private sector alternatives. Excessive and corrupt regulation of the business community stifled private sector development, while evasion of regulations through bribery resulted in erosion of safety in the workplace, environmental degradation, and other negative effects.

Government agency proliferation and lack of accountability
During the 1990s, the government allowed the creation en masse of quasi-autonomous agencies with inadequate provisions for accountability and transparency with respect to resources used and services provided. This resulted in much informality, waste, and abuse, and was a significant source of corruption in the system and loss of control over budgetary resources. The government lacked a strategic planning framework that would allow overall policy commitments, the policy priorities of individual ministries, and targets to be linked with budget allocations. The public sector pay system was not transparent and did not ensure equal pay for equal work. Local governments lacked adequate accountability mechanisms as well.

What Accountability Mechanisms Did PSAL I Introduce?

The focus of PSAL I was on strengthening the credibility of public sector institutions; increasing the capacity of the state to manage resources efficiently and deliver services effectively; and rationalizing the boundary and relationship between the public and private sectors. PSAL I included mechanisms to improve both the social and internal accountability of the Latvian government.

Social accountability

Information disclosure and public access to information. The government passed the Law on Information Access in 1998, providing for openness and disclosure of government information, and adopted related implementation regulations in 1999. However, many government officials remain unaware of the implications of the law and regulations, and ministries do not yet have sufficient capacity to respond to information requests by the public.[7] To address this situation, the Cabinet of Ministers adopted regulations that stipulate more clearly the classification of information and the institutional arrangements for ensuring access to information.

The government has also set up a unit within the Ministry of Justice that will:

- Establish an *action plan* to: (a) build capacity in public sector bodies to respond to public requests for information; (b) report on compliance with the law; and (c) educate the public on procedures for obtaining government documents.
- Develop a *system for monitoring implementation* of the law, including: (a) a mechanism for measuring fulfillment of public requests for information; and (b) publication of these measures in public sector annual reports.
- Ensure that the *annual reports* of public sector bodies include information on: (a) rights of the public to information; (b) procedures for the public to access information; and (c) measures for fulfillment of public requests for information.

The inclusion of this information in the annual reports of public sector bodies has been institutionalized. The Cabinet of Ministers adopted an instruction on public sector annual reports that requires all public institutions, including regulatory bodies and inspectorates, to prepare an annual report on their activities, beginning in the year 2000. For this purpose, the government developed clear and simple guidelines for the content of annual reports, requiring them to have a greater performance focus. Ten regulatory bodies have implemented reporting requirements that include a regulatory impact assessment, and have designed and initiated a system for monitoring compliance with the requirements.

Anti-corruption efforts. In 1997, the government formed a Corruption Prevention Council, an interministerial body responsible for the development and implementation of an anti-corruption program. Under PSAL I, the government appointed an executive head of the secretariat to the Corruption Prevention Council and provided an adequate number of qualified staff and resources. To improve the council's transparency and accountability to the public, a regulation was put in place requiring that it publish the status of all measures identified in the anti-corruption program. The council has established and published mechanisms to monitor corruption and anti-corruption efforts and piloted them, although it has experienced some difficulty in effectively establishing its monitoring capacity. In addition, the council implemented procedures for the public to report on cases of corruption. Other government anti-corruption efforts included a Law on Political Parties, submitted by the Cabinet of Ministers to the Saeima, with provisions for transparency, oversight, and audit.

Civil society has also increased its involvement in the anti-corruption effort, particularly in related monitoring activities. Delna, the local affiliate of Transparency International, has prepared a report on progress made as a result of the government's anti-corruption program and is also monitoring the privatization process of the remaining large enterprises. This information is being released publicly and will contribute to monitoring the progress of the PSAL program and preparing future reforms.

Transparency in judiciary reform. In addition to other judiciary reforms, the minister of justice has drafted instructions to require that all court decisions and rulings be made public, and to provide greater transparency in communications between judges and litigants in criminal and civil cases.

Internal accountability

A series of reforms has also been introduced to improve accountability in government administration. These include professionalization of the civil service, increasing transparency and efficiency in public expenditure management, and addressing the issue of proliferation of government agencies.

Peru Programmatic Social Reform Loan

A Programmatic Social Reform Loan is designed to support the medium-term social reform program of the government of Peru.[8] Signed in June 2001, the Peru PSRL I focused on building the foundation for transparent and participatory resource allocation mechanisms, rationalization of expenditures, decentralized implementation, and systematic performance-tracking of social programs. The first loan ($100 million) was fully disbursed in July 2001 with funds going toward protection of critical social expenditures especially beneficial to the poor during a difficult period of fiscal adjustment and political transition. It laid the groundwork for medium-term reforms, including those that increase capacity for targeting and monitoring poverty alleviation programs and those that improve public access to information on social expenditures.

The second PSRL loan to Peru, under consideration by the World Bank Board of Directors in June 2002, will help consolidate the institution-building begun under the first, focusing on depoliticization of resource allocation and utilization, further elimination of program duplication, improvement of the safety net for social risks, and strengthening of social control by civil society.

What Problems Does the PSRL Address?

Peru does not have a strong tradition of evaluation or transparency in the planning and monitoring of poverty alleviation programs. Few programs in Peru have conducted rigorous impact evaluations, and the population is rarely involved in monitoring the use and impact of public resources.[9] In addition to this weak tradition, corruption is also a problem. The collapse of the Fujimori government and the allegations of different levels of corruption—from the use of public funds for campaign financing to scandals involving prominent members of public institutions—have resulted in widespread demand in Peruvian society for greater transparency. As a consequence, anti-corruption efforts have become a priority for both the transition and elected governments.

National Poverty Dialogues and Mesas de Concertación

In preparation for the transition in government and in response to a 1997 Poverty Assessment—which suggested that duplication and lack of synergies among development actors meant that further gains in poverty reduction were unlikely—the World Bank has been promoting a space for dialogue, exchange, and partnership in Peru. In 1998, with the agreement of other donors and eventually that of the government, the National Poverty Dialogue was established. The objective was to share experiences and information and promote better use of poverty reduction resources.

After three sets of decentralized, thematic poverty dialogues between 1998 and 2001, the National Poverty Dialogue became an institutionalized, plural forum. During the transition, the government—recognizing the need to institutionalize public debate and create country ownership of development strategies—issued a presidential decree, giving the forum longevity and promoting the decentralization of efforts through plural coordinating bodies called *mesas de concertación*. These are roundtables for dialogue and collaboration that include participants from local communities, civil society, local and national government, and the donor community.

What Accountability Mechanisms Does the PSRL Introduce?

Overall, the PSRL has helped to institutionalize transparent and participatory processes of resource allocation and performance-based tracking for social expenditures, enhancing the ability of poor Peruvians to exert influence and voice in the use of fiscal resources. The PSRL has also strengthened anti-corruption efforts and promoted the empowerment of civil society and the private sector while streamlining the public sector's role. Reforms under the PSRL include mechanisms to improve both social and internal accountability.

Social accountability
Participatory processes and public oversight. An integral part of reform under the PSRL is the participation of citizens and civil society in the review and monitoring processes related to social programs. The PSRL supports efforts to build the capacity of the *mesas de concertación.*

By 2001, 75 percent of regional department development plans were agreed to by the *mesas de concertación*. In January 2001, the Paniagua Administration established a Round-Table for Attacking Poverty (*Mesa de Concertación para la Lucha Contra la Pobreza*) whose mandate is to ensure that social policies and actions are transparent, efficient, and are effective in fighting poverty.

To further advance citizen scrutiny and oversight of public services, a "score card" system allowing for public evaluation of government services was piloted in a number of cities in 2001. In addition, 75 percent of public programs have implemented service quality evaluations that include public input. At the request of the Peruvian government, the World Bank launched a conference in July 2001 on empowerment and public accountability mechanisms to draw together international best practice and provide concrete suggestions for reform.

Anti-corruption efforts and transparency. One of the key initiatives of Peru's transition government is an anti-corruption program. The first PSRL supported an assessment of the types and areas of corruption and disseminated these results to the public and public officials. To complement its anti-corruption efforts, an Institutional and Governance Review consisting of an in-depth analysis of the incentive structures that have affected Peru's current institutional and governance system was conducted in 2001.

The National Ombudsman's Office undertook a well-publicized information campaign and established a complaint mechanism, including a hotline, to discourage the political use of social programs during the 2001 elections. Numerous bodies, including the ombudsman's office, the executive, and the Ministry of Women, adopted resolutions intended to guarantee the political neutrality of their staff and the programs they administer during the pre-electoral transition.

Public access to information and public oversight. Increased public access to information about the government's use of resources and the major poverty alleviation programs is also a priority of reforms under the PSRL. The Ministry of Finance launched the Economic Transparency Website (*Transparencia Economica*) in February 2001 to give the general public access to information on government transfers to social and other development programs. In addition, district-by-district expenditures and other transfers made by a number of social programs in 2000 are published on the Internet. For example, the National Complementary Food Program

(PRONAA) has published the transfers made to each of more than 15,000 soup kitchens around the country.

The government has also launched information campaigns to ensure that the public is informed about their rights as citizens. For example, a national campaign explaining the public right to information was launched in 2001 by the Public Ombudsman's Office.

Internal accountability

Monitoring of social agencies and programs. The PSRL has assisted the government's medium-term reform program by strengthening the capacity of social agencies and programs to plan and budget based on expected results, to monitor implementation, and to determine the impact that programs have had on critical dimensions of poverty.

With support from the first PSRL, the Ministry reached agreement with the leaders of major social programs, including the Social Investment and Compensation Fund, the National Complimentary Food Program, Caminos Rurales, the National Project for the Management of Watershed Basins and Soil Conservation, and the rural electrification program, on developing a monitoring strategy and evaluation guidelines for those programs that have not conducted a systematic ex-post impact evaluation in the last two years.

Public expenditure management. To improve public expenditure management, the government instituted Multi-Annual Sector Strategic Plans and a System of Integrated Financial Management (SIAF). The Multi-Annual Sector Strategic Plans introduce performance-based budgets, while SIAF tracks public income and expenditures and provides reliable information on a regular basis. The financial administration system was created in 1999 and has consolidated income and expenditure information from the approximately 559 executing units of various ministries at the provincial level.

In January 2001 SIAF was extended to the ministries of the Interior and Defense, so that these ministries' use of funds, formerly well-guarded information, will be tracked by the Ministry of Economy and Finance. The general public also has access to the system's information on budget transfers to social programs through the Economic Transparency Website mentioned above.

At the time of publication, the SIAF is not as accessible as it might be, due to the way information is presented, the lack of computer infrastructure below the provincial level, and the time it takes to log onto the central system. The second PSRL will support improvements in SIAF and its extension to a sample number of municipal governments as well as the development by the Ministry of Economy and Finance of an integrated plan to track all transfers from the central government to local governments.

Notes

1.   O'Donnell 2000; Fox 2000.
2.   World Bank 2001c, d, e, f.
3.   See Reinikka 1999, 2001; Tikare and others 2001. See also Tools and Practices 18.
4.   This section draws from Ghani 2001a, 2001b. See also World Bank 1996b, 1997a, 1997b, 2000d.
5.   An institutional intervention is one that changes the rules of the game to alter relationships among stakeholders, remove stakeholders, or introduce new stakeholders. A catalytic mechanism is one that requires an initial push to jump-start reform but then continues to function without further intervention.
6.   This section draws from World Bank 1996a, 1999, 2000a, b, c.
7.   On information access in Latvia, see Ericsson 1999; Lubbers, Milor, and Russell-Einhorn 2001.
8.   Katherine A. Bain contributed to this section. See World Bank 2001a, 2001b.
9.   The few exceptions in evaluation are the Social Investment and Compensation Fund (FONCODES) annual beneficiary assessments as well as the ex-post impact evaluations by FONCODES, Caminos Rurales, and the National Project for the Management of Watershed Basins and Soil Conservation.

Resources

Ericsson, Fredrik. 1999. "Access to Information in Latvia: Practice, Provisions, and Proposals." Prepared for the World Bank, Washington, D.C.

Fox, Jonathan. 2000. "Civil Society and Political Accountability: Propositions for Discussion." Paper prepared for the workshop on Institutions, Accountability, and Democratic Governance in Latin America, University of Notre Dame, Kellogg Institute, May 8–9. Available: http://www.nd.edu/~kellogg/

Ghani, Ashraf. 2001a. "Russia Coal Sector Reform." Presentation given at the workshop on Voices and Choices at the Macro Level: Participation in Country Owned Poverty Reduction Strategies, World Bank, Washington, D.C., April 3–5. Available: http://www.worldbank.org/participation/ghanippt_files/frame.htm

_____. 2001b. "Russia Coal SECAL." Paper prepared for the workshop on Voices and Choices at the Macro Level: Participation in Country Owned Poverty Reduction Strategies, World Bank, Washington, D.C., April 3–5. Available: http://www.worldbank.org/participation/ghanidoc.htm

Lubbers, Jeffrey, Vedat Milor, and Malcolm Russell-Einhorn. 2001. "Preliminary Report on the Public Sector Reform Initiative in Latvia." Prepared for the World Bank, Washington, D.C.

O'Donnell, Guillermo. 2000. "Further Thoughts on Horizontal Accountability." Paper prepared for the workshop on Political Institutions, Accountability, and Democratic Governance in Latin America, University of Notre Dame, Kellogg Institute, May 8–9. Available: http://www.nd.edu/~kellogg/

Reinikka, Ritva. 1999. "Using Surveys for Public Sector Reform." PREM Note 23. World Bank, Poverty Reduction and Economic Management Network, Washington, D.C.

_____. 2001. "Recovery in Service Delivery: Evidence from Schools and Health Centers." In Ritva Reinikka and Paul Collier, eds., *Uganda's Recovery: The Role of Farms, Firms, and Government.* Washington, D.C.: World Bank.

Tikare, Seema, Deborah Youssef, Rita Hilton, Paula Donnelly-Roark, and Parmesh Shah. 2001. "Organizing Participatory Processes in the PRSP." In World Bank, *Poverty Reduction Strategy Sourcebook.* Washington, D.C.: World Bank, Poverty Reduction and Economic Management Network. Available: http://www.worldbank.org/poverty/strategies/index.htm

World Bank. 1996a. "President's Report: Republic of Latvia Structural Adjustment Loan." Report P-7019 LV. Washington, D.C.

_____. 1996b. "President's Report: Russian Federation Coal Sector Adjustment Loan." Report P-6919-RU. Washington, D.C.

_____. 1997a. "President's Report: Russian Federation Second Coal Sector Adjustment Loan." Report P-7202-RU. Washington, D.C.

_____. 1997b. "Russia Coal Sector Adjustment Loan II." Project Implementation Document 5822. Europe and Central Asia Region, Energy Sector, Washington, D.C.

_____. 1999. "Latvia Programmatic Structural Adjustment Loan." Project Implementation Document 8581. Europe and Central Asia Region, Public Sector Management, Privatization Sector, Washington, D.C.

_____. 2000a. "Draft President's Report: Republic of Latvia Programmatic Structural Adjustment Loan." Washington, D.C.

_____. 2000b. "President's Report: Republic of Latvia Programmatic Structural Adjustment Loan." Report P-7352 LV. Washington, D.C.

_____. 2000c. "Reforming Public Institutions and Strengthening Governance: A World Bank Strategy." Public Sector Group, Poverty Reduction and Economic Management Network, Washington, D.C.

_____. 2000d. "World Bank Supports Russia's Coal and Forestry Sectors." News release 2000/059/ECA, September 13.

_____. 2001a. "Peru Programmatic Social Reform Loan (PSRL)." Project Implementation Document 10052. Latin America and Caribbean Region, Human Development Network, Washington, D.C.

_____. 2001b. "President's Report: Republic of Peru Programmatic Social Reform Loan." Report P-7447-PE. Latin America and Caribbean Region, Bolivia, Ecuador and Peru Country Management Unit, Human Development Network, Washington, D.C.

_____. 2001c. "President's Report: Uganda Poverty Reduction Support Credit." Report P7442-UG. Washington, D.C.

_____. 2001d. "Uganda's Poverty Reduction Support Credit." *Bank's World Today,* June 4. Available: http://ispace.worldbank.org/todayarchive/html/060401b.htm

_____. 2001e. "Uganda Poverty Reduction Support Credit." Project Implementation Document 9653. Africa Region, Washington, D.C.

_____. 2001f. "World Bank Approves First Poverty Reduction Support Credit." News release 2001/351/AFR, June 1. Washington, D.C.

Tools and Practices 6

Participatory Budgeting

Participatory budgeting is a process in which a wide range of stakeholders debate, analyze, prioritize, and monitor decisions about public expenditures and investments. Stakeholders can include the general public, poor and vulnerable groups including women, civil society, the private sector, representative assemblies or parliaments, and donors.

Participatory budgeting can occur in three different stages of public expenditure management:[1]

- *Budget formulation and analysis.* Citizens participate in allocating budgets according to priorities they have identified in participatory poverty diagnostics; formulate alternate budgets; or assess proposed allocations in relation to a government's policy commitments and stated concerns and objectives.
- *Expenditure monitoring and tracking.* Citizens track whether public spending is consistent with allocations made in the budget and track the flow of funds to the agencies responsible for the delivery of goods and services.
- *Monitoring of public service delivery.* Citizens monitor the quality of goods and services provided by government in relation to expenditures made for these goods and services, a process similar to citizen report cards or scorecards.[2]

Increased participation in budgeting can lead to the formulation of and investment in pro-poor policies, greater societal consensus, and support for difficult policy reforms. Experiences with participatory

This note was prepared by Laura Bureš, with input from Magui Moreno Torres, under the overall guidance of Deepa Narayan.

budgeting have shown positive links between participation, sound macroeconomic policies, and more effective government. Participatory budgeting processes have been utilized in a number of different countries, including Brazil, Canada, India, Ireland, South Africa, and Uganda. Three examples of participatory budgeting—in Ireland, Porto Alegre, Brazil, and South Africa—are outlined below.

Ireland's Social Partnership Agreements

Since 1987, Ireland has developed five "social partnership" agreements in which the government and a range of civil society organizations engage in extensive consultations on economic and social objectives.[3] The idea of social partnership developed in the mid-1980s in response to Ireland's recession (1980–87), high inflation, heavy public borrowing and deficit, and loss of manufacturing base. In 1986 the National Economic and Social Council (NESC) began facilitating consultations among a number of "social partners" in a process of shared learning to achieve an inclusive overview of socioeconomic options, challenges, and tradeoffs.

The first agreement (1987–90) had a narrow macroeconomic focus and was primarily geared toward negotiating wage levels in the public and private sectors with the central goal of maintaining public finance discipline and promoting competitiveness. The process encouraged consensus building and centered around the need for the country as a whole, in the aftermath of the recession and in order to meet Economic and Monetary Union (EMU) entry conditions, to avoid creating excessive inflationary pressure through exaggerated fiscal claims on the exchequer. Trade unions were key participants in negotiating pay levels, taxes, and social welfare benefits.

In 1990 NESC identified three critical elements for a consistent policy framework within a national strategy: (a) macroeconomic policy securing low inflation and steady growth; (b) evolution of incomes that promotes competitiveness and manages conflict over distribution; and (c) structural change to adapt to a changing external environment. The NESC argued, however, that the economic strategies being employed to meet EMU conditions would succeed only with the active consent and participation of those affected by the policies. The National Economic and Social Forum (NESF), established in 1993, was brought on board to address social policy issues such as inclusion and unemployment.

While the first three agreements focused more narrowly on economic matters, the fourth (1997–2000) and fifth (2000–02) were broader in scope. The latest social partnership agreement, "Program for Prosperity and Fairness," was launched in February 2000 and outlines a comprehensive set of economic and social objectives finalized through consultations between the government and civil society organizations from November 1999 to February 2000.

Results of the Social Partnership Agreements

Social partnership has been identified as a driving force behind Ireland's economic success over the last decade.[4] This success includes a number of achievements:

- In 1999, Ireland posted a budget surplus of more than 1.1 billion Irish pounds, compared with its 1.4 billion pound deficit in 1986. As a result, expenditures on health have been increased by 150 percent, on education by 84 percent, and on welfare by 70 percent since 1987.
- The exchequer surplus reached 747 million Irish pounds in 1998, compared to a 2.1 billion pound exchequer borrowing requirement ten years earlier.
- The national debt-to-GDP ratio dropped to 52 percent in 1998 from 120 percent in 1986.
- Average annual inflation, which had been as high as 20 percent in the early 1980s, has been 2.8 percent since 1987.
- Average annual GDP growth was 4.9 percent over the period and reached 9.5 percent in 1998.
- The stock of U.S. manufacturing Foreign Direct Investment (FDI) in Ireland doubled between 1994 and 1998 ($3.8 billion to $8.1 billion), and a third of American investment in Europe is now in Ireland.
- The unemployment rate dropped from 17.5 percent to less than 5 percent in 12 years.
- Inflation-adjusted pay rates rose by about 30 percent during the 1990s—two and a half times the increase for the EU and four times that of the United States.

While it is difficult to prove direct causality between the partnership agreements and Ireland's success since the late 1980s, the stability offered by these multi-annual policy and wage commitments has been instrumental in positioning Ireland as one of Europe's fastest growing economies—the so-called Celtic or Emerald Tiger. The partnership agreements have been credited for facilitating the country's participation in the European Monetary System (EMS) and EMU through prudent public finance management, maintenance of low inflation, low interest rates, credible exchange rates, and improved competitiveness. In addition to these tangible benefits, the partnership process has built social capital and trust as partners know they will be held accountable for their commitments and will meet again in future negotiations.

Social Partnership Participants and Process

Stakeholders included

Based at the Department of the Taoiseach (prime minister), the NESC includes representatives from government,[5] trade unions, business and employer organizations, farmers' associations, and, since 1996, community and voluntary organizations. There are 19 social partners in total, selected by government to represent the four "pillars" of Irish society.

- *Trade unions:* Irish Congress of Trade Unions;
- *Business and employer organizations:* Irish Business and Employers Confederation, Small Firms' Association, Chambers of Commerce of Ireland, Construction Industry Federation, Irish Exporters' Association, Irish Tourist Industry Confederation;
- *Farm organizations:* Irish Farmers' Association, Irish Creamery Milk Suppliers Association, Irish Cooperative Organization Society, Macra na Fierme;
- *Community and voluntary organizations:* Irish National Organization of the Unemployed, Congress Centers for the Unemployed, the Community Platform, Conference of Religious of Ireland, National Women's Council of Ireland, National Youth Council of Ireland, Society of Saint Vincent de Paul, Protestant Aid.

The participatory budgeting process

Although each of the social partnership agreements has been made through a slightly different process, the agreement process generally begins with the Department of Finance's economic forecast, which is submitted to the NESC. Over a one-year period, the NESC discusses with experts the issues and parameters laid out in the forecast and, with input from other reports on aspects of socioeconomic performance, draws up a strategy report, which becomes a background paper for discussion. Formal consultation between the government and the partners over a three- to four-month period then produces a new agreement, which is a compilation of endorsed "Operational Frameworks."

The government provides the forum in which the social partnership process takes place. It invites participants and sets the limits in which partnership structures operate. The government also serves as facilitator of the negotiations. Unlike a bilateral interaction, the consultative process involving diverse groups with different interests allows each party to present its position, listen to other positions, and adjust its stance. Ireland's social partnership has been called an exercise in multiparty negotiation; yet it is in many ways a thorough attempt at broad-based stakeholder participation because partners not only influence the outcome of the agreement but are also obligated to fulfill their part of pledges made in the negotiations. Thus both government and partners are accountable to the agreement.

Participatory Budgeting in Porto Alegre, Brazil

Beginning in the late 1980s, the Workers Party in Brazil sought to encourage democracy through popular administration of government.[6] After winning several municipal elections in 1989, the party, through the mayor's office, began an experiment in engaging a wide spectrum of citizens in formulating city budgets. The participatory budgeting process put in place in Porto Alegre involves bringing together citizens from different areas and interest groups to define expenditure and investment priorities for the government budget based on criteria accepted by the community. The process also includes citizen monitoring to determine whether the previous year's budget has been implemented according to policy.

Results of Porto Alegre's Participatory Budgeting

Results on the ground

Before 1989, Porto Alegre's finances suffered from the effects of deindustrialization, in-migration, indebtedness, and a poor revenue base. Since the introduction of participatory budgeting and the major fiscal reforms undertaken between 1989 and 1991, there have been significant improvements in Porto Alegre's finances and development. The achievements between 1989 and 1996 include:

- An increase in the percentage of households with access to water services, from 80 percent to 98 percent;
- An increase in the percentage of the population served by municipal sewerage, from 46 percent to 85 percent;
- A doubling of the number of children enrolled in public schools;
- 30 kilometers of road paved annually;
- A 50 percent increase in tax revenues, as a result of increased transparency in tax rates and payments received, which has encouraged payment of taxes.

Much of the credit for these improvements was given to the participatory budgeting process. An influential business journal nominated Porto Alegre four consecutive times as the Brazilian city with the best quality of life.

Increased participation

In Porto Alegre, the number of participants involved in the participatory budgeting process rose from fewer than 1,000 in 1990 to more than 14,000 in 1996. Including informal consultations, 100,000 people—almost 8 percent of the city's population—may have engaged in these participatory processes. Sixty percent of citizens across the state were aware of the participatory budget process. Across Brazil, more than 80 other cities are now following the Porto Alegre model of participatory budgeting.

The Participatory Budgeting Process and Institutional Mechanisms

In the Porto Alegre municipal government, the mayor's office serves as the executive, and the Chamber of Deputies as the legislature. Municipalities have considerable autonomy over their revenues—raised through local taxes, tariffs, and federal transfers—and their expenditures. The executive prepares the budget, which is then ratified by the Chamber.

Within the mayor's office, two institutions—the planning office (GAPLAN) and the Coordination of Relations with the Communities (CRC)—manage budgetary consultations with city residents. The CRC works with community leaders through regional coordinators to set up discussion assemblies and to aggregate community claims. GAPLAN reconciles citizens' demands with technical and economic viability.

The city is divided into 16 regions, and policy issues are grouped into five broad areas: transportation; education, leisure, and culture; health and social welfare; economic development and taxation; and city organization and urban development. For each region, there are two rounds of plenary sessions per year on each theme to discuss citizens' priorities. Following these smaller sessions, two mass assemblies are held yearly—one to monitor the previous year's expenditures in relation to budget allocations and one to identify priorities and elect representatives.

Citizens meet in March, before the first round of formal assemblies, to gather individual requests and concerns and to mobilize the community to select regional delegates. The municipality is not involved in these intra-community discussions. The first round of meetings between citizens and the mayor follows in April to review the previous year's investment plans, discuss new proposals, and elect people to the delegates' forums for upcoming deliberations.

Between the first and second rounds (March to June), informal preparatory meetings are held with various community organizations (unions, cooperatives, mothers' clubs) to discuss demands in different sectors. Demands are ranked on an ascending scale of 1 to 5, and are then aggregated by the executive along with points earned through two other criteria: need, as measured by how much access a region has had to a particular service; and population size.

The second round follows in July when two municipal town councilors are elected from each of the 16 regions, and two from each of the five policy areas, in addition to one member each from the civil servants' trade union and an umbrella organization of neighborhood communities. These councilors make up a 44-member Council of Participatory Budgeting (COP), which serves as the main participatory institution.

Councilors then familiarize themselves with the state of municipal finances, debate criteria for resource allocation, discuss their constituents' demands, and revise the budget proposal prepared by GAPLAN and the mayor's cabinet. For these purposes, the COP convenes weekly meetings until the end of September when a final budget proposal is submitted to the legislature. From September to December, the COP follows the debates in the chamber and lobbies the legislature while working on an investment plan that outlines allocations for specific public works by region. The mayor drives the COP process by coordinating meetings, setting the agenda, and presenting information before opening the forum to negotiation with the councilors. In the end, resources are divided through a weighting system that combines citizens' preferences with quantitative criteria.

The Women's Budget Initiative in South Africa

The Institute for Democracy in South Africa (IDASA) is an independent NGO dedicated to promoting sustainable democracy in South Africa. It was founded as the Institute for a Democratic Alternative South Africa in the 1980s to support democracy and address the polarization of black and white in the country. After the 1994 elections, the organization changed its name to the Institute for Democracy in South Africa and created the Budget Information Service (BIS) to analyze how the allocation and use of public resources affects the country's poor.[7] The BIS also addressed the issue of poor information flow between the government and citizens and sought to enhance the participation of Parliament and civil society in budget planning. A particular area of concern for IDASA and the BIS was the position of women, children, and the disabled, who comprise a large proportion of poor and vulnerable people in South Africa.

In 1995 the BIS convened a small group of interested individuals to discuss the possibility of creating a South African women's budget initiative. With the support of new parliamentarians, the Women's Budget Initiative was created as a joint project of the BIS, the Parliamentary Committee on the Quality of Life and Status of Women, and the Community Agency for Social Enquiry. The Women's Budget Initiative set out to analyze the country's budget with regard to its differential impact on women and men. Analyzing the budget through a "gender lens" is, in essence, a gender audit that examines whether public expenditures are allocated in ways that promote or hinder gender-equitable patterns of revenue and resource use.

Results of the Women's Budget Initiative

The Women's Budget Initiative has led to a gender budget exercise that operates within the South African government, and to the production of a gender-focused budget manual for government officials. The initiative has also inspired similar disaggregation analyses on the impact of the budget on other interest groups such as rural people, the poor, people with disabilities, and children. The Women's Budget Initiative and spin-off projects have been successful in expanding their networks, and the involvement of project researchers in key budgetary public policy work testifies to the impact of the Women's Budget Initiative on national policy formation. The success of the initiative has led to the adaptation of its gender analysis and advocacy work elsewhere in Africa, notably in Uganda.

Process, Institutional Mechanisms, and Participants

Development of the Women's Budget process
The Women's Budget Initiative began by analyzing the South African budget from outside government. It examined whether the budget addressed women's needs and made adequate provision (financial and otherwise) for implementing gender-sensitive policies. It also identified indicators to measure whether resources were used effectively in reaching intended targets and goals. The Women's Budget Initiative looked at both revenues and expenditures, taking into account the limited financial resources available. In areas where the analysis highlighted a need for greater budgetary allocation, it identified potential savings that could be realized by reducing expenditure in areas identified as subverting gender equity.

Within a year, a parallel initiative for a gender analysis of the budget was launched within government. The Select Committee on Finance instituted special hearings on women and invited presentations by the Women's Budget Initiative and other organizations. Gender analysis research was launched three days before Budget Day and presented to key stakeholders, including parliamentarians, NGOs, the media, and others, through plenary presentations and group discussions of sectoral findings.

Information dissemination
Since 1998, analysis developed by the Women's Budget Initiative has been disseminated through materials written in accessible, popular languages, including simplified translations of key sections. Materials have also been developed for workshops and training events.

Participants in the Women's Budget process
The Women's Budget analysis is undertaken by researchers from a range of NGOs and academic institutions, who are chosen for their expertise in particular sectors and in gender issues. A reference group, which includes parliamentarians, government officials, NGO members, and sectoral experts, supports the researchers. The reference group changes every year in order to draw in the widest possible range of experience and increase involvement in the initiative.

The roles and relationships of those involved in the Women's Budget Initiative have been critical to its success:

- *NGOs* provide the expertise and staff time to collect information and produce analysis.

- *Parliamentarians* provide access to information, maintain focus on salient political issues, and act as advocates in the government.
- *Government* provides the critical link to policy. Government is also expected to provide information on its activities and report its goals and the difficulties it faces in achieving them.

Focus of the Women's Budget

The first Women's Budget was produced in March 1996 a few days before the tabling of the national budget. It evaluated national budget departments in six sectors: welfare, housing, education, trade and industry, labor, and the Reconstruction and Development Programme. It also addressed two cross-cutting budget themes: public service and taxation and the socioeconomic profile of South African women.

The initiative published its second Women's Budget in the second half of 1997. It dealt with methodology, budget reform, justice, safety and security, correctional service, energy, home affairs and foreign affairs, transport, land affairs and agriculture, and health.

The third Women's Budget, published in August 1998, covered a broad scope, including budgeting on finance, public works, public enterprises and communications, arts, culture, science and technology, constitutional development, defense, water affairs and forestry, environmental affairs and tourism, and Parliament.

In the fourth Women's Budget, from 1999, gender-impact methodology was applied to three new areas: local government budgets, employment creation, and foreign donor funding of the public sector.

Notes

1.   This section draws on Tikare and others 2001. Also see the Participation Thematic Group website at http://www.worldbank.org/participation/

2.   See Tools and Practices 16 for more information on citizen report cards.

3.   This section draws on Government of Ireland 2000 and World Bank 2001a.

4.   See World Bank 2001a. This study cites opinions and findings from, among others, *The Economist* 2000; McCarthy 1999; O'Donnell 1999.

5.   Secretaries general from five key departments and independent, government-appointed experts.

6.   This section draws on Avritzer 2000; Baiocchi 1999; MOST Clearinghouse 2001; Santos 1998; World Bank 2001b.

7.   See the website of IDASA's Budget Information Service at http://www.idasa.org.za/bis/. See also the website of the International Budget Project of the Center on Budget

and Policy Priorities at http://www.internationalbudget.org. Information in this section also draws on Krafchik 2001.

Resources

Avritzer, L. 2000. "Public Deliberation at the Local Level: Participatory Budgeting in Brazil." Paper presented at the Experiments for Deliberative Democracy Conference, Madison, Wisconsin, January 13–16.

Baiocchi, G. 1999. "Participation, Activism and Politics: The Porto Alegre Experiment and Deliberative Democratic Theory." Draft. Madison, Wisconsin. Available: http://www.archonfung.net/papers/Baiocchi.pdf

The Economist. 2000. "Hot and Sticky in Ireland." July 29.

Government of Ireland. 2000. "Programme for Prosperity and Fairness." Department of the Taoiseach. Available: http://www.irlgov.ie/taoiseach/publication/prosperityandfairness

Krafchik, Warren. 2001. "Institute for Democracy in South Africa: Budget Information Service." Presentation given at workshop on Accountability of Public Institutions to the Poor: Participatory Approaches to Public Expenditure Management. World Bank, Washington, D.C., May 21.

McCarthy, Dermot. 1999. "Building a Partnership." In B. Reynolds and S. Healy, eds., *Social Partnership in a New Century.* Dublin: Conference of Religious of Ireland Justice Commission.

MOST Clearinghouse. 2001. "The Experience of the Participative Budget in Porto Alegre, Brazil." United Nations Educational, Scientific and Cultural Organization, Management of Social Transformations Programme. Available: http://www.unesco.org/most/southa13.htm

O'Donnell, Rory. 1999. "Social Partnership: Principles, Institutions and Interpretations." *EIRI Review* (November/December).

Santos, B. De Sousa. 1998. "Participatory Budgeting in Porto Alegre: Towards a Redistributive Democracy." *Politics and Society* 26 (4): 461–510.

Tikare, Seema, Deborah Youssef, Rita Hilton, Paula Donnelly-Roark, and Parmesh Shah. 2001. "Organizing Participatory Processes in the PRSP." In World Bank, *Poverty Reduction Strategy Sourcebook.*

Washington, D.C.: World Bank, Poverty Reduction and Economic Management Network. Available: http://www.worldbank.org/poverty/strategies/index.htm

World Bank. 2001a. "Case Study 1: Ireland, Participation in Macroeconomic Policy Making and Reform." Participation Thematic Group, Social Development Department, Washington, D.C.

_____. 2001b. "Case Study 2: Porto Alegre, Brazil, Participatory Approaches in Budgeting and Public Expenditure Management." Participation Thematic Group, Social Development Department, Washington, D.C.

Tools and Practices 7

Information Disclosure

Informed citizens are better able to take advantage of opportunities, access services, exercise their rights, and hold state and nonstate actors accountable. Disclosure of information about performance of institutions promotes transparency in government, public services, and the private sector. Rules on information disclosure must be institutionalized with the help of laws concerning rights to information and a free press. Dissemination of this and other information in a timely manner, presented in forms that are appropriate and easily understood, provides the basis for the emergence of informed civic participation.

Information disclosure and dissemination have in general been underestimated and underinvested; yet important and innovative efforts are taking place in this field. This note highlights initiatives in the following areas:

- The Freedom of Information Act in Romania;
- The Program for Pollution Control, Evaluation, and Rating in Indonesia;
- The public performance audit in Manila's Metropolitan Waterworks and Sewerage System;
- Information disclosure and dissemination practices in the Kecamatan Development Program in Indonesia;
- Private sector information disclosure: the case of Nike in Vietnam.

This note was prepared by Laura Bureš, under the overall guidance of Deepa Narayan.

The Romania Freedom of Information Act

In 1999–2000, the Romanian Academic Society conducted public opinion surveys on corruption in Bulgaria, Romania, and Slovakia that showed that corruption was a widespread problem in all three countries.[1] In addition, the surveys revealed that in Romania neither the media nor citizens (especially the poor) have access to government information. In response to these findings, the Romanian Academic Society built a domestic coalition in Romania of NGOs, media, and political organizations to advance a Freedom of Information Act (FOIA) bill.

The coalition came together quickly, as the society sent an e-mail message to the NGO community calling for an emergency meeting on the FOIA. In addition, the society immediately and widely published working papers on freedom of information acts in general and its recommendations for a Romanian FOIA. Calling the coalition meeting and publishing the related papers occurred in a tight five-day window in order to raise visibility and momentum for the bill.

In January 2001, the coalition succeeded in having all essential points of its proposal included in the FOIA endorsed by the new government and the political opposition. In October 2001, the law was officially passed and made public, with implementation in December 2001.

Freedom of Information Act Provisions

The FOIA calls for regulating access to public information and radically transforming administrative culture in Romania. Under the FOIA, all public agencies are required to set up a public relations/information office responsible for assembling and publishing official documents specified by the law in a timely and user-friendly format. Official documents include organizational charts, program budgets, policy decisions, internal regulations, and procurement and contracting records. Government offices must furnish a complete activity report of the previous year's activities. The FOIA requires a 24-hour turnover of information requested by the media and a 30-day turnover for citizen requests. Denial of requests can be appealed through the bureaucratic hierarchy or through the Administrative Court. No information can be classified without a public statement of justification, and the public retains the right to sue for declassification.

The Pilot Ombudsman Project

To assist in the capacity building of the government public relations (PR) offices, the Romanian Academic Society began a pilot project in 2001 employing local journalists to work with the PR offices and ensure due process. Together, the PR office and the local journalists promote transparency through intra- and interagency communication within the government, websites, newsletters, and local media broadcasts and publications. The project also calls for local NGOs and community organizations to act as ombudsman bodies, checking reports and filing complaints on behalf of citizens in the first years after the law is passed.

Indonesia's Program for Pollution Control, Evaluation, and Rating

Although public performance audits usually focus on improving public sector performance, similar programs can promote improvements by private entities whose activity would otherwise require costly enforcement or litigation. In the early 1990s, Indonesia suffered from acute pollution problems and a shortage of funding for environmental protection.[2] Indonesia's Environmental Impact Management Agency (BAPEDAL) found its limited monitoring and enforcement capacity insufficient to effectively combat industrial pollution. In response, the Deputy for Pollution Control, Nabiel Makarim, began developing the Program for Pollution Control, Evaluation, and Rating (PROPER) in 1993. With support from the World Bank, PROPER was introduced to the public in 1995.

How PROPER Works

The PROPER system was designed to receive pollution data from factories, analyze and rate their environmental performance, and disseminate this information to the public. The rationale was that providing information about pollution in a way that nonspecialists could understand would harness the growing power of the media and public opinion to promote cleaner industry. BAPEDAL hoped that environmental performance ratings would encourage communities to join in efforts to pressure local factories for improvements and would provoke financial markets to react negatively to companies with low ratings. PROPER was intended to draw negative attention to heavy polluters and to recognize good environmental performance so as to provide an incentive for factories to operate more cleanly than required by environmental regulations.

The rating system

BAPEDAL chose to begin with water pollution because the agency already had data on factories' compliance with water regulations. Knowing that the credibility of the PROPER program would depend on the reliability of its information, the agency sought assistance from the Environment, Infrastructure, and Agriculture Division of the World Bank's Policy Research Department in creating a data management system. The system included information on each factory's economic activities, emissions control equipment, and in-house pollution monitoring. In February 1995, the analysis team sent survey questionnaires to 350 factories, then supplemented the surveys with rigorous on-site inspections. The team used a computer model to translate all the information on a particular factory into a single performance rating.

Based on the government's evaluation of a plant's environmental performance, each plant was assigned a color rating (gold, green, blue, red, or black) by PROPER. A gold rating was reserved for world-class performers on environmental standards; a blue rating was given to factories in compliance with national regulations; black was given to factories that had made no attempt to control pollution and were causing serious environmental damage. Green and red were intermediate ratings: green meant that a plant was cleaner than regulations required but not a world-class performer on environmental standards, while red meant that a company was not in compliance with regulations but was not as bad a polluter as a plant with a black rating.

Information disclosure

In the first phase of the program 187 plants, representing 13 provinces and 14 industrial sectors with effluent discharge standards, were rated for their environmental performance. Five factories were awarded a green rating (no factory was rated gold), 61 were rated blue, 115 were rated red, and 6 were rated black. Under the threat of public disclosure, the plants with red and black ratings were given until December 1995 to improve their performance. In that month full disclosure began, as plants' color ratings, names, locations, managers, and parent companies were released to the media and the public. Information was released gradually to encourage sustained media attention.

Results of the PROPER Program

In June 1995, plants that were not in compliance with environmental regulations accounted for 65 percent of the total. After implementation of the PROPER rating system and the disclosure of results, the number of noncompliant plants was reduced to 47 percent of the total by September 1996. In addition, the number of firms in compliance with regulations increased by 50 percent over this period.

PROPER used public relations incentives to promote better environmental performance. Information collected from plant owners and other evidence suggests that the main reason for improvements in environmental performance was concern on the part of factory management about the possible negative response of local communities and markets to unfavorable PROPER ratings. The program also proved to be the means by which some factory owners first learned about the environmental performance of their plants. PROPER thus increased the environmental awareness of plant owners, managers, and employees, and citizens. PROPER also led BAPEDAL to increase its factory inspections and to improve the quality and reliability of its data collection and verification.

The information provided by the PROPER system empowered citizens in local communities to negotiate better environmental arrangements with factories. It also enabled firms with good ratings to advertise their performance and earn market benefits, allowed investors to assess environmental liabilities more accurately, and helped BAPEDAL regulators focus their limited resources on the worst offenders. BAPEDAL itself also became more transparent under PROPER and received greater public scrutiny.

Improving Performance of Municipal Waterworks in Manila

The public performance audit system in Manila—part of the Philippines Water Districts Development Project—was piloted in the Manila Metropolitan Waterworks and Sewerage System (MWSS), which was privatized in 1997.[3] The goal of introducing the audit was to test a new approach to furnishing citizens and service providers with transparent information on service quality, reliability, and satisfaction.

The public performance audit was intended to alter fundamentally the way service providers and consumers interact with each other. It was hoped that the project would spark private sector interest in entering long-term contracts with Philippine water utilities, which could in turn provide much needed investment, management expertise, and client-oriented service to improve overall service delivery and coverage. The audit's emphasis on transparency was also aimed at reducing the risk that corruption would undermine regulations. Lessons learned were then to be used to implement the system fully into the Metropolitan Waterworks and Sewerage System and extend it to other water utilities in the country.

Problems Addressed by the Public Performance Audit

In water districts and other water and sanitation utilities, consumers and local politicians had limited access to information on the relative performance of the utilities and the scope for performance improvements. These utilities also lacked a well-targeted, consistent, and transparent framework of economic regulation. Furthermore, there was limited capacity at the local level to develop proposals for private sector participation and to assess the merits of unsolicited proposals for private water and sanitation schemes.

The water sector's regulatory and institutional framework was the product of incremental and ad hoc policy decisions over many years, resulting in a high degree of fragmentation. Multiple institutions held regulatory power over the water sector, and their jurisdictions were overlapping and unclear. Transparency in the design and application of regulatory rules and in mechanisms for appeal of regulatory decisions was lacking. As a result, utilities lacked clear signals about the limits of acceptable performance; there was no systematic approach to the protection of consumers from potential monopolistic abuses by water and sanitation utilities; and potential private sector investors were discouraged by the high degree of regulatory uncertainty. The Water Districts Development Project provided technical assistance to the government to improve the regulatory framework.

The Public Performance Audit System

The performance audit component of the Water Districts Development Project financed technical assistance designed to pilot and field-test a privatized public performance audit system. The project was based on the idea that poor delivery of water and sanitation services in Manila would not improve until provider incentives changed.

Under the performance audit system, independent auditors monitored, evaluated, and publicly reported the performance of the two concessionaires using a format that could be easily understood by the public, the media, and congressional leaders. The audit provided timely and reliable information to enable consumers, community leaders, and the media to monitor the benefits of privatization of the metro Manila water and sanitation services. In addition, the consistent, accurate, and independent reporting provided by the system made the concession agreements less prone to litigation. The system also allowed sanctions against concessionaires to be more easily imposed, because shortfalls in service quality were clearly and publicly documented.

Public performance audit stakeholders

The performance audit system for Manila water and sanitation services was designed to meet the needs of several groups.

- *Consumers, the media, and community leaders* wanted a simple, credible index of performance to judge service delivery;
- *Regulators* needed service quality measures to set appropriate incentives for good performance;
- *Utility managers* needed similar information for efficient service operation;
- *Environmental authorities* needed wastewater measures to check for compliance with regulations.

Information provided by the audit system

The goal of the system was to provide all stakeholders with appropriate, accurate, and timely information about the quality and cost of water and sanitation services. Reporting covered three dimensions of service quality for end-users in each billing period:

- *Water quality*: Degree of chemical, physical, and bacteriological contamination

    Chemical: Toxics, heavy metals
    Physical: Suspended solids, transparency
    Bacteriological: Total coliform, fecal coliform

- *Reliability*: Water availability as a percentage of total time in the billing period
- *Pressure*: Open-tap flow pressure.

The audit reports in each billing period were prepared for consumers in each district. Service quality measures covered all three dimensions (water quality, reliability, and pressure), and reports for wastewater discharges covered only the water quality measures.

The audit system is based on sampling for cost reasons. The concessionaire provides its own measures on key points in the distribution system (pumping stations, large mains, wastewater from treatment facilities) for each billing period, while the audit contractor randomly selects and reports measures for a sample of the same points. Both the concessionaire and the audit contractor randomly sample a significant group of households and businesses in each period to establish comparable measures of end-user service quality. Thus random sampling by the contractor monitors self-reporting by the concessionaire. Misreporting of a quality parameter (defined as a statistically significant overestimation of quality) for an area can result in automatic assignment of an unsatisfactory status to service quality for that area for a specified period. The key to the system is benchmarking on accepted standards, with ratings assigned to degrees of positive or negative deviations from the benchmarks.

Results and Follow-up

Overall, the audit found that improvements in water distribution had occurred since privatization, with 33 percent of the 10,000 households surveyed rating service as better, 55 percent as the same, and 12 percent as worse. Areas for improvement include municipalities where new pipes were laid and where water improvement programs for depressed areas were carried out. Service quality was also found to need improvement, as over 50 percent of *barangays* showed poor ratings. Water quality ratings were consistently positive, but network quality (that is, hours of service) were rated as "needs improvement" in 11 out of 15 business areas.

A forum was held in the summer of 2001, bringing together representatives from water service providers, consumer groups, the NGO community, and government involved in the audits to present the results, raise awareness, and discuss follow-up action. The information gathered in the surveys was viewed as sending important signals to government and regulatory offices for translation into improved policies and service delivery to consumers. Water service providers emphasized that the information gathered from the surveys would enable them to better prioritize their limited resources in order to address problems identified by consumers.

It was also emphasized that unless the information generated in the surveys is presented clearly and in ways that consumers can understand, it runs the risk of being misinterpreted or of creating false expectations. The use of appropriate instruments and language in communicating the findings is thus important. Plans were put in place to present the performance results to municipalities in "Road Shows," make the data available for viewing at a "Performance Café" workstation to be located at MWSS facilities, on their website, and in concessionaire business area offices.

The Kecamatan Development Project

The Kecamatan Development Project (KDP) is a community empowerment initiative designed to alleviate poverty in rural communities and improve local governance in Indonesia.[4] It was initiated in August 1998 as a three-year program, through an IBRD loan of $228 million. The program targets the poorest kecamatans in Indonesia and finances village-level development projects.[5] As a result of its successful implementation, a second, four-year phase—the Second Kecamatan Development Project (KDP-2)—began as the three-year KDP ended in early 2002. The Project is receiving $325 million from the Bank for the second phase.

KDP's goal is to develop more democratic and participatory forms of local governance by strengthening *kecamatan* and village capacities and improving community participation in development projects. The program provides block grants to kecamatans and villages for small-scale infrastructure projects and economic activities. All KDP activities are geared toward enabling villagers to make their own choices about the kinds of projects they need and want. A particular emphasis of the program is information disclosure and dissemination.

Results of the Project

In its first year of implementation (1998–99), KDP assisted 105 districts across 20 provinces and funded about 6,000 village-level projects, including roads, bridges, irrigation and clean water facilities, and economic loans for small businesses. By the end of the second year (1999–2000), the project was reaching 727 kecamatans and 11,325 villages. As of June 2001, more than 12,000 poor villages had participated in KDP, out of a total of 67,500 villages in Indonesia. The program has reached a beneficiary population of almost 10 million.

During the project's first two years, 75 percent of the funds were used to build economic infrastructure such as roads (62 percent of all economic infrastructure projects), bridges (10 percent), irrigation (8 percent), and clean water (7 percent), while the remaining 25 percent of funds was used for economic activities. Economic infrastructure built through KDP's participatory methods have cost as much as 30 percent less than traditional approaches used in the same places.

The benefits in fighting poverty have been considerable. A sample of kecamatans that were included in the first year found that 60 percent of all participants in project meetings were poor, and 40 percent were women. Nearly 5 million people received wage payments in the program's first year. Ex-post reviews show average rates of return of 30 to 40 percent to rural infrastructure built through the program, nearly all of which is captured by villagers. The project generated 4 million person-days of labor in the first year. Because the project sets wages below the local agricultural minimum, almost all of these wages have been paid to the poor and vulnerable.

Program Activities

Analysis of KDP activities shows how they are structured to enable informed community choices, local accountability, and inclusion, and are greatly assisted by a well-developed strategy for information disclosure and dissemination.

Institutional set-up

Responsibility for the project lies with the Department of Home Affairs. The program operates through elected local governments rather than through line agencies in order to make a systematic commitment to administrative decentralization in Indonesia. The core of the project's institutional arrangements lies in the relationships between the kecamatan and village levels. Already existing in each kecamatan was a Kecamatan Council of Village Heads (UDKP), bringing together the village head and leader of the village council (LKMD) from each village in the kecamatan. Under the project, villages send three additional representatives, two of them women, to the council; this was viewed as a way to introduce more transparency and accountability in the UDKPs, as well as more gender balance.

To leverage and strengthen community capacity, the project supports two facilitators per village, who are selected by the village and trained by the project, and employed for seven months of the year. Their main role is to disseminate project information to village groups (especially marginalized groups), though in some areas they do assist in developing projects. They also organize village and UDKP meetings and supervise project implementation. In addition, the project supports a facilitator in each kecamatan and another in each kabupaten (district). The kecamatan facilitator assists in a range of activities, such as helping in project design, establishing and handling bank accounts, and overall coordination. Facilitators help communities build linkages with other organizations, particularly government agencies.

Project identification and design

A village project identification and planning process selects a maximum of two projects. After being reviewed for technical feasibility by local experts, proposals are submitted to the UDKP, for discussion. The project has an "almost open" menu (only a few possibilities are excluded, such as religious buildings and environmentally damaging projects), so prioritization decisions are scarcely affected by project design criteria. Ostensibly, projects are prioritized according to three criteria: overall impact, poverty impact, and technical and financial feasibility. In practice, however, these criteria are left quite vague, so the UDKP prioritizes and approves projects according to its own criteria.

Contracting, implementation, and operation

To encourage local accountability, villages do their own subcontracting for projects whenever possible. They receive cash from the project, and pay contractors in cash. Project implementation is ultimately the responsibility of the villages, with support and supervision by project facilitators at the kecamatan and (to a lesser extent) kabupaten levels. Similarly, the village council (LKMD) monitors implementation. The village is also responsible for planning and funding the operation and maintenance of the facility, which, depending on the type of project, may be done in cooperation with local government.

KDP Information Disclosure and Dissemination

Information dissemination

Disclosure and dissemination of information about KDP take place in several ways. Workshops are held at the provincial, district, and kecamatan levels to disseminate information, raise awareness, and generate interest in the program. These workshops include community leaders, local government officials, local media, universities, and NGOs. At the village level, information is shared orally by facilitators through meetings and informal discussions as well as in writing through pamphlets, posters, manuals, and information boards. Information boards post information regarding KDP principles along with key data on types of projects to be funded, costs, progress, and expected dates of completion. On average, about 50 to 100 villagers attend the large village meetings, though in some places attendance often reaches several hundred participants.

These methods of information dissemination are supplemented by additional and unique efforts to share information about KDP. In Pugeran village, Gondang Kecamatan in East Java, facilitators found that few villagers were reading the information board. They found spreading information orally to be more effective, especially before or after the weekly Muslim prayer meetings in each neighborhood and at the regular skills training group for women. In Edera Kacamatan, Papua, the local parish priest became very interested in KDP and began disseminating information about the program in his weekly sermons. He also began placing public information boards in the front yards of churches, because the information boards in public areas were often damaged by vandalism. In the Sampang District of East Java, religious holidays can last for a few months at a time, and community members do not attend meetings at the town hall during these holidays. The facilitator in Camplong therefore began attending all of the village's celebrations and presenting KDP information there.

Information disclosure for monitoring and evaluation

Several monitoring mechanisms are in place. At the village level, village governments (LKMD and village leaders) monitor projects. There is an incentive for community self-monitoring because the failure of a project to fulfill obligations disqualifies the whole village from projects for the following year. This rule is widely publicized, creating strong accountability pressures and performance incentives for local leadership. Annual lists of kecamatans participating in the program have been disclosed by posting them on a website, which is monitored by a number of NGOs. At the province level the project has begun to hire and train journalists, local NGOs, and universities as third-party project monitors. At the national level, journalists have been contracted to write stories on the project and are given training and transport costs to visit

KDP sites. In addition, the project's performance indicators have included contracts with a host of professional journalists who provide independent reporting on site visits to KDP areas.

Lessons learned in information strategies

According to an August 2000 survey of 444 Kecamatan facilitators, 56 percent (from 250 kecamatans) reported that the information boards were functioning. A number of reports have shown that information boards have not been kept up to date, are not very interesting, or are not read by the communities, in part due to the problem of illiteracy. For the second and third years of the program, efforts were made to improve information, education, and communication by disseminating information in styles and formats more tailored to the intended audiences and users, especially community members in KDP areas. The current KDP project is conducting an ongoing evaluative review of the media used to convey information in villages, which will contribute to the information disclosure and dissemination plans of the Second Kecamatan Development Program. The Second KDP also includes an action plan for integrating gender into the program, which calls for identifying local, specific, and acceptable ways of disseminating information to women.

To further improve information disclosure and dissemination in the second phase of the program, much of the work of KDP facilitators will consist of finding and disseminating information—about available government programs, standards for projects, technical problem solving, and support for contract enforcement. Project financial information will be registered in district budgets and records. Kecamatans will prepare an "accountability speech" for the district parliament summarizing the accomplishments and faults of KDP projects. Province-based independent monitoring by NGOs and the media will be continued and expanded. The program will maintain its support of an aggressive transparency, advocacy, and disclosure program through the media, which will publish annual implementation summaries and release all audits, an official transparency policy, and assistance to community-based advocacy on disclosure.

Private Sector Information Disclosure: Nike in Vietnam

International information campaigns linked to industrial labor and environmental practices are powerful tools for holding multinational corporations accountable to local communities. In the case of a Nike Inc. subcontractor in Vietnam, an international information campaign was instrumental in improving labor and environmental practices.[6]

The Tae Kwang Vina Factory

In 1998 Nike Inc. was the world's leading producer of sports shoes and clothing, with sales reaching $9.6 billion. The company was also a leader in global outsourcing of production and, in fact, owned none of the factories that produced its shoes. In Vietnam, Nike factories (five in all) were owned by Korean and Taiwanese subcontractors and employed 35,000 people.

The Tae Kwang Vina Company was a subcontractor of Nike Inc. in Dong Nai Province. The Tae Kwang factory in the Bien Hoa 2 Industrial Estate employed about 9,200 workers, mostly women, who worked 11 hours a day, six days a week, for salaries of about $40 a month. Most of the factory's workers were recent immigrants to the province, and many had left farms for the factory. During the summer, workers sweated in a one-room plant about the size of a football field in over 100-degree heat. They were exposed to toxic solvents and glues used in the manufacture of Nike shoes, which caused dizziness and nausea. Many workers suffered from respiratory ailments, and accidents occurred in the more hazardous sections of the plant. In addition, workers were subjected to verbal and physical abuse by managers. Tae Kwang was known as a bad place to work, and most workers tried to avoid working there if they could.

Dong Nai government officials considered the factory "uncooperative" and claimed that their requests to Tae Kwang were ignored. Regulation of companies like Tae Kwang was difficult because of Vietnam's desire to attract foreign capital while establishing effective regulatory policies and enforcement mechanisms. Tae Kwang had avoided complying with national requirements for a wastewater treatment plant as well as other environmental regulations. The factory burned all of the scrap rubber from its production process to generate steam, which produced clouds of black smoke. Despite the government's requests that the plant reduce the pollution, Tae Kwang purchased additional scrap rubber from other Nike factories in Vietnam. In addition, the factory hired the son of the chairman of the Communist Party in the province to provide connections and act as a "problem solver" with the government.

Difficulties in Initiating Change at the Local Level

Because the factory was located in the middle of an industrial zone, no one officially lived near it; as a result, there was virtually no local community to complain about the problems. The people most affected by Tae Kwang's practices were the workers, and they had little power to influence the company. The union in the factory was controlled by the company, and all of its worker representatives were chosen by management. The surrounding community had little capacity, cohesion, or linkages to external actors. Furthermore, because so many of the factory's workers were recent immigrants to the province and usually stayed less than two years, the residents of the surrounding area felt little connection to Tae Kwang workers.

External Information Disclosure and Pressure

As a result of this situation, efforts by local government officials and community members proved ineffective in changing Tae Kwang's practices. However, Nike has been influenced by a range of external pressures. Networks of NGOs in the United States and Europe have had some success in pressuring Nike and Tae Kwang to improve production practices. Some of these efforts have involved using the media to educate the public about conditions in Nike factories; others have called for boycotts of the company's products, and still others have lobbied governments to force Nike to change. NGOs have also assisted in building the capacity and linkages available to factory workers and community members.

Activist campaigns targeting labor practices and conditions in Nike factories have received worldwide media attention. In October 1997, civic groups from more than 10 countries organized protests and information campaigns about Nike's production practices. In April of the following year, the effort spread to more cities in Europe and America. Fueling these information campaigns and protests were a CBS television report in October 1996 on the working conditions in Vietnamese factories, subsequent research and publicity by the Vietnamese Labor Watch, and a *New York Times* report in November 1997 that was based on research by Dara O'Rourke for the United Nations Industrial Development Organization and on a leaked Ernst & Young audit of Tae Kwang.

One of the most important players in the effort to pressure Nike and Tae Kwang to improve labor and environmental practices was the

Vietnamese Labor Watch, headed by Thuyen Nguyen and based in Washington, D.C. Mr. Nguyen and the organization began monitoring the Tae Kwang factory in 1996, meeting with workers, shoe manufacturing executives, labor union officials and representatives, and legal and foreign investment experts. The information collected was then shared with other labor and environmental NGOs, activists, and the media, and was posted on the Vietnamese Labor Watch's website.[7]

Mr. Nguyen and the Vietnamese Labor Watch gave out prepaid calling cards to factory workers at Tae Kwang and contacts around the community, so that they could call him in Washington and report problems. When such a report was made, the Vietnamese Labor Watch could then use its connections with media outlets to draw attention to the problem. In one case, a worker who was being physically abused called Mr. Nguyen on the calling card, and Vietnamese Labor Watch then arranged for a film crew to go to Tae Kwang. Within a day, the film crew had recorded abuse at Tae Kwang on videotape and distributed it to cable outlets. The calling cards proved to be a very effective though informal way of getting information about factories to the activist community and the media, and demonstrated the rapid work and influence of transnational networks.

Results of External Information Disclosure and Pressure

At Tae Kwang, these external pressures have spurred regular visits to the factory by Nike's labor and environmental inspectors as well as monitoring by third parties in accounting, health, and safety firms. The first target of these inspections was worker exposure to toxic solvents and glues. In May 1998, Nike announced a major initiative to eliminate the use of organic solvent–based cleaners and glues and pledged to comply with U.S. workplace laws in all of its factories. By December of that year, workplace health and safety conditions were much improved at Tae Kwang. Now, pressure from Nike, driven by external NGO and media pressure, is making a larger impact on the reduction of air pollution and workplace hazards at Tae Kwang than local government or community efforts had been able to achieve.

The activist community also put pressure on Nike to disclose information about its operations and the locations of its factories, information that Nike had never before released. Beginning in the fall of 1999,

Nike began disclosing information about its operations and factories in response to this pressure. The company has also begun posting audits of its factories online. The activist community has not been entirely satisfied with the disclosure of these audits because Nike has been releasing summaries rather than full audit documents; however, Nike has made great strides in information disclosure as a result of the pressure. In fact, the company provides an example of self-reinforcing disclosure and accountability: as Nike discloses information, activists put more pressure on the company to improve its standards and practices.

Nike began working toward improving its labor and environmental standards in the early 1990s, and created its code of conduct in 1992. After the attention on Tae Kwang and other factories in the mid- and late 1990s, Nike stepped up efforts to monitor factories through quarterly internal inspections by the company's own production staff (called "Safety-Health-Attitude of Management-People Investment-Environment" inspections, or SHAPE). Monitoring also included periodic visits and inspections by the Nike labor practices staff, inspections and tests by outside health and safety specialists, and the independent audits mentioned above. Nike has also created "Transparency 101," which publishes action plans and progress reports on the Nike website in response to results of the company's external and internal monitoring.

Nike has joined the Global Alliance for Workers and Communities, which conducts independent research on the attitudes and aspirations of factory workers, including those working in Nike contract factories in Indonesia, Thailand, and Vietnam.[8] Based on the results from such a study in Indonesia, Nike has developed a remediation plan and has begun implementing it with the company's Indonesian factory partners.

Notes

1.   This section is based on Government of Romania n.d.; Mungiu-Pippidi 2001a, 2001b.

2.   This section draws on Afsah, Laplante, and Wheeler 1996 and 1997; Afsah, Laplante, Shaman, and Wheeler 1997.

3.   This section draws on Renardet S.A. and Louis Berger Group 2001; World Bank, 1997a, 1997b, 1999, 2001c.

4.   This section draws on de Aenlle 2001; National Management Consultants 2000; World Bank 1998a, 1998b, 2000, 2001a, 2001b.

5.   Kecamatans are the subdistrict level of administration in Indonesia; each kecamatan includes approximately 20 villages and a population of more than 50,000 people.

6.   This section draws on Global Alliance for Workers and Communities 2000; O'Rourke forthcoming; O'Rourke and Brown 1999. For further information, see the following websites:

http://www.saigon.com/~nike/index.html

http://www.saigon.com/~nike/reports/report1.html

http://www.nikebiz.com/labor/index.shtml

http://web.mit.edu/dorourke/www/

7.   http://www.saigon.com/~nike/

8.   See http://www.theglobalalliance.org

Resources

Afsah, Shakeb, Benoit Laplante, and David Wheeler. 1996. "Controlling Industrial Pollution: A New Paradigm." Policy Research Working Paper 1672. World Bank, Development Research Group, Washington, D.C.

_____. 1997. "Regulation in the Information Age: Indonesian Public Information Program for Environmental Management." World Bank, Economics of Industrial Pollution Control Research Project, Development Economics Unit, Washington, D.C.

Afsah, Shakeb, Benoit Laplante, David Shaman, and David Wheeler. 1997. "Creating Incentives to Control Pollution." _DEC Notes_ 31. World Bank, Washington, D.C.

de Aenlle, Conrad. 2001. "Small Loans Go Far in Indonesia." _International Herald Tribune_, May 8.

Global Alliance for Workers and Communities. 2000. "Global Alliance Gives Asian Workers a Voice." Press release, September 6. Available: http://www.theglobalalliance.org/content/press2.cfm

Government of Romania. n.d. "Law Regarding Access to Public Information." Draft. Ministry of Public Information, Bucharest.

Mungiu-Pippidi, Alina. 2001a. "For an Institutional Approach to Post-Communism Corruption: Analysis and Policy Proposal Based on a Survey of Three Central European States: Romania, Bulgaria and Slovakia." Paper presented at Bertelsmann Conference on Accountability, Bucharest, May 3–5.

_____. 2001b. "'Selling' Good Governance: An Eastern European Experience." Presentation at the World Bank, Washington, D.C., May 23.

National Management Consultants. 2000. "Kecamatan Development Program: Second Annual Report, 1999/2000." Prepared for the KDP National Secretariat, Jakarta.

O'Rourke, Dara. Forthcoming. "Community-Driven Regulation: Towards an Improved Model of Environmental Regulation in Vietnam." In Peter Evans, ed., *Livable Cities: The Politics of Urban Livelihood and Sustainability.* Berkeley: University of California Press.

O'Rourke, Dara, and Garrett Brown. 1999. "Beginning to Just Do It: Current Workplace and Environmental Conditions at the Tae Kwang Vina Nike Shoe Factory in Vietnam." Available: http://www.globalexchange.org/economy/corporations/nike/vt.html

Renardet S.A. Consulting Engineers and the Louis Berger Group, Inc. 2001. "Pilot Public Performance Assessment Project: PPA Final Stakeholders Forum." Summary Report of Final Stakeholders Forum of the Pilot PPA Project, Quezon City, Philippines, June 15, 2001. Prepared for Republic of the Philippines, Metropolitan Waterworks and Sewerage System, Regulatory Office.

World Bank. 1997a. "President's Report: Philippines Water Districts Development Project." Report P-7122-PH. Washington, D.C.

_____. 1997b. "Staff Appraisal Report: Philippines Water Districts Development Project." Report 16526-PH. Washington, D.C.

_____. 1998a. "Indonesia Kecamatan Development Program." Project Implementation Document 6343. Washington, D.C.

_____. 1998b. "Project Appraisal Document: Kecamatan Development Project." Report 17397-IND. Washington, D.C.

_____. 1999. "Philippines Water Districts Development Project." Project Implementation Document 4903. Washington, D.C.

_____. 2000. "President's Report: Kecamatan Development Project." Report P7421IND. Washington, D.C.

_____. 2001a. "Indonesia: Demonstrating the Impact of Community Empowerment." *Bank's World Today,* June 26. Available: http://ispace.worldbank.org/todayarchive/html/062601b.htm

_____. 2001b. "Project Appraisal Document: Second Kecamatan Development Project." Report 22279-IND. Washington, D.C.

_____. 2001c. "Manila Public Performance Audit." Seminar, Manila, February 22. Available as online video: http://www.worldbank.org/ wbi/B-SPAN/sub_manila.htm

Tools and Practices 8

Decentralization Strategies for Empowerment

Many countries are undertaking some forms of decentralization by shifting fiscal, political, and administrative responsibilities to lower levels of government. Decentralization is driven by unique circumstances in each setting. In some countries it is linked to recent democratization, while in others it is spurred by the failure of central government to deliver basic public services. The four elements of empowerment put forward in this paper—access to information, inclusion and participation, accountability, and local organizational capacity—are often integral components of successful decentralization.

In some countries, particularly those in the Europe and Central Asia Region, central governments have decentralized responsibilities to local governments for another reason: to reduce national fiscal deficits. By pushing expenditure functions down to local governments while retaining centralized tax bases, governments maintain macroeconomic balance; yet service delivery often declines due to underfunding. In these cases, the decentralization agenda is unlikely to achieve benefits unless it is modified to empower local governments through greater resources and a sound intergovernmental framework, and empower people so they can hold their local governments accountable.

The idea behind decentralization is that moving decision making closer to people will lead to public sector decisions that better reflect

This note was prepared by Jennie Litvack and Tripti Thomas.

local needs and priorities. This in turn will lead to greater efficiency in public expenditures, improved governance, and greater equity. These results, however, are by no means automatic or easy to achieve. Efforts to decentralize usually stop at the local government level and often go no further than the provincial or state level. Decentralization is unlikely to achieve its theoretical impact unless it extends down to the population, permits informed input in public decisions, and motivates local government to respond to this input. Further, as noted below, although empowerment can help achieve benefits of decentralization and vice versa, these processes are only part of an effective poverty reduction strategy. There remains a strong role for central governments in ensuring adequate funding and incentives that target the poor, along with a legal framework that enables them to live securely.

Ukraine: The People's Voice Program

After decades of centralized control, Ukraine has begun exploring ways in which bottom-up accountability can improve governance, but the country has moved haltingly with regard to decentralization. A pilot initiative introduced in 1999, with support from the World Bank and the Canadian International Development Agency (CIDA), demonstrates how greater citizen participation at the municipal level can lead to better service delivery and higher public satisfaction. Called the People's Voice Program, this effort responds to the problem of insufficient public participation and control in the policymaking process, perceived as one of the major constraints to advancing reform in Ukraine. The program is being implemented along two fronts: (a) helping selected Ukrainian cities to improve their service delivery to households and businesses; and (b) strengthening the capacity of citizen groups and officials to interact with each other in order to strengthen the overall quality of governance in these cities.

Ternopil and Ivano-Frankivsk were the first two Ukrainian cities chosen for the pilot. Under the supervision of a local NGO, the International Centre for Policy Studies, surveys were conducted in both cities among households, the business community, and public officials to identify the key problems associated with major services, and to identify the public's priority service needs. The information gathered from the surveys, which included data on corruption, was widely distributed through the local media, public discussions, and NGOs, putting pressure on local leaders to respond to specific criticism and open channels for greater participation. Meanwhile, intensive technical assistance and training were provided to municipal officials and agencies to strengthen their capacity to listen and respond to citizen demands. Open budget hearings were introduced, task groups were set up to address the most pressing problems, and community advisory boards and working groups were established.

The results of this greater participation have been very encouraging. Better informed and mobilized community groups now play active roles in public hearings that affect critical local public decisions. Certain demands such as the reform of public education have emerged as priorities for communities in both cities. In Ivano-Frankivsk, NGOs, parents, and education officials have come together to develop proposals to improve the local education system. An interesting innovation has been the establishment of "service centers," one-stop shops where citizens can pay for all municipal services and will soon be able to file and monitor responses to their complaints. In response to the survey in Ternopil, a gender audit of regional and local government policies, practices, and services was undertaken to ensure equitable inclusion of women. As a result of the wide consultations around the audit, community clusters have emerged to focus on issues such as women's health. Other citizen working groups have formed around sectoral concerns such as housing and business development. The capacity of NGOs to raise awareness, facilitate public hearings, monitor and participate in service delivery, and become self-sufficient is also being enhanced.

The program has relied heavily upon the involvement and commitment of the city mayors and local officials. In fact, it was their initial interest and commitment that prompted the selection of Ternopil and Ivano-Frankivsk as the first pilots. These officials are now highly motivated to respond to this newly expressed citizen voice. As part of the program, a second round of surveys will be conducted in both cities to measure changes in citizen satisfaction with the public sector. In Ivano-Frankivsk, bimonthly surveys are planned for particular services.

It is expected that mayors in other cities in Ukraine will be held up to the standards set in Ternopil and Ivano-Frankivsk. In the summer of 2001, two more cities, Kupyansk and Chuguiv, conducted baseline surveys. The models developed from these four pilots will be used as the basis for expanding the program further to interested cities in Ukraine and for demonstrating to the central government the potential merits of decentralization to participatory local governments.

Guinea: Investment in Rural Government to Improve Service Delivery

Seventy percent of Guinea's population lives in rural areas, including about 87 percent of its poor, a situation exacerbated by a quarter-century of command and control dictatorship between 1958 and 1984.[1] Despite political changes in 1984, which emphasized decentralization and established 33 urban and 303 rural development committees (CRDs), the ensuing decade saw little improvement in rural poverty. Participation by rural citizens and provision of services to their localities remained low. In the mid-1990s the government recommitted itself to poverty alleviation and conducted an extensive participatory, bottom-up, strategic planning effort. Civil society representatives from across the country participated in these consultations and helped place the following priorities on the country agenda: rural development, basic education, primary health care, local entrepreneurship, and good governance.

As a follow-up to these consultations, in 1999 the Bank prepared two complementary five-year Adaptable Program Loans to support the government in its reform program: a Village Community Support Project ($22 million) to engage local communities directly, and a Capacity Building for Service Delivery Project ($19 million) to enhance public sector capacity (at both the prefecture and national levels) to respond to these communities. Taken together, these programs will help foster a range of governance, fiscal, and administrative reforms, which aim at the end of 10 to 15 years to achieve an 80 percent increase in access to and quality of all services to rural areas.

The combination of these two efforts represents a bottom-up/top-down approach that is at the heart of creating sustainable, meaningful empowerment through decentralization. The bottom-up strategy entails promoting active participation of beneficiaries in the choice and delivery of needed services. To this end the program involves an extensive public information program, as well as the establishment of administrative and financial management and information systems at the prefecture and community levels to ensure the transparent use of resources. Also included are budget tracking and citizen satisfaction surveys to stimulate transparency and participation. Participation is also being encouraged by improving communication between public officials and citizens at the point of service delivery, particularly by developing local organizational capacity in the form of parent-teacher associations, health center management committees, and farmers' groups.

The top-down effort has several components. In order for citizen groups to participate meaningfully in public decisions, responsibilities and resources need to be clearly assigned to different groups (such as levels of government and service providers). This initiative includes a revision of the framework governing roles and responsibilities of different levels of government under decentralization, and the establishment of decentralized delivery and management systems at the prefecture and CRD levels. Under a pilot initiative, some CRDs will be able to keep head taxes within their locality. Furthermore, as an initial step in increasing direct access of rural communities to the national fiscal authorities, these head tax resources will be matched by direct transfers of budgetary and donor funded resources from the center.

To reflect the growing shift in accountability to rural communities, a performance incentive system is being introduced to reward high-performing CRDs and public officials at the prefecture and central level on the basis of beneficiary satisfaction with services. Elected CRD councils are being made more representative, and Prefecture Development Councils are being established with membership elected by and accountable to CRDs, to advise on programs and budget tradeoffs across CRDs. Prefects will eventually be responsible to these elected bodies for ensuring that local service needs are met.

Mbabane, Swaziland: Two-Way Communication

Mbabane, Swaziland offers another example of how decentralization can lead to increased empowerment. Over the past few years, local authorities in Mbabane have encouraged reforms to improve municipal services and increase citizen satisfaction with public sector performance. Information dissemination has been a notable element in this endeavor. The Mbabane city council has launched a website to publicize its policies and programs and to make accessing government services more user-friendly. Information about programs to upgrade informal settlements has been disseminated through radio, print, and even street theater. In an effort to gather views on the provision of municipal services, the city council has conducted surveys of citizens, the business sector, and city employees, and has strategic plans to follow up on survey results. The city council has also established a network of outreach facilitators to encourage input from community members and groups, particularly in the context of the urban upgrade project.

As a result of these developments, transparency in public processes and accountability of local authorities is increasing. The demand for accountability is further enhanced by the devolution of tax bases, which enables Mbabane to support almost two-thirds of its budget from its own local taxes. The city council presents an annual report (available to the public) and makes information on its programs and financial flows available to citizens through community meetings, the press, and its website. Photographs of each city council member are included in the annual report, increasing the sense of personal answerability. The largely elected city council (last elected in 1998) and the indirectly elected mayor will face an increasingly informed and empowered citizenry in subsequent elections.

Philippines and Uganda: Limited Information Hampers Citizen Influence

A recent in-depth study of decentralization and governance in Uganda and the Philippines evaluated how well the different elements of empowerment were being implemented in these countries and what the impact was on delivery of social services.[2] One of the most interesting findings of the study is that independent sources of local information play a key role in enabling effective participation. In both countries, citizens were less informed about local government than about national government. While citizens in both countries rely on the media for information about national politics and corruption, they rely largely on community leaders (in Uganda) and personal contacts (in the Philippines) for such information at the local level. Econometric analysis confirms the importance of access to the media by indicating its association with better education and health care.

In addition to weak local information leading to less effective participation, local accountability is weak because officials have very limited authority to respond to local needs. Although local leaders perceive the needs of their citizens more accurately than higher-level leaders do, the reliance on earmarked transfers leaves them little scope for responding to these needs.

Decentralization: A Qualified Measure for Empowering Poor People

S ome observers have argued that decentralization reduces costs and improves targeting. Local governments and administrators are likely to have better information about local conditions and people and are thus better able to identify local households in need. Such outcomes depend on several factors, including the level of government involved, political institutions (for example, rules of the electoral system), community characteristics (including ethnic diversity, income inequality, historical and cultural factors, and so forth), and the design of the poverty program. An exciting research agenda is currently underway in the Bank's Development Economics Unit to better understand the conditions that affect the ability of programs to reach poor people in decentralized settings.

Many of the benefits of decentralization seem most likely to be achieved when decisions are made at the local level, and least likely when decision making rests at the provincial level. Local-level decentralization can lead to greater participation, more effective local decisions, better development strategies, and improved service delivery. However, if strong channels of accountability do not exist, citizen voices are unlikely to be effective even if they are heard. Even in a perfect democracy with full participation of all citizens and strong accountability of locally elected officials, decision making is unlikely to benefit the very poor and marginalized if they are a minority in the local population. Although some countries have modified their electoral rules to ensure participation by women and minority groups, this has had mixed results. In decentralized settings, decision making may be captured by the elite, and it is generally likely to favor the majority. Thus, decentralization has limitations for certain very poor groups and there remains an important role for the central government in ensuring safety nets for them, as well as an overall governance structure that provides security.

A recent careful study of Vietnam's decentralized poverty programs illustrates the need for central government to play a continued strong role.[3] Vietnam's poverty programs have expanded considerably over the past decade and have relied on administration by provincial authorities. However, since they have lacked national norms for identifying the poor across regions, and have not consistently measured or monitored local needs, there is little sign that poor people or poor communes are being targeted. Data analysis indicates that the poorer provinces are less effective at targeting their poor than are wealthier provinces. Given that growing urban-rural disparities and risks that vary by community or area (such as natural disasters) are significant components of the national poverty profile, targeting of national programs by province is a problem. Thus increasing information and participation in this situation would likely have minimal impact.

Conclusion

While there are certainly places where empowerment has made effective decentralization possible, and decentralization has facilitated empowerment, actual outcomes depend on a host of details that differ from case to case—community characteristics, local institutions, the type of decentralization, and the mechanisms of empowerment (related to information dissemination, citizen participation, group formation, and accountability). Decentralization and empowerment are partner concepts. Together they have the potential to aid the development process, particularly for the poor, yet the challenges in better understanding them as they occur in each specific context remain large.

Notes

1. This section draws on World Bank 2000.
2. Azfar, Kahkonen, and Meagher 2001; World Bank 2001.
3. Van de Walle 2001.

Resources

Azfar, Omar, Satu Kahkonen, and Patrick Meagher. 2001. "Conditions for Effective Decentralized Governance: A Synthesis of Research Findings." University of Maryland, Center for Institutional Reform and the Informal Sector (IRIS), College Park, Md.

Van de Walle, Dominique. 2001. "The Static and Dynamic Incidence of Vietnam's Public Safety Nets." Processed. World Bank, Development Economics Research Group, Washington, D.C.

World Bank. 2000. *Reforming Public Institutions and Strengthening Governance: A World Bank Strategy.* Poverty Reduction and Economic Management Network, Public Sector Group, Washington, D.C.

_____. 2001. "Decentralization and Governance: Does Decentralization Improve Public Service Delivery?" PREM Note 55. Poverty Reduction and Economic Management Unit, Washington, D.C.

Tools and Practices 9

Community-Driven Development

Community-driven development (CDD) is broadly defined as the process of giving control of development decisions and resources to community groups. Communities can be geographical entities, such as urban neighborhoods or rural villages, or groups with common interests, such as water user associations, parent-teacher associations, herders, members of a microcredit society, or women's groups. Once formed, these groups typically work in partnership with support organizations and service providers—local governments, the private sector, or NGOs—to develop and implement projects that meet their immediate priorities in education, health, sanitation, transportation, resource management, economic activities, and other livelihood issues.

CDD can be divided into four practice areas:[1]

- *Enabling environment:* Development of policy and institutional reforms oriented toward increased control of decisions and resources by community groups and/or by participatory elected local governments.
- *Participatory elected local governments:* Elected local governments make decisions on planning, implementation, operation, and maintenance in partnership with community groups.
- *Community control and management of investment funds:* Community groups make decisions on planning, implementation, operation, and maintenance, and manage investment funds.

This note is based on contributions from Philippe Dongier, Daniel Owen, Andrea Ryan, Talat Shah, Idah Z. Pswarayi-Riddihough, and Deepa Narayan.

- *Community control without direct management of investment funds:* Community groups make decisions on planning, implementation, operation, and maintenance, without directly managing investment funds.

This note first presents evidence of CDD success, and follows with four case studies:

- Malawi Social Action Fund
- Zambia Social Investment Fund
- Romania Social Development Fund
- Tunisia Northwest Mountainous Areas Development Project

Evidence of CDD Success

Experience has shown that CDD can make poverty reduction efforts more demand-responsive, increase efficiency and effectiveness, and enhance sustainability. The World Bank has undertaken both project-based and regional studies to assess CDD success in reducing poverty and improving livelihoods. An internal analysis of World Bank projects in Africa in 1994–97, for example, showed that 75 percent of projects with some level of community participation were rated satisfactory, compared to 60 percent of all projects carried out Africa during that period.[2] At the same time, only one-fifth of participatory projects in Africa were rated "sustainable," pointing to one of the major concerns around CDD practice.

As the following brief examples show, CDD approaches can be applied in widely varying contexts and address varied problems.[3]

Forest Management in India

During the 1980s, an average of 18,000 forest offenses were recorded annually in the state of Gujarat: 10,000 cases of timber theft, 2,000 of illegal grazing, 700 fires, and 5,300 other offenses. Twenty forestry officials were killed in confrontations with communities and offenders. In response, an experiment in joint management with communities was initiated. The strategy included community meetings, widely publicized creation of forest protection committees, and profit sharing in which 25 percent of timber returns went to local groups. As a result, conflicts between officials and community groups diminished, community groups assumed responsibility for patrolling forests, and productivity of land

and returns to villages increased sharply. In one year, one village of 88 households harvested and sold 12 tons of firewood, 50 tons of fodder, and other forest products, while also planting and protecting teak and bamboo trees.

Water Supply in Côte d'Ivoire

A national rural water supply program established community water groups that managed the maintenance of 13,500 water points, reducing breakdown rates from 50 percent to 11 percent at one-third the previous cost. The shift to community-level maintenance was achieved by taking away the responsibility for rural water supply from the sector agency, supporting private sector involvement in spare parts distribution, retraining technicians, and signing contracts with village groups and the water directorate for management of water pipes. The results were more sustainable in those villages that had high demand for the rehabilitated water point and in which community organizations already functioned well.

Nutrition in India

A community-based nutrition outreach program in 9,000 villages in Tamil Nadu reduced severe malnutrition in the state by one-third. Twenty women interested in health issues were hired in each village as part-time nutrition educators accountable to the communities they served. With skills and networks developed through participation in the program, these groups of women, formed initially to "spread the word," became entrepreneurs, branching off to start food production activities on their own. Earlier programs focusing only on the creation of health infrastructure had been unable to make any difference in the nutritional status of children.

Integrated Community Development in Brazil

The FUMAC project in northeastern Brazil delegates decision making for state approval of subprojects to project municipal councils, 80 percent of whose members are potential beneficiary associations and civil society groups. A study found that the subprojects executed by local contractors or communities cost 20 to 30 percent less than those executed by municipalities or government contractors. Furthermore, 95 percent of project funds are reaching targeted beneficiaries, who are mostly landless.[4]

Following are more detailed reviews of community-driven development initiatives in Malawi, Zambia, Romania, and Tunisia.

Malawi Social Action Fund

L aunched in 1996 with a total investment of $71 million over five-and-a-half years (World Bank $56 million), the Malawi Social Action Fund (MASAF) focused on alleviating rural poverty through community-based action. Targeting the 60 percent of the population that is considered poor, MASAF was the lead strategy for the Government of Malawi's Poverty Alleviation Program. Closed in December 2001, MASAF provided funding to communities for the upgrading and construction of community infrastructure such as schools, health facilities, community water points, rural-urban markets, and granaries.

MASAF II, funded for 1999–2003 at $70 million, was designed to respond to the fact that the most disadvantaged groups did not benefit significantly from the first round of MASAF financing, mainly because of the limited ability of these groups to organize themselves and approach MASAF directly. In order to better serve these groups, MASAF II partners closely with intermediary NGOs and community organizations that are already working with underserved populations to develop and support subprojects specifically designed for groups including orphans, street children, persons with disabilities, the elderly, and people affected by HIV/AIDS.

Program Achievements

The majority of projects—79 percent, or 656 projects—carried out under MASAF II are in the education sector.[5] Thirteen percent are in the water sector; 4 percent are in the infrastructure and communications sector, covering roads, bridges, and post offices; and 3.7 percent are in the health sector. Rapid progress in project implementation has meant that disbursement of all funds for community subprojects was completed three years ahead of schedule.

The program has had significant impacts in the communities where projects have been undertaken. For example, when communities controlled the type of projects they chose and implemented, they tended to select projects that better matched community needs and interests. Many communities have opted for projects such as small dams, wood lots, and water tanks. Others have identified civilian police units as a priority, to check high crime rates and protect property. Few top-down development schemes would have taken note of this preference, or even been aware of the urgent need of poor people for better policing.

Economic rates of return for subprojects have ranged from 15 percent for secondary education projects to 50 percent for boreholes, far ahead of the 10 percent standard for projects deemed "successful." Construction costs have been lowered sharply through local participation and contracting—by as much as 20 percent in the case of boreholes, for instance.

The gender impacts of the program have been quite significant, as women have benefited from increased participation and better access to services and incomes. An average of 30 percent of Project Management Committee members are women, including a significant number who hold leadership positions such as treasurer or secretary. In education, gendered impacts include higher enrollment rates and lower dropout rates and reduced attrition of older girls, helping to delay the age of marriage. Women's access to health care (especially maternal care) has improved where health facilitates have been constructed, and emergency health care has improved due to better roads built by the project. In terms of employment, MASAF has created 1,350 jobs for women, 26 percent of the total 5,111 jobs made available by the project.[6]

MASAF II and Community Empowerment

MASAF is the first social fund in Africa that empowers communities to choose projects and also gives them the responsibility for implementation, contracting, and accountability. Communities identify local priorities, contribute 20 percent of the project cost, and receive matching funds from the central government and donors. The Project Management Unit manages the day-to-day operations of the project, including appraisal and approval of subprojects and supervision of operations at the zone level. In the "Community Contracting" approach, individual subprojects are identified, executed and managed by a Project Management Committee (PMC), which is elected by and composed of community members and responsible for subproject finances. Communities also have the freedom to choose their own subproject facilitators—either NGOs or technical experts—rather than have facilitators chosen for them by the central management office.

Using a learning-by-doing approach, the program is addressing participant complaints about the project, most commonly involving delays in disbursement of project funds. Delays in releasing tranches have often halted subproject implementation for long periods of time, causing contractors and wage laborers to lose interest and money. Such delays are usually due to poor financial reporting by communities and/or delays in the processing of financial reports at the project management level. Even those PMCs that have undergone the necessary training have found it difficult to complete the required financial reports.

Access to information

The project includes an information, education, and communication (IEC) component geared to generate public support for the project and disseminate project information widely.[7] Through radio messages, posters, bus advertisements, and personal contacts, prospective stakeholders are given a clear understanding of the norms of the project, the roles they are expected to play, and their responsibilities in project implementation.

Dissemination of this information has brought about a distinct change in the relationships between poor communities on the one hand and NGOs and government district extension staff on the other. Communities have made it clear to NGOs that the communities themselves will make final decisions in choosing, designing, and implementing projects. Community attitudes toward the district administration have changed from passive acceptance of whatever is handed down to active participation in ensuring that the administration's extension staff deliver on their responsibilities in project management and implementation.

Within communities, where elites traditionally are seldom challenged, free access to project information has opened the way for pointed questions to local authorities regarding the use of funds, the quality of materials purchased, the selection of contractors, and many other community concerns. Members of Parliament who attempt to influence procurement or contracting have been, for the most part, kept at bay by the communities.

The most significant impacts of this free flow of information are better working relationships between stakeholders and increased trust. Adversarial relationships have in many cases been replaced by growing respect. For example, the fact that the project has a gender focus has been communicated widely, prompting women to insist that they should be part of project subcommittees and encouraging their active participation in decision making regarding the community's priority needs.

Accountability/enforcement

Several mechanisms to ensure accountability have been incorporated into the project design. First, Project Management Committees are democratically elected by the communities to promote accountability to their constituents in managing the implementation of subprojects. Community auditing and inter-community exchange visits enforce the accountability of the PMC to the communities at large. Also, a monitoring and evaluation system tracks the level of participation, particularly of women, in community projects, and assesses project impact on female beneficiaries. It is primarily the Project Management Committee and not the larger community that is involved in contracting and procurement, as well as supervision during implementation. In nearly all of the communities visited for the assessment, PMC members see themselves as accountable to MASAF and not necessarily to the larger community. Community leaders do not feel it is their role to actively provide oversight to the PMC.

The matching grant approach ensures that communities own the projects to which they have contributed and increases their incentives to ensure effective project management and implementation. Disbursement of funds is done in tranches of 30, 40, 20, and 10 percent, enabling good performers to be rewarded and bad ones penalized. Communities see the tranche system as both a negative and positive feature. While some PMCs note that tranching allowed them to gradually build their expertise in handling large sums of money, others consider it a burden, noting that delays in project implementation are most often linked to late disbursements. However, while decreasing the number of tranches would greatly reduce the administrative burden on both the community and the MASAF administration, it would also reduce community oversight and control.

Zambia Social Investment Fund

The Zambia Social Investment Fund (ZAMSIF) was launched in May 2000 with a commitment of $130 million, the third social investment fund for Zambia following the largely successful Social Recovery Projects (SRP) of 1991–2000.[8] ZAMSIF represents a shift from its precursors, in that it emphasizes community-driven development set within a framework of strengthened local government. Over a span of ten years (2000–2010), ZAMSIF aims to upgrade skills in the country's 57

District Councils, creating elected local bodies with assured sources of income. ZAMSIF's major innovation is a district graduation program, which rewards districts that achieve performance benchmarks with additional resources.

Project Components

ZAMSIF incorporates three major components:

The *Community Investment Fund* finances small projects for basic infrastructure (education, health, rural water supply and sanitation, roads); natural resources management projects; capacity building, basic skills training, and other activities to stimulate local productivity; and special programs targeting vulnerable groups (orphans, people with HIV/AIDS, and so on). Subprojects are identified, prepared, implemented, managed, and maintained by the community. Communities contribute roughly 15 percent of the cost of each project in cash, in kind, or as a combination. There are five levels of increasing district participation in the project cycle, corresponding to various levels of responsibility and involvement. At the final stage districts are expected to be able to perform all steps of the project cycle.

The *District Investment Fund* aims to strengthen districts' own facilitation of community-based development and strengthen the planning, management, and implementation capacity of local authorities and community members. It finances larger infrastructure investments that benefit more than one community, such as district health facilities and marketplaces. District authorities are expected to gradually take the lead in planning, managing, and financing such projects, initially by managing resources allocated on a project-by-project basis, and eventually by managing a district allocation grant. ZAMSIF is targeting investments in districts with the worst social and poverty indicators, focusing on strengthening the accountability of district staff to poor communities.

The *Poverty Monitoring and Analysis* (PMA) component aims to improve the sustainability and usability of poverty data collection and analysis. The component also finances a range of activities to strengthen the institutional, technical, and financial framework for monitoring and use of poverty information. This includes support for the development of pilot District Data Banks.

ZAMSIF and Community Empowerment

The community investment component of ZAMSIF has substantially increased decentralization of decision making and devolution of responsibilities to local levels. Further, there is a critical shift in emphasis, from community intervention as a "project" to community intervention as an ongoing opportunity for social development and increased access to information. Hence, the process of community-managed development is not tied to time-bound delivery of inputs or outputs under a micro-project, but focused on a process of community empowerment. Assistance for a community's development efforts is expected to continue with or without ZAMSIF support, and the program supports capacity-building activities that aim to encourage this.

Under ZAMSIF, the emphasis is no longer on outputs or achievements measured against targets, but on the *outcomes* of project activities. Indicators of success have changed from, for example, number of classrooms constructed to broader social and human development gains such as school attendance, teacher-pupil ratio, women's participation, and so forth. ZAMSIF's monitoring system now collects information on these outcomes, with communities taking part in monitoring the outcomes of their projects themselves. To ensure that vulnerable groups participate in and benefit from projects, communities identify these groups and take steps to involve them in decision making about the project. Activities that address their specific needs are included in the project design.

Between July 2000 and June 2001, ZAMSIF received 222 proposals and approved 72 projects countrywide, with a commitment of $6.3 million under the Community Investment Fund component. Education projects made up more than half of those financed, with a total of 44 projects receiving $3.8 million. Other projects were in the categories of health (15), water and sanitation (8), infrastructure (4), and food security (1). To reach more communities, ZAMSIF has simplified its guidelines for accessing support and has translated these guidelines into the seven major local languages.

Access to information
ZAMSIF promotes access to information about the project through information sessions with communities given by trained facilitators or NGOs, dealing with such topics as the environment, HIV/AIDS, and gender. The intent is to redress the imbalance in information access faced

by poor and isolated communities, and to catalyze new community projects to address these issues. To further project promotion, ZAMSIF is using both radio and print materials to reach communities. Future outreach plans include providing communities implementing projects with wind-up radios and encouraging them to form radio listening groups. The project will also provide pamphlets and leaflets on HIV/AIDS to every community-managed project.

In July 2001 ZAMSIF concluded an intensive nationwide awareness program that involved a series of radio programs in English and the seven major local languages and a television documentary about the project. In addition, project staff conducted "awareness workshops" at the provincial and district levels to ensure that the people for whom the project was designed knew how to access ZAMSIF funds. Information workshops were also held for members of Parliament as they are an important conduit of information to communities. Project staff noted that inquiries from communities seeking support from ZAMSIF regional and central offices increased significantly after the provincial, district, and other awareness workshops.

To support the dissemination of research and resources on poverty, a Poverty Monitoring and Analysis (PMA) Resource Center has been established at project headquarters as a "one-stop shop" for researchers, policymakers, and the public to obtain poverty-related data and resources. The PMA resource center has registered more than 120 consultants on its database, including specialists in environment, poverty, social policy, drought, food security, education, health, and gender. The resource center is also making key documents available to poverty researchers and practitioners. ZAMSIF is designing and preparing to launch a website for the PMA component that will allow the public to access most documents online.

Local organizational capacity

ZAMSIF is training 13 regional facilitators to enhance the participation of communities in all stages of the project cycle. With skilled facilitation, the quality of community participation is improving, giving voice and power to all in a community.

Communities build capacity through three mechanisms: (a) *learning by doing*, with development of manuals for project management and advice offered by district and ZAMSIF staff during implementation; (b) *training modules*, delivered by trained facilitators using participatory techniques and adult learning methods, covering topics such as HIV/

AIDS, gender sensitization, environmental appraisal and management, procurement, financial management, equipment maintenance, and so on; and (c) *skills training* for community members in, for example, home-based care, counseling, entrepreneurship, health care, and veterinary care, and other appropriate community-based services.

Accountability

Through the District Investment Fund, special attention is given to financial management and accountability. Each district is allocated a specific amount of money, based on poverty and deprivation indices, and these figures are widely known at the local level. The rate at which the district funds are used depends on how well the district administration facilitates, plans, manages, and coordinates district development. As districts improve their capacity, the benefits to the district improve. In this way ZAMSIF aims not only to build the capacity of district staff but also to improve their accountability in relation to the communities they serve.

Romania Social Development Fund

The Romania Social Development Fund (RSDF) was established in 1998 as an independent, nonprofit organization with a twofold objective: to improve the livelihood of poor rural communities and disadvantaged groups, and to increase social capital in beneficiary groups by strengthening levels of trust and organizational and self-help capacities. Using the RSDF mechanism, poor communities take the lead in articulating their priorities and in designing and implementing demand-driven subprojects. Communities are eligible to receive funding for small-scale infrastructure subprojects, community-based social services, and income and employment generation activities, with beneficiaries expected to contribute amounts equivalent to 10 to 15 percent of RSDF grants to the project.

To complement these activities RSDF provides technical assistance for increasing local organizational capacity. In the process of implementing projects, communities not only satisfy their specific urgent needs, but also increase their ability to identify and prioritize needs, to mobilize and manage resources, and to design, implement, operate, and maintain their own projects. Total RSDF funds are approximately $45 million, comprising a $20 million IBRD loan (in two phases), a Romanian government contribution of $5 million, and approximately $20 million from other donors.

Program Achievements

After two years, initial outcomes from the RSDF are encouraging:

- 1,332 subproject applications were received, of which 833 have been appraised. Of these, 290 projects were awarded funding, including 195 infrastructure projects, 56 income generation projects, and 39 community-based social service projects.
- 48 villages received "facilitation," a process that helps them determine their own assets and needs and express them collectively.
- 233 community-based organizations from villages and 21 NGOs working with disadvantaged groups have been trained in RSDF project management regulation, accounting, and procurement procedures—a step toward increasing local organizational and self-help capacity.

A beneficiary assessment completed by the project in 2000 indicates that RSDF funding has directly contributed to increased quality of life in beneficiary communities. It has also bolstered communities' confidence in their ability to address local issues themselves and increased social capital by strengthening social interaction and trust. For example, 83 percent of polled villagers who participate in RSDF projects say they are "relatively content" or "very content" about relationships among the inhabitants of the village, versus 72 percent of polled villagers not participating in RSDF projects. In contrast, the 1998 public opinion barometer showed that 57 percent of polled people were relatively or very content with other villagers.

Similar increases were reported for trust: 44 percent of polled villagers participating in RSDF projects say they trust other people, versus 33 percent of polled villagers not participating in RSDF projects. In contrast, a 1999 public opinion poll showed that 31 percent of the sample believe that most people can be trusted and the 1998 public opinion barometer showed 25 percent trust.

Program Design

Targeting

RSDF targets poor communities and, within these communities, particularly disadvantaged groups. First, poverty maps are used to identify poor counties and regions of Romania. Poor communities are then identified according to specific criteria including isolation, lack of normal access to safe water, lack of electricity, lack of railway facilities, distance to school for school-age children, and distance to a medical doctor for the majority of the villagers. Next, eligibility criteria are used to target disadvantaged groups within the communities—typically drawn from populations of children, women, and the elderly—who cannot satisfy their basic needs through their own efforts. Criteria include lack of access to universal social assistance programs and lack of assistance from family members or informal social networks. The RSDF uses intermediaries, such as NGOs, local authorities, and community-based organizations, to assist with identification and mobilization of disadvantaged groups. The types of services offered to these groups and the low subproject financing ceiling also ensure that only the poorest will be encouraged to apply.

Eligible activities

Eligible communities may receive RSDF funding for the following activities:

- *Small-scale infrastructure*, maximum RSDF grant of $75,000. This comprises small-scale rehabilitation/repair, upgrading and building works for the provision of social infrastructure such as local water supply, latrines, sewerage, and community centers, and economic infrastructure such as roads and bridge repair. A minimum contribution of 10 percent of the RSDF grant is expected from beneficiaries either in kind or in cash.
- *Community-based social services*, maximum RSDF grant of $20,000. This includes services, shelters, and life skills development for children; home care for disadvantaged elderly; shelters or services for the homeless; and legal assistance services for accessing all social protection programs. NGOs working in partnership with local authorities provide these services. Community groups are asked to contribute up to 5 percent of the RSDF grant.
- *Income-generating activities and employment opportunities*, maximum RSDF grant of $20,000. To strengthen the capacity of productive groups in poor communities, funds are provided for technical assistance, institutional support, business skills training, and assistance in network building and strengthening. Activities include processing and marketing wood, wool, fruits,

vegetables, milk, meat, or other locally available raw materials; producing and marketing handicrafts; market and storage facility rehabilitation; solar tents and greenhouses; and community bakeries. A minimum contribution of 15 percent of the RSDF grant is expected from the production group.

Role of RSDF

Identification, design, and implementation of subproject activities are managed directly by communities and disadvantaged groups. RSDF supports these efforts but limits its role to the following activities:

- Promoting and disseminating information on the activities and eligible subprojects, as well as helping target beneficiaries and disadvantaged groups to identify their needs and design subprojects;
- Designing the assessment, selection, and approval mechanism for subprojects submitted by the target beneficiaries;
- Concluding the grant agreement with the beneficiary representatives;
- Making disbursements for subproject implementation;
- Supervising and evaluating subproject implementation;
- Assessing the execution of the grant agreement through audits.

RSDF and Community Empowerment

In transitional economies, community-driven approaches such as those adopted by the RSDF present a distinct set of challenges. The philosophy of RSDF is directly contrary to the historically top-down command organization of economies and societies in the Eastern European region. Through its operations, RSDF promotes the formation and development of the kind of bottom-up informal associations that have traditionally been stifled in these countries. RSDF helps to create an enabling environment for communities to mobilize their resources and increase their physical and human capital, producing self-sustaining institutions within the communities and enhancing physical and social welfare.

Access to information

A facilitation process has been developed as an integral component of the project. The main objectives of facilitation are to inform poor rural communities about RSDF subprojects, opportunities, and eligibility criteria, and to enable them to organize and submit high-quality subproject proposals. At the same time, facilitation seeks to increase the participation of community members in the decision-making process, develop local problem-solving capacity, and stimulate local initiative.

RSDF provides information directly to potential beneficiaries through organized itinerant communication campaigns. These target poor villages within the poorest districts of Romania. Beneficiaries themselves are also directly involved in information dissemination to their communities through television, radio, and newspapers. This same information is reinforced through many communication channels. For example, television and radio reporters as well as journalists are encouraged to talk directly to project beneficiaries, and these interviews have provided the best publicity for the social fund. Today, beneficiaries' voices are regularly heard on national radio, which is the primary mass media channel accessible to poor rural communities.

Inclusion and participation

Under RSDF the inclusion of disadvantaged groups occurs at every stage of the subproject cycle. Results of the October 2000 beneficiary assessment show strong community participation in program identification, selection, and development. Under RSDF, facilitators assist communities in organizing and participating in meetings where needs and priorities are discussed.

Communities also contribute to subproject costs (usually in kind), and are responsible for subproject implementation, including procurement and contracting. In a community survey considering different aspects of an RSDF project, about 70 percent of inhabitants of communities with a financed project had at least one person in their family who contributed. It was typically more difficult to raise financial contributions from communities for small infrastructure projects, as people are more wary of contributing money than of contributing labor or materials.

In general, it was found that two factors positively influenced community participation: (a) active involvement of local authorities in helping to mobilize communities; and (b) increased social cohesion among community members, which provided social pressure and resulted in a higher level of voluntary participation. It was found that community participation, confidence in coordinators, and quality of work were superior in more cohesive communities, even when projects were more difficult.

Accountability

The RSDF encourages community organizations to elect a three-person Project Management Committee (PMC), consisting of a president, treasurer, and secretary, which becomes responsible for managing the subproject (including funds) and is accountable both to the community and to the RSDF. The whole community is involved in monitoring activities through checking the quality of work done by contractors and keeping track of funds spent and outcomes. As a result of this process, communities learn how to hold local authorities accountable for using resources judiciously through monitoring and information dissemination. In addition to being able to monitor activities of local authorities, communities that participate in RSDF come to better understand the decisions made by local authorities regarding use and allocation of public funds.

Local organizational capacity

Throughout the subproject cycle RSDF plays a critical role in increasing local organizational capacity. The facilitation process then identifies and promotes community leaders and leadership, organizes community meetings, and supports participatory decision making, assisting communities in developing the skills to identify and prioritize demands. Before implementation, the capacity of community organizations and PMCs is strengthened through training in order to develop appropriate knowledge and skills to manage the subproject. Supervision is provided during project implementation to encourage communities to become self-confident and gain control over their assets and resources.

Tunisia: Northwest Mountainous Areas Development Project

The Tunisia Northwest Mountainous Areas Development Project was prepared in 1993 (closed in 2001) as a follow-up to a successful rural development project that built basic infrastructure such as schools, clinics, roads, and potable water.[9] One of the key lessons from the first project was that sustainability of investments in the region could not be expected without the participation of local communities. Accordingly, the 1993 project, funded at $26.02 million, used an integrated participatory approach to encourage local participation, with the broad objectives of improving the wellbeing of the region's population and arresting degradation of the natural resource base. Specifically, the project aimed to: (a) promote increased involvement of village organizations in development activities; (b) promote measures to increase on-farm and off-farm income-generating activities; (c) improve the management and productivity of range and farm land; (d) promote measures to reduce erosion, runoff, and reservoir sedimentation; and (e) improve social conditions of the disadvantaged population by providing basic infrastructure and social services.

Program Achievements

Results of the program have been impressive in a number of areas, including improvements in income, basic infrastructure, education, and environment.[10]

Incomes. Family incomes from agricultural production on small farms improved, in real terms, from TD 1,113 per year in 1998 to TD 1,429 per year by 2000, a difference of TD 316 a year. Yearly incomes from medium farms improved from TD 3,141 to TD 4,135, a difference of TD 994. These represent real annual growth rates of 6.3 percent and 6.9 percent for small and medium farms, respectively.[11]

Basic infrastructure. The percentage of beneficiary populations having difficulty with access to water and/or rural roads was reduced from the baseline estimate of 48 percent to 18 percent by 2000. The average distance from potable water was reduced from 1.5 kilometers in 1996 to 0.8 kilometers by 2000. The construction and rehabilitation of rural roads contributed significantly to increasing access to basic services in these remote areas, as well as to expanding the possibilities for trading surpluses with markets outside their immediate areas.

Education. The project constructed several schools, raising the percentage of surveyed villages that were close to a school from 39 percent in 1996 to 46 percent by 2000. It is estimated that the building of schools, coupled with improvements in rural roads, contributed to reducing average illiteracy rates from baseline estimates of 60 percent to approximately 44 percent.

Environment. On the whole, there has been a significant shift to agricultural systems that are more compatible with natural resources management. The project emphasized soil and water conservation activities, which brought about increased filtration rates and higher crop and tree survival rates. In addition, as a result of the increased water retention capacity of the soils, the adoption of perennial crops increased from the baseline estimate of 45 percent to 55 percent by 2000.

The Tunisian Project and Community Empowerment

The Integrated Participatory Approach

Priority activities were identified jointly with the beneficiary populations and presented in a Community Development Plan (CDP), which was valid for a five-year period. The plan outlined the most urgent needs of the population, presented the socioeconomic context, and most important, specified how each party would participate to achieve set goals. In addition, the CDP outlined the improved technical solutions that would be used, making it a guiding tool for extension workers and specialists who would implement the activities with the communities. To implement the plan, the beneficiary populations signed yearly contracts with Sylvopastoral Development Authority for the Northwest (ODESYPANO), a Tunisian NGO.

The participatory approach was successful in encouraging the adoption of improved technical solutions, which in general was higher when the demonstrations were on farmers' lands, mainly because the farmers were able to exchange information on a regular basis. In addition, farmers participated in selecting the type of demonstration and the site, which increased project ownership at the community level. This strategy helped raise the number of households participating in the Community Development Plans. In a survey of four CDPs, for example, the number of participating households increased from 183 to 258 within five years.

Local organizational capacity

After consultations between extension workers, technical specialists, and interested local communities, the communities formed local Development Committees, which functioned as intermediaries between the program administration and the beneficiary population. Active committees—those that held frequent meetings to give and gather information, resolve internal conflicts, and train CDP members—generally resulted in a higher level of community participation in project activities, increasing the benefits of the Community Development Plans. By organizing the local communities into groups, the project was more efficient in building beneficial relationships with the local communities as well as building their capacity to participate in project activities.

A total of 162 Development Committees were established by 2000, with a total of 103 Community Development Plans prepared. More than 290 contracts signed with ODESYPANO had been completed or were under implementation. In addition, a total of 361 Integrated Action Contracts (CAI) were signed. These were designed as an interim measure in response to the rising demand from local communities to participate in development activities once the project's results became better known. The CAI allowed implementation of priorities jointly identified with the communities to be jump-started without preparation of a CDP, a process that took at least two months. Despite their timeliness in addressing the immediate priorities of a community, an evaluation of the CAIs showed that since communities using these contracts received less technical assistance and training, their programs were less likely to be sustainable. As a result, after a two-year period, the implementing unit stopped the preparation of new CAIs and the numbers of such contracts fell from a high of 104 in 1996 to only 48 in 2000.

Notes

1.   World Bank 2001a.
2.   World Bank 2000.
3.   This section draws heavily from Narayan 1995. For more recent reviews, see World Bank 1996, Rao 2001, and the CDD website at http://essd.worldbank.org/cddwk2000.nsf/gweb/home.
4.   World Bank 2000.
5.   This section is drawn from de Silva and Kamwendo 2000, which presents an assessment of local stakeholder perspectives on MASAF carried out by the World Bank in 2000.
6.   World Bank 2001b.
7.   This section draws on World Bank 1998.
8.   SRP I and II financed community-managed investments for the construction or rehabilitation of social and economic infrastructure and supported capacity building at the district level.
9.   This section draws from World Bank 2001c.
10. The project defined several criteria based on socioeconomic, technical, and environmental factors, which were measured at three intervals during implementation. A baseline survey was conducted in 1996, followed by surveys in 1998 and 2000. The 1998 survey covered 527 families in 51 Development Committees. In 2000, 259 families in 28 Development Committees were surveyed.

11. The three farm sizes considered during project implementation were: small farms, those under 5 hectares; medium farms, 5 hectares up to 20 hectares; and large farms, 20 hectares and larger.

Resources

Aiyar, Swaminathan S. 2001. "Progress of Community Driven Development in Zambia." World Bank, Community Driven Development Group Anchor, Washington, D.C.

de Silva, Samantha, and Christine Kamwendo. 2000. "Community Contracting in the Malawi Social Action Fund: Local Stakeholder Perspectives." Africa Region Findings 163. World Bank, Africa Region, Washington, D.C. Available: http://www.worldbank.org/afr/findings/english/find163.htm

Kamwendo, Christine. 2001. "MASAF Presentation: Working with Vulnerable Groups." Presentation at the World Bank, Washington, D.C., June 5.

Narayan, Deepa. 1995. "Designing Community Based Development." Social Development Paper Number 7, Environmentally and Socially Sustainable Development Network, World Bank, Washington, DC.

Rao, Vijayendra. 2001. "Community Driven Development—A Brief Review of the Research." World Bank, Development Economics Research Group, Washington, D.C.

Sandi, Ana Maria, and Christina Vladu. 2000a. "The Romanian Social Development Fund and Community Empowerment." World Bank, Washington, D.C.

_____. 2000b. "What Is the Romanian Social Development Fund." World Bank, Washington, D.C.

World Bank. 1996. "Designing Community-Based Development." In *The World Bank Participation Sourcebook*. Washington, D.C.: World Bank. Available: http://www.worldbank.org/wbi/sourcebook/sba211.htm

_____. 1998. "The Role of Information, Education and Communication in the Malawi Social Action Fund." Africa Region Findings 30. World Bank, Africa Region, Washington, D.C. Available: http://www.worldbank.org/afr/findings/infobeng/infob30.htm

_____. 2000. "The Community Driven Development Approach in the Africa Region: A Vision of Poverty Reduction through Empowerment." Africa Region, Washington, D.C. Available: http://essd.worldbank.org/cddwk2000.nsf/Gweb/AFR_vision_en

_____. 2001a. "Community-Driven Development Typology." CDD Anchor Unit, Washington, D.C.

_____. 2001b. "Good Practice in Lending: Multi-Sector Projects Incorporating Gender (Malawi Social Action Fund Project)." GenderNet, Washington, D.C. Available: http://gender/resources/examples/good_practice_lending/masaf/multimalawi.htm

_____. 2001c. "Northwest Mountainous Areas Development Project (Ln. 3691-TUN)." Report No. 22390-TUN. Middle East and North Africa Region. Rural Development, Water, and Environment Group. Washington, D.C.

_____. 2001d. "Why Community Driven Development: Key Points and References." CDD Anchor Unit, Washington, D.C.

Tools and Practices 10

Empowerment in Education

Sustained access to effective basic services—including health care, education, water, and basic infrastructure—is of primary importance in the lives of poor people. Improvements in the quality and consistency of services must be approached first of all by addressing institutional and governance models to make them more responsive to the needs of poor people. At the same time, important steps can also be taken at the local level to address the specific needs and goals of each community.

Education is an area in which expanding the involvement of community actors has led to marked improvements—higher enrollments and better quality schools. Examples from around the world show that when communities can hold teachers, administrators, and government officials accountable through formal institutional mechanisms, community members become more interested in school improvement and more willing to commit their own resources to the task. Furthermore, programs that expand the access of excluded groups to education have led to important shifts in mindset among community members and government leaders regarding the contributions that those groups can make to society. The success of small pilot efforts, often with the inspiration and involvement of devoted "champions" at different levels of government, can lead to fundamental changes in the governance of the education system at the national level. These changes include creating formal channels for the participation of local actors in the management of their

This note was prepared by Bryan Kurey, under the overall guidance of Deepa Narayan.

schools and widely expanding access to education, with a shared commitment of resources among all concerned actors.

Madagascar: Community Schooling and National Development

In the early 1990s, enrollment in primary education in Madagascar was declining due to a lack of investment, deteriorating quality, and demoralization of parents and teachers.[1] More than 2,500 public primary schools had been closed, mostly owing to a lack of teachers, and almost all 13,500 schools needed major repairs. Schools lacked educational materials and professional support. Most of all, they lacked the support of their communities.

At the end of 1993, a decision was made to closely involve local communities in the improvement of basic education in public primary schools. The idea of a school-based contract emerged from the vision of one official and his management team, a senior civil servant responsible for primary education who was transferred to one of the six provinces. With World Bank support, and prompted by the results of an education sector study, a team of innovative decision makers initiated PRAGAP, a program for strengthening pedagogical and administrative management in primary education.

The guiding principles of PRAGAP, developed during the first stages of the program, include:

- Those responsible for education at the local and regional levels are at the service of parents and pupils for the achievement of national educational objectives.
- The state cannot do everything; effective participation of parents and local authorities is a must. However, it is important that each party respect its own commitments to the letter.
- The school contract can and should contain all the actions that the local community perceives as priorities. Such actions might include, for example, the assignment of a teacher, the repair of classrooms, the construction of a home for the teacher, or the manufacture of classroom benches.
- All schools within the administrative district should benefit from being able to prepare and sign a contract. Some may decline, but all should have the opportunity to engage in such a process.

- In view of the limited budgetary resources, the government's contribution will be restricted to the provision of a sufficient number of teachers, to be matched by a complementary World Bank project in funding the repair of classrooms or the construction of new ones.[2]
- Other priorities, such as the construction of teacher housing, the sinking of a well, the provision of a water point, the accommodation of a school yard, or the building of a boundary fence, will depend on the local community.
- A minimal local contribution is demanded for each school contract, either in goods or in cash.
- Each contract can be unique, given that it is prepared and negotiated in a particular community and reflects the priorities identified by that community.

Community Mobilization

The program began in two districts in one of Madagascar's six provinces, and later expanded to 20 districts (out of 111 total) across all six provinces. All program implementers first articulated and recorded a clear vision of aims, with the primary focus being the improvement of the pupils' learning. It was recognized from the start that program administration would have to be flexible in order to respond to the real needs of the community. This required basic changes in attitude and behavior on the part of government officials, in terms of their relations both with their education colleagues at all levels and with the local village communities.

This first phase of direction setting was followed by community mobilization and training, including meetings and workshops, visits to schools, and exchanges of information and points of view. The aim was to empower parents, village leaders, and other community members to take responsibility for education in their schools. These meetings often focused on issues such as poor enrollment or attendance by pupils and teachers, dropping out and grade repetition, lack of parental involvement, weak accountability of teachers and local authorities, poor condition of school buildings, and lack of educational resources in the schools.

School Councils and School-Based Contracts

Each community was invited to set up a representative School Council as a mechanism for directly involving community members in decision making regarding the schools. Representatives included teachers, parents, and village members. The School Councils then signed contracts with local representatives of the Ministry of Education, spelling out plans to improve education in the community and specifying the commitments to be made by the local community, teachers and staff, and district and regional authorities in the pursuit of agreed plans.

In devising and implementing the school-based contracts, all parties were expected to bring to the table their expertise, vision (image of the school in one, two, or three years), resources (labor, money, commitment to send children to school), and willingness to act. Investment depended on initial actions by the local community. When the first visit to the community resulted in agreement on a few practical actions for implementation by community members, the second visit would be used to assess achievement of these commitments, and a decision would be made on further action, including whether to prepare a school contract. Entering into these contracts, which were based on community needs and availability of resources, encouraged each community to recognize its role, along with that of the central and local authorities, in the transformation and improvement of their schools.

Results

After visits to 237 schools in the two pilot districts, a considerable majority of the local communities held meetings, identified priorities, fulfilled their obligations, and prepared a school contract. Four months from the launch of PRAGAP, 235 negotiated school contracts were submitted to the authorities for their consideration. During the pilot phase of the program, achievements included the following:

- 462 primary teachers were transferred within the province of Mahajanga, and 25 public primary schools were reopened;
- New enrollments in the first year of the primary cycle increased by 26.5 percent between 1993–94 and 1994–95;
- A new organizational structure within the Provincial Directorate of Education at Mahajanga was adopted;
- Local management teams were organized in the two school districts.

The average cost of each school renovation was estimated at $481 for an average of 103 pupils (1994–95), or approximately $4.70 per pupil, including construction materials and direct administrative funds for the management of the program.

These early positive outcomes motivated the management teams at the district, provincial, and national levels to extend the PRAGAP approach to the other five provinces of Madagascar. In the 20 school districts of phase two of PRAGAP, enrollments in year one of the first cycle increased by 28 percent between 1993–94 and 1995–96, almost twice the increase observed at the national level over the same period.

The lessons of PRAGAP served as the basis for formulation of a new national education policy, in place since 1996. This policy stresses the absolute priority of primary education, the importance of improving the quality of education and training at all levels, and the need to mobilize the energies and commitments of parents, communities, and beneficiaries, as well as the private sector and civil society. In December 1997, the government of Madagascar adopted the Second National Improvement Plan for Education, based on three principles:

- *Centered on the child:* each action or activity has to be measured for its impact on the child and his or her learning;
- *Based on the school:* the school in its community and environment is seen as the fulcrum for change and action; and,
- A *bottom-up approach:* information and data drawn from a school's experience should be used by local partners to make continuing improvements in the quality of learning.

Preparation of the second national plan, as well as its dissemination among national and international partners, led to the institutionalization of the school-based contract at the primary level throughout the system, as well as to similar institution-based contracts in higher education and vocational training. From 1998 to 2000 the PRAGAP approach was gradually adopted and applied to all programs and projects in more than half of all school districts in Madagascar.

El Salvador: Community Managed Schools Program

After a decade of civil war, approximately one million of El Salvador's children were not in school in the late 1980s.[3] The national enrollment rate for basic education was around 80 percent, and poor rural communities in particular suffered from a lack of schools and teachers. In 1989, Cecilia Gallardo de Cano took the role of Minister of Education as a reform proponent from the "modernizing" wing of the conservative ARENA party. Under her leadership, the Ministry of Education identified expanding access to and quality of basic education as a central policy objective, both to strengthen national unity and to promote long-term economic development.

The ministry began a comprehensive reform of El Salvador's traditional education system, with the objectives of decentralizing the education bureaucracy, improving the quality of education, expanding coverage at all levels, strengthening administrative capacity, and promoting participation by private and nongovernmental actors. One of the first steps was the piloting of a new decentralized model of service provision in rural areas, the Community Managed Schools Program (EDUCO). The program initially targeted the poorest 78 (out of 221) municipalities and was driven by the urgent need to quickly restore basic education services.

The three main aims of the EDUCO program were to:

- Increase the supply of educational services in the poorest rural communities;
- Promote the participation of local community members in their children's education;
- Improve the quality of pre-primary and primary schooling.

The EDUCO program built on the demonstrated willingness of communities to participate. While providing technical assistance to build capacity, it delegated the management of new rural preschool and primary schools to parents and community organizations. In the course of developing the program, the ministry began, for the first time, to work with local NGOs that supported program implementation.

Community Education Associations

The program emphasizes the direct involvement of parents in their children's education. To facilitate this involvement, each EDUCO school has a Community Education Association (ACE), composed of and run by elected parents and community members. The ACE is legally responsible for running the school, including its budget and personnel. It can hire and fire teachers and is responsible for supervising their performance and attendance.

The Ministry of Education transfers funds directly to the ACE's bank account, and the association administers these funds according to its assessment of the educational needs of the school. The bulk of the transfer is used to pay teachers' salaries according to their contract with the

ACE. ACEs are able to raise additional revenues by negotiating with other government agencies and international donors as well as by mobilizing local support, including in-kind support.

Information Dissemination, Consultation, and Communication Strategies

By 1993, the pilot program demonstrated clear results in restoring services to the poor and empowering local communities. Enrollment rates rose in rural parts of the country. Parents reacted very positively to being taken seriously and given key responsibilities, such as the hiring and firing of teachers. However, despite the success of this pilot, the Ministry of Education found little support for the program at the national level. The EDUCO experience had changed some attitudes and perceptions among education officials, but the new approach was not well understood outside the ministry. There had been little public discussion or consultation when the program was developed. In general, policy changes were made in an unsystematic way, contributing to a lack of transparency and continued skepticism on the part of teachers, communities, and political opposition groups.

In light of this, the Ministry of Education began to organize seminars with teachers and other key stakeholders to discuss the EDUCO experience and its use as a model for broader efforts to promote a decentralized approach. The teachers' association feared that new authority given to parents might lead to arbitrary hiring and firing, and they expressed strong opposition. These concerns were addressed through dissemination of the EDUCO experience, through creation of new job opportunities for teachers, and by having EDUCO teachers defend the decentralized approach, citing the increased involvement and support of parents.

Between November 1994 and February 1995, a social assessment was undertaken during preparation of a ministry project to support basic education reform in El Salvador. In the absence of formalized communication channels, the assessment provided valuable feedback to ministry officials about the perceptions and misperceptions of key stakeholders. Local consultants conducted focus groups, in-depth interviews, and a case study to learn the views of Ministry of Education staff, teachers, parents, and students.

Parents were suspicious of government motives and expressed concern that the ministry was planning privatization of education or a

closer link to municipal governments, which were seen as highly po-
liticized and as lacking the capacity to manage education. The study
revealed a high level of mutual distrust between the government and
approximately 110 NGOs active in the education sector. However, it
also demonstrated that the end of the civil war and the new emphasis
on democratic procedures were beginning to have a positive impact
on government accountability.

The ministry declared 1995 as the Year of Consultation on the Reform Process. The government established a National Commission for
Education, Science, and Development, which helped to launch a national dialogue about education, and from that dialogue produced a
report outlining a broad, conceptual approach to reform.

Results

The commission's report provided the conceptual basis for a detailed,
ten-year plan for the Ministry of Education that formalized broad commitments for expanding access to education. Although some key reforms in curriculum and other areas had been undertaken previously,
this marked the start of a more formalized, comprehensive reform process. The plan defined a set of measures and programs in support of
four objectives: (a) increasing access to education and improving literacy; (b) improving the quality of education; (c) promoting the formation of values; and (d) modernizing institutions. New legislation prepared and approved in 1995 included the Law on Higher Education,
the Law on Teacher Promotion/Profession, and the General Law on
Education. Reforms were undertaken within the ministry to address
administrative bottlenecks.

As implementation began in 1996, the government launched a formal communications program. Its goals were to build public support
for reforms, open permanent channels within the ministry and with the
public, and receive feedback from key stakeholders, including the ministry, parents, teachers, students, and NGOs.

Overall, enrollment rates in rural areas of El Salvador increased
from 76 percent in 1991 to 83 percent by 1993. By 1999, more than
237,000 children were enrolled in the EDUCO network of schools, up
from 8,400 in 1991. In these schools dropout rates have plunged, and
fewer students fail. The portion of students repeating grades fell from
23 percent in 1994 to 15 percent in 1998. The World Bank has supported the program through three loans totaling $148 million.

India: Uttar Pradesh Basic Education Project

In 1992 the government of India presented an educational reform proposal to the World Bank with the objective of assisting Uttar Pradesh (UP), one of India's poorest states, through a statewide primary education initiative targeted at improving the status of women and girls.[4] With the female literacy rate in UP third lowest in India, and the estimated enrollment rate of children aged 6 to 10 fourth lowest, the UP Basic Education Project aimed to increase female enrollment, reduce dropout rates, improve academic achievement, and strengthen community ownership of schools.

Mechanisms for Community Participation

From its inception, the project sought community involvement. Surveys and focus group discussions identified a wide range of educational issues at the village level, from caste discrimination to the language of instruction to the impact of weather on educational opportunities. In some villages, girls were not attending school because of their responsibility to care for younger siblings. In other places, the issue was girls' safety.

One of the key elements of the UP pilot project was the development of local Village Education Committees (VECs). These committees directly involve all interested community members, including women and minority groups, in the process of making decisions and setting goals for the schools. VECs are involved in school construction, community mapping, monitoring teacher attendance, and processing funds from the government.

Capacity Building for Sustainability

By the mid-term review in 1993, the UP project had developed an inservice teacher training program, which was also decentralized at the level of village blocks and clusters. These local efforts were supported by improved capacity building for Institutes of Education and Training at the district level and through the creation of a State Institute of Educational Management and Training.

The government of India independently hired educational specialists who shadowed World Bank staff working on the project to learn from their expertise and ensure the sustainability of the program. The government had been accustomed to running top-down programs, so developing a program that took its direction from the ground up was a new approach. Local politicians have promoted the UP project's educational objectives; they were pleased to find an approach that worked at the community level and that they could champion as their own regardless of which government was in power at the state level.

Results

The results of strengthening community involvement in schools through VECs in the UP Basic Education Project have been impressive. Targets set for female participation in primary education were exceeded. The enrollment gap between boys and girls decreased, and dropout rates for girls were halved. Learning achievement improved in 8 of the 10 districts, particularly in the second grade, and as a result of this project, 2 million girls are in school who otherwise would not be.

In reviewing the outcomes of the UP project, the government agreed that the decentralized approach worked effectively and decided that the project was exactly the kind of primary education program needed nationally. In 1995, the program was scaled up to the national level through the District Primary Education Project.

Bangladesh: Female Secondary School Assistance Project

In its fourth five-year plan, the government of Bangladesh set a goal of raising the female literacy rate from 16 to 25 percent and ensuring that women participate in all aspects of national life.[5] The principal objective was to create employment opportunities for women in primary and secondary schools, health care, family planning, agriculture extension departments, and self-employment programs run by nongovernmental organizations. The Bangladesh Female Secondary School Assistance Project (FSSAP), initiated in 1993 as part of that plan, is an example of a targeted project designed to encourage greater participation and inclusion of girls in schooling, and in the process change mindsets regarding the value and contributions of females to society.

Specific economic, cultural, and religious factors in Bangladesh combine to depress demand for girls' education. As a result, many girls either never enroll in school or withdraw from school earlier than boys do. Educational attainment of women in Bangladesh is among the lowest in the world, with only 20 percent of women able to read and write, according to the 1991 census. During the early 1990s, the disparity of access between girls and boys was most significant in secondary schools. Only one-third of students enrolled in secondary school in 1990 were girls, and the number of girls completing secondary school was less than half the number of boys. Low female secondary schooling is largely due to the fact that, unlike primary school, secondary education requires payment of tuition fees, in addition to other costs such as transportation, books, uniforms, school supplies, and examination fees. In a culture where daughters are considered economic liabilities, many parents are not willing to make such investments in their education.

Project Design and Expansion

The FSSAP, budgeted at about $88 million, has a twofold objective: to reduce constraints to enrolling girls in secondary education, and to promote positive community values regarding the education of girls. Of the program's six components, the most important is a stipend program for girls, ranging from $12 per year in grade 6 to $36 per year in grade 10, which addresses the direct costs of educating girls in secondary school by assisting with personal and tuition costs in all grades and book and examination fees in upper grades. Other components include: (a) salaries of additional teachers, particularly females; (b) occupational skills training for girls related to market demand in both wage and self-employment; (c) activities to promote public awareness regarding the benefits of female education; (d) toilets, tubewells, and water supply and sanitation programs at schools; and (e) capacity building at national and local levels.

Initially, the FSSAP was to be implemented in two overlapping phases in 118 rural *thanas* (subdistricts), with 59 *thanas* starting in 1994 and another 59 in 1997. These *thanas* were identified using combined criteria of income level, female literacy level, and female attendance level. During the first phase, community support became so widespread that the first applicants were about double the original estimate. The government of Bangladesh decided not only to implement the FSSAP in all 118 *thanas* in 1994, but also to expand the stipend concept into a national Female Secondary Stipend Program in 460 rural *thanas*. In addition to the government's contribution, support for the program is provided by the World Bank through IDA ($68 million), by the Norwegian Agency for Development Cooperation, and by the Asian Development Bank.

Project Mechanisms for Enhanced Image and Inclusion of Girls

During the project design, mechanisms were put in place to encourage the direct involvement of both schools and parents in the process of changing community mindsets and behavior regarding female education. In order to receive the stipends associated with the program, schools are required to sign cooperation agreements with the government confirming participation in the project. Once registered, the schools have the following obligations:

- Help create public awareness and encourage girls to enroll;
- Issue warnings to girls not fulfilling the requirements;
- Accept the tuition fees from the project at a rate decided by the Ministry of Education;
- Assist eligible students in filling out the student application form;
- Maintain a roster book, assigning a unique identification number to each applicant.

Similar mechanisms are at work in the design for parental involvement. Eligibility for and continuation of stipends depends on parents agreeing that their daughters will:

- Attend school for at least 75 percent of the school year;
- Obtain a grade of at least 45 percent in the annual examination;
- Remain unmarried throughout the secondary school certificate exams.

In addition to setting up schools and involving parents as agents of social transformation, the program is designed so that girls contribute to their own empowerment by taking responsibility for the payment of fees beyond tuition. The tuition part of the stipend is paid directly to the school where the girl is enrolled, but the rest of the subsidy is paid directly to the girl in two annual installments through a savings account in her name at the nearest Agrani Bank branch in the project district. The girls are responsible for paying all fees beyond tuition, such as session fees and examination fees, directly to their schools immediately on return from the bank. The image this promotes of girls bringing resources into the community and paying their own way is a significant departure from traditional norms.

Results

The growth in girls' secondary school enrollment in the project thanas is far above the most optimistic projections. Since inception, the number of girls enrolled in the program has increased each year and for every class the program has covered. In project areas, enrollment more than doubled from 462,000 in 1994 to more than one million by 2001. By July 1997, the gap between girls' and boys' enrollment in the project area had been virtually eliminated, and close to 100 percent of primary-age girls are now in school. In addition, the overall proportion of 13–15 year old females who married in project areas declined from 29 percent in 1992 to 14 percent by 1995, and for girls aged 16–19, from 72 percent in 1992 to 64 percent in 1995.

In March 2002, as a result of the impressive success of the FSSAP program, the World Bank approved a second round of the project, FSSAP II, with an IDA credit of $120.9 million. Up to 1.45 million girls are expected to participate in schools covered under FSSAP II. In addition to expanding the stipend program, FSSAP II will include components to improve access to and quality of education to *all* students in 5,000 schools in the project areas. This will involve teacher training and support, and incentives focusing on learning outcomes. The number of female secondary school teachers is to be increased, and mechanisms are being introduced to encourage participants and communities to take a more active role in ensuring better educational results and improved management of their schools.

Colombia Education Voucher Program

In Colombia, low government spending on secondary education has greatly limited the availability of public secondary schools to poor people, forcing them to choose whether to spend their limited incomes on private schooling or let their children go without a secondary education.[6] About 14 percent of fifth-grade students drop out of the system; many of them would have continued in school if a public school were available or private schooling were affordable. Colombia's targeted education voucher program was launched in 1992 with the aim of increasing low-income students' participation in secondary education.[7] By providing vouchers to students lacking access to public secondary schools, the program allowed these students to enroll in selected private schools with excess capacity.[8] In five years of implementation, the program enabled more than 125,000 children living in the poorest areas of Colombia to attend secondary school.

Targeting Poor People

The design of Colombia's program avoided some criticisms commonly made against voucher plans. The program guaranteed that levels of funding for public schools would not decrease, even if their enrollments should fall, thus mitigating concerns that vouchers draw resources from already underfunded public schools. In addition, by law, only poor people qualified for the program. Strict eligibility requirements were imposed for both students and secondary schools. Students had to reside in a poor neighborhood, one located in the two lowest strata of a neighborhood stratification scheme that ranked neighborhoods from poorest to richest. During the application process, students' families had to verify their socioeconomic status, usually by presenting a utility bill containing the status classification of their neighborhood.

The program was a partnership between local governments and the national government, supported in part by the World Bank, with participating municipalities paying 20 percent of the costs and the national government contributing the remaining 80 percent. It was designed to offer municipalities a short-term, cost-effective, efficient option for expanding access to secondary schooling. The National Ministry of Education signed an agreement with each participating municipality setting forth the terms and conditions of the voucher and the financial and administrative arrangements. Municipalities determined the number of vouchers required, certified that private schools met the requirements for participation, and jointly monitored the progress of the program with the Colombian Institute for Education Credit and Training Abroad (ICETEX), a public institution mainly handling administration of study-abroad programs. ICETEX charged 3.5 percent of the central government's share of program costs to pay for meetings between students and schools, publicity efforts, implementing the voucher system, and monitoring the program.

Results

Throughout the program, demand for vouchers exceeded supply in almost all participating municipalities. In most of these cases, a lottery was used to select recipients. Depending on location, between 20 percent and 90 percent of qualifying applicants received vouchers. The program significantly increased educational opportunities for poor people, with a considerable increase in enrollments at a low cost to the government. By 1995, about 90,000 vouchers were being used by students in 1,800 private schools in 217 municipalities, and by the end of the program, more than 125,000 students had been reached.

Three years into the program, voucher recipients were 15 percentage points more likely to have attended private school and were about 10 percentage points more likely to have finished eighth grade, primarily because they were less likely to repeat grades. Students who participated in the program scored 0.2 standard deviations higher on standardized tests than those who did not. Furthermore, voucher students were less likely to be married or cohabiting as teenagers, and worked about 1.2 fewer hours per week, suggesting an increased focus on educational achievement.

Notes

1.   This section draws on Viens and Lynch 2001a, 2001b.

2.   Known by its French acronym CRESED, the project contributed $39 million to support the initial phases of PRAGAP, with the primary goal of establishing institutional bases in subsectors concerned with curriculum, teacher training, and the management of education systems.

3.   This section draws on El Salvador Evaluation Team 1997 and World Bank 2000.

4.   This section draws on World Bank 2001.

5.   This section draws on Liang 1996; World Bank 1999; and World Bank 2002.

6.   This section is taken from a summary write-up provided by Harry Patrinos (HDNED). It draws from Angrist and others 2001; King and others 1997; King, Orazem, and Wohlgemuth 1998; and Patrinos 1997.

7.   The voucher program is formally known as Programa de Ampliación de Cobertura de la Educación Secundaria (PACES).

8.   The maximum voucher value was initially set to correspond to the average tuition of low-to-middle-cost private schools. Vouchers became less generous over time, not keeping up with inflation, and participants had to supplement vouchers with additional payments to cover school fees.

Resources

Angrist, Joshua, Eric Bettinger, Erik Bloom, Elizabeth King, and Michael Kremer. 2001. "Vouchers for Private Schooling in Colombia: Evidence from a Randomized Natural Experiment." NBER Working Paper w8343. National Bureau of Economic Research, Cambridge, Mass.

El Salvador Evaluation Team. 1997. "El Salvador's EDUCO Program: A First Report on Parents' Participation in School-Based Management." Working Paper Series on Impact Evaluation of Education Reforms No. 4. Ministry of Education, National Research and Evaluation Division, El Salvador, and World Bank, Development Economics Research Group, Poverty and Human Resources, Washington, D.C.

King, Elizabeth, Peter F. Orazem, and Darin Wohlgemuth. 1998. "Central Mandates and Local Incentives: The Colombia Education Voucher Program." Working Paper Series on Impact Evaluation of Education Reforms No. 6. World Bank, Development Economics Research Group, Washington, D.C.

King, Elizabeth, Laura Rawlings, Marybell Gutierrez, Carlos Pardo, and Carlos Torres. 1997. "Colombia's Targeted Education Voucher Program: Features, Coverage, and Participation." Working Paper Series on Impact Evaluation of Education Reforms No. 3. World Bank, Development Economics Research Group, Washington, D.C.

Liang, Xiaoyan. 1996. "Bangladesh: Female Secondary School Assistance." Draft. World Bank, Human Development Department, Washington, D.C. Available: http://www.worldbank.org/education/economicsed/finance/demand/case/bangladesh/bangladesh_index.htm

Patrinos, Harry Anthony, and David Lakshmanan Ariasingam. 1997. *Decentralization of Education: Demand-Side Financing*. Directions in Development. Washington, D.C.: World Bank.

Viens, Daniel, and James Lynch. 2001a. "PRAGAP: The Birth of an Innovation. Community Schooling and National Development in Madagascar." World Bank, Washington, D.C.

_____. 2001b. "Madagascar: A Developmental Approach to Community-Based School Management." Africa Region Findings 175. World Bank, Africa Region, Washington, D.C. Available: http://www.worldbank.org/afr/findings/english/find175.htm

World Bank. 1999. "Pioneering Support for Girls Secondary Education: The Bangladesh Female Secondary School Assistance Project." South Asia Brief. South Asia Region, Washington, D.C.

_____. 2000. "Reform of Basic Education in El Salvador." Action Learning Program on Participatory Processes for PRSP. Participation Thematic Group, Social Development Department. Available: http://www.worldbank.org/participation/web/webfiles/eseducation.htm

_____. 2001. "A Social Development Saga: India Uttar Pradesh Basic Education and India District Primary Education Projects." Social Development Notes 55. Environmentally and Socially Sustainable Development Network, Washington, D.C.

_____. 2002. "Bangladesh: Girls Education Gets US$121 Million in World Bank Support." Press Release 2002/232/SAR. World Bank, Washington, D.C.

Tools and Practices 11

Institutional Innovations to Support Micro, Small, and Medium Enterprises

Many governments of developing countries perceive micro, small, and medium enterprises (SMEs) as engines of employment, poverty alleviation, and broad-based economic growth. Growth and development of SMEs in developing countries can increase poor people's opportunities, security, and empowerment.

This note presents examples of two types of commercially viable innovations that increase productivity and growth of SMEs in developing countries: business networks and clusters and venture capital to small enterprises through a combination of equity investments and technical assistance.

SME Network and Cluster Development

In order to better compete in the marketplace, micro, small, and medium enterprises in the same or related industries can form business collectives. Partnerships among businesses in geographic proximity are called "clusters," while businesses that team up to work on a joint development objective are called "networks." The term "networking" characterizes the overall process of building business relationships, whether through clusters or networks.

This note was prepared by Radha Seshagiri, under the overall guidance of Deepa Narayan.

SMEs team up for sound economic reasons, including the opportunity to procure raw materials and other resources more efficiently, the availability of customized business development services, the abundance of clients attracted by the cluster, and the presence of a skilled labor force. Such partnerships reduce costs for individual enterprises through economies of scale and raise profits through industry development. Cooperation among firms can also create a learning environment in which firms can exchange ideas and knowledge to improve products and profits. The following examples explore how business networks and clusters can be supported, yielding benefits to both firms and economies.

Broadening SME Networking in Nicaragua

In 1995, the United Nations Industrial Development Organization (UNIDO) and the government of Nicaragua formed a partnership to develop a strategy for strengthening small and medium enterprises in the country. The technical assistance program promotes networking, understood as relations between enterprises (and between enterprises and institutions) that allow the SMEs to overcome their isolation and achieve new collective competitive advantages unattainable by individual firms. The program also helps develop local institutions that facilitate the networking process by helping the SMEs to forge a joint entrepreneurial vision and build capacity to implement that vision through common development projects. These network brokers act as "system integrators" at the local level, facilitating the development of relationships between the enterprises and optimizing the use of available technical and financial services.

The joint Nicaragua-UNIDO initiative to foster the growth of Nicaraguan SMEs emphasizes local capacity building. The national consultants working on the project are local professionals with no international experience and no direct knowledge of cluster or network practices or policies. The project therefore invests in training for them to upgrade and specialize their skills, which is expected to result in improved services to the enterprises. Project consultants are also responsible for training "network brokers" to expand network creation capabilities and multiply results throughout the country. Network brokers are selected from locally active institutions, especially entrepreneurial ones, and from other technical assistance projects.

The project also seeks to diversify its activities to include the training of new network brokers, the promotion of industrial districts or clusters, and the promotion of industrial integration along production chains (large enterprises subcontracting to SMEs, with emphasis on upgrading the small firms that serve as suppliers).

The initiative has resulted in the growth of clusters and networks among Nicaraguan SMEs. Twenty networks were created within two years by a team of seven national consultants, assisted by short-term international consultants. More and more local institutions are demanding the services of network brokers. The project was invited to assume an important role in the National Committee for Competitiveness and Sustainable Development, made up of high-level policy makers and representatives from the private sector and academia, and is contributing to the national dialogue around design of an overall SME development policy.

The early support for and involvement in this business networking project by the Nicaraguan government has been important to its success. First, the project has had easy access to local policy dialogue and formulation around business development and has been able to propose business networking as a key SME development strategy for Nicaragua. Network promotion has now become one of the main instruments of the government's approach to private sector support. Second, public sector involvement has made the project a model of interinstitutional coordination and, as a result, has enabled the project to have greater access to local people and resources. Third, public sector involvement has brought about a much clearer prospect for sustainability of the project. The long-term expectation is that the networking project will be taken over by the public sector counterpart and eventually become an independent agency.

EcoHamaca: networking hammock producers

One successful example supported by the Nicaragua-UNIDO initiative is EcoHamaca, a network of 11 small enterprises in Nicaragua producing handcrafted hammocks. Each enterprise employs about 15 people and competes with the other hammock producers in the local market. After consultations with UNIDO experts at the beginning of 1997, the producers were convinced of the need for closer collaboration in order to develop and carry out an export strategy. They subsequently applied for UNIDO support in March 1997. By August of that year, the group had gained formal legal status as a producer association, with a standing constitution signed by all 11 members.

Through the UNIDO networking project, producers received technical assistance to help standardize their production so that they could collectively improve the quality and design of their products, develop pricing systems, and produce quantities suitable for export. In order to offer a more eco-friendly and exportable product, the group changed the wood used for the poles from cedar, which is close to extinction, to other, more abundant, exotic species and shifted from chemical to natural dyes. The producers have agreed on the common brand name, "Made in Masaya," in order to promote a local identity. By 1999, the network was exporting more than 3,000 hammocks a month, with regular customers in Finland, Peru, Sweden, and the United States.

In order to advance their common work and maintain their competitiveness, EcoHamaca has hired a manager whose tasks include identifying more formal training opportunities for the producers, securing additional technical and financial assistance from local SME support institutions, and developing a stronger marketing strategy that capitalizes on the Internet.

Hand-Block Printed Textile Cluster of Jaipur, India

Jaipur, Rajasthan, India is home to a group of artisans specializing in hand-block printing, a form of fabric printing that uses ethnic designs and traditional, eco-friendly vegetable dyes to produce colorful textiles. More than 550 small firms engage in both hand-block and screen printing and employ almost 10,000 workers. In the 1980s and 1990s, as national and international demand for hand-block textiles grew, traditional hand-block printers in Jaipur failed to keep up. Increasing competition from substitute products also began to squeeze the artisans out of the market.

UNIDO conducted a diagnosis of the artisan group in 1996 and offered recommendations to help revitalize these small businesses.[1] The recommendations included developing clusters—interlinked similar enterprises in a particular sector—in order to promote cooperation and collaboration and thus achieve greater gains than would be possible for the enterprises individually. UNIDO also recommended fostering cooperative relations between the public and private sectors to develop a coordinated industrial policy, identify and implement coherent actions, and support entrepreneurship. For the hand-block artisans, the result has been a revitalization of their business cluster, greater access to international markets, and a restructuring of activities to meet growing demand.

Revitalizing the hand-block cluster
UNIDO's study assessed constraints to the cluster and the potential for growth. It identified an unexploited potential for traditional artisans in

the cluster to target profitable national and world markets. Constraints included lack of an active association, limited capacity, and inadequate access to financial services. The resulting action plan aimed to promote traditional production methods and improve the living standards of the artisans. The plan envisaged restructuring the cluster and improving linkages among the different enterprises; enhancing the design, production, and marketing capacity of the firms; developing a product image to meet market demand; and improving business support services.

Has it worked?

As a result of the UNIDO intervention, one dormant artisan association, Calico Printers Co-operative Society (CALICO), has been revitalized. Its membership has increased from 26 artisans in 1997 to 120 by 1999, and a common showroom has been created. In addition, after two years of UNIDO assistance, four new formal networks (three of which are made up of women producers) and four informal networks had been created. The Consortium of Textile Exporters (COTEX) has also been formed. By 1999, of the 155 firms involved in the whole hand-block cluster, 40 had expanded their capacity; 20 had been exposed to international markets; 25 had improved their design capacities; 80 had been registered with various institutions to provide regular market linkages; 15 had received bank credit; 22 had trained in visual merchandising; and 55 had trained in marketing and entrepreneurship.

India's National Bank for Agriculture and Rural Development played a key role in the growth of the cluster. Following the bank's 1998 contribution of 15 percent of costs for the cluster artisans to participate in a product fair in Jaipur City, collaboration within the cluster improved considerably. Other agencies, working in partnership with UNIDO, also made contributions. Small Industries Development Bank of India (SIDBI) and the National Institute of Design initiated activities related to marketing training, design development, technical training, and introduction of an innovative credit mechanism. SIDBI has also adopted the cluster for further intervention under its Rural Industrialization Program.

Commercial banks have also begun playing a role in development of the hand-block cluster. Lending by commercial banks to these small-scale businesses was suspended in 1991 following a flood that deprived the artisans of their collateral. Once the hand-block cluster was reestablished with UNIDO assistance in 1997, the president of CALICO, a respected businessman from Sanganer, successfully negotiated an agreement with the banks for the resumption of lending to the small businesses. CALICO smoothed the financing process by providing collateral on behalf of its members to secure the loans and by screening applications before submission to the commercial banks. In a matter of months, 15 loan agreements were signed between local banks and CALICO members. The supply of loans has increased so dramatically that bank managers have been known to reach out to CALICO to inquire about upcoming projects and identify potential loan recipients.

The cluster has progressively relied on fewer subsidies as it has developed. UNIDO's contribution declined from 50 percent in the first product fair in 1998, to 7 percent at the last fair, a year-and-a-half later.

Small Enterprise Assistance Funds (SEAFs)

S mall Enterprise Assistance Funds is a U.S.- and Dutch-based NGO that aims to foster economic development and entrepreneurship in developing and transitional countries. Spun off from the CARE International development organization in 1989, SEAF began by pursuing operations in Central and Eastern Europe, then expanded to Latin America. It is now extending its operations to Asia. With $140 million under management in 2001, SEAF has made more than 160 investments valued at about $45 million, and manages a network of 14 commercially driven investment funds around the world. Individual investments range from $100,000 to $1.5 million, with SEAF holding a minority equity position of 25 to 49 percent.

SEAF funds companies that are too small to interest most mainstream foreign investors, commercial banks, or public development banks, typically those with 10 to 100 employees and annual revenues of $200,000 to $2 million. Its approach is similar to that of a venture capital firm. As an active shareholder, it provides donor funded technical assistance and fee-based services to help the firm grow, and exits the firm when it has reached a point of maturity, usually after five to seven years.

While SEAF is a nonprofit with a development objective, it manages each of its investment funds as separate, for-profit entities. At the end of 2000, the average company in SEAF's portfolio saw a revenue increase of 80 percent. Employment growth was also strong: 7,000 jobs have resulted from the funds' investments. As of April 2000, SEAF had sold nine of its 37 investee companies, earning a 32 percent return.

SEAF typically begins operations in a particular country or region by launching an SME equity fund to serve emerging enterprises and then targeting promising firms that need outside capital and management support to grow. Once it identifies a firm, SEAF takes a minority equity position in the firm and helps it grow by providing technical assistance. SEAF's "equity plus assistance" model provides technical assistance along with funds to develop capacity in SME management and expertise, and builds a relationship with firm managers to achieve growth. Technical assistance in financial management, marketing, accounting, and other fields is provided to the firm for a fee. Specialized consultants funded by donors are also available if needed. SEAF has found that this customized support to firms has helped small firms grow rapidly. It recovers approximately 50 percent of its costs through fees and return on equity, while the remainder is financed by loans or grants from development institutions.

Examples of SEAF Investments

Bolivia: Jolyka Flooring Company

In August 2000, SEAF helped to restructure the management operations of Jolyka, a small company in Cochabamba, Bolivia, that uses sustainable timber from managed Amazon forests to produce high-quality flooring. After an initial investment of $860,000, SEAF helped the company restructure its balance sheet and negotiate its debt to achieve greater profitability. The new structure of the company has helped production, with annual revenues rising from $850,000 to $2.2 million. Jolyka employees now number 115, up from 75 since SEAF invested in 2000. SEAF has also helped to negotiate contracts with major U.S. firms and has introduced Jolyka to trade shows in North America. International exposure has helped make Jolyka among the top 70 exporters in Bolivia.

Propelled by international recognition for its high-quality, eco-value product, Jolyka expects to reach $4,000,000 in sales in 2002. To promote the sustainable timber industry in Bolivia, Jolyka's founders created the Jolyka Foundation in 1998 to work with indigenous people, teaching them marketing and sales as well as sustainable forest management.

Poland: Holding Centrum Bookstore

Holding Centrum Bookstore in Poland, in which SEAF invested in 1996, is a typical example of a company that has benefited from SEAF assistance. In addition to financial support, SEAF provided input into the company's initial attempts at computerized inventory control and management systems. Technical assistance grants from donors also helped the firm grow. In 1996, Holding Centrum was a promising business start-up with 86 employees, run from its founder's apartment. By 2001, the company had grown into a nationwide chain with seven distribution centers, 50 bookstores, 446 employees, and annual revenue of $17.6 million.

Estonia: Regio Maps

Technology company Regio was the first firm in Estonia to receive assistance from SEAF, which provided Regio with strategic management advice to help expand its production and operations. Regio had focused its operations on sales of paper and digital maps. When SEAF invested $140,142 in 1998, acquiring a 28.6 percent stake in the company, it recommended moving into higher-value-added services and improving financial management, marketing, and business organization. In 2000, SEAF facilitated negotiations with the Finnish industrial group DONE to purchase Regio, which resulted in a Euro 3.9 million sale of 100 percent of Regio's shares.

IFC's Role

In 1996 SEAF began working with IFC through a $600,000 line of credit. Since IFC's subsequent 1998 investment in SEAF Macedonia, the two have collaborated to improve the efficiency and reduce the management costs of SEAF's operations. Since 1999, IFC has invested $17 million in four different SEAF-managed funds. SEAF received $850,000 from IFC's SME Capacity Building Facility in March 2001 to help the organization scale up and expand to several countries and regions.

Note

1.   UNIDO's 1996 survey of small-scale enterprise clusters in India found that there are 350 industrial clusters and approximately 2,000 rural and artisan-based clusters throughout the country. These clusters account for approximately 60 percent of manufactured exports from India (Clara, Russo, and Gulati 2000).

Resources

Ceglie, Giovanna, and Marco Dini. 1999. "SME Cluster and Network Development in Developing Countries: The Experience of UNIDO." Paper presented at the International Conference on Building a Modern and Effective Development Service Industry for Small Enterprises, organized by the Committee of Donor Agencies for Small Enterprise

Development, Rio de Janeiro, Brazil, March 1999. Available: http://www.ilo.org/public/english/employment/ent/papers/cluster.htm

Clara, Michele, Fabio Russo, and Mukesh Gulati. 2000. "Cluster Development and BDS Promotion: UNIDO's Experience in India." Paper presented at the International Conference on Business Services for Small Enterprises in Asia: Developing Markets and Measuring Performance, Hanoi, Vietnam, April 2000. Available: http://www.ilo.org/public/english/employment/ent/papers/unido.htm

International Finance Corporation. 2000. "Partner Profile: Small Enterprise Assistance Funds." *SME Focus* 1 (2): 6. Small and Medium Enterprise Department, Washington, D.C. Available: http://www.ifc.org/sme/html/sme_publications.html

_____. 2001a. "The Power of Partners." *SME Focus* 2 (2): 1–3. Small and Medium Enterprise Department, Washington, D.C. Available: http://www.ifc.org/sme/html/sme_publications.html

_____. 2001b. "Partner Profile: SEAF." SME Fact Sheets, March. Small and Medium Enterprise Department, Washington, D.C. Available: http://www.ifc.org/sme/html/sme_publications.html

United Nations Industrial Development Organization. "Cluster Development in India." Document 331112. Available: http://www.unido.org/doc/331112.htmls

Tools and Practices 12

Institutional Innovations in Financial Services for the Poor

Poor people represent a largely untapped market for financial services. While some institutions are extending microfinance (very small savings, credit, and other financial services offered to a poor clientele), the supply is still far below demand. In recent years, a number of public, private, and nonprofit institutions have developed innovative ways to address the financial needs of the poor by introducing to the marketplace new products that enable outreach to a much larger and more diverse population.

This note highlights five examples of institutional innovations in provision of sustainable financial services to the poor:

- Accion International
- Bangladesh Rural Advancement Committee (BRAC)
- Information and communications technology applications
- Micro Enterprise Bank–Kosovo (MEB-Kosovo)
- Consultative Group to Assist the Poorest (CGAP).

ACCION International

A pioneer in microfinance, ACCION International supports a network of independent institutions that between 1991 and 2001 provided more than $3 billion in loans to two million low-income borrowers in the Caribbean, Latin America, and the United States. It is an

This note was prepared by Radha Seshagiri, under the overall guidance of Deepa Narayan.

NGO with a private sector approach, one with a proven technical assistance model that helps poor people raise their incomes through entrepreneurship.

ACCION's work has demonstrated that, under the right regulatory conditions and with proper management and technology in place, microfinance can both serve the poor and earn profits—sparking the interest of some commercial banks to enter the field. The key, ACCION believes, lies in the strong technical support it provides to its network. ACCION considers its clients to be skilled business people, not objects of charity. With access to the basic tools of business—capital and training—ACCION's clients can work their own way up the economic ladder, with dignity and self-respect. As their businesses grow, ACCION's clients gain security and self-esteem and participate more fully in the economic, social, and political life of their communities, thus empowering themselves. One ACCION study in Latin America showed that family income increased an average of 30 percent after a few small loans.

With 27 years of microfinance experience in one hemisphere, ACCION took its model to Africa for the first time in 2001. Support from the World Bank Group's SME Capacity Building Facility is enabling ACCION to help new microfinance partners in South Africa and Mozambique, while scaling up existing networks in Guatemala and Brazil. In each case the facility provides $100,000 to support ACCION's work, for a total of $400,000. In South Africa, ACCION and local partners will create a new microfinance institution in the country's North West Province. In Mozambique the work will center on strengthening a cooperative credit and savings bank called Tchuma in the Maputo area, where only 5 percent of potential poor clients are currently being reached. ACCION also began work in Benin and Zimbabwe in 2001.

The International Finance Corporation endorsed ACCION International by making its first direct investment in an ACCION affiliate, Compartamos of Mexico, in 2001. In the last 10 years Compartamos has developed a highly profitable lending portfolio serving 60,000 Mexican borrowers, mostly women. With technical assistance provided by ACCION and funded by the U.S. Agency for International Development, Compartamos spun off its microfinance operations into a separate for-profit entity, Financiera Compartamos SA. IFC is now supporting this new institution through $1.63 million in loans and equity investments, taking over 15 percent of the newly issued shares and helping to triple its number of borrowers by 2006.

BRAC: Extending Financial Services to the Extreme Poor

B angladesh is home to more than 25 million people who are considered "extremely poor."[1] Women are particularly disadvantaged: they suffer from higher mortality rates, poorer health conditions, more limited access to employment, and lower literacy rates than do men (female literacy is 29 percent compared to male literacy of 45 percent).[2]

In 1985 the Bangladesh Rural Advancement Committee (BRAC) pioneered an innovative program to help extremely poor Bangladeshis, mainly illiterate and landless women, many of them widowed or abandoned. The Income Generation for Vulnerable Groups Development (IGVGD) program, jointly administered by the government of Bangladesh and BRAC, gives the extreme poor the opportunity to generate income, build skills, and become independent entrepreneurs.

The IGVGD program has grown to become a national program. From 1991 to 2001, the program expanded to provide food grain assistance and savings and credit services to over a million participants. Nearly two-thirds of participants have moved out of absolute poverty, become mainstream microfinance clients, and no longer require government safety net programs.[3]

How It Works

IGVGD enables the extreme poor, previously excluded from participation in financial institutions, to access mainstream microfinance programs. In partnership with central and local governments and the World Food Program, BRAC devised this program to help the extreme poor generate income through poultry farming, an activity in which more than 70 percent of rural landless women are directly or indirectly involved. The government and the World Food Program provide an 18-month stipend of free wheat while BRAC provides training in income-generating activities, human rights and legal education, nutrition, essential health care, and credit. Through this package of support, the program prepares women to earn a regular income after the subsidy ends.

The IGVGD mechanism is designed to facilitate the entry of the poorest Bangladeshis into regular credit programs, and acts as a transition from a safety net to a longer-term development program. The IGVGD program has three main elements: food grain assistance, skills training, and financial services in the form of savings and credit. Elected representatives of local government first identify recipients of free food grain. BRAC then chooses households from this group to participate in the IGVGD program according to the following criteria: (a) they are headed by widows or abandoned women; (b) they own less than half an acre of land; and (c) they earn less than 300 taka ($6) per month.

Participants begin the program by training in poultry and livestock rearing, vegetable gardening, and other related topics. They also begin saving a minimum of 25 taka ($5) per month with BRAC and attend weekly meetings. Once training is completed, BRAC provides credit to the beneficiaries as initial investment capital in two loan cycles. The first loan is for 2,500 taka ($50); once it is repaid, participants are given a second loan of 4,000 taka ($80). Once the second loan is repaid, participants are "graduated" to BRAC's regular microfinance program, the Rural Development Program.[4] Evidence indicates that about 80 percent of participants stay on for the second loan while about two-thirds move on to regular microfinance membership.[5]

Results to Date

The program's combination of training, financial assistance, and food grain assistance has enabled participants to graduate from reliance on the government safety net to participation in regular financial services programs. From 1991 to 2001, the IGVGD program has grown to provide food grain assistance and savings and credit services to more than a million participants. Nearly two-thirds of participants have moved out of absolute poverty and have become mainstream microfinance clients, and have not slipped back into requiring government safety net programs.[6] During the June 1998 to June 1999 cycle alone, 180,900 women received training while 97,230 graduated to regular employment with the assistance of small loans from BRAC.[7]

The IGVGD program has had considerable success in reaching the extreme poor of Bangladesh. A recent longitudinal survey tracked household economic changes in IGVGD participants, starting before participation (1994), at the end of the program (1996), and three years later (table 5-1). Data suggest that in the early 1990s, while 16 percent of total households and 53 percent of the extreme poor did not own land in rural Bangladesh, nearly 80 percent of IGVGD participants were landless. By 1996, this number had fallen to 62 percent of participants. Similarly, 87 percent of IGVGD households owned no blankets (compared to 37 percent of the total extreme poor), a number which had fallen to 75 percent by 1999.[8]

Most participants have moved out of extreme poverty to become independent, viable entrepreneurs. The participants' overall income has risen considerably after participation in BRAC's IGVGD program, by more than 30 percent on average. Notably, the percentage of households engaged in begging declined dramatically, from 18 percent in 1994 to 2 percent in 1996, to 0 in 1999. Overall, program participants sustained their economic improvement, even three years after the program ended.[9]

Information and Communications Technology Applications

Innovations in the delivery of financial services to poor people are emerging through the application of technologies that greatly increase efficiency and bring previously inaccessible services to poor people at

Table 5-1 Household Economic Changes among IGVGD Participants

Indicator of household economic status	1994 (pre-program)	1996 (end-program)	1999 (+3 years)
Households without blankets (percent)	86	—	75
Households without beds (percent)	42	40	36
Monthly income preceding survey (Tk)	75	717	415
Households earning more than Tk 300 (percent)	7	64	31
Households saving with NGOs (percent)	11	34	37
Households begging (percent)	18	2	0
Landless households (percent)	78	62	—
Households with no homestead land (percent)	27	13	—
Functionally landless households (percent)	94	72	—

— Not available.
Source: Hashemi 2001.

lower costs. Two such examples are highlighted below: Smart card technology and ATM services for poor people.

Smart Cards: Innovative Banking Services for the Poor

Smart cards, an emerging ICT tool, can be used effectively by financial institutions to reach poor people. A smart card is a plastic card, akin to a credit card, with an embedded microchip on which both borrowers and lenders can record loan activity in lieu of tracking transactions on passbooks, collection sheets, and loan ledgers. It allows the development of client history through an electronic record. Smart card transactions are much faster than traditional teller transactions. They are also easy to use, do not require literacy, and protect against fraud by forgery. Further, the cards leave a "transparent and tamper-proof" audit trail for reconciling accounts, thereby reducing central accounting time.[10]

Microfinance institutions with a scale of operation classified as small and medium spend on average between 35 percent and 50 percent of their portfolios on overhead costs.[11] By lowering costs, smart cards have the potential to greatly increase the efficiency of all MFIs, and particularly small and medium MFIs, while at the same time allowing them to reach large numbers of poor people.

While commercial banks previously shied away from small business services due to high transaction costs, with technological innovations many banks have now become interested in doing business with poor people. Financial institutions in India and Swaziland are using smart cards with an embedded microchip containing information on the client's credit history in order to reduce transaction costs and build credit history.

India: Swayam Krishi Sangam

Swayam Krishi Sangam (SKS) is a microfinance institution that operates in the Narayankhed area of Medak District in Andhra Pradesh, India, an arid area with many poor villagers trapped in perpetual debt to moneylenders. A recipient of one of the first CGAP Pro-Poor Innovation Challenge Awards, SKS was founded in 1998 by Vikram Akula, a son of Indian immigrants to the United States, who was inspired to expand financial services to the poor after visiting Muhammad Yunus and the Grameen Bank in Bangladesh.

SKS targets the poorest 20 percent of the population by focusing its activities on the poorest regions and selecting individuals through key informant interviews and village surveys. A typical participant is a woman from a household that has an annual income of less than Rs. 20,000 ($450).[12]

SKS offers its clients two savings and four loan products that were designed through participatory processes. It provides general and seasonal loans at an interest rate of 20 percent, consumption loans from group funds at 0 percent interest, and emergency loans also at 0 percent interest. Most members take out a $50 general loan their first year and $100 their second year, and use the funds for enterprises related to land and livestock.

In August 2000, SKS started using smart cards at one of its four branches to improve the tedious process of recording all financial transactions at group meetings, which often took 90 minutes per meeting. SKS integrated the smart card into various stages of its operations. Staff members carry a handheld computer to group meetings in order to download collection information from the branch office computer. Members have a smart card that electronically holds their information and records transactions. A read-only computer is available in the village so that members can check their accounts.

SKS plans to expand use of the technology to its other branches, and estimates that the time and financial savings will be substantial. The smart card will allow staff to hold three meetings a day instead of the current two, and even with the additional costs of the cards and terminals, each branch will save about $2,000 annually. Computerization of financial records will also minimize errors and provide management with immediate client-level information.

Swaziland: Swazi Business Growth Trust

In Swaziland, the Swazi Business Growth Trust, with donor assistance, issues smart cards to its small business clients. Clients use the smart card to obtain funds and repay loans at commercial bank branches around the country that have smart card reading terminals.[13] SBGT maintains a line of credit with the commercial banks that provide this service free of charge to SBGT. SBGT downloads daily transaction information complete with cash flow analysis, which allows accurate and easy monitoring of disbursements and repayments.

The system enables SBGT to act as a "virtual bank" with smart card terminals within the nationwide banking network. SBGT invested approximately $100,000 in the smart card technology and banking software. Future plans are to make transactions available by telephone and online and to expand services to include savings.

ATM Services for Poor People: E Bank, South Africa

Standard Bank of South Africa has been a pioneer in demonstrating that a commercial bank can use market information and technological innovations to offer a bundle of services needed and valued by poor people at a fee high enough to cover costs. In 1993, Standard Bank created the affiliated E Bank to deliver basic banking services to the urban poor. E Bank offers services designed for low-income populations and convenient to access while keeping bank costs low. E Bank combines the innovative technology of modified ATM services with staff trained to help clients with basic electronic banking.

E Bank offers a single savings account (no checking, no passbook), and all accounts of more than R 250 ($56) earn interest. Clients can obtain cash and deposit savings, and will soon be able to safely transfer money to relatives and others in the system around the country.[14] Depositors with regular minimum balances become eligible for drawings and prizes and automatically receive a modest amount (R 1,500 or $333) of life insurance coverage.

E Bank outlets are nontraditional kiosks, conveniently located and open to the sidewalk, decorated with vibrant colors, and having video displays for entertainment or instruction. The ATM screen shows graphic as well as text prompts. Each kiosk has three or four assistants who speak several local languages.

More than 150,000 customers created E Bank accounts within the first year of operation. Costs of developing, marketing, and operations were borne by E Bank customers and E Bank barely broke even at the time. In 1996 it was merged with Standard Bank and renamed Auto Bank E and E Plan. A resulting feature is that E Plan cards can be used as point-of-sale cards at certain retail stores including Pick and Pay, the largest in the country. The fixed cost of managing E Plan accounts is half that of the traditional low-balance Plus Plan.

In May 1997, Standard Bank converted 570,000 low-balance customers to the E Plan. In addition, E Bank attracted 600,000 new account holders in the 10 months between late 1996 and mid-1997. After three years in operation there are approximately 1.4 million E Plan account holders using 70 Auto Bank E centers. In 1997 there were about 18.5 million Auto Bank E transactions, comprising 24.6 percent of all Standard Bank transactions. By 2002, the Bank expects more than 50 million Auto Bank E transactions, representing 42.5 percent of all transactions.

Kosovo Micro Enterprise Bank: A Microfinance Model

During and after the recent conflict in Kosovo, the Micro Enterprise Bank (MEB-Kosovo), established in late 1999, emerged as a key player in the provision of financial services. The first and only regulated commercial institution in post-conflict Kosovo, MEB-Kosovo has taken in $53.2 million in deposits and built a loan portfolio of $1.2 million, comprising 311 loans to small and medium enterprises since its inception.

Despite the 100 new accounts that are opened each working day, demand still exceeds supply. After just six months of providing financial services to low-income clients, Micro Enterprise Bank was already showing a profit. Although the bank operates in one of the world's most difficult business environments, strong repayment rates took its initial portfolio of $500,000 in small loans to nearly $5 million by the end of 2000.

The success of the Micro Enterprise Bank in Kosovo has served as a model for other IFC support to financial institutions. IFC formed a successful partnership with a German firm, Internationale Projekt Consult GmbH, to start Micro Enterprise Bank of Kosovo. The bank turned a profit in its first six months, and the partnership has been extended through an $85 million package of grants and equity investment to start up commercially viable microcredit banks in several other countries, including Bulgaria, Georgia, Ghana, Kazakhstan, Macedonia, Moldova, the Philippines, and Romania. Start-up costs include training, fundraising, and management support services.[15]

The facility supports an initial period for set-up operations, using grant money.[16] During the start-up phase, the microfinance institution builds relationships with the formal financial sector and puts into place best-practice management systems to bring about commercial viability rapidly. "The banks are profit-oriented, but do not aim for short-term profit maximization," said Dr. Claus-Peter Zeitinger, managing director of IPC. "They seek a reasonable balance between social and economic goals."[17]

Consultative Group to Assist the Poorest

The Consultative Group to Assist the Poorest is a consortium of 27 bilateral and multilateral donor agencies that support microfinance, with the World Bank as a major financial supporter. Its mission is to improve the capacity of microfinance institutions to deliver flexible, high-quality financial services to the very poor on a sustainable basis.

CGAP's work focuses on five main areas, or strategic themes:

- Supporting the development of microfinance institutions;
- Supporting changes in the practices of member donors to improve their microfinance operations;
- Increasing the poverty outreach of MFIs;
- Improving the legal and regulatory framework for MFIs;
- Facilitating commercialization of the industry.

To achieve these goals, CGAP serves MFIs, donors, and the microfinance industry by providing technical assistance and strategic advice, by developing and disseminating technical guides and services, by delivering training, and by performing field research on innovations. CGAP also has a small grant facility that provides funding for these activities and for strategic investments in MFIs. CGAP's training and capacity-building programs are increasing technical and managerial capacities at the local level, through national workshops and networks such as those held recently in Benin/Togo, Cameroon, Ghana, and Mali.

Notes

1. Extreme poverty is defined as food consumption of less than 1,740 calories a day (Hashemi 2001; Saleque 1999).
2. Saleque 1999.
3. Hashemi 2001; Saleque 1999.
4. BRAC's Rural Development Program has reached 3.3 million poor landless people since 1977.
5. Hashemi 2001.
6. Hashemi 2001; Saleque 1999.
7. Bangladesh Rural Advancement Committee 2001.
8. Hashemi 2001.
9. Hashemi 2001.
10. Nelson 1999.
11. MicroBanking Standards Project 2001. Criteria for classification of scale of operations vary by region, based on size of gross outstanding loan portfolio. See additional analysis tables, p. 53 for more details.
12. SKS believes there has been up to 20 percent leakage into the next higher decile of the population, but this still makes SKS clients considerably poorer than most MFI clients.

13. The current cost is $1,000 per unit (a $500 version is being developed).

14. It costs Standard Bank R 4.58 per month to maintain an account. Transactions per account average about 2.8 per month. E Plan transaction fees are high relative to income and higher than the market on some transactions. Average daily balances for E Plan accounts are R 320 ($71).

15. IFC 2000b.

16. The IFC also offers an SME Capacity Building Facility in developing countries for small business projects that are innovative, replicable, sustainable, and involve close partnerships with outside organizations. The initiative was launched in September 2000 with a $7.1 million allocation from IFC (IFC 2001). IFC also offers project development facilities, or regionally based capacity-building facilities, to strengthen small enterprises through provision of technical assistance and capital.

17. IFC 2000b.

Resources

Bangladesh Rural Advancement Committee. 2001. "BRAC Development Programme: Rural Development Programme." Available: http://www.brac.net/pov3.html

Baydas, Mayada, Douglas Graham, and Liza Valenzuela. 1998. "Commercial Banks in Microfinance: New Actors in the Microfinance World." CGAP Focus Note 12. Consultative Group to Assist the Poorest, Washington, D.C. Available: http://www.cgap.org/html/p_focus_notes12.html

Hashemi, S. M. 2001. "Linking Microfinance and Safety Net Programs to Include the Poorest: The Case of IGVGD in Bangladesh." CGAP Focus Note 21. Consultative Group to Assist the Poorest, Washington, D.C.

International Finance Corporation (IFC). 2000a. "IFC and Internationale Projekt Consult Finance Microcredit Start-ups in Developing Countries." Press release 00/115, June 22.

_____. 2000b. "Micro Enterprise Bank, Kosovo: Financial Institution Building in a Post-War Environment." *SME Facts* 1 (14). Small and Medium Enterprise Department, Washington, D.C. Available: http://www.ifc.org/sme/acrobat/14-Kosovo.pdf

_____. 2001. "The SME Capacity Building Facility." *SME Facts* 2 (9). Small and Medium Enterprise Department, Washington, D.C.

Ledgerwood, Joanna. 1998. *The Microfinance Handbook*. Washington, D.C.: World Bank.

MicroBanking Standards Project. 2001. "Focus on Productivity." *MicroBanking Bulletin* 6 (April): 53–70.

Nelson, Eric R. 1999. "Financial Intermediation for the Poor: Survey of the State of the Art." African Economic Policy Discussion Paper 10. Development Alternatives, Inc., Washington, D.C.

Paulson, Jo Ann, and James McAndrews. 1998. "Financial Services for the Urban Poor: South Africa's E Plan." Policy Research Working Paper 2016. World Bank, Development Research Group, Washington, D.C.

Saleque, Md. A. 1999. "Scaling-up: Critical Factors in Leadership, Management, Human Resource Development and Institution Building in Going from Pilot Project to Large Scale Implementation: The BRAC Poultry Model in Bangladesh." Paper presented at workshop on Poultry as a Tool in Poverty Eradication and Promotion of Gender Equality, Denmark, March 1999. Available: http://www.husdyr.kvl.dk/htm/php/tune99/5-Saleque.htm

Zaman, Hassan. 1999. "Assessing the Impact of Micro-credit on Poverty and Vulnerability in Bangladesh." Policy Research Working Paper 2145. World Bank, Development Research Group, Washington, D.C. Available: http://econ.worldbank.org/docs/244.pdf

Tools and Practices 13

Poor People's Organizations

One of the most important and most overlooked development assets is the capacity of poor people to mobilize and organize for collective action.[1] Membership-based organizations and networks of poor people have emerged in many places in response to the common needs of specific groups: rural producers, home-based workers, slum dwellers, indigenous people, and landless workers, among others. Poor people's exclusion from decision making at the local, national, and global levels, especially in the face of rapid changes brought about by globalization, gives impetus to the formation of these organizations and to their efforts to make their voices heard. When successful, such groups have been able to effectively represent their members in local and even national forums. Some have then reached out to similar groups in other countries, recognizing both the power of numbers and the commonality of problems poor people face.

This note begins with a description of the World Bank's experience with rural producers' organizations (RPOs). It then describes some successes and good practices of these and other poor people's organizations in three major areas:

- Development of processing, marketing, and alternative employment;
- Management of collective goods;
- Networking and coalition building for influencing decision making.

This note was prepared by Pierre Rondot and Marie-Helene Collion, with contributions from Bryan Kurey and Deepa Narayan.

The emergence of vibrant, representative poor people's organizations such as those described below is enabling poor people to connect with and influence national and global actors.

World Bank Experience with Rural Producers' Organizations

Seventy percent of the world's poor live in rural areas, where agriculture or agriculture-related activities are the mainstay of their livelihoods. The rural poor have limited access to services or means of production, and limited influence, if any, in local, national, or global decision-making processes. To lift themselves out of poverty and improve their livelihoods, rural producers around the world have organized themselves into rural producers' organizations. RPOs are key actors for any development strategy aimed at reaching the rural poor.

A 1993 review of the World Bank's role in the development of cooperatives and rural organizations concluded that inappropriate policy frameworks and government interference were the major reasons that many cooperatives failed to develop as viable and efficient organizations.[2] This was true despite significant investments of financial resources and technical support from donors. Projects with rural producers' organizations were negotiated exclusively between the Bank and governments. They failed to analyze institutional issues, were overly complex, and provided very limited capacity building, most of it for government services. The review concluded that cooperatives must be seen as private sector enterprises and that government's primary role should be not only to control or regulate, but also to establish a conducive policy environment for their growth.

In June 1999, the Bank organized a consultative workshop to hear the views of RPO representatives and NGOs providing support to RPOs. The goal was to better understand why supporting RPOs is important, what types and activities of RPOs should be strengthened, how RPOs could be supported, and what the role of the World Bank should be.[3] In addition, as part of the process of revising its Rural Development Strategy, the Bank commissioned a study to identify the potential role of RPOs in its future rural development strategy.[4]

The findings from both the workshop and the study emphasize that RPOs are not only key economic actors, but also vehicles for the empowerment of rural people and for their inclusion in policy dialogues at the local, national, and global levels. Partnership with rural development actors and the private sector—including RPOs—is necessary to achieve rural development, but it is a fledgling process that requires long-term support. Some areas for programmatic emphasis include the following:

- *Promoting a conducive environment*
  - Promote a conducive legal environment in which private initiatives (collective and individual) are supported by appropriate legislation that is effectively enforced.
  - Promote effective decentralization that provides a favorable environment for RPOs to generate locally relevant answers to their needs.
  - Promote decentralized rural finance institutions.
  - Promote institutional reforms in the delivery of public services to ensure client-responsive services and accountability to users.
  - Strengthen the capabilities of service providers.
  - Promote a dialogue among donor agencies to harmonize approaches and procedures in support to RPOs.

- *Empowerment of rural producers' organizations*
  - Promote the establishment of forums for RPOs at the local, regional, and national levels (when they do not already exist), where rural producers can meet, establish their priorities, and exchange experiences.
  - Finance a regional and national RPO capacity-building fund, in which allocation decisions are made by RPOs themselves.
  - Finance "professional facilitators" to help RPOs organize themselves and help them define transparent procedures to allocate resources and operate their forum.
  - Obtain recognition of RPOs from governments and end the mistrust directed toward them by public services.
  - Ensure that RPOs are recognized as partners by governments and donors, and that they actively participate in:
    - Preparation and negotiations of rural development policy or strategy (CAS, PRSPs, and so on);
    - Preparation, implementation, monitoring, and evaluation of rural development projects.

Activities of Poor People's Organizations

Development of Processing, Marketing, and Alternative Employment

Poor people's organizations have the potential to play important roles in improving and expanding access to markets and opportunities. Among other services, they can coordinate production activities of rural producers and workers in the informal sector, provide marketing and/or advocacy services, and execute capital-intensive investments in infrastructure or processing equipment.

Dairy cooperatives in India

Dairy cooperative development in India began in Gujarat with the establishment of the milk company AMUL in 1946 in response to limited opportunities for traditional milk producers.[5] Operation Flood built on this experience when formation of cooperatives became a government priority for agricultural development in the 1970s. Beginning in 1974 with three projects in Karnataka, Rajasthan, and Madhya Pradesh, and following with two national dairy projects funded through the late 1980s, the World Bank lent more than $500 million to develop the milk industry through cooperatives (made up of district unions combined into state federations). The projects have focused on capacity building (strengthening cooperative institutional structures and training) and support to activities and infrastructure development for increasing production and marketing. The overall objective was to promote viable cooperative businesses, owned and managed by producers, for collecting and marketing milk products in order to expand rural incomes and improve dairy productivity.

The national federation comprises 96,000 village milk cooperatives with some 10 million members. Sixty percent of milk suppliers are landless, small, or marginal farmers. The federation and its members produce 16.5 million liters of milk daily, generating an annual additional income of $90 for each family. Per capita milk consumption has almost doubled, and the milk cooperative business has created an estimated 250,000 off-farm jobs, most of them in rural areas.

Investment has been heavy, and some observers have been concerned about the cooperative being overprotective and monopolistic; there are also concerns that it could use its political power inappropriately. However, these problems seem to be outweighed by the impressive results of the program, due largely to committed membership and farmer-controlled organizations at the local level, sound management, influential and charismatic leaders, strong accounting systems, and effective and profitable services provided to members.

Vila Paraná, Brazil

Vila Paraná is one of 22 communities settled in 1973 through the Projeto de Colonização of Serra do Mel, in the northwestern part of the state of Rio Grande do Norte in Brazil.[6] Attracted by a variety of incentives offered by the state government, 1,196 families received individual plots of 50 hectares each, of which 15 hectares were already planted with cashew nut trees. Since then, much development has taken place in Serra do Mel. Cashew nut plantations occupy a total area of 25,000 hectares, with annual production of unprocessed cashew nuts as high as 10,000 tons.

In the late 1980s, farmers in Serra do Mel began to process cashew nuts using small, semi-artisanal family units developed with the help of the Associação de Apoio às Comunidades do Campo (AACC), one of the most active NGOs in Rio Grande do Norte. These individual family units had difficulty competing in the market. At the end of 1998, the association representing the 46 families of Vila Paraná presented a request, through the local FUMAC council, for a subproject to set up a larger cashew nut processing and marketing center (*central*) for the community.[7] The proposal was approved and financed by the World Bank–supported Rural Poverty Alleviation Program, at a cost of R$15,400. Individual producers now take their cashews for further processing, grading, and marketing in the *central*, selling their processed cashew nuts at an average price of R$9.20 per kilogram, compared to the R$7.50 per kilogram received previously from intermediaries.

The *central* employs 25 people from the community, 19 of them women. Each receives a monthly salary that is 13 percent higher than the minimum wage in Brazil. When asked if local intermediaries can still buy unprocessed cashew nuts in the area, the president of the association replied: "Maybe elsewhere than Vila Paraná, because here no producer sells his cashew nuts outside the *central* anymore." In January 2000, Dutch businessmen visited Vila Paraná and, recognizing the high quality of the cashew nuts produced in the *central*, initiated contractual arrangements that will allow the association to export its production to Europe.

Self-Employed Women's Association, India

In December 1971, Ela Bhatt, a lawyer and social activist who was then head of the women's wing of the Textile Labor Association (TLA), along with Arvind Buch, president of the TLA, founded SEWA in Ahmedabad, India. In April 1972 SEWA was registered as a trade union, making it the first trade union to address the needs of poor women workers in the informal sector, working at home, or trading and vending in the streets.[8] Any self-employed female worker in India can become a member of SEWA by paying an annual membership fee of 5 rupees (about 12 cents). Every three years SEWA members elect representatives to a new trade council made up of worker-leaders, and this committee then elects the executive committee.

SEWA has 212,000 members across India, with 84 cooperatives, 181 producers groups, 1,000 savings groups in nine districts of Gujarat, and about 100,000 women depositors in the SEWA Bank. About 30,000 poor women participate annually in the SEWA Academy, where they explore their contribution to the national economy, their roles and responsibilities as women, their own organizations, and the values and vision behind their movement. SEWA also has a "barefoot managers" training program, and health and life insurance programs. On behalf of its members it has won high court rulings to improve work conditions of urban vendors. SEWA is exploring options to access large loans and venture capital to finance its insurance, information technology, and banking activities. Based on its 20 years of experience, SEWA has reached out across national boundaries and actively participated in the emergence of cross-country networks of common interest.

Management of Collective Goods

It has recently been acknowledged that people whose livelihoods depend on the sustainable management of collective goods are most motivated to manage them, and if formally organized, have the capabilities to do so adequately. Impressive cases exist in which governments have adopted new policies to transfer management of irrigation schemes or other collective resources to farmers' groups, resulting in notable improvements in the sustainability of those resources. In urban areas, it has been found that slum dwellers organizing and pooling their resources can bring about collective ownership of property and more secure land tenure.[9]

Water users' associations in Albania

Following the breakup of state farms and cooperatives in Albania, and the subsequent privatization of the agricultural sector, there was no organization to take over the operation of irrigation systems and the distribution of water.[10] The formation of water users' associations (WUA) began under the World Bank–financed Irrigation Rehabilitation Project in 1994. The first WUAs were organized by village unit, but since several villages might share a single source of water, they were reorganized on the basis of water source to avoid disputes. WUA members are full-time farmers who grow wheat, vegetables, alfalfa, and maize.

The state-run water enterprises, which operated the primary and secondary levels of the irrigation systems, had become overstaffed and inefficient; farmers had lost confidence in them and were reluctant to pay water charges. The idea of allowing WUAs to manage the overall irrigation systems evolved as a solution to this problem. The WUAs became responsible for all costs involved in operating the system, and paid reduced charges to the water enterprises according to their level of responsibility.

Although it started only in 1994, the program has had considerable success. By 1997, there were 187 WUAs covering the entire project area of 98,000 irrigated hectares. By 2001, 408 water users' associations had grouped into 21 federations covering 200,000 families, or one-third of the entire population. The associations are self-financing and manage entire irrigation schemes; they have improved delivery of water to those at the end of irrigation schemes and increased cost recovery from zero in 1994 to $700,000 in 2000.

Hill community forestry in Nepal

In 1978 the government of Nepal passed legislation handing over to local communities a substantial amount of public forest land and hilly areas.[11] Local management of both public and locally owned forest was to be achieved through the *panchayats* (villages), under agreed forest management plans. The *panchayats,* however, proved ill-suited to undertake local forest management. Although forest management committees were formed, they seldom functioned as representative discussion and decision-making bodies. The system was revised to incorporate features of the indigenous control and management systems traditionally practiced by many communities. These systems were based on user groups rather than on whole communities. These groups established management rules that were enforced by use of forest watchers, and included social sanctions.

The focus on user groups was formalized, with more authority and responsibility progressively devolving to these groups under Nepal's 1993 Forest Act. Ownership of the land remains with the state but trees legally belong to the user groups. Management control rests solely with the users of the resources, who develop their own operational plans, set the prices at which the produce is sold, and determine how surplus income will be spent. By June 1997 there were 6,000 user groups, managing 450,000 hectares, with another 6,000 waiting for formal registration.

Issues still arise within user groups, between them, and with the forest department; some of these issues have to do with difficulties in securing access to forest areas from officials, domination by local elites, politicization, and pressures from the forest department. Nevertheless, the Nepal experience has been encouraging: recent studies have demonstrated that managed forests have often thrived with active user group management.

Regional producer groups in Burkina Faso

The World Bank is piloting an RPO capacity-building program in Burkina Faso as a component of the National Agricultural Services Development Project II (PNDSA II).[12] The project, approved in 1997 with a World Bank commitment of $47.3 million over six years, is using a community-driven development approach in nine pilot provinces (out of 45) to encourage RPOs in each province to form a regional forum of RPOs. Within these forums, RPOs carry out several activities, including: (a) exchanging experiences and discussing common issues or problems; (b) setting up priorities for productive investment or services; and (c) selecting capacity-building subprojects identified and prepared by RPOs, to be financed on a cost-sharing basis. Projects accepted by the regional RPO forum are implemented by the RPOs that prepared them, with funds transferred directly to them. They may contract with service providers of their choice when necessary. Members of the RPO forum are RPO leaders, selected by their peers.

In order to benefit from project support, local RPOs need legal status and a bank account. The PNDSAII supported efforts by the Ministry of Agriculture to: (a) revise the existing laws relating to cooperatives and local *groupements* so that these traditional farmers' groups could be registered as legal entities; (b) translate information on the new law into local languages and implement its dissemination; and (c) facilitate the registration of RPOs.

Implementation and roles. Responsibilities are distributed as follows. *Local RPOs* prepare capacity-building subproject proposals on themes that they choose, selecting one of the following instruments: training, advisory services, communication, participation in a national or international RPO meeting, small productive investments, or on-farm research and development. They then submit these proposals to the RPO regional forum. If a proposal is accepted, the local RPO implements the subproject activities on the basis of a contract between the project management unit and the RPO, and reports implementation progress to the RPO provincial forum.

The *RPO provincial forum* adapts the proposed procurement and disbursement manual; organizes sessions to discuss RPOs' priorities, exchange experiences, and review and select additional proposals made by RPOs; and monitors implementation of financed subproject proposals.

A *professional facilitator* (NGO) is recruited to help RPOs form regional forums. Its functions include: (a) local diffusion of information regarding the project, its objectives, its procurement and disbursement mechanisms, and the total amount of funds available for RPOs per zone; (b) facilitation to RPOs in selecting their representatives at the local and provincial levels; (c) elaboration of governing rules for the provincial forum; (d) revision/adaptation of a simplified procurement and disbursement manual with RPOs leaders; (e) training RPO leaders and members of the regional and local forums in the review, selection, and subsequent monitoring of subprojects; (f) monitoring the process; and (g) drawing lessons.

Subproject proposals selected by RPO regional forums are sent to a national *financial management unit*. Documents in the proposal package include the subproject proposal, the approval from the RPO regional forum, and the RPO's bank account statement. On the basis of the documentation received, the national financial unit prepares a contract with the RPO and transfers funds according to the contract. The financial unit also organizes technical and financial audits of financed subprojects on a random basis.

Summary of results after two years of implementation

- Of the 4,009 local RPOs eligible, 1,480 submitted a subproject, and 908 of these were selected by the regional forum.
- The project financial management unit signed 201 contracts and transferred an estimated $351,000 to 201 RPOs (an average of

$1,700/project/RPO). RPOs contributed up to 20 percent of the total costs of subprojects.

- The rate at which the proposals are being submitted is exceeding the capacity of the Bank and the national financial management unit to process them. A total of 707 RPO subproject proposals, for an estimated amount of $1.2 million, are awaiting contracts and initial disbursement. The national financial management unit cannot disburse funds quickly enough because of administrative problems within the Bank and national administrations.

Scaling up. RPOs in Burkina Faso have demonstrated their capacity to identify and formulate subproject proposals, select service providers, and implement their subprojects. The Burkina Faso government and the donor community have decided to expand this approach to the entire country. The same approach has also been tested in Senegal, with similar results.

Influencing Public Policy Decision Making

In many different settings, poor people's organizations are forming networks and coalitions to present a united front and strengthen their influence and bargaining positions in decision making at the local, national, and global levels.

The National Rural Exchange and Cooperation Council (CNCR), Senegal

In March 1993, nine national federations of rural producers in Senegal joined to create CNCR, with the goal of representing rural producers in any formal negotiations related to rural development. By 2001, CNCR had grown to include 19 national rural producers' organizations, representing 3 million rural producers in all regions of Senegal. CNCR is recognized by the government of Senegal as a legitimate institution representing rural producers and can negotiate on their behalf. Driven by the conviction that rural people are responsible for their own destiny, its activities center on three objectives:

- To promote dialogue and exchange of experiences among the leaders of farmers' organizations in order to strengthen the farmers' movement and its federations·
- To represent farmers' interests in negotiations with the government or other national or international partners.

- To contribute to the promotion and sustainable development of family farming.

CNCR is actively involved in rural development policymaking, holding regular meetings with the president of Senegal (once a year), with the prime minister (once every three months), and with the minister of agriculture (once a month). The group is also involved in designing, implementing, and monitoring several World Bank and other non-Bank-funded projects, including the National Rural Investment Project and the Agricultural Services and Producer Organizations Project.

CNCR's successes show that negotiations between national policy bodies and representatives of poor people's interests can have a significant impact on ensuring the promotion of policies favorable to people at the local level. For example, in 1994, as the credit borrowing rate varied between 13.5 percent and 17.5 percent in rural areas in Senegal, CNCR informed the national rural credit bank (La Caisse Nationale de Credit Agricole) and the Senegalese government of the difficulties these high interest rates were causing for Senegalese farmers. As a result, in 1995 the interest rate for farmers was reduced to 7.5 percent. Also in 1995, CNCR raised with the Ministry of Agriculture the issue of the low productivity of soil in Senegal. CNCR and the ministry reached agreement by which the government arranged for the systematic provision of free rock phosphate (a slow-release fertilizer) to farmers and their organizations, greatly improving soil productivity. In return, farmers' groups agreed to arrange for the distribution of the fertilizer to rural areas across the country.

Society for the Promotion of Area Resource Centres (SPARC)

Formed in Mumbai, India, in 1984 by Sheela Patel, SPARC works to form partnerships between professionals committed to grassroots activism and communities of pavement dwellers.[13] Within India, the NGO works in alliance with Mahila Milan, a network of women's collectives initially formed by women pavement dwellers, and the National Slum Dwellers Federation (NSDF), a network of leaders from urban slum settlements. SPARC's role in this alliance is to help build local capacity through the creation and mobilization of community-based organizations, sponsor training and people exchanges, promote gender inclusiveness in decision making, and create an information base on the poor and their problems.

SPARC projects enable poor people to organize themselves, learn from each other, and take action on collective concerns, including advocating for policy change, obtaining land, and managing their settlements. In Mumbai, for example, SPARC's work with Muslim women in the Bayculla slum resulted in the creation of Mahila Milan in 1986, which trains and supports women in savings and credit groups and other productive activities. SPARC worked with the new community organization to educate and train slum dwellers—mostly women with children—to collectively avert or deal with demolition or eviction, helping to break isolation and create solidarity within the community. SPARC guaranteed a credit line of 3,500,000 rupees (about $70,000) from the Ministry of Women and Children in Delhi to help Mahila Milan establish a "Housing Bank" for its members to save and borrow money for secure shelter and/or emergency needs. Members started out saving about 5 rupees a day (about 10 cents). By 2001, about 600 families had saved an average of 5,000 rupees (about $100) for future permanent housing. Another 600 families had saved 1.6 million rupees (about $33,000) in a crisis savings fund. About 1,800 members have taken out individual loans of up to 5,000 rupees (about $100).

After almost twenty years, SPARC has expanded its partnership model to 36 cities across India, always working in alliance with poor people to build local organizational capacity. The alliance—SPARC, Mahila Milan, and NSDF—has convinced the government to provide alternative land for slum dwellers and to stop mass demolitions of slums without notice. It has demonstrated new models of urban upgrading in World Bank–financed projects, including resettlement of slum dwellers living directly next to railway lines.

In addition, SPARC is actively involved in regional and international networks of slum dwellers' associations and participates in a global campaign for secure tenure for poor city dwellers. On a regional and global scale, SPARC is a lead member of Shack/Slum Dwellers International. This global network of national slum dweller federations from 12 countries works to strengthen grassroots efforts against homelessness and negotiates with governments in support of shack/slum dwellers' rights. A key SDI project is enabling slum and shack dwellers to participate in exchange visits to other villages, towns, and countries and share their experiences and ideas. In 1992, SPARC undertook an international exchange with SDI member South African Homeless People's Federation—an experience that has supported the mutual development of both communities. South Africa has 85 women's savings groups with 60,000 members who have saved $1,750,000 and are setting up their own federation. The model has spread to Zimbabwe where

17,000 people are saving, and more recently to Namibia where there are 6,000 people saving.

Via Campesina

This international farmers' movement, whose name means "the peasant way," is based in Honduras and coordinates more than 50 peasant organizations of small and middle-scale producers, agricultural workers, rural women, and indigenous communities from the Americas, Africa, Asia, and Europe.[14] Its objective is to develop solidarity and unity in diversity among organizations of small farmers in pursuit of economic and social justice. It also aims to strengthen women's participation in formulating proposals to improve livelihoods.

The organization was founded in April 1992 when several peasant leaders from Central America, North America, and Europe gathered in Managua, Nicaragua, at the Congress of the National Union of Farmers and Livestock Owners. In 1999 Via Campesina launched its Global Campaign for Agrarian Reform. In Toledo, the Philippines, peasant families had started to benefit from agrarian reform by receiving land previously belonging to a huge estate. However, armed struggle with the landlords, who had tried to reclaim their land, resulted in the burning of some peasant houses, the eviction of peasants, and the killing of members of peasant organizations. An international campaign in support of the Toledo families was mounted through hundreds of letters sent to the Philippine Ministry for Agrarian Reform. Confronted with this international pressure, officials forced the landlords to turn over the land to the peasants.

Another global action by Via Campesina is the International Solidarity and Resistance Caravan. More than 450 farmers from Brazil, India, and Europe came together in 1999 in an international caravan that made its way through 12 European countries. The purpose was to confront the most powerful countries of the world to demand a new framework for international economic relations, one in which the world's wealth would not be concentrated in a small group of transnational corporations. Via Campesina has also been a major mobilizer against the World Trade Organization. In Seattle in 2000 members from several continents protested against transnational companies and announced their decision to fight genetically modified food. On April 17, 2002, Via Campesina organized an "international day of farmers' struggle" to promote farmer-based agricultural production and show solidarity against genetically modified organisms and the corporations that produce them. There were protests in more than 20 countries around the world.

The International Federation of Agricultural Producers (IFAP)

Founded in 1946, the International Federation of Agricultural Producers is an international organization grouping nationally representative general farmers' organizations from around the world.[15] IFAP has nearly 80 member organizations in 52 countries and 42 associate members in 30 countries. It represents all of the agricultural producers in the industrial world and hundreds of millions of farmers in developing countries, and is financed and governed entirely by its member organizations.

Established to facilitate cooperation between agricultural producers' organizations, with a view to ensuring the security of the world's food supply, IFAP also works to improve the economic and social status of all who live by and on the land, and to promote the creation and strengthening of independent farmers' organizations in every country. In pursuit of these objectives, IFAP:

- Acts as a forum in which leaders of national farmers' organizations can meet to exchange information and ideas, highlight mutual interests, and take coordinated action to further those interests. IFAP has five permanent standing committees on agriculture in developing countries, representing Africa, Asia, the Mediterranean, North and South America, and Central America/Andean region/Caribbean.
- Keeps members informed about international events and issues of concern to farmers' organizations.
- Promotes the creation and strengthening of independent, representative organizations of agricultural producers around the world through such tools as the Corporate Development Committee, which supports the development of organizational capacity among poor people's rural organizations in developing countries.
- Acts as the recognized representative of the world's farmers, bringing the concerns of agricultural producers to the attention of international meetings of governments and other bodies, including the United Nations Food and Agricultural Organization, the Organisation for Economic Co-operation and Development, the World Trade Organization, and the World Bank.

IFAP has been influential in many international conferences. During the 1995 U.N. World Summit for Social Development in Copenhagen, for example, as a result of IFAP's efforts, the world's governments recognized farmers' organizations as an essential element of civil society.

At the 1992 Earth Summit in Rio de Janeiro, IFAP presented a declaration in which the world's farmers committed themselves to environmental conservation. According to a German farmers' organization, this declaration had an important impact not only on the international bodies involved with IFAP, but also on national governments. "In Germany, we referred strongly to this resolution in order to influence national politics and to prove to our government that German farmers shared the same point of view as other farmers worldwide."[16]

IFAP has also worked since 1989 to strengthen the links between farmers' organizations and research institutes, organizing a series of consultations that resulted in the farmers' real needs being considered in research programs. Since then, projects linking farmers' organizations and research institutes have been implemented in Burkina Faso, Kenya, Zambia, and Zimbabwe.

Notes

1. This introduction is taken from Narayan and Shah 2000.
2. Hussi and others 1993.
3. Rondot and Collion 2001.
4. CIRAD/ODI 2001.
5. This section draws on Candler n.d. and World Bank 1997.
6. This section draws on van Zyl, Sonn, and Costa forthcoming.
7. FUMAC refers to municipal community schemes created under the World Bank–financed Rural Poverty Alleviation Projects in northeast Brazil. Through the FUMAC, decision making for subproject approval is delegated to project municipal councils, with 80 percent of members comprising potential beneficiary associations and civil society representatives.
8. The section draws on Narayan and Shah 2000.
9. See also Tools and Practices 9 on Community Driven Development.
10. This section was prepared with the assistance of David Groenfeldt. It draws on INPIM 1998 and Konishi 2001.
11. This section draws on World Bank 2001.
12. This section is based on personal communication with the project facilitator and on quarterly reports of CECI (Canadian Centre for International Studies and Cooperation).
13. This section draws on Narayan and Shah 2000. "Pavement dwellings" are seemingly makeshift structures that exist mainly on sidewalks and other paved areas in cities. For more information see the SPARC website at www.sparcindia.org
14. This section draws on Narayan and Shah 2000.

15. Information in this section is drawn from the International Federation of Agricultural Producers website at www.ifap.org

16. IFAP 2002.

Resources

Beaudoux, Elian, Andre Borque, Marie-Helene Collion, Jean Delion, Dominique Gentil, Charles Kabuga, Jurgen Schwettman, and Ashih Shah. 1994. "Farmer Empowerment in Africa through Farmer Organizations: Best Practices." Departmental Working Paper 14. World Bank, Africa Technical Department, Washington, D.C.

Candler, Wilfred. n.d. "Operation Flood: The Cooperatives' Role." PowerPoint presentation prepared for the World Bank, Rural Development and Agriculture Sector, Animal Resources Thematic Team. Available: http://essd.worldbank.org/rdv/RDVWeb.nsf/Animal/dairy_master

CIRAD/ODI. 2001. "The Role of Rural Producers' Organizations in the World Bank Rural Development Strategy: Reaching the Rural Poor." Cirad-tera 17/01. Centre de Coopération Internationale en Recherche Agronomique pour le Développement (CIRAD) and Overseas Development Institute (ODI), Montpellier, France.

Delion, Jean. 2000. "Producer Organizations–Donors Partnership in Project Implementation: Risk and Precautions from a Social Perspective." World Bank, Agriculture Knowledge and Information Systems, Thematic Team on Producer Organizations, Washington, D.C.

Hussi, Pekka, Josette Murphy, Ole Lindberg, and Lyle Brennernan. 1993. *The Development of Cooperatives and Other Rural Organizations: The Role of the World Bank*. Washington, D.C.: World Bank.

INPIM 1998. "Country Updates: Albania." INPIM Newsletter No. 7. May 1998. Washington, D.C. Available: http://www.inpim.org/Library/Newsletters/newsletters.html

International Federal of Agricultural Producers (IFAP). 2002. "About IFAP." Paris, France. Available: http://www.ifap.org/about/federate.html

Konishi, Toru. 2001. "Albania Irrigation Rehabilitation Project: In the Context of Community Driven Development." Presentation given at World Bank seminar on Community Driven Development in ECA:

Experience with Water Users' Associations, May 27, 2001. Environmentally and Socially Sustainable Development, Social Development Department, World Bank, Washington D.C.

Narayan, Deepa, and Talat Shah. 2000. "Connecting the Local to the Global: Voices of the Poor." Framework paper prepared for workshop on Local to Global Connectivity for Voices of the Poor, December 11–13. World Bank, Poverty Reduction and Economic Management Network, Poverty Reduction Group, Washington, D.C.

Rondot, Pierre, and Marie-Hélène Collion, eds. 2001. "Agricultural Producer Organizations: Their Contribution to Rural Capacity Building and Poverty Reduction—Report of a Workshop, Washington, D.C., June 28–30, 1999." World Bank, Rural Development Department, Washington, D.C.

van Zyl, Johan, Loretta Sonn, and Alberto Costa. Forthcoming. "Decentralized Rural Development, Enhanced Community Participation and Local Government Performance: Evidence From Northeast Brazil." Cited in Luis Coirolo, Keith McLean, Mondonga Mokoli, Andrea Ryan, Parmesh Shah, and Melissa Williams, *Community Based Rural Development: Reducing Poverty from the Ground Up*. Washington, D.C.: World Bank.

World Bank. 1997. "India, Second National Dairy Project." Implementation Completion Report 16218. Rural Development and Agriculture Sector, Animal Resources Thematic Team, Washington, D.C.

_____. 1999. "Zimbabwe Farmers' Union." Case study prepared for workshop on Agricultural Producer Organizations: Their Contribution to Rural Capacity Building and Poverty Reduction, June 28–30. Rural Development Department, Washington, D.C. Available: http://wbln0018.worldbank.org/essd/essd.nsf/producer/casestudies

_____. 2001. "A Revised Forest Strategy for the World Bank Group." Draft paper prepared under the Forest Policy Implementation Review and Strategy. Environmentally and Socially Sustainable Development Network, Washington, D.C.

Tools and Practices 14

Legal and Judicial Reform

By mid-2002, there were more than 400 World Bank–financed projects with legal and judicial reform components, with 30 freestanding projects approved in five regions. These have resulted from recognition of the fact that the rule of law and a functioning judicial system are important not only for the investment climate, but also for protecting poor people and their livelihoods.[1] Typically, World Bank legal and judicial reform projects are implemented over two to five years through institution building, technical assistance, learning and innovation, or Adaptable Program Loans, as well as through grants from the Institutional Development Fund and advisory work by the Legal Department.[2] This section examines the empowerment impact of four innovative legal and judicial reform projects undertaken by the Bank in the Latin America and Caribbean Region.

Guatemala Judicial Reform Project

In October 1999, a $33 million Adaptable Program Loan was approved for the Guatemala Judicial Reform Project for five years, through June 2004. The project aims to create a more effective, accessible, and credible judicial system that will foster public trust and confidence and improve consistency and equity in the application of the law.

Extensive input from a wide range of stakeholders, in the government as well as in civil society, informed the project design. An

This note was prepared by Talat Shah, with input from Waleed Malik, under the overall guidance of Deepa Narayan.

innovative collaborative participatory assessment involved more than 1,000 individuals, including judges and representatives from government agencies, law schools, the private sector, and civil society. This unique process of citizen participation in judicial reform helped identify the problems to be targeted: poor performance of the court system, limited citizen access to justice, corruption, poor institutional management, and negative public perception of the judicial branch. Designed to address these problems, the project has mainstreamed the idea that citizens, as users of judicial services, have a right and obligation to contribute to the design and implementation of reforms. As a result, the reforms that are in place help to bring the law closer to the people.

Impact

In the two years since its inception, the project has made significant strides toward strengthening the judicial system and improving public access to the law. The project supports a 50 percent increase in the budget for the judicial branch, enabling the hiring and training of 30 new judges, many of them women. In addition, the number of regional courts has been increased, allowing many more people than before to actually go to court. Court processes and plans have been simplified and made user-friendly. For example, before the reforms it used to take 5 to 6 months to register power of attorney or file for a divorce. Through court reengineering, the same processes now take only 24 hours.

Several mechanisms enable better access to justice by indigenous Guatemalans, a widely underserved population who live mainly in rural and remote areas. Language training for judges and interpreters in indigenous languages has made the justice system more accessible and responsive to the indigenous population. With the demonstrated success of the initial language training, the demand for this training among judges and court personnel has increased tremendously.[3]

In addition, the project has expanded Guatemala's justice of the peace program into locations where judges are absent. In 2001, justices of the peace made up 50 percent of all judges in Guatemala. They also have increased power to vet and mete out cases, expediting case management. This single reform has significantly increased productivity and efficiency throughout the judicial system.

In addition to process improvements, Guatemala passed a judicial ethics code in April 2001 that has helped generate some unprecedented rulings. For example, the Guatemala Supreme Court voted to send a military general to jail for killing a religious official. The Supreme Court also denied immunity to a senior Congressman (also a former general), stating unequivocally that he must face trial under international human rights law. Previously, the public believed that military and political officials were above the law. Such rulings hold great symbolic value and communicate to the public that judicial reform is serious and accountable.

Access to Information

The Guatemala Judicial Reform Project includes a comprehensive social communications component to promote public access to legal information as well as to improve information and communication within the judicial system. With project support, a Supreme Court Public Information Center was established in the capital city in 2001. Similarly, information centers are also being established in other urban centers. In addition, public education campaigns spread the word about the "new" judiciary. A public website was created to provide the public with direct access to judicial procedures and rulings.[4] Through the website, members of the public can register a complaint or receive regular judicial updates by e-mail.

Several mechanisms are in place to improve information flow within the judiciary and help professionalize court personnel. A judicial systems Intranet has increased communication among judges and other court officials, and has been particularly useful for judges in rural and remote areas. A digital divide program is under development (pilot testing was carried out in 2001) to provide distance education to judges in remote areas and promote knowledge sharing across the judiciary.

Inclusion and Participation

An independent Public Defender's Office has been established to open up opportunities for poor people to have equal access to the law. Alternatives to courts, such as mediation and conciliation centers, have been successfully piloted and are to be expanded throughout the country. Pilot mediation centers in indigenous areas have been very well received by the local population, and public demand is high for the expansion of such centers to other underserved areas.

A first workshop on cultural sensitivity training for judges in indigenous areas was held in January 2001 in Santa Cruz del Quiché.

Sixty-one judges and auxiliary staff from 5 of the 21 Quiché municipalities took part in the participatory program that included interac-
tive and practical activities, role playing, presentations, and group discussion. The major concerns voiced by participants were related to
language and cultural barriers to justice, because Guatemalan formal
courts operate exclusively in Spanish. Participants recommended training in the Quiché language for local judges and their staff. At the end
of the workshop, participants reported feeling better equipped to integrate cultural sensitivity into their work.[5]

Accountability

A new anti-corruption program has been instituted through the project
to promote public oversight of the judiciary. The program includes preventive and control measures that streamline procedures for discipline of
judges, require information disclosure on judges and judiciary personnel,
and promote community participation in identifying concerns with the
judicial system and correcting wrongdoing. In addition, groups involved
in the initial broad stakeholder consultation continue to be involved in
various aspects of project implementation, monitoring, and evaluation.

Lessons Learned

This project demonstrates how broad stakeholder consultation can help
identify critical areas for judicial reform and start a process to regain
public confidence in the judicial system. The experience also demonstrates that projects designed using participatory methods are more likely
to have participatory practices mainstreamed during implementation
and evaluation. In part, reaching poor people requires using local languages and establishing branches and services in closer proximity to
poor people themselves. Transparency and information dissemination,
in combination with technical improvements, are important for legal
and judicial reform to be sustainable.

Venezuela Supreme Court Modernization

Prepared in 1997 through a participatory methodology, the Venezuela Supreme Court Modernization Learning and Innovation Project
was supported by a $4.7 million loan through June 2001. The project
was designed to strengthen the judiciary and make it more accessible to
the public. The design incorporates the results of extensive stakeholder

assessments, carried out through one- and two-day workshops with judges, judges' assistants, administrative staff, and civil society organizations.[6]

Impact

The project has improved the functioning of the judiciary and has increased public access to the judicial system. Constitutional changes facilitated by the project ensure that the judiciary receives at least 2 percent of the annual federal budget, has financial and political independence, and is open to scrutiny by the public. The project promotes coordination among formerly adversarial judicial sector agencies to foster mutual understanding, identify policy gaps, and capitalize on opportunities for collaboration.

Access to Information

Both judges and the public have better access to information because of reforms espoused by the modernization project. A criminal procedure code instituted in July 1999 eliminated secret trials and introduced less complicated and oral procedures to promote transparent processes and use of resources. A CD-ROM on the new code was prepared to facilitate training of judicial sector employees and dissemination of the new regulations. Venezuelan judges now participate in an international virtual network of knowledge sharing for judges called IUDICIS. Participation has meant that Venezuelan judges are better informed about the law and, as a result, feel more ownership of and pride in their work.

For public benefit, the Supreme Tribunal has launched a public website and has begun publishing its decisions online.[7] Public information windows have been set up in renovated courts to enable the public to track their cases and obtain information about the judicial system. Some information locations are fully automated, providing the community with instant access to the judiciary. The Venezuelan public can also watch a new television show that discusses how people can obtain greater access to justice and raise their awareness of the law.

Accountability

While Venezuelan judges themselves have taken the lead in implementing the modernization project, a Supreme Court Civil Society Unit was also created and provided with adequate staff, training, and resources as a forum for public dialogue and partnership. One unique form of civil society participation is that as new supreme court justices are appointed, they are subject to citizen scrutiny through direct review and press coverage. In a 2000 appointment process, the names of short-listed candidates for judgeships were published in Venezuelan newspapers and over the Internet with the purpose of soliciting citizen feedback before final selections were made. A similar process is being developed to carry out public evaluation of all judges throughout the country.

Local Organizational Capacity

As a result of civil society consultations, in the first year of the project a group of 45 NGOs formed the umbrella organization Alianza Social para la Justicia, whose members are active participants in judicial reform activities. The World Bank helped coalesce the NGOs into this umbrella group, which became more unified in its priorities and concerns and began to present joint plans for reform and implementation. The Internet was a useful tool in helping the NGOs come closer together, share information, and work as an alliance. Alianza has introduced new ideas and has shown a commitment to public pressure for change. The umbrella structure has also enabled alliance members to share and compile information, strengthen their organizational capacity, and improve their outreach and communication skills.

Lessons Learned

This project demonstrates the importance of linking strong public support with government commitment, leadership, and technical capacity to create building blocks for judicial change. Modernization through partnership between civil society and judges has begun to show some valuable returns, benefiting courts and communities alike with high-quality justice.

Ecuador Judicial Reform Project: Legal Aid for Poor Women

In April 1995, the World Bank approved a $10.7 million loan for the Ecuador Judicial Reform Project to support case administration, mediation centers, an education program on legal rights and procedures, and remodeling and development of court infrastructure. A subproject on Legal Aid for Poor Women, funded with $256,780 over two years, supported the creation of five legal aid clinics in the cities of Quito, Guayaquil, and Cuenca to help poor women and their children exercise their legal rights and improve their socioeconomic condition. By design, each of the five legal aid clinics was established and operated by one of the following local and national Ecuadorian NGOs: Centro Ecuatoriano de Promoción y Acción de la Mujer, Fundación Maria Guare, and Corporación Mujer a Mujer.

Impact

Over two years, from April 1998 to March 2000, the pilot program provided legal consultation and representation, counseling, and dispute resolution services to almost 17,000 poor women for a project cost of about $15 per client. The majority of women in Quito and Guayaquil who sought legal services used them either to obtain child support, to stop domestic violence, or to file a case. The project also indirectly assisted another 50,000 beneficiaries, most of whom were the children or other relatives of the women clients.

An evaluation of the legal aid subproject revealed that women did better when they used NGO legal services than when they used private lawyers to litigate their claims.[8] For example, women using NGO legal services obtained child support awards that were on average 20 to 50 percent higher than awards obtained by women who adjudicated traditionally. In addition, legal aid clients obtained restraining orders in a shorter period of time: two or three days rather than the weeks typically needed by private lawyers. The public reputation of the NGO centers is so positive that demand has outstripped supply. Even middle- and upper-class women would like to be able to use the services.

The work and outreach of the legal aid clinics has helped build community awareness of domestic violence as a human rights violation. It has also strengthened NGO relationships with the media, increased the judiciary's respect for the NGOs, and initiated policy change processes. For example, the Municipality of Santa Elena is vetting a proposal for a new family code and a strategic development plan that includes a gender perspective.

Access to Information

The legal aid clinics facilitate women's concerns by educating them about their rights. They use an extensive outreach methodology employing radio programs, brochures, flyers, information tables at community events, meetings with women's groups, and other public activities to reach out to the general public and, more specifically, to poor women. Mobile brigades on Saturdays and Sundays bring services directly to distant areas where lawyers and legal offices are usually not available.

Local Organizational Capacity

The pilot program promoted local organizational capacity by improving staffing, technology, and training of local NGOs delivering legal services. These NGOs are the critical partners in the implementation of the legal aid clinics. Early on, service teams from each clinic participated in workshops on mediation, litigation in crisis situations, child support, defense of women's and children's rights, coordination of community resources, gender and justice, abuse prevention, and education and training.

The expanded organizational capacity of these NGOs is reflected in the remarkable improvements in the quality, range, and geographic scope of services to poor women. For example, high demand for services has resulted in extended hours so that the centers can assist many more clients. Participating NGOs have also developed a database of cases which now produces a wealth of information on the needs and characteristics of the beneficiary population. This information will be useful for future initiatives supporting women's access to law and justice as well as their public health needs.

Lessons Learned

This project demonstrates that legal aid clinics are an important complement to the formal court system and help underserved populations obtain fair access to justice. By providing legal, psychological, and medical assistance, the clinics demonstrate the importance of using an integrated approach to helping poor women find lasting solutions to their problems. The sustainability of providing legal aid services to poor populations remains a critical challenge. In this instance, there is no long-term financing mechanism in Ecuador for legal aid clinics for women despite their undeniable success. Because poor women do not have the resources to pay for transportation or court fees even when legal services are free, alternative financing mechanisms must be identified. As the pilot program has completed (June 2002), project staff are seeking a private partner to help finance the clinics and are considering the possibility of providing services on a sliding payment scale.

Peru Urban Property Rights Project

Most of Peru's urban poor live as squatters on publicly owned lands and have no formal rights as citizens or property holders. Recognizing this problem, Peru began to initiate legal reforms to support property rights in the late 1980s and early 1990s. In 1996 then-President Fujimori announced a public commitment to formalize 1.6 million urban properties by 2001. Formalizing property rights involves issuing and registering land titles to squatters through legal and institutional improvements in the legal and bureaucratic system. Without secure property rights, the urban poor are not able to claim the social and economic benefits of land ownership. For example, they are unable to use their homes or lands as collateral for loans or pass their property on to their children. In addition, credit providers have no incentive to offer financial services to this population.

With the creation of an autonomous national agency responsible for formalizing existing property in poor urban settlements, 200,000 such properties were registered by early 1998. As a result of simplified and more transparent procedures, the cost of registering and titling property was reduced from $2,000 to $50, and the length of time necessary for the process dropped from 15 years to six weeks or less. In August 1998 the World Bank approved the $38 million Urban Property Rights Project to support the creation of a low-cost, user-friendly system of formal and sustainable property rights in selected predominantly poor settlements in Peruvian cities. Building upon Peru's existing national program, the project made a commitment to register an additional one million properties in eight urban areas by 2001.

Impact

Through regulatory reforms, the Peru Urban Property Rights Project has dramatically reduced the cost and time required for registering property. The urban poor can more easily and affordably register their property and become "legitimate" citizens. The institutional reforms have been very effective. By August 2000 the project had helped almost seven million Peruvians secure land titles collectively worth more than $4 billion. By introducing the newly formalized urban properties into the organized capital markets, the property values have increased by more than $1.7 billion since the start of the project.[9]

A social assessment involving repeated consultations with key stakeholders and beneficiaries at all levels was used as an iterative process to devise, test, and adapt land titling strategies at the neighborhood level. With the introduction of formal property rights, communities are being affected in different ways. For the first time, Peruvian women have equal rights to property under the law. However, the impact on neighborhood organizations has been mixed. In some areas, they have been weakened with individual ownership, while in other cases communities are better organized to provide social services to residents. The project has earned a high political profile in Peru because of its widespread success in providing tangible assets to poor people.

Access to Information

The project supports regular and multidirectional informational flows. For example, regular stakeholder consultations and weekly visits to participating communities are scheduled in order to solicit public feedback about the project. The outreach process is also active with the two relevant public agencies, the Commission for Formalizing Informal Property (COFOPRI) and the Urban Lands Registry (RPU), visiting beneficiaries in their communities rather than waiting for citizens to visit them.[10] Community leaders facilitate the formalization program by organizing community meetings, which precede COFOPRI's door-to-door collection of ownership information.

The advantages of registering property are being widely publicized, as is the process for formalizing ownership. People are encouraged to provide information about their property to the government agencies charged with titling and registration, and residents are organizing themselves to obtain registration certificates and to produce evidence of ownership. Registration is conducted house by house to verify that applicants are the true owners of each property.

Accountability

Through social and economic monitoring, the project is able to track the impact of property formalization on local communities. The general director of the project (who is also the national coordinator of formalization) is accountable for outcomes. A project management committee, with equal representation from COFOPRI and RPU, oversees implementation and the attainment of project goals, and makes any strategic decisions needed. Conflicts among community members are resolved in an assembly. Problems of leadership, land ownership, and conditions of occupancy are among the issues discussed. The establishment of a property arbitration system eliminates the incentive to turn to the courts to challenge or block the granting of a title. A mediation and conciliation system is being developed for settling disputes between squatters and private owners.

The project concept was developed a decade ago by Hernando de Soto at the Instituto Libertad y Democracia (ILD), a Peruvian research institute. The World Bank and the ILD worked together to expand the concept nationally and encourage the development of local organizations and institutions that could undertake the project. The $13.07 million institutional-strengthening component finances efforts to bolster the administrative and institutional capabilities of RPU and COFOPRI so that they can be sustainable and viable.

Local Organizational Capacity

A continuous participatory process has involved a wide range of stakeholders from all sectors. Neighborhood organizations in new informal urban communities, which have been responsible for acquisition and distribution of land, have been impacted by the reforms. In some cases, the property formalization process has weakened neighborhood organizations; in other cases, the organizations have evolved in function and now provide social services to the community. Urban settlements have also seen the growth of voluntary functional organizations (community kitchens, mothers' clubs, parents' associations, sports clubs) normally run by women and providing a safety net to poorer people. This has strengthened the role of women in these communities.

Lessons Learned

A key to the urban property rights project's success is the careful analysis of citizen needs through studying and listening to poor people's concerns. The iterative process of devising, testing, and adapting land titling strategies at the neighborhood level has led to the development of a streamlined and responsive land registration process. The project helps integrate low-income families into the wider urban landscape and creates rights and obligations that enable small property owners to develop a greater sense of partnership with the government and private sector.

Notes

1. Dietrich 2000; Hammergren 2000; Van Puymbroeck 2001; and World Bank 2001b.
2. For an overview of World Bank legal and judicial reform projects, see World Bank 2001b.
3. Ohman 2001a.
4. The Guatemala Judicial Extranet is at http://www.organismojudicial.gob.gt/index.html
5. Ohman 2001b.
6. Malik 2001.
7. The Venezuela Supreme Court website is at http://www.tsj.gov.ve
8. Rodríguez 2000.
9. Panaritis 2001b.
10. Established in 1996, the Commission for Formalizing Informal Property (Comision de Formalizacion de la Propiedad Informal, COFOPRI) is a decentralized public institution responsible for promoting access to formal ownership and registered title in order to guarantee the right of individuals to privately hold property. The Urban Lands Registry (Registro Predial Urbano, RPU) was formed in 1996 to register properties located in squatter settlements and low-income neighborhoods, and has technical, administrative, economic, and financial autonomy. Since 1996, RPU and COFOPRI have registered more than one million titles and formalized more than 1.4 million properties (Panaritis 2001b).

Resources

Dietrich, Mark K. 2000. "Legal and Judicial Reform in Central Europe and the Former Soviet Union: Voices from Five Countries." World Bank, Legal Vice Presidency, Washington, D.C. Available: http://www4.worldbank.org/legal/publications/ljr_eca.pdf

Hammergren, Linn. 2000. "Can Law and Institutions Give Voice to the Poor?" *PREM News,* June 12. World Bank, Washington, D.C.

Malik, Waleed H. 2001. "Challenges of Forging Civil Society Partnerships for Judicial Reform." Washington, D.C.: World Bank. Available: http://www1.worldbank.org/publicsector/legal/venezuelapaper.doc

Ohman, Nina. 2001a. "Cultural Sensitivity: Judges in Indigenous Areas #1110." First Interim Progress Report to Development Marketplace (March). Washington, D.C: World Bank. Available: http://www.developmentmarketplace.org/report1.pdf

_____. 2001b. "Cultural Sensitivity: Judges in Indigenous Areas #1110." Second Interim Progress Report to Development Marketplace (June). Washington, D.C: World Bank. Available: http://www.developmentmarketplace.org/ProgressReporttwo1110.pdf

Panaritis, Elena. 2001a. "Do Property Rights Matter? An Urban Case Study from Peru." *Global Outlook: International Urban Research Monitor* 1 (April): 20–22. Woodrow Wilson International Center for Scholars and the United States Department of Housing and Urban Development, Washington, D.C.

_____. 2001b. "Real Property: A Basis for Market Development (Establishing Property Rights in Peru)." The World Bank, Urban Land and Real Estate Unit, Urban Development Department, Washington, D.C.

Rodríguez, Marcela. 2000. "Empowering Women: An Assessment of Legal Aid Under Ecuador's Judicial Reform Project." World Bank, Legal Vice Presidency, Washington, D.C. Available: http://www4.worldbank.org/legal/publications/Empowering-Women-web.pdf

Van Puymbroeck, Rudolf V. 2001. *Comprehensive Legal and Judicial Development: Toward an Agenda for a Just and Equitable Society in the 21st Century.* Washington, D.C.: World Bank.

World Bank. 2001a. "Argentina Legal and Judicial Sector Assessment." World Bank, Legal Vice Presidency, Washington, D.C. Available: http://www4.worldbank.org/legal/publications/argentina-final.pdf

_____. 2001b. "Initiatives in Legal and Judicial Reform." World Bank, Legal Vice Presidency, Washington, D.C. Available: http://www4.worldbank.org/legal/publications/initiatives-final.pdf

Tools and Practices 15

Institutional and Governance Reviews

Strengthening public institutions underpins the World Bank's work in all sectors. Most Bank activities engage public sector institutions that are, or should be, supporting policymaking and service delivery, and providing oversight and accountability.[1] Institutional and Governance Reviews (IGRs) are analytical reports that focus on the functioning of key public institutions. They have three features. First, they take performance failures in policy management, service delivery, or accountability as the starting point for their analysis. Second, they use standardized toolkits, surveys, and quantitative measures of performance wherever possible.[2] Third, and most fundamentally, they analyze the feasibility of reform recommendations with a rigorous assessment of political realities and constraints to reform.

The purpose of IGRs is to inform the Country Assistance Strategy and operational priorities by identifying institutional weaknesses that are contributing to measurable performance problems, by helping to improve the design of projects, and by providing a basis for rigorously prioritizing reforms according to institutional or political feasibility. IGRs should be undertaken upstream of the CAS or major lending operations. They are prepared for the country team, providing a basis for dialogue between the Bank and counterparts.

This note was prepared by Nick Manning and Laura Bureš.

Confronting Politics

IGRs would not have been produced in the Bank just a decade ago. Their examination of political issues and motives—reinforcing the vital point that short-term, purely technical applications will not solve problems that have deep political roots—and their use of empirical data to make comparisons between institutional arrangements and to monitor officials' behavior are signs of growing openness and candor within the Bank and among an increasing number of client countries. IGRs can provide an analysis of the relevant political dynamics and show how the structure of political institutions and the behavior of political actors drive public sector performance and increase or decrease the prospects of achieving those development objectives.

A well-executed analysis of the relevant political dynamics is fundamental to an IGR. The Bolivia IGR, for example, convincingly showed how the structure of political institutions and the behavior of political actors drive the operation of that country's public administration, and hence the service-delivery performance of its public sector. It showed that the intrusion of political factors and incentives into administrative practices and outcomes has benefits and costs.

Such analyses raise significant challenges and expose sensitivities both on the client side and on the part of the Bank. Reformers committed to good governance welcome robust analytic reports and their contribution to productive political discourse. At the same time, there are necessarily sensitivities around such politically delicate topics. The degree of explicitness in IGRs thus will vary considerably.

"Best Fit": Emphasizing Alternatives and Tradeoffs

IGRs respond to the challenge of moving away from the "best practice" model that has proved less than successful in fostering institutional reform. In the best-practice approach, problems in formal institutional arrangements are highlighted, and advice and incentives to address the problems are provided. Governments are urged to make their civil services more meritocratic and their budget processes more performance-focused, but they are not provided with any pragmatic guide as to how those changes could be introduced, given political realities.[3] A "best fit" approach, by contrast, asks, "What would work here?"

Recent research on the effectiveness of aid concludes that aid in the form of money has a large impact only when countries have already begun to make substantial progress in reforming their policies and institutions. In such settings, donor support should be geared less to project financing and more to economic and sector work that in the long run lays the groundwork for institutional and policy reform.[4] Successful reformers among IDA countries typically have gone through a period of intensive policy dialogue with the Bank and other stakeholders, without the formality of adjustment lending (and without a great deal of donor financing).[5] The implications of these findings for the Bank's operational work are clear: in countries with weak institutions and poor policy performance, the Bank's focus should be on ideas, not money.

In pursuing "best fit," IGRs seek to provide governments with ideas about the tradeoffs between approaches, rather than to dictate which approach to follow. The Bolivia IGR, for example, set out three alternative arrangements: public action by a centralized bureaucratic hierarchy, by an insulated autonomous agency, or by decentralized and participatory local governments. Opening up the agenda in this way provides a fertile basis for exploring what sequence of actions—including the relative emphasis accorded diverse alternatives—offers the best prospects for sustainable success.

The Pioneers

IGRs have been undertaken in Armenia, Argentina, Bangladesh, Bolivia, the Organization of Eastern Caribbean States, and Peru, and are planned for southeast Europe (fiscal 2002). Their styles have varied according to the nature of the problem being addressed, the stage of the country dialogue, and the resources available to the country team. Some have been sweeping and others more incremental in their recommendations. The Bolivia and Bangladesh IGRs are described in more detail below.

The Bolivia IGR

The Bolivia Institutional and Governance Review, issued in August 2000, aimed at understanding the country's public sector and identifying challenges and possible directions for an ambitious second-generation reform program.[6] The IGR recognized the achievements of the last 15 years in public sector reform, including the government's current Insti-

tutional Reform Project, and identified informality as the most significant obstacle facing the Bolivian bureaucracy.[7]

Bolivia findings: informality as the primary obstacle to institutional development

The review found informality to be a problem in several areas of public
administration, including public expenditure and personnel management. The underlying causes of this were identified as stemming from
political dynamics in the country, which produced a system of patronage and clientelism. In particular, the IGR cited:

- Politicians' interest in obtaining electoral support from and ex-
  erting control over the bureaucracy by distributing public jobs
  and other types of rents and placing "persons of confidence" in
  critical bureaucratic posts;
- A weak private sector that failed to generate employment opportunities for the middle class, encouraging some segments of
  the population to seek employment in the public sector;
- A fragmented party system that forced political parties to negotiate coalition agreements.

While Bolivia's coalition governments had passed some key reforms
and were the basis for democratic stability, this was achieved at the cost
of deteriorating public services at the local level due to excessive
politicization of the government bureaucracy and its weak institutional
capacity. As additional obstacles to a properly functioning government,
the review faulted deficiencies in formal rules and procedures, weakness of supporting institutions, the Ministry of Finance's focus on fiscal
discipline at the expense of strategic allocations and efficiency, and delays in the implementation of the Statute of Public Officials.

In *public expenditure management,* the review found the clearest
indication of informality in the lack of credibility of annual budgets.
Significant deviations between approved and executed budgets were the
result of inadequate central control over details of resource allocation
and use, combined with unrestrained, opportunistic spending behaviors by line agencies. Analysis of budget data for 1990–92 and 1994–96
showed that 15 to 20 percent of approved agency budgets were reallo-
cated across agencies.

In *public personnel management,* the IGR found several areas of
informality. One example was the widespread use of consultants for
line functions. Because regular government employees had low salary
levels, agencies had difficulty attracting qualified personnel and there-

fore were in the habit of hiring consultants to circumvent the government's formal wage policy. Other forms of informality included civil servants' tendency to give in to outside political pressure in fear of losing their jobs or salaries, deliberate destruction or concealment of agency-related information at times of government change, and use of nonwage budget items for salary supplements.

The review found implementation of the *Law of Financial Management and Control*, which provides the legal framework for regulating public administration, to be incomplete and uneven. The law had been created to introduce results-oriented management practices and strengthen central oversight; however, the IGR demonstrated that there was little evidence that such reforms had been implemented. The failure to implement the law more fully was primarily the result of limited commitment on the part of the Ministry of Finance and resistance from public officials. The IGR survey showed that in the nine years since promulgation of the law, public officials had not internalized its norms and values; most did not believe the law encouraged officials to focus on results or improved their agency's efficiency.

The IGR also found *micro-institutional causes* of informality in weak mechanisms for management control and regulatory enforcement. The laxness or indifference of agencies such as the Controller General of the Republic and the Ministry of Finance contributed to weak central oversight. In addition, unavailability of information on agency performance, transactions, and compliance with rules made it impossible for any central oversight body to exercise effective control over public agencies. For example, the Treasury did not have timely information on budget execution to adjust disbursement during a fiscal year, and the Controller General could not audit line agencies' accounts effectively because it had no adequate financial statements to audit.

Analysis of participatory reforms

The IGR analyzed Bolivia's experience with the 1994 Popular Participation Law, which empowered communities in some municipalities to oversee the actions of local municipal governments and to hold them accountable. Some of the participatory mechanisms created by the law included:

- Regular election of town councils to five-year terms in office, which provided the most basic means of citizen control through electoral accountability. The council could remove a poorly performing mayor from office after a year by a three-fifths vote of censure.
- Establishment of "vigilance committees" that could issue pub-

lic statements on how co-participation funds were budgeted and invested. The committee could file a complaint or petition the national Senate if problems were found and not resolved.

- Establishment of rights and duties of territorial base organizations, including the ability to propose, request, and control the performance of public works and provision of services. These organizations were required to account for all actions undertaken on the community's behalf and elect representatives to the vigilance committee.
- Introduction of a participatory investment planning process.

One year after the Popular Participation Law was enacted, an Administrative Decentralization Law was passed to redefine the role of administrative departments. Deliberative and oversight functions of departments were now carried out by departmental councils, and council members were elected from each province by town councilors. Departmental councils had a legal mandate to approve departmental budgets, reports on resource expenditure, and development projects and public investments.

Shortcomings of Bolivia's participatory reforms. The review found that departmental councils were weak in practice, with little power to take initiative. There were several reasons for this weakness: the prefect presided over the council presidency; the council had no budget of its own; and members had no means of hiring technical support. Popular Participation's planning process was not working well as an accountability mechanism at the local level, because it was difficult to get people to participate and planning meetings tended to produce lists of projects rather than planning strategies.

The oversight and participatory instruments created by the Popular Participation Law were sometimes co-opted by political parties and interest groups, which weakened transparency and accountability. The IGR's case studies demonstrated a conflict-ridden struggle to gain partisan control over municipal resources—in elected officials' decisions about how to distribute co-participation funds and what projects to carry out, in the oversight and participatory roles played by the vigilance committees and the territorial base organizations, and in the use of the vote of censure. Political parties were found to exert disproportionate influence in local affairs, undermining civil society's oversight mechanisms.

The IGR survey found high turnover of mayors, instability in council membership, limited roles and impact of civil committees at the local level, limited power of vigilance committees, and bypassing of vigilance committees by mayors. The survey also showed signs of politicization of intergovernmental relations, as party alliances and divisions largely determined relations between prefectures and municipalities and between mayors and prefects. Strong political party clientelism was discovered in the hiring of departmental personnel, while job stability and merit-based promotion did not exist. The IGR survey revealed weak citizen participation at the departmental level, as four of six prefectures reported they had not taken steps to promote participatory governments.

Positive outcomes of Bolivia's participatory reforms. In their localities, Bolivians pressed their demands through their territorial base organizations and vigilance committees, despite shortcomings of the system. A degree of community representation was created that had been weak or nonexistent in the past, and communities pressured mayors for equitable distribution of resources. Electoral accountability was improved as local officials were now elected throughout the country, providing opportunities for traditionally marginalized groups to participate in municipal government. Bolivian municipal governments were empowered to a greater extent than they had been in the past, as they were developing plans, investing resources in major public works, improving public services, mobilizing resources, and responding to community pressure.

Recommendations of the Bolivia IGR

The IGR classified institutional reforms as urgent priorities for the government. It found signs of "reform fatigue" among citizens, whose quality of life had not improved very much in 15 years of reform efforts. The review warned that, unless the state began to provide better public services and alleviate poverty more effectively, the credibility of the current regime might be threatened, and it pointed to recent social protests as one indication of the fragile legitimacy of the Bolivian government.

In response to the pervasive problem of informality, the IGR provided four central recommendations:

- Depoliticize personnel management in the public sector;
- Strengthen central oversight capacity in financial and personnel management;
- Learn from the recent successful experiences of the autonomous

regulatory agencies (superintendencies) and replicate those successes in other public sector institutions;

- Use "citizen voice" as a means of exercising social control over public administration.

Depoliticization. The IGR argued that "depoliticization" of Bolivia's administration lay at the heart of further reform. However, given the strong incentives to maintain a coalition government, a depoliticization process was likely to be successful only if it were initiated and sustained with the explicit participation of the major political parties. The IGR also noted the importance of transparency in the depoliticization process and, to this end, recommended that the government establish reasonable parameters for political appointments agreeable to major political parties; provide information to Congress and the public about the number of political appointees in each agency; and commit to decreasing the scope and magnitude of political appointments over time.

Oversight mechanisms. The IGR emphasized the importance of establishing effective oversight mechanisms in the core areas of personnel and financial management and institutional mechanisms for sharing management information within the public sector. The review argued that a strong central oversight body, autonomous and insulated from short-term partisan political considerations, was essential for implementing a depoliticization strategy. The IGR also recommended reconsidering the institutional arrangement for overseeing procedural compliance in financial management and discussed the need for predictability in budget allocations, recommending greater coordination between the Ministry of the Presidency and the Ministry of Finance in developing a performance-oriented management and evaluation system.

Learning from past success with autonomous regulatory agencies. The IGR public officials' survey showed that autonomous regulatory agencies in the country had achieved a much higher level of organizational development than the rest of the public sector. However, the review warned that "autonomization" could create other costs to efficient public administration, such as ambiguous accountability arrangements, duplication of functions, and difficulty in coordination. Therefore, the review recommended autonomous agencies in cases where political independence was important for agency success, but not in service delivery agencies.

Citizen voice for social control. The IGR recommended that participatory reforms be adapted for the national level. It advised a government strategy of engaging the private sector, civil society, and the media as supporters of the reform agenda, consulting with them on reform implementation, and providing them with information on institutional performance in the public sector to enable them to monitor progress and exert pressure for continued reform. To this end, the IGR recommended that the Ministry of Finance and the Controller General adopt a more open policy of information disclosure.

The Bangladesh IGR

The Bangladesh IGR of September 2000 analyzed the underlying causes of Bangladesh's poor governance, the consequent weak performance of its public institutions, and reasons for the government's slow response to reform proposals.[8] The review focused in particular on the available mechanisms for holding government agencies accountable to the public. Drawing on prior economic and sector work and integrated economic and social analysis, it described the vested interests and underlying incentives, both formal and informal, operating within the bureaucracy and political leadership to explain the deep-seated opposition to public sector reform. The report examined these factors at both the national and local government levels and proposed measures to improve accountability for the delivery of public services.

The report gave high priority to reforms that would promote the rule of law and enhance the security of citizens, especially the poor. It also emphasized the importance of finding ways to strengthen the voice of civil society and to build partnerships for better governance involving the press, NGOs, independent research centers, and private business. A central theme of the IGR was that successful public sector reform must benefit all stakeholders.

Bangladesh findings: sociopolitical obstacles to improved governance

Overall, the IGR found that reform initiatives had frequently failed in Bangladesh, because they had promoted technical solutions when the main obstacles to improving public sector management were sociopolitical. The review noted three obstacles to public sector reform in particular:

- Pervasive clientelism in public service;
- Organized interest groups, some illegitimate, determining political decisions;
- Major discrepancies between the private agendas of principal public actors and their formal public agendas.

According to the IGR, clientelism in Bangladesh's public service operated within clearly defined hierarchies, and the government's "rules of business" for conduct in public service were increasingly disregarded. The well-organized interest groups that determined political decisions included the military, the bureaucracy, private business, trade unions, religious groups, NGOs, and donors. However, the activities of some of these interest groups were illicit and included bribery, extortion, harassment, and the use of musclemen. The political, business, trade union, and bureaucratic power structures had been partially captured by an underworld that used strong-arm tactics to enforce its power. In the districts, the powerful often gained support from the police and members of the judiciary for their own benefit, to the disadvantage of the poor. Poor people meanwhile were dependent on patron-client relationships for their survival.

Corruption and fraud on the part of public officials were widespread, while economic losses from inefficiencies in the public sector were huge. The IGR estimated that the revenue loss from corruption and inefficiency in the customs and income tax departments exceeded 5 percent of GDP. More than 40 percent of commercial banks' loan portfolios were overdue, and much of this money would likely never be recovered. Investors were discouraged by the country's poor governance. In addition, the physical insecurity of poor people and women of all classes, as well as the rapid deterioration of the natural environment, adversely affected the quality of life in Bangladesh.

Recommendations of the Bangladesh IGR
The Bangladesh IGR made several recommendations to improve governance in the country's public sector:

- Strengthen systems of both internal and social accountability by reinforcing the role of Parliament, reforming the judiciary, tightening public financial accountability, promoting transparency, and strengthening civil society;

- Increase decentralization;
- Reinvigorate administrative reform by focusing on incentives, performance, merit postings and promotions, a credible oversight system, and delegation of authority over personnel and financial matters;
- Take advantage of the potential of e-government;
- Mobilize support for reform.

Strengthening systems of accountability. The IGR's recommendations for strengthening public accountability are described in more detail below.

To reinforce the role of the Parliament, the IGR advised several steps. It recommended that parliamentary committees undertake investigative work when appropriate. As one example, the IGR suggested that the committee overseeing the health ministry gather data on the operation of health facilities around the country, produce a written report, and commit to engaging with civil society and the media. The review also suggested that the government respond to outstanding queries in recent reports of the Public Accounts Committee and the Public Undertakings Committee. It recommended that the Parliament debate these reports and allow the press to witness and report on such deliberations. The IGR also supported creating a greater separation between policymakers and the bureaucracy, so that bureaucrats could be required to come before parliamentary committees to justify their actions.

To improve the judicial system in Bangladesh, the IGR recommended computerizing court records and case management, upgrading facilities, supporting initiatives to improve management of physical and human resources, and improving the training of justices, including preparing them to deal with technical cases (as in environmental or commercial law). The review further called for streamlining court procedures and providing adequate resources to ensure more prompt and effective enforcement of the law.

To tighten public financial accountability, the IGR called for a phased, medium-term program of five to ten years. It identified several top-priority measures, including: providing top-notch policy advice to the minister of finance; establishing a resource management unit to monitor the implementation of the budget and improve the quality of budget data; providing urgent practical training to the economics, budgeting, and planning staff; and computerizing and rationalizing the payroll and pensions system.

To promote transparency, the IGR focused on protecting the independence of the press, building its capacity, and allowing independent radio and television. The review recommended that public agencies issue regular reports on their activities, submit them to Parliament, and make them available to the public. It advised that such reports describe clearly defined annual work programs and budgets with performance targets and objectives that could be monitored. Accounts and audits would be published within six to nine months of the end of each fiscal year.

Notes

1. World Bank 2000c.
2. See http://www1.worldbank.org/publicsector/toolkits.htm for recent work on toolkits. Details of public officials surveys are available at http://www1.worldbank.org/publicsector/civilservice/surveys.htm
3. World Bank 2000c.
4. World Bank 1998.
5. Devarajan, Dollar, and Holmgren 2001.
6. This section draws on World Bank 2000a.
7. Informality is defined as the gap between "ideal" or "desirable" behavioral patterns prescribed in a set of formal institutions (laws, rules, and organizational norms) and actual behavioral patterns that obtain without following the letter or spirit of the existing formal rules.
8. This section draws on World Bank 2000d.

Resources

Devarajan, Shantayanan, David Dollar, and Torgny Holmgren. 2001. *Aid and Reform in Africa: Lessons from Ten Case Studies.* Washington, D.C.: World Bank.

World Bank. 1998. *Assessing Aid: What Works, What Doesn't, and Why.* Washington, D.C.: Oxford University Press.

_____. 2000a. *Bolivia: From Patronage to a Professional State. Bolivia Institutional and Governance Review, Volume 1: Main Report.* Report 20115-BO. Poverty Reduction and Economic Management Network, Latin America and Caribbean Region. Washington, D.C.

_____. 2000b. "Fixing ESW: Where Are We?" Draft report prepared by Operations Policy and Strategy Group for the meeting of the Committee on Development Effectiveness, Washington, D.C.

_____. 2000c. *Reforming Public Institutions and Strengthening Governance: A World Bank Strategy*. Washington, DC: World Bank.

_____. 2000d. "Taming Leviathan: Reforming Governance in Bangladesh, An Institutional Review." South Asia Region, Poverty Reduction and Economic Management, Washington, D.C.

_____. 2001. "Assessing the Quality of FY01 ESW: Approach Paper." Quality Assurance Group, Washington, D.C.

Tools and Practices 16

Citizen Report Cards

Citizen "report cards" are social accountability mechanisms based on citizen surveys of the performance and quality of government services. They allow citizens to monitor state performance. In addition, they:

- Provide quantitative information from the perspective of public service users, which can help government agencies make changes and improve service;
- Assist in prioritizing reform efforts and allocating public resources;
- Aggregate and communicate poor people's realities to government officials, decision makers, and the public;
- Foster voice, discussion, and debate, and build demand for reform;
- Treat users of public services as clients or customers whose voices matter in the design, delivery, and assessment of government services.[1]

The citizen report card was developed by civil society in Bangalore, India in 1993 in response to concern about the quality of public services.[2] The methodology used in the Bangalore citizen report card has since spread and is currently being used countrywide in India as well as in other countries, including the Philippines, Ukraine, and Vietnam.[3] Citizen report cards are also used to assess the performance of public agencies in Canada, Denmark, Ghana, Sweden, the United Kingdom, and the United States. Different country contexts have led to different models for institutionalizing report cards (table 5-2).

This note was prepared by Laura Bureš, with input from Magui Moreno Torres, under the overall guidance of Deepa Narayan.

Table 5-2 Implementing Report Cards

Administering agency	Advantage	Examples
Civil society organization	Builds public pressure for reform	Public Affairs Centre, Bangalore
Government service provider agency	Ownership of the process by the agency	United Kingdom, Canada
Government oversight agency	Most comprehensive in process and product	United States

Examples of public sector report card experiences from Bangalore, India, Ukraine, and the Philippines are discussed below.

Bangalore's Report Cards on Public Services

In 1993 Dr. Samuel Paul and a small advisory group of local leaders initiated the first report card on Bangalore's public services. Based on a sample survey of middle-income and poor (slum dweller) households, the report card assessed public services from the perspective of the user. It was not an opinion poll, but rather reflected people's actual experiences with a range of public services. The exercise was then institutionalized as a core function of the Public Affairs Centre (PAC), a nonprofit organization in Bangalore founded in 1994 and dedicated to improving the quality of governance in India. PAC completed a second report card in 1999 to provide a comparative assessment and benchmarking device to gauge whether public services improved or declined between 1993–94 and 1999.[4]

Findings

The 1999 report card showed that most public services in Bangalore had improved to some extent in the five years since the first report card.[5] Slum dwellers reported improvements in service quality for all agencies, although in varying degrees. Yet the second report card's findings revealed a generally low level of citizen satisfaction with government services, with less than 50 percent of respondents satisfied in most cases.

Among slum dwellers, the services that were rated satisfactory by more than 70 percent were: public transport (83 percent), primary schools (74 percent), electricity (73 percent), and public hospitals (73 percent). The lowest satisfaction ratings were for the police (only

25 percent satisfied). Problems with services most frequently involved garbage collection, drainage, streetlights, roads, and telephones.

Nearly two-thirds of the poor reported that they were willing to pay more for services if quality and reliability were improved. More than half were willing to pay more for water and health services. Only five percent were aware of anti-poverty programs meant to benefit them, making the percentage of poor people who attempted to use the programs very low. In any case, applicants rarely succeeded in getting benefits.

The report card demonstrated that corruption remained widespread in most agencies with few exceptions. The incidence of corruption in almost all agencies increased between 1993–94 and 1999, and the average amount paid in bribes rose dramatically in four of 10 agencies. The proportion of slum dwellers paying bribes declined by 22 percent, but the average amount paid increased by 71.5 percent. In addition, more people visited agencies in 1999, but their rate of success in having their problems solved declined. For slum dwellers, the incidence of problems rose from 22 percent in 1993–94 to 34 percent in 1999, while problem resolution declined from 38 percent to 1.3 percent.

Outcomes

After the publication of the first report card, civil society groups in Bangalore took on a range of government reform activities. Media coverage of the report card's results contributed significantly to informing the public and drawing attention to problems with government services. Public agencies became engaged in the efforts sparked by the report card, and some agency leaders initiated collaborative programs with citizen groups and their networks. In some cases, service providers adopted the report card approach as an internal monitoring device. In telephones, electricity, and water supply, bill collection was streamlined and decentralized. Increased competition in services (such as cellular phones) also spurred improvements between the first and second report cards.

The second report card also attracted wide media attention and public interest and stimulated civil society to put further pressure on local government to improve performance. Agency leaders acknowledged that their responses to the report cards were stimulated by public pressure to improve services, and many officials now view report cards as a guide to better delivery of services and greater public accountability. As a result of Bangalore's success, a number of cities and countries have replicated or adapted the report card method.

Methodology

The first report card was based on surveys of approximately 480 middle-income and 330 low-income (slum dweller) households. Focus group discussions were held, and pre-tested questionnaires were used to collect data on respondents' levels of satisfaction with a range of public services. The second report card was based on a sample of 1,339 middle-income and 839 low-income households and used similar scales for responses as those used in the first report card to allow appropriate benchmarking. A multi-stage stratified sampling plan ensured representativeness. The field work was conducted by Gallup MBA India Pvt. Ltd., a market research agency. The report cards covered water supply and sewage, power, telephones, ration shops, police, public buses, the regional transport office, hospitals, and the development authority. The survey of the slum dweller sample covered primary schools but did not ask about telephones, the regional transport office, or the development authority.

Lessons Learned

To move from the report card to reform and improvement of public services, the Public Affairs Centre recommends a number of steps based on its experience:

- Identify critical services/agencies and design both short- and long-term reform strategies;
- Build support constituencies and partnerships and determine capacity/resource requirements;
- Find "quick wins" to build momentum for reform;
- Focus on services and agencies rather than on individuals;
- Identify a "local champion" to support and encourage the report card process;
- Use an independent and technically competent local NGO or professional organization to carry out the study, and establish local ownership of the process.

The People's Voice Program in Ukraine

Inspired by Bangalore's experience with citizen report cards, the People's Voice Program was created in Ukraine to promote public participation in building an open, accountable, and effective government by bringing together the supply and demand sides of reform. The

International Centre for Policy Studies (ICPS) is the lead local institution for the program and works with a number of local partners to gather and disseminate information on public services through citizen surveys for improved service delivery. The project is a World Bank pilot initiative, funded in partnership with the Canadian International Development Agency.[6] Two Ukrainian cities, Ternopil and Ivano-Frankivsk, were selected because their mayors had agreed to be "local champions" and their city governments had shown willingness to cooperate. ICPS implemented the program in the spring of 1999 with the goals of monitoring local service delivery through the public sector scorecard approach and supporting local reform initiatives.

Findings

Although some public services, such as the post office, telephone company, local schools, and infrastructure, received positive evaluations in the People's Voice surveys, the study revealed widespread dissatisfaction with service quality. In general, survey respondents found the performance and integrity of public agencies to be no better than "average" (a rating of 3 on a scale of 1 to 5). Problems were most frequently cited in the housing authority and health services. Citizens who interacted with agency officials about service problems found them neither helpful nor friendly. The highest frequency of bribe taking was in hospitals, road police posts, and visa offices. Over a third (36 percent) of respondents reported that they paid bribes "on their own initiative"; 28 percent paid because bribes were solicited by officials, while 36 percent paid on the advice of others. Despite dissatisfaction with services, 93 percent of citizens had never filed a complaint because they believed that doing so would be futile. While 80 percent of citizens were aware of government rules and regulations, 50 percent claimed that these rules and regulations were not followed by public agencies.

Entrepreneurs who were surveyed indicated that they encountered a number of problems in their interactions with the public sector. They cited arbitrary interpretation and enforcement of regulations as significant obstacles, as well as the high costs of regulatory compliance and tax inspections. Respondents indicated that 40 percent of senior managers' time was spent dealing with government. These problems were considered greater than those related to corruption. The respondents found municipal government to be hostile toward business, and they had little confidence in the court system for resolving commercial disputes in a fair, honest, and timely manner. The survey revealed problems (late or insufficient payment) in public procurement. The entrepreneurs also indicated dissatisfaction with the lengthy process of business registration.

Outcomes

In response to the dissemination and public discussion of survey results, the People's Voice Project has generated dialogue among citizens and public officials in the cities of Ternopil and Ivano-Frankivsk. The free flow of information has resulted in unprecedented actions by municipal authorities and by citizen groups for improved public services. For example, municipal officials in Ternopil set up several task groups to develop concrete solutions to the most critical problems identified by survey respondents. The surveys also mobilized Ternopil residents to pressure the local government to create "service centers" as one-stop shops where people can pay for all of their municipal services. The service centers are also intended to become clearinghouses for filing and monitoring citizen complaints.

The project has supported the establishment of NGO coalitions and citizen action groups in both cities and improved the capacity of its NGO partners by providing training in human resource management, strategic planning, media relations, and coalition building. Because citizens in both cities have identified education as a primary area of concern, NGOs, parents, and education officials have held dialogues and are developing proposals to improve the local education system. In Ternopil, these dialogues have produced the "City Blueprint for Education," plan for 2005. The city of Ivano-Frankivsk convened the multi-stakeholder Ivano-Frankivsk Education and Advisory Council in October 2001. In addition, community advisory boards have been established in both cities to create an agenda of issues and needs for citizen engagement to further educational reforms. In both cities, other citizen working groups are focusing on strategies to improve transport, housing, and business development.

In summer 2001, the People's Voice Program expanded to two additional Ukrainian cities—Chuguiv and Kupyansk—conducting surveys on the quality of public services involving citizens, business representatives, and public servants. In both cities, the public evaluated service quality as less than satisfactory, with the most problematic institutions for citizens being local housing offices, public health clinics, and the city energy department.

Methodology

The study's methodology used pre-tested surveys with standard questionnaires conducted through face-to-face interviews with random samples of 500 households and 100 entrepreneurs.[7] The surveys asked citizens and business people about their experiences with the following government agencies: the post office, health services, phone service, housing authority, school authorities, state savings bank, office of social benefits, tax inspection, road police, hospital, local executive committee, customs service, visa department, police, and courts.

Lessons Learned

ICPS identified several factors as very important in implementing the project effectively:

- Commitment and engagement of city mayors and local government officials;
- Close cooperation with local NGOs;
- Establishment of local NGO coalitions working in different sectors;
- Additional surveys over time to reassess services, monitor progress, identify lessons learned, and recommend steps for the future.

The Filipino Report Card on Pro-Poor Services

The Filipino Report Card on Pro-Poor Services was conducted in the spring of 2000 as a follow-up to the World Bank's Philippines Poverty Assessment.[8] It was based on a national survey of client satisfaction with public services designed to help the poor. The survey asked poor Filipinos about constraints they encountered in accessing public services, and about their views on the quality and adequacy of services and the responsiveness of government officials. This information provided insight into citizens' priorities and problems and raised the issue of how different services could better meet people's needs.

Findings

The survey findings showed that poor Filipinos used health facilities less than those with higher incomes, despite the fact that a larger percentage of the poor were sick. One in five poor households that used private facilities did not have access to government facilities, especially in poorer and more remote areas. Satisfaction with health care was lowest in urban areas. Payment for health care by poor people was almost entirely out-of-pocket, as insurance coverage was low overall. High prices for medicine were especially burdensome.

In education, about 10 percent of school-age children (ages 7 to 12) were not in school during the period of the survey. Dropouts were mostly from poor families, with the reasons most often related to illness or physical disability, followed by economic need and poor academic performance. Very few poor and middle-income households used private schools, which charged tuition fees 10 times as high as public school tuition. Families spent about 2 percent of income on enrollment for each child in school.

Water supply services reached about 64 percent of the Filipino population. About a third relied on self-provision from their own wells or rainfall collection. Seventy-five percent of poor people were without access to home-piped water, and most of them had not applied for access. Their median per capita daily water consumption was barely 30 liters and was lower among the small percentage that relied on water vendors. Water supplied by all sources was considered unsafe for drinking.

Half of the households sampled considered their housing inadequate. The urban poor were less satisfied with their housing than the rural poor. Only 53 percent of poor households owned the land on which their house stood, although a large percentage (81 percent) owned their home. Only 6 percent of poor households applied for housing assistance, while larger percentages of the middle- and high-income groups applied for assistance (9 percent and 14 percent respectively). In addition, the approval rate for assistance was lower among the poor than among the higher-income groups.

According to the survey, rice was important to the welfare of poor people. Although the availability of subsidized rice was limited, poor people purchased more subsidized rice than those classified as middle-income. Yet higher-income people purchased more rice in general and thus benefited more from the subsidy on the whole. Survey respondents recommended geographical targeting of the poor.

Outcomes

The Report Card is being used by President Gloria Macapagal-Arroyo's administration to revise the Philippines Medium Term Development Plan and to develop new poverty alleviation strategies and programs. The Department of Budget and Management intends to institutionalize client feedback and "performance-based budgeting" so that all public agencies will use the information generated by the survey and other measurement tools for allocating funds. This is an unprecedented measure to obtain regular citizen feedback on key public services, bringing citizens directly into the budget allocation process.

At the time of writing, a number of "localized" report card initiatives were also underway in various cities throughout the Philippines, and the report card model is being replicated in other countries, including Albania, India, and Vietnam.

Methodology

The report card survey was undertaken by the World Bank in collaboration with Social Weather Stations, an independent survey research organization in the Philippines. The survey was carried out in March and April 2000 and included a sample of 1,200 households distributed across the four regions (National Capital Region, Luzon, Visayas, and Mindanao) in proportion to population. The questionnaire asked for information on awareness, access, use, and satisfaction related to pro-poor public services in five areas: health care, primary education, housing, water, and subsidized rice distribution.

Lessons Learned

Similar assessments in the past have failed to make a lasting impact, because they were one-time exercises that lacked follow-through. Incentives for reform and improvement are more likely to increase if service providers know they will be monitored again. The Philippine experience points to the need to institutionalize the report card system as a process to be repeated periodically to assess progress (or lack thereof) in service delivery.

Notes

1.   World Bank 2001b.
2.   This section draws on Paul and Sekhar 2000 and on material from the Public Affairs Centre, Bangalore, India, available at http://www.pacindia.org. See also World Bank 2001a and the website of the Participation Thematic Group at www.worldbank.org/participation/

3.   In India, the recently completed Millennial Public Service Survey reached more than 36,000 people across 24 Indian states. See Paul 2002.

4.   For more on benchmarking, see Kingdom and Jagannathan 2001.

5.   See Paul and Sekhar 2000 for detailed findings.

6.   See the website of the International Centre for Policy Studies at http://www.icps.kiev.ua/pvp/home_e.html. Also see Ternopil Urban Development Agency, Peolpe's Voice Project, and International Center for Policy Studies 2000; UFE Foundation and others 2000.

7.   The program also surveyed a sample of civil servants.

8.   World Bank 2001b. See also http://www.worldbank.org/participation/philsocial.htm for information on the Philippines "social weather stations" system.

Resources

Kingdom, Bill, and Vijay Jagannathan. 2001. "Utility Benchmarking: Public Reporting of Service Performance." Viewpoint Note 229. World Bank, Private Sector and Infrastructure Network, Washington, D.C.

Paul, Samuel. 2002. *Holding the State to Account: Citizen Monitoring in Action*. Bangalore, India: Action Aid Karnataka Projects—Books for Change.

Paul, Samuel, and Sita Sekhar. 2000. "Benchmarking Urban Services: The Second Report Card on Bangalore." Public Affairs Centre, Bangalore, India.

Ternopil Urban Development Agency, People's Voice Project, and International Center for Policy Studies. 2000. "Educational Policy Reform in the City of Ternopil." Ternopil, Ukraine.

UFE Foundation, World Bank Institute, International Centre for Policy Studies, and Canadian International Development Agency. 2000. "People's Voice Project Survey in Ternopil: Report, July 30, 1999." Ivano-Frankivsk, Ukraine.

World Bank. 2001a. "Case Study 1: Bangalore, India, Participatory Approaches in Budgeting and Public Expenditure Management." Participation Thematic Group, Social Development Department, Washington, D.C.

_____. 2001b. "The Filipino Report Card on Pro-Poor Services." Draft. Participation Thematic Group, Social Development Department, Washington, D.C.

Tools and Practices 17

World Bank
Corruption Surveys

In recent years, research and analysis have provided overwhelming evidence that corruption is a regressive tax on the poor. Corruption distorts public resource allocation and impedes access to basic services such as health and education. It discriminates against small and medium enterprises in their access to markets. Evidence shows that poor people tend to spend a larger proportion of their incomes on bribes than do citizens in other income categories. Corruption undermines the legitimacy and functioning of the state, affecting even its ability to ensure basic security of life and property.

In 1996–97 the World Bank began exploring the use of surveys as a means to "measure" corruption. Illicit and secretive, corruption by its very nature is difficult to quantify using survey instruments. In fact, for many years it was thought that data on corruption were impossible to capture. But experience over the last few years has shown that if designed, targeted, and implemented well, surveys can elicit from victims and even perpetrators of corruption—including households, the private sector, and public officials themselves—perceptions of, as well as experiences with, corruption across the range of public sector institutions. Thus far, the Bank's experience has demonstrated that:

- Surveys can help diagnose the extent and source of institutional dysfunction in a country, help set reform priorities, and inform policy dialogue;

This note was prepared by Tripti Thomas.

- They can help quantify the economic and social costs of corruption, and evaluate the quality of public service delivery and of the business environment;
- They represent an empirical approach that turns the policy debate away from a focus on individuals toward a focus on institutions;
- Surveys allow the establishment of baselines against which progress in anti-corruption efforts can be measured;
- Surveys can also provide public information on corruption, which in turn can encourage attention by the executive, parliamentary scrutiny, and greater participation of civil society to stimulate the demand for better governance and measures against corruption.

Since its initial efforts in 1996–97, the Bank has developed and adapted a range of survey instruments and applied them in a variety of contexts, countries, and regions. A few key efforts are highlighted below.

Global Surveys of the Private Sector

Surveys of Firms for World Development Report 1997

One of the Bank's first attempts to use surveys to understand the causes and consequences of corruption was a survey of firms carried out to inform *World Development Report 1997: The State in a Changing World* (WDR97).[1] This large-scale survey, covering more than 3,600 firms in 69 countries, aimed at understanding the institutional framework faced by the private sector. Entrepreneurs from a range of small to large firms were asked to evaluate different institutional conditions in their country, such as the security of property rights, the predictability of rules and policies, judicial reliability, problems with corruption and discretionary power in the bureaucracy, and disruption due to political transitions.

Analysis of the survey data flagged the enormous extent to which corruption disrupts private sector activity and development. Respondents in all countries except the high-income Organisation for Economic Co-operation and Development (OECD) countries rated corruption in their countries as among the top three impediments to doing business. As noted in WDR97, "Overall, more than 40 percent of entrepreneurs reported having to pay bribes to get things done as a matter of course. In industrial countries, the figure was 15 percent, in Asia about 30 percent, and in the CIS over 60 percent... Furthermore, over half the respondents worldwide did not regard a bribe as a guarantee that the promised service would be delivered."[2] It was also found that general arbitrary action by governments (including corruption and red tape) forced businesses to spend excessive amounts of time on negotiating laws and regulations with public officials, rather than on productive activities.[3]

The World Business Environment Survey

The World Business Environment Survey (WBES), initiated in 1999–2000, was intended to build and expand upon the WDR97 survey approach. Under this effort, surveys of at least 100 firms in each of at least 100 countries are envisioned, in order to develop a global dataset on corruption from the perspective of business. The survey instrument is designed to elicit detailed information about bribes in public procurement and bribes as a share of firm revenues. While the dataset is intended primarily for global comparisons, individual country analyses, such as those in a May 2001 report on West Bank Gaza, have also been gleaned from the survey results.[4] One of the best large-scale examples of the WBES effort has been the Business Environment and Enterprise Performance Survey (BEEPS).

Business Environment and Enterprise Performance Surveys

Commissioned jointly by the World Bank and the European Bank for Reconstruction and Development, the BEEPS involved surveys of more than 3,000 enterprise owners and senior firm managers in 22 transition countries in the Europe and Central Asia Region (ECA) of the World Bank. Among other things, BEEPS aimed to identify the many forms of corruption across transition countries. For the first time, it provided the basis upon which empirical evidence could be gathered on the means through which firms influence the state, leading to introduction of the concept of "state capture" into the anti-corruption lexicon.[5] Whereas administrative corruption refers to the abuse of existing rules, regulations, laws, and policies for private gain, the term "state capture" refers to the actions of individuals, groups, or firms in both the public and private sectors to *influence the formation* of laws, regulations, decrees, and other government policies to their own advantage as a result of the illicit and nontransparent provision of private benefits to public officials.[6]

The report *Anti-corruption in Transition: A Contribution to the Policy Debate* used the BEEPS data to explore reform options for the 22 transition countries, using a typology of corruption based on the relative levels of administrative corruption and state capture in each country.[7] The options for reform are presented as integral parts of a multipronged strategy for combating corruption. This multipronged strategy includes addressing institutional restraints, political accountability, a competitive private sector, civil society participation, and public sector management. The recommendations of the report are increasingly being integrated into country analysis, strategy, and policy dialogue in ECA.

Country-Specific Corruption Surveys

While the surveys discussed above have primarily involved the application of a single survey instrument to firms across a range of countries, country-specific instruments have also been developed. One such approach has entailed simultaneous surveys of households, firms, and public officials to develop multidimensional profiles of corruption in a country. The surveys of households and firms help establish the status of governance conditions in the country and identify the costs (for example, in the form of lost public revenues, investments, and poverty impacts) of weak governance and corruption. The surveys of public officials also try to get at the sources of weak governance, such as levels of pay, incentive structures, and reporting mechanisms. Given the nature of the phenomena under observation, a triangulation approach is favorable because it allows for corroboration of responses across the different groups of respondents.[8]

First Steps in Albania, Georgia, and Latvia

The triangulation approach was pioneered in the ECA region in 1998. Albania, Georgia, and Latvia were the first countries in which such surveys were used, primarily because they were among the first to request assistance from the World Bank on anti-corruption. The analysis of these surveys and comparisons of the results across the three countries revealed in particular that each country faced unique patterns of problems and that the problems had different institutional causes in each country. Notably, the surveys revealed that bureaucrats in all three countries purchased positions based on expected illicit gains, and that private enterprises would be willing to pay higher taxes rather than deal with corruption.[9]

The results of these surveys were widely disseminated in each of the countries and led to broad public debate. Albania subsequently launched an anti-corruption program, tackling, among other things, patronage in judicial appointments and the civil service, two key sources of corruption. In Georgia, where the surveys pointed to excessive licensing and regulations as prime causes of corruption, subsequent Bank assistance has helped put in place the legal and institutional framework for procurement, licensing, and tax reform. The surveys in Latvia revealed high-level corruption as a serious problem. Accordingly, a key feature of Latvia's governance PSAL entails the strengthening of institutions to expose and resolve the conflicts of interest that lie at the core of high-level corruption in the country.

Expanding Country Coverage and Adapting Approaches

Country-specific surveys have since been conducted in a range of countries including Bolivia, Bosnia and Herzegovina, Cambodia, Ecuador, Ghana, Paraguay, Peru, Romania, and Slovakia, and in Uttar Pradesh in India. Smaller-scale surveys have also been conducted at the local and municipal levels, including in Ukraine and Venezuela. In each case, the surveys have been adapted to the particularities of the country environment. In Poland, a different approach was taken with a view to using the process of data collection to build momentum behind the results and encourage ownership of the reform process. Existing surveys conducted by reputable local organizations, polls, audits, and other existing reports and research supplemented a large number of targeted and face-to-face interviews with parliamentarians, judges, government officials, business people, academics, media workers, and NGO representatives.[10]

Although the surveys differ in approach and methodology, there has been common agreement on the wisdom of garnering perspectives from many segments of society, including public officials. Another underlying commonality has been that in all cases the surveys have been conducted at the request of the client governments. In most cases, the survey results have helped inform anti-corruption strategies, formulated in collaboration with a wide range of stakeholders. Workshops and other mechanisms for building coalitions across all segments of society to formulate, implement, and monitor strategies for change have also been an important common feature in most cases.

Surveys of Public Officials

Surveys of public officials, while not directly targeted at measuring corruption, have nevertheless proved useful in getting at the same questions of the incentives, costs, causes, and consequences of corruption. Through a set of stand-alone surveys, conducted by the Bank with funding from the Bank Netherlands Partnership Program, more than 7,000 public officials have been surveyed in 16 countries, including Albania, Argentina, Bangladesh, Bolivia, Bulgaria, Guyana, Indonesia, Kenya, Macedonia, Moldova, and countries of the East Caribbean region. These surveys form part of a broader effort to inform work on civil service reform in these countries, and have primarily been used to analyze the institutional factors underlying poor performance in public organizations in developing countries. They have solicited direct input from public officials about the signals they receive from policies, the flow of resources, their perceptions of the formal and informal rules in their organizations, and the consequences of adhering to or breaking these rules.

While these surveys have not been targeted toward measuring corruption per se, the survey questionnaires include explicit questions about perceptions of corruption in the public officials' agencies and in the public sector at large. As with the surveys discussed above, the design has been adapted to fit each country context, and each survey has been followed by a report presenting country-specific findings. Among the varied country results, concerns about poor accountability and corruption emerge as common themes. Solutions for reform, some suggested by the public officials themselves, are being incorporated into economic and sector work such as Institutional and Governance Reviews, and are informing civil service reform strategies in the participant countries.

Practical Considerations in Using Surveys for Anti-corruption

Costs and Resources

The costs of conducting country-level surveys vary widely among countries depending upon country size, the level of domestic capacity, local conditions and the scope and complexity of the survey exercise. Nevertheless, some cost ranges may be noted. The tripartite country-level corruption surveys have typically cost between $30,000 and $50,000, with

an additional $50,000 to $100,000 for the processes of country dialogue, design, analysis, dissemination, and linkage to country programs.
The public officials surveys funded by the Bank-Netherlands Partnership Program have generally cost between $40,000 and $50,000.

Funding for these surveys has largely been provided by bilateral
donors such as USAID and the Dutch government. The Bank has mostly
funded staff time for dialogue, analysis, outreach, dissemination, and
linkages to country programs.[11]

Challenges and Considerations

Data from surveys, as noted above, can be a powerful tool to gauge the
extent and nature of corruption and governance problems; to identify
practical areas for policy change; and to build the impetus for reform
and empowerment. However, data on corruption can also be used inef-
fectively, or worse still, abused. In using anti-corruption surveys, therefore, some considerations are key:

- Survey methodologies must be carefully designed and adapted,
  and the analysis must be conducted in a rigorous fashion.
- Surveys should only be implemented in appropriate country
  environments. Ownership on the part of in-country stakeholders, as well as the capacity and political commitment to follow
  up on survey findings, is critical to ensure the utility of survey
  exercises and the credibility of the reform processes during which
  survey exercises are undertaken. Identifying and building constituencies for reform before embarking on a labor-, time-, and
  resource-intensive survey is a precondition for effectiveness.
- Public dissemination of survey results is obviously crucial, but
  the process of dissemination must be carefully considered, and
  just as importantly, owned and agreed to by the client government. In addition, cross-country comparisons must be made with
  care, given the many different underlying methodologies, as well
  as the delicate relationships of trust that enable the Bank to conduct corruption surveys in its client countries.

Note

1. World Bank 1997, p. 36.
2. World Bank 1997.

3.   World Bank 1997.

4.   Sewell 2001.

5.   Hellman, Jones, and Kaufmann 2000.

6.   World Bank 2000b.

7.   World Bank 2000b.

8.   Kaufmann, Kraay, and Zoido-Lobatón 2000.

9.   World Bank 1998.

10. World Bank 1999b.

11. Numerous World Bank units have developed materials, websites, and other resources that are easily accessible to staff and external audiences looking for country reports, lessons, and experiences, and information on methodologies. See, for example, http://www.worldbank.org/publicsector/acticorrupt, http://www.worldbank.org/wbi/governance, and http://www.worldbank.org/publicsector/civilservice

Resources

Hellman, Joel, Geraint Jones, and Daniel Kaufmann. 2000. "Seize the State, Seize the Day: An Empirical Analysis of State Capture and Corruption in Transition." Policy Research Working Paper 2444. World Bank, Development Research Group, Washington, D.C.

Hellman, Joel, and Daniel Kaufmann. 2001. "Confronting the Challenge of State Capture in Transition Economies." *Finance and Development* 38 (3). International Monetary Fund, Washington, D.C.

Kaufmann, Daniel, Aart Kraay, and Pablo Zoido-Lobatón. 2000. "Governance Matters: From Measurement to Action." *Finance and Development* 37 (2). International Monetary Fund, Washington, D.C.

Manning, Nick, Ranjana Mukherjee, and Omar Gokcekus. 2000. "Public Officials and Their Institutional Environment: An Analytical Model for Assessing the Impact of Institutional Change on Public Sector Performance." Policy Research Working Paper 2427. World Bank, Development Research Group, Washington, D.C.

Narayan, Deepa, Raj Patel, Kai Schafft, Anne Rademacher, and Sarah Koch-Schulte. 2000. *Voices of the Poor: Can Anyone Hear Us?* New York: Oxford University Press.

Sewell, David. 2001. "Governance and the Business Environment in West Bank/Gaza." Middle East and North Africa Working Paper 23. World Bank, Washington, D.C.

World Bank. 1997. *World Development Report 1997: The State in a Changing World*. New York: Oxford University Press.

_____. 1998. "New Frontiers in Diagnosing and Combating Corruption." PREM Note 7. Washington, D.C.

_____. 1999a. "Using Surveys for Public Sector Reform." PREM Note 23. Washington, D.C.

_____. 1999b. "Corruption in Poland: Review of Priority Areas and Proposals for Action." World Bank, Warsaw.

_____. 2000a. "Cambodia Governance and Corruption Diagnostic: Evidence from Citizen, Enterprise and Public Official Surveys: New Empirical Tools for Anti-corruption and Institutional Reform." Report prepared by the World Bank for the Royal Government of Cambodia. World Bank Institute, Washington, D.C.

_____. 2000b. *Anti-corruption in Transition: A Contribution to the Policy Debate*. Washington, D.C.: World Bank.

Tools and Practices 18

Public Expenditure Tracking Surveys

When assessing service delivery, most surveys examine the effects of policies or interventions on households and their demands for and perceptions of the quality of services. Inputs and outputs on the supply side—such as the flow of public funds and school enrollment rates—are left for official statistics or administrative records. The Public Expenditure Tracking Survey (PETS) and Quantitative Service Delivery Survey (QSDS) are two new tools that seek to document service delivery on the supply side, and have proven effective in increasing both the accountability and the effectiveness of service providers. In both instruments, the facility or frontline service provider is typically the main unit of analysis, in much the same way that the firm is the unit of observation in enterprise surveys and the household in household surveys.

Diagnostic surveys such as these can provide vital information for decision makers when institutional weaknesses inhibit a more regular flow of information. They are particularly helpful in identifying areas where actions are needed to improve the relationships among different levels of government involved in service delivery; illustrating areas where information asymmetries exist among agencies; and highlighting opportunities for more effective means of accountability within agencies,

This note was prepared drawing from work by Ritva Reinikka and Jakob Svensson (2002), compiled by Bryan Kurey.

among agencies at different levels, and between agencies and end users. When surveys are strategically designed, their findings can help induce policy change by making it easier for policy makers to find solutions. This note describes these tools in more detail and highlights their recent application in Uganda, Tanzania, Ghana, and Honduras.

What Are the PETS and QSDS?

When increases in public spending do not appear to be generating improvements in the delivery of basic services, two explanations are possible. One possibility is ineffective transfers of funds among public sector agencies, such as leakage of funds that prevents spending from reaching the intended end producer. A second possibility is deficiencies in the capacity of end-users to create valuable goods and services, along with waste and corruption.

Because of this, micro-level tools are needed to reveal provider behavior and illuminate the translation of public spending into services, where the quantity and quality of services reflect the public funds spent on them. PETS and QSDS have recently been tested in several countries to document frontline service delivery from public, private not-for-profit, and private for-profit providers. The PETS and QSDS approach focuses on provider behavior in general, including issues of incentives, oversight, accountability, and multiple-principal multiple-agent dynamics in the public sector.

As information on actual public spending is generally unavailable in many developing countries, the PETS was designed to provide the missing information from different tiers of government and frontline service facilities. It focuses on collecting micro-level data on the characteristics of the service facility, and the nature of financial flows from facility records, outputs, and accountability arrangements. In this process, a PETS can also help uncover where and to what extent corruption and abuse are leading to breakdowns in service delivery systems. Nearly all applications of the PETS so far have been in the health and education sectors, although the survey can be applied in other areas as well.

In the QSDS, quantitative data are collected both through interviews and directly from the service provider's records. Facility data can be "triangulated" by also surveying local governments, umbrella NGOs, and private provider associations. The compilation of facility-level quantitative data typically requires much more effort than, say, a perception survey of service users, which makes the QSDS both more costly and time-consuming to implement than its qualitative alternatives.[1] The PETS and QSDS can be conducted in conjunction, and their combination allows a direct evaluation of the effect of wider institutional and resource-flow problems on frontline service delivery.

In general, the surveys have two broad uses. First, they serve as diagnostic tools on service delivery, enabling the analysis of public expenditure priorities to take into account the implementation capacity of governments. Second, these surveys provide primary data on service providers for empirical research, data that up to now have been severely lacking on questions of incentives and moral hazard.[2]

PETS in Practice

Several countries have already implemented diagnostic Public Expenditure Tracking Surveys, while the QSDS is just beginning to be applied in a number of countries. This section reviews the experience gained from the use of PETS in Uganda, Tanzania, Ghana, and Honduras.

Analysis of these surveys provides several key findings, particularly related to information and accountability:

- *Information.* The surveys show that the flow of funds to the frontline and the efficacy of service delivery agencies are seriously hampered by information asymmetries, both among agencies at different levels and between agencies and end-users. Further, as access to and ability to acquire information differ among segments of society, actual benefits may also be unequally distributed. In addition, the surveys show that cash budgeting, deemed necessary in a number of low-income countries to bring about fiscal discipline, has serious negative side effects in that it produces volatile monthly releases of funds, aggravating the informational disadvantage that beneficiaries typically have. This may lead to substantial leakage of funds.
- *Accountability.* Nonwage expenditures are found to suffer more from leakage than salary expenditures. Furthermore, the sources of leakage can be located at different tiers of government. In Uganda and Tanzania, the most serious leakage arose at the local government level, while in Ghana it occurred before the resources reached the local government.

Uganda

In 1996, Uganda became the first country to carry out a PETS, prompted by the observation that despite a substantial increase in public spending on education since the late 1980s, officially reported primary enrollment remained stagnant. The PETS compared budget allocations to actual spending through various levels of government, including front-line service delivery points, in primary education and health care. It also collected quantitative data on outputs produced by schools and health clinics, as well as data on facility characteristics. Adequate public accounts were not available to report on actual spending, so the surveys of 19 districts (out of 39), 250 government primary schools, and 100 health clinics collected a panel dataset on spending (including in-kind transfers) and outputs for 1991–95.

The school survey showed that, on average, only 13 percent of per-student nonwage funds distributed annually by the central government reached schools during the survey period. Eighty-seven percent either disappeared for private gain or was used by district officials for purposes unrelated to education. Most schools (roughly 70 percent) received very little or nothing. In fact, based on yearly data, 73 percent of the schools received less than 5 percent, while only 10 percent of the schools received more than 50 percent of the intended funds. Although the trend showed improvement over time, by 1995 only 22 percent of funds reached the schools.

The survey confirmed that public primary education was mostly funded by parents who contributed up to 73 percent of total school spending in 1991 (42 percent at the median level of school spending). While the government's share increased during the survey period, by 1995 parents still financed 60 percent of total primary school spending on average; furthermore, parental contributions continued to increase in real terms despite higher public spending.

The survey quantified the adverse effects of asymmetric information on the flow of funds. Because local government officials have an informational advantage regarding the amount of funds received as transfers, they can obtain rents at the expense of Parent Teacher Associations (PTAs) simply by reducing the amount of funds actually used for the school. Following publication of the survey findings, the central government began publishing the monthly intergovernmental transfers of public funds in major newspapers and broadcasting the information on radio, and required primary schools to post information on inflows of funds for all to see. This not only made information available to PTAs, but also signaled to local governments that the center had resumed its oversight function, thus creating incentives for increased accountability among local agencies. Initial assessments of these reforms a few years later, through two locally implemented follow-up PETS, show that the flow of intended capitation grants improved dramatically, from 13 percent (on average) reaching schools in 1991–95 to about 80 to 90 percent reaching schools in 1999 and 2000.

Tanzania

Tanzania implemented two Public Expenditure Tracking Surveys in 1999 and 2001 to investigate the suspicion that serious problems existed in the flow of funds from the central government via the local authorities to frontline service facilities. The first Tanzanian PETS, which covered 45 primary schools and 36 health facilities in three districts, found that local councils diverted a large part of funds disbursed by the center for nonwage education and health expenditures—57 percent in education and 41 percent in health care—to other uses as well as for private gain. Salaries appeared to be less prone to diversion, but payrolls were populated with ghost workers and frontline staff suffered delays in pay.

The second PETS covered four primary schools and four clinics in each of five districts. Considerable delays in disbursement of funds were found at all levels of government, particularly for nonwage expenditures and in rural areas. Rural districts received a smaller share of the intended resources than urban districts. One important cause of this was cash budgeting, leading to volatile transfers due to fluctuations in revenue, which in turn gave rise to information asymmetries as it became increasingly difficult for beneficiaries to know the amount of their monthly allocation or entitlement. Council staff took advantage of these information asymmetries in their relationship with service facilities. Similarly, highly aggregated government records were found to undermine transparency in public spending.

The findings of the two PETS were disseminated during the subsequent national budget consultations, but they have not yet had as strong a catalytic effect on central government oversight or transparency arrangements as the PETS in Uganda. The Treasury has begun regular dissemination of itemized local government budgets to members of

Parliament and regular publication of budget allocations for selected pro-poor spending programs in both Swahili and English-language newspapers, covering allocations for ministries, regions, and local authorities.

Ghana

Ghana implemented a PETS in 2000 to estimate the leakage of funds in the transfer from central government via districts to basic education and primary health care facilities. The Ghana PETS covered four districts in each of the 10 regions, with interviews of 40 district education officers and 40 district health officers, and a survey of 119 primary schools, 79 junior secondary schools, and 173 primary health clinics. The survey found that only about 20 percent of nonwage public health expenditure and 50 percent of nonwage education expenditure reached frontline facilities. As observed in Uganda and Tanzania, the leakage in salaries, in contrast, was much smaller.

Contrary to the Ugandan and Tanzanian experience, a large proportion of the leakage seemed to occur between line ministries and district offices during the process of translating public expenditures from funds into in-kind transfers. The in-kind nature of transfers gave rise to information asymmetries and lack of accountability within the delivery system, and discouraged opportunities for feedback from frontline facilities regarding their resource needs or complaints. The possibilities for leakage were found to be much greater when the value of the materials distributed was unknown to their recipients.

The PETS opened an avenue for interministerial collaboration and provided a practical approach for assessing frontline expenditures and service delivery. However, it has not yet been able to catalyze a strong response to reduce leakage.

Honduras

Honduras used the PETS to diagnose moral hazard with respect to frontline health and education staff, demonstrating that issues related to staff behavior and incentives in public service—such as ghost workers, absenteeism, and capture of multiple jobs by employees—can have adverse effects on service delivery. The hypothesis of the PETS was that the central payroll office in Honduras has no means of ensuring that public employees really exist and that they actually work where they are supposed to. The objective of the PETS was thus to quantify the incongruity between budgetary and real assignments of staff and to determine the degree of attendance at work.

In the health sector, 2.4 percent of staff were found to be ghost workers. Absenteeism was found to be a generic problem, with an average attendance rate of 73 percent across all categories of staff (meaning that only 73 percent of staff members were at work in the five days prior to the survey). Thirty-nine percent of these absences were without legitimate reason (such as sick leave, vacations, and compensation for extra hours worked). In addition, multiple jobs were prevalent, especially for general practitioners and specialists: 54 percent of specialist physicians held two or more jobs, of which 60 percent were in a related field. Slightly over 5 percent of staff members had migrated to posts other than those to which they were assigned in the central database, while 40 percent had moved since their first assignment.

In the education sector, 3 percent of staff members were found to be ghosts, while only 5 percent of primary school teachers were unknown in their place of work. Absenteeism is less of a problem than in the health sector, with an average attendance rate of 86 percent across all categories of staff and 15 percent of all absences unexcused.

As the PETS study was carried out fairly recently, there has not yet been much follow-up within government on the findings.

Notes

1.   Examples of these survey instruments can be found at http://www.publicspending.org (tools).

2.   For further information on the diagnostic, data collection, and research benefits of the PETS and QSDS, along with the potential for capacity building, see Reinikka and Svensson 2002.

Resources

Ablo, Emmanuel, and Ritva Reinikka. 1998. "Do Budgets Really Matter? Evidence from Public Spending on Education and Health in Uganda." Policy Research Working Paper 1926. World Bank, Africa Region, Macroeconomics 2, Washington, D.C. Available: http://www.econ.worldbank.org/docs/539.pdf

Reinikka, Ritva. 1999. "Using Surveys for Public Sector Reform." PREM Note 23. World Bank, Development Economics and Poverty Reduction and Economic Management, Washington, D.C.

_____. 2001. "Recovery in Service Delivery: Evidence from Schools and Health Centers." In Ritva Reinikka and Paul Collier, eds., *Uganda's Recovery: The Role of Farms, Firms, and Government.* World Bank Regional and Sectoral Studies. Washington D.C.: World Bank.

Reinikka, Ritva, and Jakob Svensson. 2002. "Assessing Frontline Service Delivery." World Bank, Development Research Group, Public Services, Washington, D.C. Available: http://www.worldbank.org/wbi/publicfinance/documents/seco/reinikka_assessing%20frontline.doc

Tools and Practices 19

Private Enterprise Surveys of the Business Environment

Recognizing the private sector's efficiency at allocating resources and spurring economic growth, the World Bank Group seeks to identify obstacles to private sector development. Listening to the problems of active entrepreneurs is an important step toward identifying needed reforms in the enabling environment and support systems for private enterprise. Surveys give greater confidence in the Bank's conclusions and credibility to its recommendations. Recent initiatives in the Bank have attempted to bring greater uniformity to the questions asked and the implementation methodology of private enterprise surveys in order to better leverage resources to generate internationally comparable indicators of investment climate conditions.

The use of surveys offers a number of advantages that complement other methods in identifying business experience in, and perceptions of, the local investment climate. Bank staff often have limited sources of information on the local business environment: official statistics, contacts with public officials, discussions with a limited number of experts and representatives of large firms, as well as the collection of other existing data. In the context of brief missions often centered in the seat of government, Bank staff have limited opportunities to obtain a complete and objective understanding of the views and experiences of the entire business community. A properly structured survey can help to

This note was prepared by Andrew H. Stone.

break out of this blind box. Surveys can generate a rich body of fact (and anecdote) that illuminate: (a) the relative priorities for reform as perceived by businesses; (b) the private costs imposed by constraints in the enabling environment and support systems (and/or their impact on firm-level performance); and (c) the functioning of policies "on the ground" in a country's unique institutional environment.

For example, the Pakistan Private Sector Assessment Survey (1995) showed that Karachi firms lost an average of 25 working days a year to ethnic and political unrest. The unreliability of the electric power supply cost Pakistani firms an average of 21 working days a year, and two-thirds of firms owned generators to compensate for faulty public power supply. These generators cost an average of $240,000 to purchase (although prices varied widely) and $62,000 a year to operate.

The results of uniform questionnaires uniformly administered may also be compared across countries to better evaluate responses using international comparators, and to begin to understand patterns in economic and institutional problems facing private enterprise both by location and over time. For example, the 1999–2000 World Business Environment Survey (WBES) was implemented in 80 countries around the world. Econometric analysis of the results of the WBES shows that perceived severity of policy uncertainty and instability as a constraint and perceived severity of corruption as a constraint are both negatively associated with firm-level sales growth and foreign direct investment at the national level.[1]

Hence, the use of properly designed survey instruments should enhance the credibility of Bank analysis and recommendations in the eyes of governments, the business community, and other donors. However, for results to be useful, care must be taken in the design of a questionnaire ("survey instrument"), the selection of a sample, the administration of the survey, and the analysis and interpretation of the results. While surveys can be performed economically, it is unwise to cut corners in planning and implementation.

Equally important, survey results must be kept in perspective. The value of this new source of information in no way argues for the abandonment of other sources, such as traditional economic analysis. Firms' responses have certain biases—in general they would like lower costs and less competition—suggesting that results should always be weighed against other information sources and interpreted with common sense. In other cases, the main contribution of surveys is to make private sector priorities clear. For example, although "taxes and regulations" ranks high on the list of constraints in most regions, the majority of African firms responding to the WBES did not place this even among their top five problems. Instead, the issues of financing, corruption, infrastructure, inflation, and "street crime/theft/disorder" led the priorities of private enterprises in Africa.

In addition, private enterprise surveys can document the state of business practice, including financial management, personnel management, technological innovation, and marketing. Information on business practice can help the Bank to understand both where enterprises are starting from (which will shape the design of interventions) and what services they would find useful.

Detailed studies and panel studies, such as the Regional Program on Enterprise Development (RPED) conducted in Africa and the series of studies described in Tan and Batra's *Enterprise-Led Training in Developing Countries'* allow econometric analysis of the determinants of firm-level productivity and performance in various dimensions, such as investment, growth, and exports.[2] If repeated, they can allow the tracking of trends over time. An RPED study using cross-country data from Ghana, Kenya, and Zimbabwe, for example, finds that access to short-term working capital increases value added in firms by as much as 40 percent.[3]

Survey Design

The focus of a survey can be determined by:

- Collecting and reviewing existing knowledge about the private sector through relevant documents and discussions with operational staff, and in the process, learning what experts currently understand to be the priorities for promoting private sector development;
- Identifying gaps in knowledge on key issues and on the role and structure of the private sector.

Increasingly, however, the World Bank Group relies on standardized core questions applied across multiple countries to represent the experiences and perceptions of businesses in comparable ways across countries and over time.

In the field, surveys should be accompanied by traditional information described above. Most surveys to date have relied on some form of stratified random sampling. Strata have been chosen either broadly to represent the entire economy (such as by sector, location, and/or size), or more narrowly to investigate priority areas of the economy (such as the manufacturing sector), or to highlight phenomena of special interest (such as industries with long contracting horizons versus those with short ones, nontraditional exporters, and so on). Across or within selected strata, a list of industries is acquired, which constitutes the sample frame. Then a random, structured, or stratified selection method is employed. In cases where available lists are known to have systematic biases, nonrandom methods (such as quota sampling) or area-based methods have been used to improve representation of smaller or less formal enterprises, or to highlight characteristics of certain groups (such as foreign investors).

Good sample design requires careful implementation and a sufficient budget. However, business environment enterprise surveys have generally been performed under strict time and budgetary constraints. Therefore, the instrument itself has been kept short, so that it can be completed in a single one- to two-hour sitting with an entrepreneur and to ensure that randomly selected entrepreneurs will complete their responses. In order to achieve this brevity, survey designers have been forced to make tradeoffs between breadth and depth. In general, the breadth approach is more useful for charting unknown terrain, while the depth approach is more useful in countries where the terrain is known, but economic or institutional details in a few areas are unknown. Some efforts have used much longer surveys, but have asked only a limited amount of time from each of several individuals associated with the enterprise (such as the director, the chief financial officer, workers, and so on).

Questionnaires are usually divided into sections, beginning with simple (and safe) background information and moving on to a series of substantive areas of the designer's choosing, such as "regulation," "finance," and "infrastructure." A typical sequence of questions would move from the general to the specific to the comparative. For example, a section of a questionnaire on regulation often begins with an open-ended question such as: "What are your three worst problems with regulation and regulatory agencies?" This allows researchers to gain an unbiased overview of what is bothering entrepreneurs before they possibly bias that view by suggesting specific issues of concern. Next, detailed questions, combining short-answer questions and multiple choice, address the specific agenda. Finally, either at the end of each section or at the end of the entire survey, a ranking question can elicit the relative importance of the constraints just discussed. In a "nested" approach, each section of the questionnaire ends with a ranked constraint question on a particular category (such as regulation, infrastructure, or finance). Then, either at the beginning or the end, each category of constraints is compared in a ranking question, which also adds general constraints not previously covered in the detailed sections of the survey (such as some macroeconomic and political constraints).

A critical concern of surveys has been to evaluate business costs—particularly the burden imposed on businesses by the fiscal and regulatory environment and by inadequate public infrastructure, financial systems, and other services. Initially surveys focused on relative costs, using ranked responses. This methodology rests on the hypothesis that the constraint rankings assigned by firms reflect the (unobserved) incremental costs associated with the constraints. Therefore, constraint scores reveal the ranking of the shadow prices for different constraints. Such rankings allow comparisons, and enable investigators to determine the enterprise characteristics associated with high and low constraint scores, as well as to identify the collective business perspective on priorities for reform. For example, the WBES survey is based on a nested structure of constraint and qualitative rankings, with a general constraint question and specific sets of questions on regulatory constraints, financial constraints, quality of public services, and so on. However, ranking does not assign a monetary equivalent to the constraint score.

Increasingly, surveys have also focused on obtaining quantitative estimates of costs. Direct cost estimates prove particularly useful for the analysis of regulatory burden and other costs involving discrete payments or expenditures of time by the firm. Direct questions address expenditures of money or time on particular activities or items, such as the cost of business licenses or the operating cost of a generator to compensate for poor public power supply. In addition, questions may concern lost days of business due to, for example, inspections, power interruptions, or strikes. Indirect questions attempt to get entrepreneurs to assign values to items without well-defined monetary or labor costs. Contingent valuation questions ask entrepreneurs what percentage of gross sales they would sacrifice to be free from particular constraints.

As noted above, enterprise surveys are increasingly designed to maximize comparability with work in other countries or periods. The use of "core" groups of questions in surveys is beginning to allow international comparisons of the severity of, and costs imposed by, different constraints in the investment climate.[4] For valid comparisons to be drawn, sample design must also be standardized.

Survey Implementation

B efore a survey is launched, the questionnaire itself must be tested to ensure that the questions are comprehensible to respondents, that they elicit the desired information, that none of the questions seriously offends or threatens respondents, and that completing the entire survey does not take too long. Testing surveys identifies problems and creates opportunities to improve questions and adjust language and questions to local usage and local institutions—a step that can increase respondents' enthusiasm.

Survey costs vary substantially depending on a number of conditions, including the length and design of the survey itself, the number of firms to be included, the number of different economic sectors examined, and the number and dispersion of locations at which the survey will be administered. Costs also depend on who administers the survey. For multicountry surveys, the use of international survey firms may bring greater standardization, but also increases costs. Local consultants usually bring with them important local knowledge, language skills, and the ability to quickly mobilize local surveyors, and they cost much less than international consultants or Bank staff. However, the feasibility of using them depends on local supply conditions and the intensity of supervision they require.

In assessing a local consultant, the following factors are key:

- Experience carrying out enterprise surveys or, next best, public opinion or market research surveys;
- Knowledge of business issues from an entrepreneurial and a policy perspective;
- Access to sources of information on firms required to construct the sample frame;
- Access to firms;
- Ability to mobilize, train, and supervise surveyors (enumerators);
- Ability to control quality in survey implementation, data entry, and analysis;
- Ability to analyze or assist in analyzing results both quantitatively and qualitatively.

Even with experienced local consultants, proper orientation and training are key. Very few have administered a World Bank private enterprise survey, so the type of questions being asked and even the subject of the survey may be unfamiliar to them. It is important to orient them to the purpose of the survey, the etiquette of interviewing, the importance of confidentiality, and the correct methods of recording and encoding data. It is useful to illustrate the value of surveys with examples from past Bank work. Completed forms must be checked to ensure accurate and consistently recorded responses. Inadequate supervision may lead to large data losses because of errors in entry, unreadable responses, or incomplete forms.

Before responses can be analyzed, they must be put into a tractable form, generally by entry into a spreadsheet, database, or statistical software program. In the process, most responses are coded so that a number represents a particular response (for example, 0 for "no" and 1 for "yes"). Clearly, the accuracy of this process is vital to the usefulness of all the work that precedes it. Data should be scanned for obvious errors, and entries should be checked against the actual survey forms from which they were recorded. In general, effective reporting on survey results combines quantitative analysis with qualitative interpretation.

Ongoing International Initiatives

Different survey instruments are appropriate for different purposes. Some recent examples include:

- The World Business Environment Survey focuses on perceptions of factors external to a firm. Based on samples from about 100 firms in some 80 countries, the WBES covers perceptions of the national business environment as shaped by local economic policy; governance; regulatory, infrastructural, and financial impediments; and the quality of public services.
- The Regional Program on Enterprise Development in Africa studies and Firm Analysis and Competitiveness Survey (FACS) focus on selected factors, both internal and external to the enterprise, and relate them to firm productivity and performance, based on detailed firm-level financial data.
- Regulatory and administrative costs surveys document time and monetary costs of various procedural requirements, such as tax and customs compliance, business registration, obtaining land and premises, and complying with product conformity assessment procedures. These have been implemented in a number of Eastern European countries.
- The SME mapping survey, which adds to the WBES core details on financing, business services, and business information.

In a major recent initiative, the World Bank Group has created an Investment Climate Unit (ICU) to standardize its approach to assessment through surveys and indicators.[5] This unit has already generated a standard core instrument for investment climate assessment, drawing on the best elements of each of the above mentioned instruments. The core survey provides the basis to link investment climate conditions to firm-level productivity. Additional modules of questions are under development to evaluate regulatory compliance costs, SME and foreign investor concerns, and details of financing and labor issues. The ICU is now working to develop a standard methodology for a core survey sample design.

Using Results

In order to use survey results appropriately, staff should understand their applications and limitations. Firm-level surveys fill gaps in existing information by supplying firm-specific information. In general, survey data is better at identifying problems than identifying solutions, so the survey represents only one step in improving the business environment.

However, properly designed surveys have a distinct legitimacy with local businesses and policymakers, and thus make an excellent focal point for consultations on policy and projects. In order to make survey results useful to clients and country strategy and operations, surveys should be followed up by direct consultation with both government counterparts and the private sector on priority issues and implications arising from the survey.

In 2000–01, the FACS India survey was carried out by the World Bank in collaboration with a leading local business association, the Confederation of Indian Industries. Results were discussed at two seminars (in Bangalore and Hyderabad) in 2001 involving representatives of government, business, NGOs, and donors. Further consultative conferences in Delhi, Bombay, and other locations will disseminate findings and discuss their implications for policy reform.

Notes

1.   For more information, see the WBES website at: http://www.worldbank.org/beeat/resources/assess-wbessurvey-alt.htm

2.   Tan and Batra 1995.

3.   Biggs and Srivastava 1996.

4.   Several standard survey modules can be found at: http://www1.worldbank.org/beext/resources/assess-wbessurvey-alt.htm

5.   See the ICU website at http://rru.worldbank.org

Resources

Biggs, Tyler, and Pradeep Srivastava. 1996. "Structural Aspects of Manufacturing in Sub-Saharan Africa." World Bank Discussion Paper 346. Africa Technical Department Series, Washington, D.C.

Tan, Hong W., and Geeta Batra. 1995. "Enterprise Training in Developing Countries: Incidence, Productivity, Effects, and Policy Implications." World Bank, Private Sector Development Department, Competition and Strategy Unit, Washington, D.C.

Tools and Practices 20

Participatory Poverty Diagnostics

In order to devise effective and appropriate strategies for poverty reduction and economic and social development, it is essential to understand levels of poverty, how poverty occurs, why it persists, and how it can be alleviated.[1] A variety of data collection instruments, including household surveys, is necessary to understand the multidimensional nature of poverty and the realities that determine the opportunities and barriers poor people face in their efforts to move out of poverty. This note describes the methods and value of Participatory Poverty Assessments for understanding poverty and presents examples of participatory poverty diagnostics conducted in Tanzania, Vietnam, Uganda, and Guatemala.

Participatory Poverty Assessments

A Participatory Poverty Assessment (PPA) is an iterative, participatory research process that seeks to understand poverty in its local, social, institutional, and political contexts, incorporating the perspectives of a range of stakeholders and involving them directly in planning follow-up action. While the most important stakeholders involved in the research process are poor men and women, PPAs can also include decision makers from all levels of government, civil society, and the local elite in order to take into account different interests and

This note was prepared by Laura Bureš, with input from Bryan Kurey, under the overall guidance of Deepa Narayan.

perspectives and increase local capacity and commitment to follow-up action. Because PPAs address national policy, micro-level data are collected from a large number of communities in order to discern patterns across social groups and geographic areas.

PPAs are usually carried out by NGOs, academic institutions, government extension workers, or local consulting firms. They use a variety of participatory research methods, including community mapping, flow diagrams showing links and causes of deprivation, seasonal calendars, matrix analysis, and rankings of wealth or wellbeing. They incorporate anthropological methods, including semi-structured interviews with key informants about poverty-related issues and institutions. While PPAs and more traditional quantitative poverty diagnostics should be viewed as complementary, two underlying principles make the participatory approach different from other research approaches. First, the PPA methodology engages respondents actively in the research process through the use of open-ended and participatory methods. Second, it assumes that the research process will empower participants and lead to follow-up action.

The design of a PPA depends on the purpose of the study being conducted. PPAs have become increasingly common since the early 1990s. In 1994 only one-fifth of the World Bank's country-level poverty assessment reports incorporated PPA material. In 1995 one-third included PPAs, and between 1996 and 1998, PPAs were included in half of all Bank poverty assessments.

The Tanzania Participatory Poverty Assessment

In 1995 the government of Tanzania, the University of Dar es Salaam, and the World Bank conducted a PPA involving more than 6,000 people in 87 villages across Tanzania.[2] The World Bank and the British Overseas Development Agency provided financial assistance for the project.

Methodology

The PPA combined qualitative and quantitative data collection methods and tools, including participatory tools such as community mapping, group discussions, and Venn diagrams, key informant interviews, and household survey instruments. The issues explored included how poor Tanzanians view and experience poverty, perceptions of inflation and other trends over time, the effects of liberalization on the rural

poor, access to and use of formal and informal credit and savings institutions, the role of social capital in household welfare, and the relationship between poverty and the natural environment.

Different sampling techniques were used for a household survey focusing on expenditures, along with a range of participatory tools. To
establish credibility and ensure that the PPA was broadly representative
of rural areas as a whole, 100 villages were selected throughout the country. These villages were part of the National Master Sample framework
that had been established by the government's Planning Commission. All
national-level studies in Tanzania—including a human development survey conducted by the government and the World Bank—are done in these
villages to allow researchers to generalize findings to the national level
and to ensure that findings from one survey can be compared and con-
trasted with data from other studies. The 15 households selected in each
village for the household survey were the same as those randomly selected for the national agricultural survey. Six to 12 discussion groups of
men, women, and youth were also conducted in each village.

Before the PPA team entered a village, the community was informed
so that village leaders and community members would be available to
meet with the team during their stay. To ensure that group discussions
were not dominated by the more powerful community members, the
team supervisor met with local elites while the research team focused
on the broader community.

Participatory data collection tools

Two participatory methods were used in the Tanzania PPA. SARAR (Self-
esteem, Associative Strength, Resourcefulness, Action Planning, and Responsibility) relies on visual exercises to generate discussion and involvement. Participatory Rapid Appraisal (PRA) is based on open-ended
dialogue and community-level analysis. Various participatory tools were
administered in discussion groups of men and women, usually segregated
by gender to conform to local culture and to ensure that women felt the
freedom to speak frankly. These participatory tools included:

- *Mapping.* Groups were asked to draw a map of their community, marking key features of the village and drawing in households that were labeled according to wealth status later in the
  process.
- *Poverty characteristics and wealth ranking.* Once trust was established between the PPA team and the village group, people
  were asked to identify characteristics of five different wealth

groups, from very rich to very poor. After consensus was reached on the defining characteristics, people used colored stickers to classify households into these categories.

- *Seasonal analysis.* People were asked to draw a matrix, with months on the horizontal axis and activities or resources on the vertical. Discussions focused on how people coped across seasons, over years, and during periods of hardship.

- *Trend and price analysis.* Groups plotted changes they had noticed in availability of services and prices of food and important commodities at the beginning of the liberalization process (a decade earlier) and when basic food commodities were liberalized in 1991.

- *Venn diagrams.* Groups were asked to draw a large circle representing the community and circles of various sizes representing village-level groups and institutions. Size indicated importance, overlapping circles represented overlapping membership, and lines between them indicated interaction. Discussions focused on the membership, structure, and functioning of village groups and the relationships among them.

- *Problem identification.* Drawings by local artists and community members were used to depict a variety of problems and issues. People were provided with blank paper to draw a problem they faced if it was not already depicted. Participants ranked the five most important problems affecting their lives through a voting exercise, and these issues were then discussed in depth.

- *Story with a gap.* This activity began with two pictures, one showing a poor, unproductive farm and the other a prosperous farm. Using the pictures, people discussed the situation of their own farms. The discussion then moved on to how to turn a poorly functioning farm into one that works well. Pictures were drawn to represent the crops and ecology of different agro-ecological zones.

- *Gender analysis.* A local artist drew three large pictures of a man, a woman, and a couple. People were then handed more than 30 smaller pictures of different objects including land, a house, household items, babies, and young children. The group was asked to arrange these pictures under the man, woman, or couple to indicate who owned which possessions during marriage. Then people were asked what happened to property in situations of divorce, separation, or death of a husband.

- *Key informant interviews.* Much of the information obtained through groups was also asked of key informants, who included village officials, schoolteachers, and others. In each village, discussions were held with two or three key informants. Information that did not tally was further cross-checked.
- *Household surveys.* A two-part household questionnaire was developed, including a Social Capital and Poverty Survey (part one), and the household expenditure and consumption module of the 1993 Human Resources Development survey (part two). Part one focused on social capital issues, agriculture, savings and credit, environmental issues, and three measures of poverty, including wealth rankings and household asset indices.
- *District-level workshops.* Because district officials implement many of the programs that affect the poor, each PPA team held a one-day workshop at the district level to brief district officials about the study, explore their attitudes toward knowledge about poverty, learn the reach of their programs, and share preliminary findings from the field. These officials also participated in mapping and story-with-a-gap techniques related to poverty and agriculture in their district.

Data analysis

The PPA study drew on the content analysis and field notes of 29 fieldworkers who generated more than 100 notebooks of village-level data. Fieldwork was done by six teams who received training for three weeks in the various participatory data collection tools. Team members were drawn from the University of Dar es Salaam, other research institutes, and government ministries, as well as from respondents to a newspaper advertisement. Each team was headed by a senior social scientist, half of them men and half women, and the work was supervised by a World Bank sociologist. In addition, the study relied on approximately 1,500 household questionnaires as well as regional reports written by team supervisors.

All data gathered through participatory methods were subject to systematic content analysis, and statistics were obtained, where appropriate, through a step-by-step aggregation of village data. Field teams checked the quality of household survey data, and a private firm in Nairobi, Kenya, entered the data into a computer. Data were cleaned and checked for accuracy. Statistical analysis consisted of a step-by-step process involving frequencies, cross-tabs, index construction, and model testing.

Findings

The Tanzania PPA provides a unique example of a case in which a PPA was done in the same villages and using the same samples as a household survey. As a result, it proved particularly useful in comparing the findings and benefits of both quantitative and qualitative methods. In this case, with the exception of findings on availability of drinking water and the status of female-headed households, the aggregate results of the two approaches turned out to be very similar, with the PPA generating more subtle and detailed findings in a number of areas, some of which had been previously overlooked.

The PPA's overall findings revealed inflation in prices in rural areas, widespread need for rural credit, and people's desire to save. The study found that while many poor Tanzanians faced hardship as a result of cutbacks in government subsidies, most favored expanded opportunities to improve their livelihoods rather than a return to subsidies. In defining categories of wealth, land ownership was nearly always the first characteristic mentioned. Poverty was associated with skipping meals, sending children to neighbors' homes to eat, and poor performance in school. The causes of poverty most frequently cited were farming problems, sickness or chronic poor health, and drunkenness.

While the household survey showed that female-headed households were doing better at each expenditure level, the findings from the PPA were the opposite, that is, that female-headed households were classified as less well off than male-headed households at every level of wellbeing. Further analysis revealed that female-headed households owned fewer assets and experienced greater insecurity and vulnerability. However, female-headed households appeared to do more with fewer assets than male-headed households, using a range of coping strategies, particularly petty trading. Girls were more likely to be withdrawn from school for various reasons, while educating boys was considered to be a better investment. For women, the dissolution of marriage and widowhood were identified as major sources of financial difficulty. Local customs often caused women to be left destitute after divorce, despite formal laws intended to protect women's inheritance of property.

The household survey did not pick up availability of water as a problem. However, water problems emerged high on the list of priorities identified through participatory methods. Further comparisons of information from both data sets revealed that the household survey did not reflect seasonal dimensions of water availability and the unreliable functioning of water sources.

Perhaps the most striking finding was the contribution of village-level social capital to household incomes: an increase of one standard deviation in social capital at the village level was found to increase household expenditures per person by at least 20 to 30 percent. By comparison, a standard deviation in schooling of nearly three years per person increased income by less than 5 percent.

The Vietnam Participatory Poverty Assessment

In 1999, four Participatory Poverty Assessments were implemented in Vietnam in an effort led by the World Bank in partnership with NGOs and other donors:[3]

- The Vietnam-Sweden Mountain Rural Development Program conducted PPAs in two districts of Lao Cai Province, an upland area with a high proportion of ethnic minorities living in remote villages.
- Action Aid, a British NGO, coordinated PPAs in six districts of Ha Tinh Province in the north-central coastal region, a typhoon-prone area with very poor natural endowments.
- Oxfam GB carried out PPAs in two districts of Tra Vinh Province, a coastal region with a large ethnic minority population and growing problems of landlessness.
- Save the Children Fund (U.K.) coordinated PPAs in three poor urban districts in Ho Chi Minh City.

Methodology

Each of the four implementing agencies took responsibility for planning and undertaking the research in its site, but all of the PPAs used common techniques and covered certain common subject matter in order to facilitate the compilation of a national perspective. The process of designing the studies was facilitated by the institutional knowledge of the PPA study agencies and their experience with participatory techniques. All of the teams made use of a variety of participatory research tools (described in greater detail in the Tanzania example above), including focus group discussions, semi-structured interviews, wealth/wellbeing rankings, matrix and preference ranking and scoring, flow diagrams, and institutional ranking and Venn diagrams.

All together, the four PPAs engaged more than 1,000 households. All the research teams worked with men and women separately. All teams also interviewed elderly people separately, and two teams worked with children separately.

Comparison of Results: PPA and the Vietnam Living Standards Survey

The PPAs were analyzed and synthesized at the same time that the quantitative household survey data from a second round of the Vietnam Living Standards Survey were being analyzed. In areas where the PPA research themes and Living Standards Survey data overlapped, findings generally coincided closely, with a few notable exceptions, and the PPAs and household surveys reinforced the same key messages overall. The quantitative data revealed robust, nationally representative trends, while the qualitative, participatory studies helped to indicate explanations for some of these trends.

Findings of the two methods differed in two important areas. First, while the survey found female-headed households to be better-off than male-headed households in percapita expenditure terms, the position of female-headed households was routinely described as being poor and vulnerable in the PPAs. Second, the scope and nature of urban poverty did not appear to be a pressing problem according to the survey. However, urban poverty did figure as an issue of importance in the PPAs.

Additional findings included high indebtedness and growing landlessness, strong demand for off-farm economic opportunities, vulnerability due to health shocks, lack of information on government decisions and programs, domestic violence, and vulnerability of women and children within households.

Involving Government and Establishing Credibility

The amount of collaborative work between the Bank, government agencies, other donors, and NGOs in implementing the PPAs led to wide circulation and use of PPA findings. The Vietnamese government became involved in the process through a Poverty Working Group, which was initiated by the Bank and included the Ministry of Planning and

Investment, the Ministry of Labor, Invalids and Social Affairs, the Ministry of Agriculture and Rural Development, the Ministry of Finance, the General Statistics Office, the Committee for Ethnic Minorities and Mountainous Affairs, the Women's Union, and the State Bank of Vietnam.

Many government officials joined the Working Group highly skeptical of the value of PPAs, but the workshops, presentations, meetings with local government, and connections with the global *Voices of the Poor* project played important roles in establishing the credibility of the research methodology and findings. Government ownership of the process was also encouraged through the production of a joint PPA report. During the PPA process, the Poverty Working Group met one day each month to discuss methodology and findings and review early drafts of its poverty assessment. The group also traveled to all four PPA provinces for workshops to discuss and debate PPA findings when the studies were completed.

Provincial workshops were very important for building local government support, for raising interest in the findings among local officials, and for addressing their questions and concerns about the research. The involvement of the World Bank and the Poverty Working Group were especially important in this regard. World Bank meetings with local authorities at an early stage raised awareness of the studies at the local level and reinforced the idea that donors and central policymakers took participatory information seriously.

A workshop that evaluated the impact of the PPAs found that all stakeholders—poor communities, communes/wards, districts, provinces, central government, NGOs, and donors—experienced changes in knowledge, understanding, and attitudes in many areas as a result of the PPA studies. Some of these changes included: a better understanding of the nature and causes of poverty; increased commitment to consulting with the poor and to participatory research, planning, and monitoring; greater willingness to acknowledge sensitive issues such as domestic violence and marginalization of some social groups; and increased demand for better social services, programs, and grassroots democracy.

Additional Studies and Policy Changes

A number of additional studies and policy changes were initiated as a result of the PPA findings and process. They include:

- A Health Sector Review studying the high costs of curative health care;

- A Public Expenditure Review, investigating high health care costs, local revenue-raising, the high direct costs of education for the poor, and the fees and voluntary contributions related to commune-level financing;
- Inclusion of both poor households' lack of access to information on legal rights and the "knowledge of the poor" as issues addressed in the government's poverty reduction strategy;
- New criteria in some Ho Chi Minh City districts for including long-settled but unregistered migrants in the city's Hunger Eradication and Poverty Reduction activities;
- A study of constraints to the development of the off-farm sector in Tra Vinh;
- A study of the marginalization of ethnic minorities in upland areas;
- Development of a more integrated approach to dealing with community-wide shocks and disasters, in which the government has asked donors to become involved.

The Uganda Participatory Poverty Assessment Project

The idea of undertaking a PPA in Uganda emerged during the World Bank's Country Assistance Strategy consultation in 1998.[4] The government began planning for the Uganda Participatory Poverty Assessment Project (UPPAP) with initial funding from the U.K. Department for International Development (DFID), the World Bank, and UNDP. It was designed as a three-year initiative whose objectives were twofold: (a) linking poverty analysis to policy decisions by strengthening the participatory poverty assessment capacities of government (both central and district level) and civil society organizations, and (b) enriching and verifying quantitative data used in poverty monitoring.

Oxfam agreed to become the implementing partner for the project and identified nine research institutions and local NGOs, which it invited to join the UPPAP Technical Committee and carry out the participatory research. The first round of assessments began in September 1998 in 36 rural and urban sites in nine pilot districts. The location of the PPA project within the Ministry of Planning and Economic Development (which merged with the Ministry of Finance in 1998) kept the poverty agenda at the forefront of government policy and has been identified as a key factor in the Uganda PPA's success.

Methodology

Twenty-four rural and 12 urban sites in nine of the most disadvantaged districts were selected as the sample for the UPPAP in order to capture the multiple facets of poverty in the country. In each district, at least one urban and up to three rural communities were chosen. The research for the PPA included focus group discussions, case studies, and key informant interviews.

Findings

The participatory research of the PPA brought to light several issues that had been previously overlooked or had been given insufficient priority from a policy perspective. Among these issues were:

- The importance of local responses to local needs. Poverty in Uganda proved to be location- and group-specific.
- The importance of information flows. There was a limited flow of information about government policies, both between different levels of government and between government and communities. Ugandans were largely unaware of their rights.
- The importance of involving communities. People in all communities expressed interest in participating in making policies that would affect their lives, but lacked the information, mechanisms, and forums to do so.

Policy Responses to the PPA

The report from the first phase of the project revealed a number of outcomes of the PPA process. PPA findings have been extensively used in the development of influential government documents, including the revised PEAP in 1999/2000, the annual Background to the Budget 1999–2000, and the biennial Poverty Status Report. The Plan for Modernization of Agriculture now includes the poor as primary producers, focusing interventions on their constraints and priorities for reducing poverty. The mid-term expenditure framework process used PPA findings for reviewing public investment programs and sector expenditures, and the government allocated additional resources to providing clean water in response to poor people's priorities. PPA findings have been incorporated into education and health sector reviews as well.

The Poverty Monitoring and Analysis Unit published its first biennial Poverty Status Report in 1999, which presented the latest trends and analysis drawing on both governmental and nongovernmental sources, including PPA results. This unit also began to compile indicators that the PPA had revealed to be important, such as vulnerability, risk, and security. Poverty indicators identified by poor people through the PPA have also been included in national household surveys.

To respond to specific, regional, or local needs expressed in the PPA, flexibility has been introduced in the utilization of conditional and equalization grants by districts, and grant utilization procedures have been modified accordingly. The Poverty Action Fund has been reoriented to monitor the effective utilization of conditional grants and the impact on the poor. Local governments, particularly in the nine partner districts where the study was conducted, have also begun to internalize participatory poverty assessment principles.

On a broader level, the PPA raised awareness on the part of politicians and civil servants about the concerns of the poor through PPA-related dialogues, briefing documents, public presentations, regional workshops, and the media. In addition, the PPA led to greater insight into the obstacles to poverty reduction efforts, awareness of the regional differences in problems, and greater openness about sensitive issues, such as corruption at all levels of government.

The PPA raised critical questions among some NGOs about the design and implementation of their own projects. Civil society organizations have also used the PPA findings to support their participation in the process of revising the PEAP. Research institutes have begun to mainstream participatory poverty assessment principles into their work as well.

Phase 2

A second phase of the Uganda Participatory Poverty Assessment Project aims to support capacity building for participatory planning at the district level. Local NGOs that were involved in the first phase have asked to go back to the same communities in order to allow follow-up and continuity in the process. The main objectives of this second phase of the PPA will be to look at the need to revise priorities; to examine the implementation of Community Action Plans; to help communities identify the best channel for flow of funds; and to raise awareness among communities about how to access funding, through government structures as well as other sources.

The Guatemala Poverty Assessment

The Guatemala Poverty Assessment (GUAPA) is an on-going multiyear program of analytical work and technical support to provide a better understanding of the multiple dimensions that characterize poverty and exclusion and to identify related policy implications.[5] The GUAPA is one of the first country-level studies to build on the three pillars of poverty reduction identified in *World Development Report 2000/2001*—opportunity, empowerment, and security—using both qualitative and quantitative data to explore the multiple dimensions of poverty. Begun in May 2001, this comprehensive investigation will contribute to the World Bank's country assistance program and strategy, and foster institutional development and capacity building in counterpart agencies for greater ownership and sustainability of the process.

Gathering Information on the Multiple Dimensions of Poverty

The GUAPA uses quantitative data to draw conclusions about general tendencies and patterns, and qualitative information to understand the processes that perpetuate poverty, inequality, and exclusion. The main source of quantitative data is the Living Standards Measurement Survey (ENCOVI). Qualitative information has been collected under the Qualitative Poverty and Exclusion Study for 10 rural ENCOVI villages whose populations represent five different ethnic groups. The multiple dimensions of poverty are analyzed through a basic analysis of poverty and inequality and investigation of three major components: opportunity, vulnerability, and empowerment.

Basic analysis of poverty and inequality

The first phase of ENCOVI analysis involved production of a standard profile of poverty and inequality and analysis of their determinants. The profile of poverty and inequality uses monetary indicators of poverty, nonmonetary social indicators (health, education, and infrastructure), and qualitative definitions based on the perceptions of communities. ENCOVI data on monetary welfare indicators were used to construct a profile of inequality. Determinants of poverty and inequality are analyzed using multivariate regression analysis. This quantitative analysis is supplemented by qualitative information on the perceptions of communities as to the "causes" of poverty, prosperity, and inequality.

Opportunity

A series of background papers were prepared on the different facets determining opportunity as a key dimension of poverty. Topics covered include livelihoods and poverty; education and poverty; health, malnutrition, and poverty; poverty and modern utility services; social protection; transport; exclusion; and vulnerability.

Vulnerability

Work to understand vulnerability and security in the context of Guatemala focuses on several factors. The study identifies key vulnerable groups and constructs a typology of these groups, including their characteristics, poverty status, living conditions, and the main risks they face. In addition to this, investigation is made into risks and shocks, informal mitigation and coping mechanisms, and formal risk management and social protection interventions.

Empowerment

In relation to empowerment, the GUAPA explores the following topics:

- *Perceptions of poverty and exclusion.* This includes household and community perceptions of exclusion, institutions, interactions with officials, and living conditions, changes in these issues over time, and priorities and aspirations for the future.
- *Social capital.* Issues include: (a) a typology of the types and degree of social capital at the household and community levels; (b) community relations with the "outside world," including other communities and formal institutions; (c) the effects of other social forces (such as conflict, crises, and so on) on social capital; (d) the correlation between social capital and poverty/prosperity; and (e) the uses of social capital.
- *Other topics include:* voice, participation, and citizenship issues, and conflict, crime, violence, and justice.

Findings

The GUAPA highlights the extremity of poverty in Guatemala, where over half of the population lives in poverty. Over 81 percent of the poor and 93 percent of the extreme poor live in rural areas. Malnutrition is strikingly high, with 44 percent of children under five stunted.

Guatemala ranks as one of the most unequal countries in the world, with the top quintile of the population accounting for 54 percent of total consumption. Disparities in assets constitute the main sources of inequality in the country, with education accounting for over half of all inequality. Patterns of land ownership are among the most highly unequal in the world.

Opportunity

Poor people are highly constrained in terms of opportunities and livelihoods. Growth in Guatemala, while averaging 3.9 percent per year between 1950 and 2000, has not been pro-poor, and has not favored the sectors that primarily employ poor people, such as agriculture. Close to two-thirds of salaried poor workers receive less than the minimum wage.

Vulnerability

Primarily because of their low asset bases, poor people in Guatemala are extremely vulnerable to shocks. Eighty-eight percent of the extreme poor and 86 percent of the poor suffered losses in response to shocks, compared with 83 percent of the non-poor. Further, the effects of shocks are felt not only in income, but also in reductions in community assets, psychological and social wellbeing, and health and education. Existing social protection programs are poorly targeted and inefficient, and as a result, when shocks occur government assistance does not reach poor people. Poor people are thus forced to cope with shocks by reducing consumption (a strategy reported by 40.9 percent of the poorest quintile) or by seeking other forms of self-help (39.4 percent of the poorest quintile), such as supplying more labor, selling or mortgaging assets, or drawing down savings.

Empowerment

A weak public sector has been an obstacle in Guatemala's efforts to improve living conditions and promote a more inclusive society. Problems include a weak tax base, poor public expenditure management, poor targeting of public spending, insufficient accountability and responsiveness, and high centralization. Corruption is also a serious problem. Households in the ENCOVI survey ranked corruption/bad government as the second main cause of poverty in Guatemala. Using key indicators of governance, Guatemala ranks worst in Latin America in voice and accountability, political instability, and rule of law.

Social capital is concentrated among the more privileged groups in society, with inequalities favoring those in urban areas over rural areas, men over women, the non-poor over the poor, and the educated over the non-educated. Poor people do have strong connections within villages (bonding social capital), however they have little bridging social capital linking them to other communities or to formal institutions. Participation rates in within-village organizations (18 percent) are over three times higher than those for organizations linking individuals and communities to others outside their communities.

Notes

1.   This introductory section draws on Narayan with others 2000 and Robb 2000; for more information, see also Norton and others 2001.

2.   This section draws on Narayan 1997.

3.   This section draws on Turk 2001; World Bank 1999, 2000, 2001a.

4.   This section draws on Narayan with others 2000 (p. 26); Robb 2000; World Bank 2001b.

5.   This section draws on Clert and others 2001; Lindert 2000; World Bank forthcoming.

Resources

Clert, Carine, Michael Woolcock, Ana-Maria Ibanez, and Kathy Lindert. 2001. "Social Exclusion and Empowerment in Guatemala: A Quantitative and Qualitative Study." Draft of Proposed Framework and Issues Paper being developed under the Guatemala Poverty Assessment Program. World Bank, Washington, D.C.

Lindert, Kathy. 2000. "Guatemala: Reducing Poverty and Exclusion. World Bank's Poverty Assessment Program: 1999–2002." Draft of Approach and Concept Paper being developed under the Guatemala Poverty Assessment Program. World Bank, Washington, D.C.

Narayan, Deepa. 1997. "Voices of the Poor: Poverty and Social Capital in Tanzania." Environmentally and Socially Sustainable Development Studies and Monographs Series 20. World Bank, Washington, D.C.

Narayan, Deepa, with Raj Patel, Kai Schafft, Anne Rademacher, and Sarah Koch-Schulte. 2000. *Voices of the Poor: Can Anyone Hear Us?* New York: Oxford University Press.

Norton, Andy, with Bella Bird, Karen Brock, Margaret Kakande, and Carrie Turk. 2001. "A Rough Guide to PPAs: Participatory Poverty Assessment, An Introduction to Theory and Practice." Overseas Development Institute, London.

Robb, Caroline M. 2000. "How the Poor Can Have a Voice in Government Policy." *Finance & Development* 37 (4): 22–25.

Turk, Carrie. 2001. "Linking Participatory Poverty Assessments to Policy and Policymaking: Experience from Vietnam." Policy Research Working Paper 2526. World Bank, Development Research Group, Washington, D.C.

World Bank. 1999. "Vietnam Development Report 2000: Attacking Poverty." Report 19914-VN. Poverty Reduction and Economic Management Unit, East Asia and Pacific Region, Washington, D.C.

_____. 2000. "Vietnam: Managing Public Resources Better. Public Expenditure Review 2000." Report 21021-VN. Poverty Reduction and Economic Management Network, East Asia and Pacific Region, Washington, D.C.

_____. 2001a. "Case Study 3: Vietnam—Process Document of the Country Experience." Case study prepared as part of the Action Learning Program on Participatory Processes for Poverty Reduction Strategies. Participation Thematic Group, Washington, D.C. Available: http://www.worldbank.org/participation/web/webfiles/vietnam.htm

_____. 2001b. "Process Document of the Country Experience—The Case of Uganda." Case study prepared as part of the Action Learning Program on Participatory processes for Poverty Reduction Strategies. Participation Thematic Group, Washington, D.C. Available: http://www.worldbank.org/participation/web/webfiles/uganda.htm

_____. Forthcoming. "Guatemala Poverty Assessment." Poverty Reduction and Economic Management Unit and Human Development Sector Management Unit, Latin America and the Caribbean Region, Washington, D.C.